THE
CREATIVE
SOCIETY

HOW THE FUTURE
CAN BE WON

Published by
LID Publishing Ltd
Garden Studios, 71-75 Shelton Street
Covent Garden, London WC2H 9JQ

31 West 34th Street, Suite 7004,
New York, NY 10001, US

info@lidpublishing.com
www.lidpublishing.com

A member of:

BPR
Business Publishers Roundtable

www.businesspublishersroundtable.com

Printed in Great Britain by TJ International Ltd.

ISBN: 978-1-907794-88-9

Cover and page design: Laura Hawkins

THE
CREATIVE
SOCIETY

HOW THE FUTURE
CAN BE WON

LARS TVEDE

LONDON   MONTERREY
MADRID   SHANGHAI
MEXICO CITY   BOGOTA
NEW YORK   BUENOS AIRES
BARCELONA   SAN FRANCISCO

CONTENTS

WOW!

INTRODUCTION

Creativity, seen from Space

"**W**ow! That's where we live. On that tiny, lonely ball!" That is the emotional reaction astronauts often describe having, when they first look back at Earth from outer space. Just listen, for instance, to Alan Shepard after his visit to the Moon with Apollo 14:

"If somebody had said before the flight 'Are you going to get carried away looking at the Earth from the Moon?' I would have said: 'No, no way.' But yet when I first looked back at the Earth, standing on the Moon, I cried."

The Moon is 384,000 kilometres away, and seen from that distance, Earth is "the blue planet". However, if astronauts revolve around the Earth at a distance of just 200-300 kilometres, they can distinguish mountains, glaciers, deserts and major lakes beaming with many beautiful colours.

However, even from here, it is still very hard to detect signs of human civilization. "The scenery was beautiful, but I could not see the Great Wall," said China's first astronaut Yang Liwei, in 2003. If he had not known better, it could have been a beautiful, but uninhabited, planet.

However, this was only when he saw it from the sunny side. On the shadow side, the signs of civilization suddenly became obvious, because here the planet beamed with artificial light, as if it were a starry sky in itself. This, he would know, was the consequence of some species that had conceived of electric power grids, glass, lamps and more: telltale signs of creativity, in other words.

What if a spaceship from another civilization came by, and its travellers saw this night image? Perhaps they would also think "Wow!" Then one might say: "There must be an intelligent species here!" to which another might respond: "And it found the key to civilization, just like we did!" They might also pass by the Moon and notice footprints, a little flag and, oddly, a golf club and two golf balls (we shall get to that later) and conclude that an intelligent species had definitely been there.

After these initial observations, they might again turn their attention to the Earth at night and notice that there was most light near rivers and coasts. They would also note that large parts of the globe were dark. "Are these areas uninhabitable?" they would perhaps ask one another. "Or has civilization not yet spread to the intelligent beings in those places?"

NASA'S EARTH OBSERVATORY

We Earthlings know the answer. Some of the dark areas are indeed uninhabitable, but others are actually densely populated by our own species. In most of Africa, for instance, there is almost no light at night - at least not enough to be easily seen from space - and yet, it is home to more than a billion people.

Nevertheless, one of the world's fastest-growing economies over the past decades has actually been Botswana, which is, yes, African. In daylight, this country does not look particularly lush from a satellite, but its purchasing power per capita grew more than eight-fold during the 30 years from 1980 to 2010, which led it to becoming twice as rich as China. At night, the satellite view of rays of light emanating from its capital Gaborone provides a rare, shining gem within the African continent: these guys overtook China!

This is impressive, but here's something odd: right next-door to this successful state is Zimbabwe, where GDP per capita in 2010 was around $400 – equating to less than a thirtieth of Botswana's. This seems very strange, not least because the average income in Zimbabwe back in 1980 was not much lower than income in Botswana. But after 1980, the Zimbabwean standard of living almost halved, while Botswana experienced its aforementioned success. In 2009, Zimbabwe's inflation reached no less than 489,000,000,000%, which led it to drop its own currency and convert to US dollars. To put all this misery in perspective, the country's average life expectancy decreased from 65 years in 1980 to 34 in 2010. After the government had, with considerable difficulty paid wages in January 2013, it announced it had $ 217 left.

Not $217 million. No, no: $217.

Botswana and Zimbabwe provide an extreme example of neighbouring countries that have evolved very differently, but it is not unique. For instance, in 2010, Israel had an average income that was approximately six times higher than that in Syria (and this was before the latter descended into civil war) and approximately five times higher than income in Jordan or Egypt. The US population was more than three times richer than their neighbours in Mexico, and the people of Hong Kong were about six times richer than their peers in China.

Yes, plenty of direct neighbours have oddly different economies, and here's another strange tale: In 1900, Argentina was the world's twelfth richest country, ranking just above Sweden and, over the following five decades, it was neck-and-neck with Germany.

Yes, really. It was.

However, by 2013 Argentina had slipped down the ranks to number 73 in terms of purchasing power, clearly overtaken by ... yes, Botswana![1]

Strange. And this is perhaps even stranger: In 1922, Great Britain ruled more than a fifth of the planet and an even greater part of its population and economy, even though England itself accounted for less than 0.2% of its land masses and just 1% of its population. However, around 50 years later, almost all its empire had disappeared, inflation was above 20%, its top tax rate 83% and 98 % on investment profits, and the country had to get emergency loans from IMF to avoid imminent bankruptcy. How did that happen?

The international literature about how poor countries may succeed is enormous, and for instance, the famous american political economist Francis Fukuyama has described how nations could "get to Denmark", which to him was an example of a country that had been very successful at building its institutions.[2]

How to succeed is an interesting subject, but it is also interesting to consider how you "get to Argentina" with its history of serial bankruptcies and chaos. Scientists in the West have made countless studies of how poor countries grow richer, but they have been rather less interested in how rich countries become poorer. Perhaps they should investigate this because, as we shall soon see, that route is often taken. But the relative lack of interest in this question tells us, arguably, that people in the West do not believe significant economic decline could happen to them.

But it could. Just consider this: There have been approximately 200 great empires in history and they are all gone now, every one of them! What happened, for example, to the Inca Empire? The Aztecs? Babylonia? The Moguls? The Ottomans? Egypt was once the world's most developed civilization, but then the lights went out, and one may argue that the country has been stagnant or in decline for more than 1,000 years. The city of Baghdad in Iraq was once an intellectual powerhouse and home to the world's largest library. The Egyptian city of Alexandria and Cordoba in southern Spain have also been right up there at the top and had very large libraries too. All three libraries were later burned down on purpose. The Athenian civilization was once the shining light of the world, but the same cannot be said of modern Greece or its capital Athens.

More food for thought: 1,000 years ago, China was far richer than northern Europe. The Chinese had poetry clubs and art catalogues while Denmark, for example, was a rather rustic place, to put it mildly. However, then the Chinese economy went into decline and, in 1980, living standards had deteriorated to the level of Somalia's, while Denmark had become the shining example of a country, cited by Francis Fukuyama.

Why?

This book's main thesis is that empires and civilizations have predominantly flourished when they have stimulated human creativity, and that they have mostly decayed or collapsed, when they have blocked creativity - which they have strong tendencies to do sooner or later. Their successes and failures are much harder to explain through comparing resources, whether fertile land, useful plants and animals or mineral resources, as many authors have tried to do. In fact, we see an amazing tendency for countries with notably few natural resources (such as Japan, Singapore and Switzerland) to fare especially well in the long term.

Nor do climatic differences offer reliable explanations for most differences in wealth and human development. It is true that hot central Africa has, on average, been less successful than north and South Africa, but there are plenty of examples of the opposite. Furthermore, warm countries such as Malaysia, Taiwan, Costa Rica and Hawaii have done pretty well, and hot, humid Hong Kong and Singapore have exhibited explosive economic growth. In antiquity, most of the world's richest civilizations were in fact in warm or tropical regions, and people in the Middle East were better off than those in northern Europe - and that was before the discovery of oil.

Why was the industrial revolution launched in wet and windy Scotland and not in fertile, temperate France instead? And if climate is so important, how do you explain the rather considerable difference between the way in which Australia was run by Aboriginal peoples compared with British invaders? Furthermore, in the 15th century, the Aztecs were richer than Indians in North America. A thousand years ago, it even seems that Africans were better off than Europeans, or at least at roughly the same economic level.

Moreover, today there are plenty of communities in the colder zones that are destitute. In parts of Albania, Turkmenistan, Ukraine and Belarus, for example, life is often tough and poverty rife.

Of course, there is a third potential explanation: people. While it may be a "hot potato" in academic circles, many laymen may assume that the economic differences are largely caused by differences in intelligence - they may be racist, in other words, assuming that some races are more intelligent than others. However, as we shall see in Chapter 11, the "cause and effect" relationship is the other way around: civilisation stimulates intelligence more than intelligence stimulates civilisation.

So no, it is not in differences in climate, mineral resources, soil quality, presence of beneficial organisms and plants or racial differences that we will find most of our answers. Resources and environment cannot explain why certain countries have periodically been at the forefront of the economic rankings, have fallen back and then recovered again, as China and Great Britain have done. Nor can theories based on natural factors explain why many of the countries with the richest mineral resources or the best land have the poorest people. And they certainly can't explain the rise and fall of Argentina.

The scientist Jared Diamond proposed some of those flawed explanations, but he added another one that sounds more interesting: Eurasia (the combined continental landmass of Europe and Asia) is a predominantly east-west orientated super-continent, which has enabled people to intermingle within a very wide area called "the Fertile Crescent", throughout which the climate is much the same. The Americas, on the other hand, is more North-South orientated, so intermingling involved passing through many different climates as well as a fairly narrow bottleneck in Central America. For sure there is a valid argument there regarding economic outcomes, say, 4,000 years ago, but it doesn't explain why the "fertile crescent" today include countries as varied as Albania, Afghanistan and Germany and the Americas includes nations as different as Bolivia and Canada.

In this book we will see that there is only one geographical factor which, in fact, does seem to correlate rather well with success internationally and over the very long term: the presence of navigable coastlines and rivers. We shall study that issue later but please note that the importance of this resource does not lie in fishing, drinking water or irrigation. Instead, such water access is important because it facilitates trade and migration. It enables, in other words, voluntary win-win transactions under competition. Singapore, with its plentiful coastlines, didn't become one of the world's wealthiest nations because of fishing or farming and, in fact, today it imports both fish and drinking water. No, it became wealthy because it was good at trading and exchanging ideas, and its access to the seas was very helpful in that respect. So its success was a question of transactions, not resources: It was about creativity.

Creativity is the main key to long-term success, but what is required to access it? As we shall see in the subsequent chapters, creativity occurs spontaneously, when a few, essential elements are present in a dynamic system - in any dynamic system, in fact, whether it is an ecosystem, a business sector, a civilisation or something else. When such a combination is present in a system, magic development starts to happen in the form of spontaneous, creative development. No plan or intention is needed for it to work - it just happens. We can observe such self-organizing processes take place right before our eyes in natural ecosystems, in commercial markets and in human civilization, and over time, the results can be amazing.

Within this book, we will look, initially, at the general principles of spontaneous creativity. These are introduced in the first chapter, elaborated on in the second and should be fairly clear by the time we reach the end of the third chapter. After this, we will use these principles as a frame of reference.

Along the way we will see how the Western nations, hundreds of years ago, started an incredible, creative chain-reaction that led to massive improvements in people's lives - even though no-one seemed to plan specifically for general creativity. In fact, if anything, there were lots of leaders who made plans for curtailing the creativity once it had started; they just couldn't succeed in halting it, for reasons we shall hear later.

One of the arguments we will examine is that creativity (and the change it brings) is not just a pleasant feature of a civilization, but a necessary one. Stagnant societies, it seems, simply cannot survive in the long-term, partly because stagnation tends to create some nasty cultural changes.

Since creativity is essential to successful civilizations, we will study it further in the second part of the book, as well as examining why the West became so much more creative than all other civilizations.

The book's third section is about one of the most fascinating consequences of civilization - and especially of Western civilization: the so-called civilizing process. After that, we move on to some reasons that many people now want us to prepare for a static society: concerns about lack of innovation opportunities, ever-increasing capital concentrations, resource depletion and the environment.

This brings us to parts five and six, in which we will study current problems such as debt crises, structural unemployment, irrationality, anti-technology bias and much more. Summing up all of this, we will see there is a real risk that many Western nations have chosen the road "to Argentina".

The book's final section contains a number of specific suggestions about how we could make Western societies – any society, in fact - much more creative and dynamic than ever before. Of course, it is the author's hope that readers will think of extra and varied solutions that are better.

All of this is rather a big story, and we will take it right from the beginning; from the time, when pre-humans or apes started to evolve in unusual ways that would eventually make them creative. Embedded in this story is another one which will lead us to the reason why we developed civilization and thus also to why parts of our planet are now lit up at night (and why there is golf gear on the Moon). As aliens in a spaceship passing Earth would observe, we did indeed find the key to civilization, and we shall now study what that was.

PART I

HOW CREATIVITY DEVELOPS

Deciduous forests and coral reefs; ant hills, butterflies
and flocks of birds; hummingbirds; elephants.

How creative nature is! And yet, as naturalist Charles Darwin
explained to us, such marvels could happen absolutely
spontaneously through random change combined with natural
selection and competition. This simple combination, he said, can
create spontaneous creativity.

He got that right, but the explanation does not reveal from where
the winner's strength typically comes. In this section, we shall look
at the fundamental drivers of spontaneous creativity and success,
and at how they helped create civilisation. We shall also study a
number of the (often surprising and amazing) effects creativity
has had on civilisation, culture and life. And as we do that, we will
stumble upon the key to civilization.

CHAPTER 1:
When creativity began

CHAPTER 2:
The taming of life

CHAPTER 3:
The dynamics of ideas

1.
WHEN
CREATIVITY
BEGAN

Please think for a moment about your mother, and imagine she is standing two steps away from you at this very moment.

Now think of your grandmother standing another two steps away, just next to your mother. There are three of you now. Then add her mother – your great grandmother – two further steps away.

Including yourself, that's four people standing in a row and, as the average generation in human evolution has been approximately 25 years, you and these three women would, statistically, represent 100 years of evolution.

Go on, imagine the next four mothers – we are now approximately 200 years back in time. And then imagine the next mother and the next again and so on; all in a line: About 210-240 mothers along this line, you might be surprised to learn that all the women are black, even if you are white, and if we go about 1,700 mothers down the row, the women would look distinctly African, even if you are Asian or Inuit. In fact, these women would live in Africa.

If you go more than 8,000 mothers back, the womens' brains would start to appear smaller and their bodes more hirsute and, even further down the row, you would note that the women become physically smaller and start to look more and more ape-like. Around 200,000 - 300,000 mothers back, your ancestral mothers are entirely ape-like; small, hairy all over, walking on knuckles. These would be the common ancestors of humans and chimpanzees, and some scientists call them the CHLCA for "chimpanzee–human last common ancestor".

Approximately 99% of the genetic material of modern humans and chimpanzees is identical, but 1% can evidently make a big difference and, when you speculate about what happened to separate us from chimps, there are some peculiarities you have to explain. The first is that hominins, which include pre-humans, have survived for as long as they have done. The average lifespan of mammal species on the Earth has been between three and four million years, but our species is probably 5-8 million years old already, if we count from CHLCA.

The second peculiarity is that we have developed our brains so fast - none of the millions of other species on Earth did anything remotely like that.

So what happened? The first critical factor is that pre-humans only lived in Africa, which had a very volatile climate, where many areas would alternate between humid jungle and dry savannah. These cycles meant that the populations of pre-humans oscillated between doing pretty well (jungle) and pretty badly (savannah), and when they did badly, they were reduced to small, isolated groups. Whenever this happened, there was more inbreeding, which led to accelerated genetic mutation. However, whenever times improved, populations grew and reconnected, resulting in a "battle of the genes" with the best ones winning.

This oscillation between isolation in small groups and reconnection to larger networks was effective. As paleoanthropologist Ian Tattersall of the American Museum of Natural History has commented, "(...) a population needs to be small if it is to incorporate any substantial innovation, genetic or cultural. Large, dense populations have too much genetic inertia to be nudged consistently in any direction. Small, isolated populations, on the other hand, routinely differentiate."[3]

To put this another way, the innovation itself happens in small units, but, for it to spread, these units must connect with others from time-to-time. This is exactly what happened for our pre-human ancestors because, as Tattersall elaborates: "When conditions improved once more, the altered populations would have expanded again and come into contact with others. If speciation had taken place, competition and selective elimination would have likely occurred." When previously isolated tribes connected and interbred, their children would have combinations of their recent mutations, which would often be disastrous, but sometimes very beneficial.

However, superimposed on this climate cycle was an overall trend towards colder climates and thus a gradual shift towards less forest and more savannah. Some of our CHLCAs stayed in the forests, while others moved to the open ground; possibly by staying put while the forests moved.

Because the CHLCAs on the more open land began walking upright on two feet instead of crawling and swinging in trees, there was genetic selection for different body-shapes. However, as those in open areas were more visible to large predators, their males found it difficult to guard a harem, so they each began to guard only their own female and her children. This may have been especially pronounced during hard times, where the females had to scatter around bigger areas in search of food (this is called the female-spacing hyphothesis).

When a male stays with the same female, we call it pair-bonding, and this only happens in around 10% of mammals. There is a reason why it's relatively rare, because it can have limitations, but it also stimulates a capability for personal affection which provides a good basis for social-bonding and co-operation.

Something else happens: with pair-bonding, each child has a pretty good idea who its extended family is, since it knows the identity of its own father. To understand why this is important, consider chimpanzees, which, unlike humans do not have pair-bonding. Like primitive humans, chimpanzees live in tribes that are "patrilocal", which means that males stay put, but females move to other neighbouring tribes. Also like humans, chimpanzees frequently attack such tribes and kill members indiscriminantly. However, human pair-bonders came to recognize some of these tribe members as their own sisters or children, so became more hesitant in their killing. Pair-bonding didn't stop raids on other tribes, but it did lead to less agression and greater co-operation. We can see clear examples of this in more recent history, where European kings would marry their children to children of neighbouring kings in order to avoid wars with them.

Before we discuss co-operation in further detail, we need to look at a simple concept called social spaces. This comprises three layers, where the inner one is our known family, whose members we may help, even if we gain nothing directly in return. The second layer is our friends and members of the tribe/culture with which we identify and have ongoing social relationships. We will help these, but we generally expect some reciprocity. Combined, these two circles constitute our social network.

The third layer is everyone else, about whom we may not give a hoot or might actively be hostile too, even though (or because) we have never met them. When we include this layer, we have our entire social space. When pair-bonding started, our forefathers would - unlike chimps – understand that some members of their inner circle in fact lived among others in what they had thought of as their outer circle. So these people became middle circle, which meant that their social networks expanded.

The greater the number of "others" whith whom you can co-operate, the more advantageous it becomes to be co-operative, and we know today that human babies in simple tests show a far higher inclinations to help other humans than do small chimpanzees in terms of helping peers.[4]

Something else happened. Because our ancestors had literally come down from the trees, they had hands instead of hooves, and these hands were flexible because they had been used for holding on to branches while picking

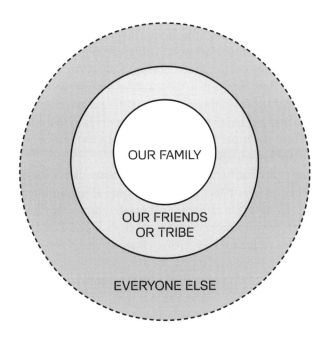

THE SOCIAL SPACE. THE BETTER PEOPLE ARE AT COOPERATING BEYOND THEIR INNER CIRKLE, THE MORE SUCCESSFUL THEY WILL BE.

fruit and so on. As they moved into the savannahs, the pre-humans began walking mainly on two legs, which meant their hands were available for other activities, which offered up many opportunities; especially as they gradually developed opposing thumbs. This enabled pre-humans to do very simple stone-cutting, which seems to have started approximately 2.6 million years ago; they would surely have used branches as weapons. This stimulated so-called gene-culture co-evolution, whereby those best at using tools had the highest survival rates, which meant there was also a hand-brain coevolution.

To sum up, the reason our species has survived for so long already and that our bodies, and especially our brains, have developed so quickly is a combination of five factors: 1) the frequent isolation in small units which altered genetic drift; 2) the reconnections into bigger networks for competition; 3) the increased personal compassion and expansion of networks after pair-bonding; and 4) the fact that they could still mate after they had been separated due to compatible DNA.

Here is something to think about: anthropologists and other scientists tell us that our species, which we call Homo sapiens, has existed for approximately 200,000 years - before that, there were pre-humans. They also say that the sizes of our brains haven't changed much through all this time – in fact, people had slightly bigger brains in the Stone Age than they have now; the brain evolved from 1,500 cm3 to 1350 cm3. And yet, it is less than 5,000 years ago that some of our ancestors began to develop civilization.

Isn't that odd? How was it that they walked around with these big brains for close to 200,000 years without even inventing a bicycle? What happened 5,000 years ago that pushed them from living in caves to flying aeroplanes and watching satellite television? What was the key to civilization?

Well, as we just noted, it wasn't brains.

And it wasn't physical strength either. Humans didn't suddenly become stronger 5,000 years ago. In fact, it has never been about our physical abilities, because we are, by nature, a rather fragile species, as we also were 5,000 years ago. In line with sea cucumbers, common jellyfish and Daddy Longlegs, we lack such impressive features as strong claws or sharp teeth with which to defend ourselves; in biological terms, we are pretty much unarmed. Also, we cannot fly and, if we could, we would probably catch a cold anyway, because we lack the fur, scales, and feathers that might protect our highly sensitive skin. We cannot run or swim particularly fast, and to top it all, human females find it very difficult to give birth to our children, which are helpless for an incredibly long period of time.

We are, to put it bluntly, a bunch of rather wimpy sops, if not helpless weaklings and, as such, we answer pretty well to the standard description of animals destined for extinction: large enough to be eaten and slow enough to be caught. Considering things from that perspective it is no wonder that our early ancestors - as we shall soon see – came to the brink of extinction time and again. In fact, they were probably skinned alive and eaten by stronger creatures on a regular basis.

To understand how physically weak and vulnerable our species really was, we can start with our distant forefathers Homo ergaster. These ape-men lived as one species in Africa and then, approximately 1.4 million years ago, they split into two sub-species named Homo antecessor and Homo erectus, respectively. The latter later spread into Asia where, over a long period (perhaps between 70,000 and 30,000 years ago) they went into decline, until they only consisted of a tiny enclave on the island of Flores in Indonesia. These creatures (Homo floresiensis) were, when full-grown, just over one metre tall, and they died out 12-17,000 years ago, so quite recently, actually. There may have been other human sub-species and other attempts to leave Africa that we have yet to discover. For instance, we have one 40,000 year-old finger bone from Siberia that has deviant DNA suggesting it might be yet another sub-species now known as Denisova hominins.

The adventures of the people dying out on Flores and the Denisovans dying out we-dont-know-where, were not very uplifting but, meanwhile, our ancestors in Africa kept going, and some of them migrated to Europe approx-imately 1.3 million years ago. However, these emigrants also perished around 70,000 years later.

So that was yet another failure but fortunately our African pre-human ancestors were still around, and while most just stayed in Africa, a few made another excursion into Asia, where these also died out as in the previous attempt.

Yet another group migrated into the mostly harsh and cold Europe, where they survived several ice ages while evolving into a more physical-ly-robust, bigger-brained sub-species called Homo neanderthalensis or simply "Neanderthals".

These guys actually looked rather promising. In fact, if aliens had landed on Earth around that time, they could easily have assumed they were the future.

While all this took place, there was steady progress in Africa, since its Homo species' average brain mass also grew – the ape-men became gradually less ape and more men. Their brains more than doubled in size due to the aforemen-tioned gene-culture and hand-brain coevolutions.

This produced results. At some point between 400,000 and 1.5 million years ago, some of our ancestors began doing something no animal had ever done: they learned to control fire to keep warm and to cook food. This meant their stomachs and intestines had less work to do digesting food which freed up energy and space for other things, such as supporting the bigger brains which had enabled the smaller digestive systems in the first place. Brains use about 20% of our energy, so they don't come cheap, but the gene-culture co-evolution made it practical.

There was more: Probably around 700,000 years ago, a genius invented the stone axe, and perhaps 500,000 years ago, the first tents made of skin were developed. This was followed by the wooden skewers some 400,000 years ago. These inventions were actually amazing when you consider that we were still at ape-man stage. But, then again, please note that it took them more than 300,000 years to come up with just four inventions. After this, though, their creativity started to accelerate :[5]

◆ 250,000 BC: Fine stone cutting
◆ 230,000 BC: Funerals
◆ 200,000 BC: Knives and rope

So this was another four inventions within a mere 50,000 years – still not a blazing speed, but faster. In the meantime, our ancestors changed so much genetically that, as already mentioned, from approximately 200,000 years ago, our ancestors started to look so much like us that we call them Homo sapiens. Meanwhile our (yes, now its "our") creativity kept improving, and although it still wasn't overwhelming, we do notice a continued acceleration:

◆ 100,000 BC: Serrated blades and domestication of wolves
◆ 90,000 BC: The needle made of bone
◆ 70,000 BC: Art and clothing

Now we are talking about five inventions within just 30,000 years! Furthermore, we also see for the first time how one invention (clothing) depends on three previous ones, since our knives could cut a coat up into pieces, while our needles and rope enabled sewing these together to create the clothing.

We are moving through history at a good pace here, but now we have to make another detour to introduce one more little model: the creative design space.

This relates to how innovation occurs: innovation is mainly about combining existing things in new ways. The creative Homo sapiens and Apple co-founder Steve Jobs put it succinctly:

"Creativity is just connecting things. When you ask creative people how they did something, they feel a little guilty because they didn't really do it, they just saw something." [6]

Such a process becomes hyper-exponential. If, for example, we only have products A and B, then we can combine these in three different ways (if we ignore doublet combinations). However, if we double the number of existing products to four (A, B, C and D), the number of possible combinations rises from 3 to 14. So, if the number of creative building blocks grows in a linear fashion, it leads to an hyper-exponentially-increasing number of possible combinations. We can call this inventory of ideas ready to be recombined a "creative design space" and it was the process of re-combining within this that began around 70,000 years ago; the first time we know of where someone combined three prior innovations (knife, needle and rope) to make a new one (clothing).

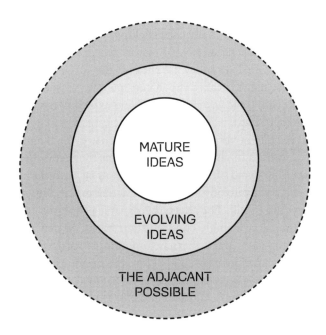

THE CREATIVE DESIGN SPACE. SINCE INNOVATION IS LARGELY RECOMBINATIONS OF PREVIOUS IDEAS, THE MORE IDEAS WE HAVE ALREADY IMPLEMENTED, THE MORE NEW POSSIBILITIES WE HAVE WITHIN THE ADJACENT POSSIBLE.

The inner circle in the illustration above represents old technologies and concepts that no longer evolve very technically (such as knives, axes and ropes). Most of the change that happens in this area equates to a fashion shift – the technical concept of a knife changes very little, but we keep coming up with new artistic variations.

The next cirle illustrates newer ideas that are still evolving a lot technically (such as cars and airplanes). Within this area you will typically also see many applications developing around some core ideas; miniature versions of a similar creative design space. For example, the smartphone can now be seen as a relatively mature core technology, but the software applications for it continue to evolve very rapidly.

The outer ring represents what US biologist and complex systems scientist Stuart Hauffman has called "the adjacent possible" – it is what could, in principle, be assembled by recombining existing elements from inside the two inner circles, but which hasn't yet been assembled. We shall study much of that later, but it includes creative computers and some amazing biotech stuff.

Back to our ancestors. One thing many anthropologists assume about them is that they probably learned to use language more than 50,000 years ago (plus/

minus a lot). Perhaps they initially used clicking sounds to communicate, and maybe that was all it was, because we do know that some of the most isolated and primitive tribes in Africa today use clicks as the core element of their language. One of these tribes is called the !Kung- people ("!" stands here for such a clicking sound), and their way of life may give us a clue to what life was like before people left Africa.

It's like this: In spite of very low population density, the !Kung people tend to run out of resources in any given location, but they solve this by moving around. Between 30% and 40% of their food is meat, and the rest is plants. Since they have virtually no possessions, they are all materially equal, and they share what they find or kill. They keep their sparse properties in leather bags, and women often carry a single child on their backs. When a woman gives birth, she leaves the men, and if there is something wrong with the baby, she kills it. They rarely have the next child before the previous one has learned to walk far enough because, as an anthropologist once calculated, a woman will, on average, carry each of her children almost 8,000 km on her back before he or she learns to walk. Just to put this into perspective: The distance from the French coast towards the English Channel to the south of Spain is in the region of 3,000 km, so it's there, back and then some with a child on your back.

One more thing: the !Kung people don't trade or, at least, they didn't until they met modern people. That is important and we shall come back to it soon.

So this is how we think ancient people lived: Sparse population, often isolated, but then reconnected, primitive life, harsh conditions, no possessions, sharing almost everything, walking a lot, killing the weak and no trade. Harsh and primitive, but they did survive.

They only just survived, though, and approximately 70.000 years ago, humans almost became extinct, because genetic analyses tell us that, at this time, the global population probably fell to just 2,000 to 20,000 survivors - several scientists believe they were down to 5,000 individuals, which would have qualified them for a status on the "Red List" of endangered species. Perhaps this population decline was triggered by a gigantic volcanic eruption in Sumatra, which covered the sky with ash for several years and led to a dramatic temperature drop, but it could also have come from a devastating epidemic or war.

But they survived and recovered, and continued to innovate, as the next four inventions came in just 10,000 years – faster than ever before:

◆ 60,000 BC: Herbal medicine
◆ 50,000 BC: Boats, flutes, bone spearheads

Around this time, (around 50,000 years ago) their way of life had changed in ways that make anthropologists call them "modern" from then on, since their remains were fairly similar to what the !Kung people leave behind today, which apparently is modern to an anthropologist.

Now the story takes a twist, because a few thousand years later something happened that has puzzled scientists ever since they first learned about it. The event began when approximately 42,000 years ago, a small group of Homo sapiens left Africa, just as some of their ancestors had done several times much earlier. There is broad consensus that there may well have been several attempts to do this, but that only this group achived it at the time. Based on DNA analysis, some scientists believe that it was a single group consisting of approximately150 individuals that left Africa and then spread.[7]

Having crossed the Strait of Arabia they continued a (seemingly) very slow migration to India, after which some of them walked towards Europe. These migrations were spread out over many generations and their progress was so slow that, on average, they barely travelled more than a half-to-two kilometres a year - maybe 10 – 30 km within a generation. Europe's new immigrants, at this stage, only numbered a few thousand, and anthropologists and archaeologists believe they typically arrived in clans of 20-30 individuals, each of which was loosely associated with a few similar clans.

Why did they migrate to Europe? It seems unlikely that it was a particularly attractive landscape because it was Ice Age and the Alps, for example, were buried under glaciers, which in some places were about a kilometre thick. In addition, a large part of Scandinavia and half of the British Isles was also covered in ice, and the lands just south of these regions could best be described as Arctic desert. The vegetation in the rest of Europe was mainly low and sparse; something in line with that of Iceland or northern Siberia today.

There was another problem: the Homo sapiens group was heading in the direction of the aforementioned Neanderthals. That sounds dangerous, because these people were very muscular, stocky and robust. In fact, their skeletons, of which we have found many, were stronger than those of Homo sapiens and tended to show physical impact damage reminiscent of the ones you see today at the rodeo riders (in other words, the kind of damage you can expect if you tangle with large animals or enemies from your own species).

Furthermore, the Neanderthals were well adapted to life in Europe. Because they were short and dense of build, they could keep warm more easily than the more slender Homo sapiens. The latter were all black at this time, while Neanderthals had fair skin and red hair which helped with absorption of calcium as the body synthesizes vitamin D from sunlight. In Europe, they had managed to survive four ice ages and they had probably learned to use clothes long before Homo sapiens.

Furthermore, Neanderthals do not seem to have been dim: their brains were bigger than those of Homo sapiens and they made tools as Homo sapiens did, including spear tips made of stone. Something that looks like a whistle has also been found in one of their caves, so perhaps they played music, and we know they buried their dead.

So Homo sapiens (humans) were slowly approaching these tough dudes, and it was almost inevitable that these two sub-species of the genus Homo had to fight. The winners should have been a foregone conclusion: the mighty Neanderthals.

The scene was set for an epic power struggle. As the newly arrived Homo sapiens first met Neanderthals in Europe, the latter had already lived there for approximately 300,000-400,000 years; they were the home team. In fact, Neanderthals had existed as a breed for 500,000 - 600,000 years and Homo sapiens only for approximately 200,000 years, when the two sub-species now ran into each other.

Various archaeological finds suggest that they definitely fought. For example, we have a Neanderthal cranium where one can see that the meat has been cut with a tool in the same way as Homo sapiens then cut deer meat. The crop marks indicate that even the tongue had been cut off - presumably to be eaten. Presumably, they had clashed once before, since earlier Homo sapiens had lived in the area we now know as Israel but, 80,000 years ago, Neanderthals walking east-ward apparently overcame them (unless they simply perished by themselves). So it would seem that the Neanderthals had won the first round. What was different this time?

This is what has puzzled scientists for so long: The earliest European skeleton of Homo sapiens found, to date, was in modern Romania and is 34,000 – 36,000 years old. Relatively soon after - perhaps around 30,000 years ago - Neanderthals became extinct. Actually, a few scientists have claimed they didnt really disappear, because non-Africans have, on average, approximately 3% Neanderthal genes,which suggests cross-breeding whether through rape or via free will. Bear in mind, though that some or all of this shared genetic material may be down to our common ancestors rather than inter-breeding. How, then, is it possible that Neanderthals came first and completely dominated the area, but that today 97% of their ancestors' genes is non-Neanderthal?

So here's the odd scenario in a nutshell:

1. Neanderthals lived in Europe for 300,000-400,000 years, surviving four ice ages.
2. They were perfectly adapted for their environment, extremely strong and robust and had bigger brains than Homo sapiens.

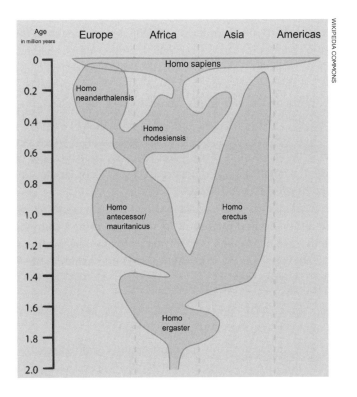

WIKIPEDIA COMMONS

MAP OF MIGRATIONS OF HOMO SAPIENS AND THEIR PREDECESSORS THROUGH TWO MILLION YEARS. AS THE GRAPH SHOWS, IT WAS CERTAINLY NOT EASY FOR THE EARLIER HOMO SPECIES TO BREAK AWAY FROM AFRICA.[8]

3. Homo sapiens arrived in Europe about 80,000 years ago but subsequently disappeared - they were probably defeated by Neanderthals in the Middle East.
4. Homo sapiens arrived again in Europe approximately 34,000 - 36,000 years ago and prevailed.
5. Within just a few thousand years after the second arrival of Homo sapiens, Neanderthals had been squeezed into a corner of Europe, then a corner of Spain, before becoming extinct.

Over time, there have been made many theories. Some researchers have suggested there was a crucial difference between the two species' form of intelligence which gave Homo sapiens an advantage despite their somewhat smaller brains. At one time, a specific candidate for the crucial difference was even considered, a specific variant of the gene FOXP2, which helps us to talk. However, new DNA analysis demonstrated in 2009 that Neanderthals actually had the same variants of this critical gene.

Another theory about Neanderthal disappearance assumes that the frequent climatic changes in Africa from which Homo sapiens had just emigrated, made them more flexible than Neanderthals. Nowadays, climate change has become a fashionable theme, but if we look at the current case, this explanation borders on the ridiculous, because there were also large variations in the seasons as well as long-term climate variability in Europe, and glacial weather fluctuates much more than hot weather. In addition, if you live close to a kilometre-tall ice wall, it is really not that easy to tackle cold days. And it was precisely Neanderthals and their predecessors - not Homo sapiens - who had practised this for 300,000-400,000 years.

When you inhabit an entire continent like the Neanderthals did, but end up living on a tiny, natural fortress at its very edge after a competing species has arrived, then your problem is hardly lack of resources or disease. No, you are fleeing a stronger enemy – in this case, Homo sapiens. But how could Homo sapiens be stronger?

We need help here, so let's introduce three renowned biologists to the stage: Richard Dawkins, Robert Wright and Matt Ridley.

Professor Dawkins is probably the most famous of the three. He received a doctorate in zoology from Oxford University in 1966 and has spent most of his career as a lecturer and, later, professor at Oxford University. In 1974, he published his book *The Selfish Gene,* in which he pointed out a curious phenomenon: intuitively we believe that people who survive "pass on their DNA".[10] Okay, Dawkins claimed, that is true in a literal way, but just think about this: when we die, our genes don't, if we have children. After all, before our death our DNA has been smart enough to make copies of itself, which then live on in our offspring. These children's bodies will eventually also perish but, before this happens, our genes will, typically, again have managed to copy themselves. Seen from that perspective, the genes use us.

Dawkins therefore described the genes as "selfish", though he apologized several times in the book since, of course, genes do not possess selfish feelings or any feelings at all. But they are automatic self-copying machines, like viruses, and, as such, they have, through natural selection, found a way to replicate themselves – and yes, they use our bodies for their purpose.

This may sound like sophistry, but it explains the fact that many individuals are willing to sacrifice themselves in order to protect their children or family: in doing so they also protect their DNA. Of course, this is not how we see it ourselves. We see it as saving our loved ones but thereby we lose our own lives, whereas our genes win out, and love is a lovely little trick DNA came up with to ensure its own duplication once pair-bonding became useful.

Dawkins's book was an immediate bestseller, and it revolutionized the thinking of many biologists. But, funnily enough, it had, towards the end, a rather short chapter, in which he pointed out, almost as an after-thought, that something similar could be seen within human ideas and behaviour. Based on the Greek word "mneme", meaning memory, he noted that there are numerous small ideas or behavioural traits in our various communities, which replicate themselves as genes do and which thereby manage to survive every individual or even their civilizations. These "memes", as he called them, were therefore also selfish self-copy machines, which also used people as their carriers.

Memes are the concepts, behaviours or sayings we use in our everyday lives, which we often consider self-evident, but they also include specific details of our behaviour and elements of our cultural style. In contrast to genes, a single meme is sometimes able to penetrate an entire community within days or weeks. Interestingly enough, we are not even aware of many of our memes. For example: children can be good at grammar, which is a set of memes, without being able to explain them. Shared memes help us to interact with people we have not met before, as if they were a kind of social glue.

There are many interesting examples of how memes can survive for centuries or millennia, until their original cause is completely forgotten. In Spain, for instance, it is customary to hang smoked hams in the ceiling of restaurants and bars, but you don't see the same in, say, France or Italy. This is a meme that evolved during the Spanish Inquisition, where Muslims and Jews were given the choice to convert to Christianity, emigrate or be robbed, tortured or burned. Many chose to convert and, to dispel any doubts during the Spanish Inquisition, they began to hang hams from their ceilings, since Jews and Muslims cannot eat pork. To this day, the Spanish maintain the meme of hanging hams from the ceilings of their bars and restaurants, even though most are not aware of the reason behind it. The bodies perished, but the memes survived.

That was a bit about memes, but now we need to introduce our next philosophical biologist: Professor Robert Wright. He graduated in socio-biology at Princeton University and has since written various highly acclaimed books covering game theory, religion, the human mind and more. His book *Nonzero* published in 2000 was described by Fortune Magazine as one of the 75 most important books ever written about the business (even if it isn't a business book at all).[11] In this book he argued that the main driver of biological and cultural progress was cooperation.

Cooperation? Do we not all know from Charles Darwin, that the logic of progress is the survival of the fittest, which actually seems to mean a brutal jungle-law that does not sound like co-operation at all? Yes we do, but Wright's argument was not opposed to this.[12] It was rather an elaboration, in which he pointed out that the evolution of life from the very beginning has been driven by the benefits of what one may call "nonzero" "zero-sum" or "win-win" transactions. Whenever the biological building blocks, such as molecules, organelles, cells or individuals randomly discovered new opportunities for collaboration, their chances of lasting survival through replication improved tremendously.

This brings us right back to our social spaces and creative design space, because recombination and co-operation is kind of the same thing. In other words, the best co-operators became the fiercest competitors. Human bodies are walking creative design spaces, which implies a tonne of co-operation. Just think about it; our bodies are molecular military alliances, if not huge metropolises of cooperating cells. The human body depends of various bacteria, and we cannot survive without these. It also has more than a billion different types of immune cells. Each of these is only found in very small numbers, but if the body is attacked by an alien element, they will quickly multiply through a complex collaboration between its many cells and enzymes to take up the fight and protect the entire metropolis of cells (and thus the selfish DNA).

So co-operation is key, and it can evidently extend beyond the individual. Just imagine this: a caveman named Fred Flintstone meets another named Frank Fisherman. Fred is good at making flint axes and Frank at making fishing nets. So Fred and Frank now swap an axe for a net. We call this a nonzero transaction (where nobody gets nothing) or a win-win transaction (both are happy). But there may be more to it, because as the two exchanged goods, they also exchanged information and ideas. When Frank comes home to his cave, it may well be that he has been inspired by Fred to make his first flint axe, and vice versa. In other words; the exchange of goods was a voluntary win-win transaction that could not be reused, but the accompanying exchange of ideas or memes was another win-win transaction that could be repeated indefinitely.

Think of it this way: While we were still sleeping peacefully on Saturday morning, the baker around the corner was baking bread and he was doing his best because otherwise the clients would choose another baker. Two hours later, as we arrived in the shop and asked for bread, he smiled and passed it across the counter, and we said "thank you". Then we paid him, and he responded with a "thank you".

None of the parties involved in such a transaction is likely to be personal friends with any of the others and many may not even know one another. This means we conducted a 1) depersonalized 2) voluntary 3) win-win transaction 4) under competition.

Here comes the point: The concept of making voluntary exchange transactions with strangers is mankind's greatest idea – it is far more significant than, for instance, the control of fire or invention of the wheel. It is bigger, because trade is what we can call a meta-idea - it's a great idea for coming up with more ideas. Furthermore, because it can be conducted outside the small circle of our friends and family, and because it is voluntary (each person is free to do it with someone else or not at all), it can mutate with blazing speed if there is no specific resistance, which makes it an incredible engine of creativity. Why? - Because:

◆ When you trade in a "market" with strangers beyond the inner layers of your social network, there is no longer any forgiveness for a bad product or attitude, and you have to compete on harsh terms against others.
◆ When there is competition, people wonder about how to get the best deal or make the most competitive offer. So it makes them think hard and become selective and demanding.
◆ While the social networks leads to more trade transactions, trade transactions also increase social space.

It is not difficult to see what this leads to. It leads to more of the same, where products and services get ever better.

Trade can happen because people desire money, status, security, fun or anything at all; it does not matter in the case of this argument. What counts is that innovation happens when we make voluntary win-win transactions in a competitive environment. .

Let's turn the argument upside down and consider how life was (and occasionally still is) without it. In primitive society, where livelihoods predominantly relied on using limited natural resources, people were encouraged to create win-lose (yes, win-lose) transactions with all but their most immediate friends and family. Members of a tribe would help each other, but they would fight intensively for food, loot, territory and women against other tribes with whom they were not family-related. They would not co-operate beyond the core of their social group.

This was how life was for almost anybody in the distant past. However, after trade was invented, you could gain by doing something for others – even if you didn't know them. The more cooperative you were, the more you would gain. And if you could think up a completely unfulfilled demand and be the first to fulfill it, you might gain even more.

This changed the mentality from seeking win-lose transactions to pursuing win-win transactions and in particular innovative win-win transactions. So people started to expand the circles of people with whom they would co-operate and, with this, came greater exchange of ideas and an ever-growing creative design space.

In this we have our key to civilization. Come to think of it, this key is, in fact, so obvious that we almost certainly can assume that if there are intelligent beings on other planets who have developed civilizations, that is also how it started for them. Trade must be the universal key to civilization.

One man who saw a lot of this long before our biologist Robert Wright was the philosopher and economist Adam Smith, whose book The Wealth of Nations, published in 1776, first described how it is mainly voluntary win-win transactions that drive progress of civilizations. In fact, he contrasted this with slavery, which he not only considered unfair, but uneconomical: " ... I believe, that the work done by freemen comes cheaper in the end than that performed by slaves," he said. Furthermore, while he thought it was useful to colonize new land, he believed it made no sense to maintain central control over it forever, since it made the people there unfree. He compared this with the Greek colonies of antiquity in Italy and elsewhere, which had ruled themselves. The original city state from which the colonizers came viewed each colony as "an emancipated child over whom she pretended to claim no direct authority or jurisdiction". No, people should rule themself, be free and do things voluntarily. As Smith famously explained:

"It is not from the butchers, the brewers, or the baker's benevolence that we get our dinner, but from their own interests."

So there we have our baker again, but please note: no shared ideology is necessary among those who co-operate. A model for a good society doesn't need to be any more emotionally attractive than an engineers' model for an engine. It just needs to work well, and voluntary win-win transactions under competition really does work.

When we co-operate with people beyond our personal social network, we may be dealing with strangers who we do not like, and the principle will work anyway. Cavemen Fred Flintstone and Frank Fisherman can both be stupid, selfish pigs - they may still co-operate well through trade, if it is in their mutual interest. And that co-operation may give each of them new ideas, lead to specialization and encourage greater work effort.

Is it a shame if they dont like each other particularly? No, it is actually best so, because if friendship becomes a part of it, we end up with nepotism and tribalism, which restrict competition, choice and creativity.

Come to think about it, there actually is something emotionally appealing about this whole concept after all. If a Frenchman buys something from China, he does not know those who made it and they do not know him, but they co-operated anyway and, in a global economy, everybody seems to work for everybody else. That is why it is somehow beautiful (and why the concept of self-sufficiency isn't).

It is important to understand that trading is different from the widespread symbiosis that is essential to ecology and nature, such as when bees fertilize flowers in return for nectar or when small fish, rather heroically, clean the teeth of sharks. Natural symbiosis does not include any examples of two creatures in the wild that randomly meet and then spontaneously negotiate the exchange of two different objects. Nor is symbiotic exchange in nature versatile in the sense that the same creatures may negotiate the exchange of something entirely different the next time.

But human interaction is now versatile, and here we come back to one of Robert Wright's two central insights: evolution is a gigantic multi-player game where the winners overwhelmingly are those who are best at facilitating co-operation, i.e. facilitating win-win transactions (Adam Smith saw the same). Building on that, his second insight is this: Since those cultures and civilizations best at stimulating win-win transaction become strongest, there will, for all mankind, be a general trend towards more win-win and less win-lose. It is this to which Wright's book's subtitle - *"The logic of human destiny"* - referred: man's logical destiny is to enable yet more win-win transactions (we probably lost Adam Smith there). Many civilizations will, at some point, begin to head the opposite way, of course, but these will (sooner or later) find themselves in the trash bin of history alongside other nations that preferred central command and forced transaction to decentralization and voluntary action.

Let's now return to the question of why Homo sapiens (man) beat Neanderthals, and here we need to introduce our third super-biologist: Dr Matt Ridley. Like Dawkins, he took a Doctorate in zoology from Oxford University. Then he served for a number of years as the science editor of The Economist magazine. He has also written a number of books about genetics and society.

In 2010, he published a book called *The Rational Optimist,* in which he argued that the crucial difference between Homo sapiens and Neanderthals didn't lie in their external circumstances or genetic differences, but in their memes. But what differences might those be, and how can we trace differences in the memes of cavemen tens of thousands of years ago?

Ridley's answer was very simple: examination of excavated objects from Neanderthal dwellings showed these always came from their immediate neighbourhood. For example, if archaeologists found axes, they would always be made with the types of stones that could be found fairly close to that particular habitat. In Homo sapiens' European settlements, on the other hand, archaeologists would often find objects that had clearly come from far away, so could only have be acquired via trade with strangers.[13]

Before the invention of trade, both Homo sapiens and Neanderthals must typically have seen all strangers as a threat to their own safety and their reaction would often have been to kill before being killed – win-lose, in other words. But these dynamics must have changed after they developed the concept of trading. Instead of planting his stone axe in the stranger's skull, a man would perhaps seek to swap it for fifteen beautiful seashells.

So, as Ridley suggested, that was in all likelihood the answer to the conundrum: when Homo sapiens and Neanderthals clashed 24,000 – 36,000 years ago, the former had invented trading, and latter hadn't. As we saw earlier, there was no evidence of trade between Homo sapiens in Africa and previous attempts to migrate from Africa had thus been made by tribes which did not yet trade. But when Homo sapiens later ran into Neanderthals again, it became a struggle between traders and non-traders.

Undertaking trade facilitated more peaceful networking among Homo sapiens which in turn, made it possible for them to exchange ideas, memes and information, and it enabled them to co-operate in warfare by assembling larger armies to defeat small groups of Neanderthals one at a time. Furthermore, as they were now traders, the Homo sapiens would probably have fought each other a lot less than the Neanderthals fought one another.

So it was, in all likelihood, memes, rather than genes, that eventually led our ancestors to victory, and it was different approaches to transactions, that really mattered, and not environment or resources.

What were Homo sapiens trading? The early European trading objects included flint and seashells and, later, came salt, amber, zinc, copper, gold, silver, furs, jadeite axes, textiles, oils, gemstones, wine, pottery, trained horses, walrus ivory, slaves, silk, glass and more.[14]

This was attractive stuff, which brings us to the point that trade encourages diligence. Many scientists have formulated theories stating that increased leisure time frees up time to create the elements of an effective culture. Maybe so, but, as we shall see repeatedly in the course of this book, most people do very little if they do not identify a clear incentive. When anthropologist Robert Carneiro visited the Kuikuro tribe in the Brazilian jungle, he noted that they had far more food than they needed. In fact, it took them only a few hours a day to gather the necessary fruits to survive. So what did they do with their remaining time?

Nothing, they were just dozing. But when the Europeans showed up with lots of exciting things that could be bought in exchange for Cassava (root vegetables native to the area), the tribe's Cassava production went through the roof. The possibility of trade gives people an incentive to work harder. Trade is a perpetual generator of creativity. As such, it is also what scientists sometimes call a "change agent".

Nothing progresses without change agents. Nature provides strong genetic change agents through oxidation, virus infection, radiation, sunlight, cosmic rays and other means. These have changed our genes, mostly for the worse, but occasionally for the better, and competition combined with these change agents has taken us from strands of DNA in a primordial soup to the very complex beings we are today.

Like natural evolution, the effects of voluntary win-win transactions between people accumulate. When the British first crossed the Atlantic to begin the colonization of North America, they sailed in ships that were inspired by early shipbuilding traditions of the Normans, north Germans and Vikings. They had gained their knowledge of navigation from astrological observation plus their alphabet from the Greeks and their algebra from the Arabs. Their cannons, gunpowder and compasses were Chinese ideas, their maps were printed with a German technology, and their number system was developed in India. If they had not previously driven intensive international trade, they could never have combined all these amazing innovations and technologies and would thus never have been able to colonize North America.

Trade is such a strong idea that today its effect is clearly visible from space at night. It is simply brighter in places where voluntary and international trade is most common. The clearest example of this is seen when astronauts fly over the Koreas at night. They will note that North Korea, with the exception of some light in its capital and a few other places, is simply pitch black at night, whereas the sister state of South Korea is bathed in light. Although the two countries have similar ethnic populations, population density and natural resources, and although until 1945 they formed a united and homogeneous country, the economic difference is now huge, as the differences in light intensity demonstrate.

And that difference keeps growing. A study showed that South Korea's light intensity increased by 72% between 1970 and 1999, while North Korea over the same period decreased (yes, fell!) by 7.4%.[15] Former US president Jimmy Carter visited North Korea in 2011 and reported afterwards that approximately one third of the children there were malnourished and that authorities had just halved people's daily rations to just 700 calories. The recommendation in the West is 2,000 calories for women and 2,500 for men, and the health hazard boundary is located at 500-800 calories.[16]

So here we have two neighbours with the same common history, climate and natural resources and one of the world's most homogeneous ethnic populations, and yet one has, within three generations, become 20 times richer than the other.

South Korea is a global trading nation. North Korea has based its society on socialism combined with a principle they call "juche". This means self-sufficiency.

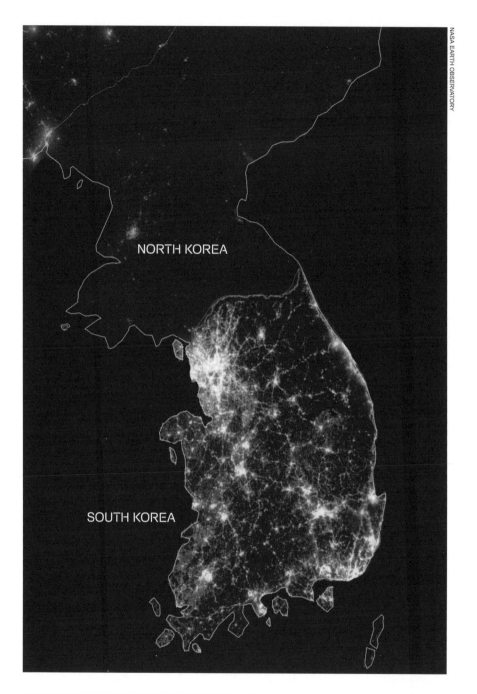

NASA EARTH OBSERVATORY

NORTH AND SOUTH KOREA FROM SPACE. THE NORTH IS A CENTRALIZED SOCIETY PURSUING SOCIALISM AND SELF-SUFFICIENCY. THE SOUTH IS AN OPEN MARKET ECONOMY ENDORSING GLOBALIZATION.

Of course, we can never prove beyond doubt that Homo sapiens out-competed Neanderthals because only the former had invented trade. But it sounds a lot like the North Korea/South Korea story and, one thing we do know, at least from recent history: voluntary co-operation under competition is the primary source of creativity, civilization and prosperity. Ideas for improving such co-operation lead us forward, and ideas that prevent it lead to stagnation, decline or collapse. In fact, as Ridley has pointed out, there are no examples anywhere in the world of communities that lost ground, in terms of their economy, once they had opened up free trade - even in cases where their neighbours did not reciprocate. The strongest supporters of free trade have often sprinted from their neighbours - just think of Hong Kong, Singapore, Taiwan, South Korea, Mauritius, Botswana and Chile.

2.
THE TAMING
OF LIFE

Nature seems to try almost everything. Over the course of billions of years it has created an unimaginable quantity of the most intricate, and sometimes distinctly odd, life-forms. In fact, in some cases, one wonders how certain creatures managed to survive competition (the peacock and sloth spring to mind), but when you study the cases in more detail, you find good explanations. Until, that is, you get to the sausage dog, or "Dachshund" (pictured below These are very cute, but they are are still half a dog high and a dog-and-a-half long, and their little legs are plainly ridiculous. So how on earth did nature select them? What was it thinking?

THE DACHSHUND. HOW COULD THIS ANIMAL POSSIBLY COMPETE WITH FOXES AND WOLVES, ETC?

We shall come to the answer to this question within a few pages, and it illustrates a bizarre consequence of civilization. It is about what memes do to genes and, therefore, we must briefly consider how genes work and how scientists study them. Let's begin at the beginning: living creatures' genetic codes are stored in DNA strands present inside all our cells except in the red blood cells. A creature's genetic code is written with combinations of four chemical compounds: adenine, thymine, cytosine and guanine, where each is always paired with another. We therefore speak of base pairs, and human DNA contains about 3.2 billion of these. Think of them as the letters in a cookery book that contains the recipe for a human being. Or, to be more precise, a recipe for making proteins which are the essential building blocks of life for humans.

This cookery book has approximately 20,600 chapters, which we call genes. Each gene is responsible for a specific chemical function (sometimes, however, several features or parts of a function). The sum of all these genes is what we call our genome. Our genome and our DNA is thus, in a sense, the same, but the first refers to the code (software) and the other to the molecule (hardware).

Most living being's DNA strands are strikingly similar. For instance, depending slightly on how you calculate it, there is approximately 99% overlap between human and chimpanzee DNA, and our DNA is even approximately. 50% identical to that of a banana.

The first time we managed to sequence/decode (map the atomic sequence) of a human DNA strand was between 1990 and 2003. This project seemed enormous at the outset and involved thousands of scientists and laboratory technicians. Initially, this progressed unbelievably slowly with no end in sight, and, given the technology used in 1990, it would probably have cost $300 billion and taken generations to complete, but towards the end in 2003, the cost was approx. $ 300 million and the speed far higher. It ended up lasting 13 years and costing three billion dollars.[17] Since then, both the cost and time consumption for a decoding DNA strand has reduced dramatically, and this has led to an explosion in our knowledge of the biochemistry and history of life.

There are various methods for investigating how our genes have evolved through the ages and from where they come. The two used most commonly are studying the DNA of so-called Y-chromosomes and examining the DNA of our mitochondria. Y-chromosome is found in male mammals and its DNA is never mixed with the DNA from a woman. Therefore, it shows a broken line of direct copying from the males of a species.

Similar benefits are found by examining the DNA in mitochondria. These are organelles inside each of our cells, and they have their own DNA, which is only copied from women. Interestingly, it is now assumed by most experts that these mitochondria are actually former bacteria, which are now co-habiting with the human cells – so there we have the ultimate symbiosis as described by Robert Wright.

The fact that Y-chromosome DNA is purely male and mitochondrial DNA purely female gives us an interesting tool for examining genetic history. An example: In the last chapter we saw that, according to researchers, the human population dropped to between just 2,000 and 20,000, approximately 70,000 years ago. The scientists reached that conclusion by looking at the variability of mutations in our Y-chromosomes and mitochondria.

So now we have come to the subject of mutations. All species are under constant genetic development. Such mutations may be caused by the change agents we mentioned earlier, such as oxidation, but there is much to indicate that viral infection plays a particularly important role. Unlike bacteria, viruses will routinely poke around inside animal and plant cells and certain types of them have a habit of exchanging sequences of DNA with their host cells. Genetic fragments – even some fairly large ones - can thereby spread to other species, and thus, for example, it has been observed how a major DNA sequence has been copied from snakes to gerbils. This could have happened because a virus infected first a snake and then a gerbil and brought a DNA string from one to the other.

Our own DNA's 3.2 billion base pairs were written in the course of more than 4.4 billion years (counting from the first single-celled organisms to humans today) which, on average, means the addition of a new base pair every 17 months.

The vast majority of mutations are harmful, and the typical person may be carrying around ten deleterious mutations - new or inherited from ancestors - which can be more or less problematic. On average, there are 100 new mutations in each child, of which two or three have a real impact. That's a problem but, in the long term, it is the rarer favourable mutations that, through natural selection are most likely to be passed on. As Robert Wright pointed out, such favourable mutations often enable some new form of co-operation between atoms, molecules, organelles, cells, organs, individuals or species.

Let's not forget the question of how nature has selected the sausage dog (Dachshund to the owners). Can that really be an example of survival of the... fittest?

Actually, yes it can be, because it survives due to its co-operation with humans, which actually makes it mightily strong - so strong in fact that, in the US, there are approximately 100,000 registered sausage dogs but only 9.000 grey wolves (fortunately there are many more grey wolves in Canada, but still).

This brings us to an interesting fact, because the Dachshund is a direct descendent of the grey wolf and can still (presumably with some technical difficulties) breed with these. In fact, all living dog breeds descended from the grey wolf. The oldest trace we have of dogs is a discovery from 2010 of the remains of a 33,000 year-old dog in south Siberia. The following year, a skeleton of a dog was found in the Czech Republic that was estimated to be 26,000-27,000 years old. Someone may have liked this little guy, because he or she buried it with a bone from a mammoth in its mouth, which tells us, what the dog liked.

In addition, we have found footprints from a child who was walking with a dog in the French Chauvet cave approximately 26,000 years ago. As for the Dachshund, we have seen precursors depicted in ancient Egypt.

All of this suggests that human beings have lived with dogs for more than 30,000 years, but how did it start? Undoubtedly, very badly. Humans have been obvious victims of wolves, and it was probably normal for a pack of wolves to stalk people and, in an example of the ultimate win-lose transaction, pick them off one-by-one when they were isolated from their companions, perhaps doing you-know-what, or when everyone was asleep.

But the relationship between man and wolf must have changed. One possibility is that people occasionally found abandoned wolf cubs and became attached to them. A more obvious possibility is that wolves learned they could gain food leftovers if they lived close to people - even without fighting with them – which may be why they settled near human settlements. The people, in turn, perhaps discovered these wolves not only kept away mice and rats, but would fend off hostile tribes and, for that matter, other wolf packs that were less co-operative. Your enemy's enemy is your friend, as they say.

The result was that the win-lose transactions (wolf-eats-human-for-lunch) gave way to win-win transactions (wolf-keeps-guard-and-gets-food-leftovers). So this is not exactly trade as we define it, but it is certainly voluntary co-operation and it must have led to a genetic selection in favour of the wolves that were most accommodating and which, somehow along the way, learned to bark to warn off intruders (wolves don't bark).

To test the creation of a dog out of a wild species, the Russian scientist Dmitry Belyayev decided, in 1959, to breed silver foxes to become dog-like, where he continually bred the foxes that seemed most friendly until he had some that routinely tolerated humans. After 40 years and 35 breeding generations, they were all as friendly as dogs. As a side effect of this, they also changed their appearance: his tamer foxes had lighter skin, rounder heads, somewhat smaller brains and often soft ears, and they continued to wag their tales after becoming adults, which wild foxes do not normally do. They became, in other words, dog-like and it only took 40 years to achieve this.[18]

Dmitry Belyayev also tried a similar experiment with rats and it worked the same way. After 60 generations bred from the same rats, he had created two populations with completely different personalities. When you entered a room where the violent ones were caged, they would scream at the visitor and hurl themselves against the bars in anger. In the room where the friendly were kept, it was completely different. These rats would calmly stick their heads through the bars of the cage to have their heads petted.

Dogs are good at interpreting our signals, whereas wild wolves and foxes are largely incapable of this, just as they are unwilling to accept instructions. It is these traits that, through symbiosis and, later, more deliberate breeding, have been developed by man: dogs are genetically modified wolves that remain puppy-like, even when they reach physical maturity. We have civilized them.

And as we did this, something else developed: increased diversity. The original grey wolf has evolved into approximately 160 sub-species of dog (so far), and this is an example of a general rule: a system based on voluntary win-win transactions will, spontaneously, create diversity. If we co-operate, we will request an ever-growing range of services from one another, and this will evolve into an expanding creative design space and wider social networks, both of which open up extra possibilities. From being enemies, the wolves became guard dogs and pets, and then perhaps hunting partners, and so on. Today, we breed dogs specialized in herding sheep, hunting foxes or birds, warding off intruders, being nice to children, fitting in a handbag, looking cute, elegant, sporty, aggressive or deliberately silly. And because of this diversity, the diversity of the products we make for dogs has also grown exponentially, from collars to food, shelters, shampoo and thousands of other examples, such as racing tracks for greyhounds (but not for sausage dogs; perhaps because of human impatience).

The same happens in nature as a whole, and the number of animal and plant species has therefore grown significantly since the first living cells came into being. One of the reasons for that is a phenomenon called character displacement, whereby differences among similar species which live within the same geographical area tends to be accentuated automatically, which drives them towards speciation.

So Robert Wright's "co-operation under competition" creates diversity; diversity increases the creative design spaces and social design spaces and this creates new opportunities for co-operation. The reason why there are now millions of species on Earth (not counting viruses and bacteria) is that co-operation has many possible business models, and this number grows exponentially with the number of different participants co-operating. Because of this phenomenon, immense creativity can occur without it being planned centrally.

Why do many plants expend so much energy on making big, colourful flowers that smell like perfume and contain rich nectar? Why do some plants produce delicious fruits, only to drop them on the ground, where they may rot? What's the point of a flower or a peach?

It is all marketing, of course. Plants promote themselves to bees and butterflies via their flowers or to fruit-eating animals with their fruits, because that is how their selfish genes can spread themselves. Their DNA has made these

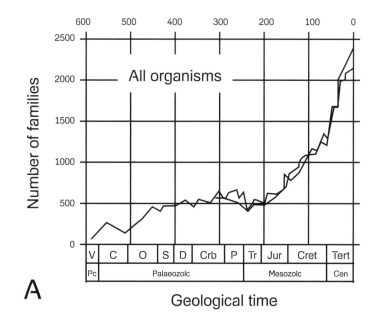

A

Geological time

NUMBER OF ANIMAL AND PLANT FAMILIES OVER GEOLOGICAL TIME. THE TREND HAS RISEN MASSIVELY BECAUSE COOPERATION CREATES DIVERSITY.[19]

species highly adapted for co-operation with other species, and flowers were, in a sense, largely shaped by the multiple desires of butterflies and bees, just like dogs were shaped by the multiple desires of men.

That also explains why puppies and kittens often look so ridiculously loveable; it is because they depend on the care of their parents and now us. On the other hand, fish and other animals that are on their own from the moment their eggs hatch are, typically, simply small copies of adults, because being cute is no advantage to them. Being fast is important, though, and they normally are.

Virtually all life-forms are constantly taming some other life-forms, and man has tamed many more life-forms than wolves. At one point some people changed from having a nomadic lifestyle to forming permanent settlements, presumably so that women did not have to carry their children around for thousands of kilometres, and also to enable the storage of goods and development of better shelters. This, in turn, created the condition for agriculture, which occurred a few thousand years later.

When farming began, however, a whole series of genetic adaptations followed. When people picked up plants with seeds to take them home, the seeds that made it home were those most firmly attached to the plants - the other seeds were more likely to drop off en route. Hence began an unplanned genetic modification of the plants, under which they increased their tendency to hold on to their seeds; this also made it easier to collect these seeds before they blew away. At the same time came a selection of plants with more, and larger, seeds.

Over time, our crops changed in order to co-operate with us, to about the same extent as the wolves that became dogs. Modern corn is descended, for example, from a grass called teosinte, which still grows wild, but the two no longer resemble one another at all. Modern bananas are sterile and cannot set seed. Wheat descended from three different grass species that were crossed, and it contains alien chromosome fragments and mutations deliberately provoked by radioactive and X-ray irradiation and genetic modification by exposure to chemicals. As with bananas, you will never see wheat growing wild in nature, because it cannot survive there.

And so it goes on: all our livestock and just about everything we eat is genetically modified by us, over thousands of years, to such a high degree that, like the sausage dog, much of it could never survive without us. In fact, pretty much the only indigenous foods we eat today (as they were before the introduction of agriculture) are fish, hunting game and certain nuts and berries.

However, the story does not end there, since our ideas and memes have not only modified the genes of plants and animals around us, but also our own genes. It is quite obvious that people have developed genetically, because after our (perhaps 150) ancestors migrated from Africa, they evolved into Asians, jungle Indians, Europeans, Aborigines and Inuits and so on, all of whom look rather different. Races constitute a statistical cluster of genetic traits which US scientist and author Jared Diamond and the American Anthropological Association claim do not exist; however, assuming they do, we will note how each is highly-adapted to its environment. For example peoples who live in mountains have more blood cells and bigger lungs; those living in hot climates have darker skin and those with risk of frost bite have shorter noses.

Once people gained control of fire and began cooking, their stomachs and intestinal systems grew smaller. Their skeletons also became thinner in a process known as grazialization and their jaws shrank, which is why we now need to have our wisdom teeth extracted. Furthermore, as people developed weopens such as bows and arrows and spears, they no longer needed to fight in close combat with their prey, so their muscles grew smaller too - thus saving energy. And given that people began to live with animals, they were very often infected with diseases by them, which stimulated gene alterations that made them more resistant.

Although agriculture provided a number of practical advantages, it also resulted in some immediate drawbacks. For instance, farmed food contained

MAN-MADE GENETIC MUTATION OF MAIZE (CORN). TO THE LEFT IS TEOSINTE; TO THE RIGHT IS MAIZE, WHICH HAS EVOLVED FROM TEOSINTE OVER THOUSANDS OF YEARS AND IN THE MIDDLE IS A HYBRID BETWEEN THE TWO. AS THE PICTURE SHOWS, MAN HAS MODIFIED TEOSINTE VERY SUBSTANTIALLY.[20]

MAN-MADE MUTATIONS OF BRASSICA OLERACEA (CABBAGE, BROCCOLI, KALE, CAULIFLOWER, BRUSSELS SPROUTS, SAVOY, AND CHINESE KALE) ARE ALL PLANTS THAT MAN CULTIVATED OUT OF THE WILD CABBAGE PLANTS SHOWN TO THE LEFT. THE PARTS OF THESE CULTIVATED, DERIVATIVE PLANTS THAT WE LIKE TO EAT ARE MAINLY THE COMPLETELY- DEFORMED MUTATIONS THAT HAVE BEEN CULTIVATED BY MAN. FOR INSTANCE, THE WHITE STUFF IN A CAULIFLOWER (RIGHT) IS AN EXTREME MUTATION THAT MAN HAS DELIBERATELY CULTIVATED. MUCH OF THIS HAPPENED THOUSANDS OF YEARS AGO. FOR EXAMPLE, THE BROCCOLI IS THOUGHT TO HAVE BEEN DEVELOPED BY THE ETRUSCANS LONG BEFORE THE ROMAN EMPIRE. [21]

less protein than the meat from hunting, and plant proteins did not have the nutritionally-optimal composition of amino acids that virtually all meat has. Second, the farmers had less food variation, which could result in a lack of vitamins and minerals and, finally, their teeth decayed. The consequence was that the first farmers were less healthy than their immediate ancestors.

Then their genes started to compensate. The decline in meat consumption was reflected, in particular, by a lack of vitamin D. Our access to this vitamin is a little bizarre, because we can partly get it from food, which sounds fairly normal, but also by exposure to the sun, but if you lived up north and neither got enough meat nor sun, you could get vitamin D deficiency. The genetic solution was to make the skin and hair of northerners lighter to allow greater sun exposure. In fact, studies indicate that northern Europeans had dark skin until 5,300-6,000 years ago, by which time virtually the entire population, within relatively few generations, mutated to become fair-skinned.[22]

One of the key new mutations provoked by our farming culture concerned the ability to digest milk. In all mammals, including humans, it is inherently normal that the body loses its ability to digest lactose (a sugar contained in milk) after childhood. However, beginning approx. 8,000 years ago, people started keeping cows. Although, initially this was probably for their meat and hides, and later for use as draft animals, at some point someone had the idea of drinking their milk. Approximately 80 generations later, a mutation that made it possible to digest cow's milk sugar started to spread.

This ability to digest milk created a virtuous circle, because milk endowed perhaps five times greater nutritional benefits from a cow than did its meat alone. This was reinforced as people began to breed selectively the cows that gave the most milk.

Please note that, up until this point, the idea of exploiting cow's milk can be described as the mining of a resource. However, it became so powerful because it stimulated interpersonal transactions: if you had milking cows, you could feed many more individuals per unit area, which enabled military concentration and increased trade and division of labour. Human co-operation with cows thus stimulated human co-operation with other humans and therefore stimulated their creativity. It comes back to Robert Wright's theory of co-operation yet again.

With the transition to agriculture came a change in our work methods. It was no longer important to be able to chase animals in the wild but advantageous to be able to work long hours in the fields or to build stone fences, houses and so on. For the same reason, there was a change in the gene known as ACTN3, which controls our muscle composition. Muscle fibres comes in two versions - one that provides explosive muscle power, as seen in sprinters, and another that lends us endurance, as required by marathon runners. All people have a combination of both muscle types, but apparently we gained a greater share of the endurance variant after the introduction of agriculture.

Agriculture has probably also changed our genes in ways that affect our mentality. We can illustrate this through some trials of a game. It is very simple:

"You will be offered some money that you have to share with someone else. You must decide in what proportions. If the other refuses his part, the deal is off and both of you get nothing."

The outcome of this simple game has often been used by anthropologists to describe the willingness of people in various societies to co-operate voluntarily. However, it becomes more interesting in tribal communities, such as in Indonesia and South America. In an experiment in those communities, some anthropologists classified tribes based on how much they traded with outsiders - i.e. their market integration. Some traded a lot, whereas others didn't. Then the anthropologists asked members of each tribe to play the game, wherein the amount at stake corresponded to approximately two days' worth of income, so that it had real economic interest of the participants.[23]

The results were very interesting: People behaved far more selfishly within the communities that had least trade with the outside world. Among the very isolated Machiguenga Indians in South America, the first player's average offer was, for example, 26% and the most common offer just 15%, and in only one instance was such a low offer rejected by the other player. So the first player was typically very selfish and the second accepted that as normal.[24]

In addition to categorizing tribes by market integration, anthropologists also made a scale reflecting the extent of division of labour in each community, and this also showed a clear correlation, so that those who were most dependent on cooperation in everyday life gave the best offer to their counterparty in the game. This is an expression of one of the most general observations of our development process: civilization and trade gives people a greater tendency to respect others. The taming process does not only involve genes, but also memes.

This has important implications for the ability to act and to create a functioning state. The economist Paul Zak has found that every 15% increase in the tendency for mutual trust among people in a society leads to an additional annual increase of GDP per capita growth of 1%, annually.[25] A high degree of mutual trust makes it easier for people to make voluntary transactions, and general trust among people in a society increases if they are used to make voluntary transactions.

When someone shows us clear trust, we secrete a substance called oxytocin, which makes us more confident about these people - so we reward trust with trust. In fact, it has been discovered that the inability to secrete this substance correlates with sociopathic, narcissistic and generally reckless or egocentric behaviour. Given that the development of civilization requires mutual trust , it seems likely that our genetic ability to secrete and respond to oxytocin has increased, as our civilization has evolved.[26]

In a hunting society, where physical goods came from either prowess in hunting big game or making raids against neighbouring tribes, the most aggressive men acquired the most food and thus easier access to women. This created selection pressure for aggressiveness, fearlessness and what psychologists today call sociopathic behaviour (psychopats). A study of the warlike Yanomami Indians of the Amazon found, for example, that men who were murderers had far more children, on average, than non-killers: [27]

Age	Children per murderer	Children per non-murderer
20-24	1,00	0,18
25-30	1,57	0,86
31-40	2,83	2,02
41+	6,99	4,19

It should be mentioned that this study was done by anthropologist Napoleon Chargnon, who expected to find a romantic, peaceful tribe, but described his very first and rather shocking encounter with them as follows:

"I saw a dozen burly, naked, sweaty, hideous men staring at us down the shafts of their drawn arrows! Immense wads of green tobacco were stuck between their lower teeth and lips making them look even more hideous, and strands of dark green slime dripped or hung from their nostrils-strands so long that they clung to their [chests] or drizzled down their chins. My next discovery was that there were a dozen or so vicious, underfed dogs snapping at my legs, circling me as if I were to be their next meal. I just stood there holding my notebook, helpless and pathetic. Then the stench of the decaying vegetation and filth hit me and I almost got sick."[28]

Chargnon discovered that approximately 40% of the Yanomami men had committed at least one murder. As he tried to map their family trees he collected their names only to be informed later, by another tribe, that they had all lied to him, since the names they had given included, for instance, "long dong", "eagle shit", "arsehole" and "fart breath".

Brutality and rudeness has been ingrained in the memes and genes of primitive hunter-gatherer societies, but the transition to rural communities changed the natural criteria for success significantly. People now had to learn how to plan for the future. They needed to learn to postpone gratification and wait patiently for the fruits of their labours. They had to be good at interacting with strangers and with each other and to operate within more structured and complex social models. This meant that being genetically predisposed to peaceful co-operation was suddenly an advantage and being an uncompromising aggressor became a liability; being scary, covered with slime and calling strangers "dog fart" wasn't very helpful in this respect. We have therefore achieved so-called "self-domestication". Just as we domesticated and adapted plants and animals to civilization, we have actually domesticated ourselves culturally and genetically.

Let's close this chapter with two observations about our brains. As we already saw, brains grew as our ancestors evolved from ape-men to Homo sapiens, but declined since then by a size roughly equivalent to a tennis ball. The same happens when you domesticate foxes or turn wolves into dogs.[29] The likely reason is that the wild animals have to decide everything for themselves, whereas their domesticated cousins look to their owner for answers. The implication is that as you are tamed and learn to live co-operatively with others, you don't need to be as smart to live smarter.

The other observation is that people's skulls, on average, grew thicker after the invention of the stone axe, indicating that it was often used for win-lose transactions. But about 40,000 years ago, as trading was spreading, our skulls again began to thin across the globe – other than among Australian Aborigines and Native Americans on the tip of South America.[30] Accordingly, creativity and later civilization flourished as people began to read each other's thoughts rather than smash in each other's skulls.

The general conclusion from the examples in this chapter, however, is that, if you want to stimulate the creative development of a society, you must focus on facilitating voluntary win-win transactions under competition. If you do that, people will implement one good idea after another and build a growing social ecosystem. Additionally, they will - without even noticing it - develop their own ability to cooperate constructively. They will self-domesticate, in other words. This is obviously important but, as we shall see in the next chapter, co-operation under competition alone is not enough to ensure strong creativity and progress.

3.
THE
DYNAMICS
OF IDEAS

What we have found out so far? First, there is the resources-versus-transactions consideration, where we saw that original differences in human intelligence or natural resources such as climate, soil, minerals or natural flora and fauna were not very important for long-term success. Instead, it was primarily our ability to expand social networks and stimulate creativity that counted.

Early societies were mainly what we may call "extractors", and when they made their first institutions, these would easily become extractive too. However, over time, some civilizations became more "combiners" instead – they focused more on trade – and in order to do that they would eventually develop more inclusive institutions. Some people may have become good at growing potatoes, and that is a good skill. But others learned to trade them and, as the Swedish economist Johann Norberg, explained: "Trade is like a machine that turns potatoes into computers, or anything into anything: who would not want to have such a machine at their disposal?" While the potato growers grow their food from soil and water, the traders grow their creative design spaces from people and ideas, and that is how creativity and prosperity grows big, and it also how self-domestication gets stimulated.

In the previous chapter we noted that the human age of creative transaction was kicked off by the invention of trade, which included depersonalization of interaction whereby we could co-operate within our total social space rather than only within our personal network. Such trade created ideas and products and this became part of an expanding creative design space. Once that expanded, it increased the number of previous inventions that could be recombined, and so on, forever and ever. So it was a self-feeding loop.

Meanwhile another self-feeding loop started. When people undertook more voluntary win-win transactions with one another, they became more trusting and co-operative. This was surely a cultural phenomenon, but almost certainly also genetic. In either case, we managed self-domestication, which increased our talent for co-operation, which again fostered more diversity in our products and transactions, which expanded the creative design space, and because people found that attractive, they also build ever bigger creative social spaces.

We have also touched upon the fact that, as described by Adam Smith in 1776, it was the pursuit of self-interest combined with trade that made everything grow. When Darwin, 83 years later, published *On the Origin of Species,* it was actually a kind of rediscovery of the same principles in nature. Nature was selfish, like business people are, and the most effective also gained market share here.

As we have seen in previous chapters, Dawkins brought a new perspective to both theories by explaining how genes and memes managed to wander from one carrier to another in rather selfish ways; Wright contributed the idea that both nature and civilization predominantly found success by improving ability for co-operation. The striking aspect is, of course, that nature and culture follow some identical rules. Being selfish is rather natural in both systems, as in the selfish gene, the selfish meme and the selfish baker, and this selfishness could lead to great results even if it doesn't sound sympathetic or welcome.

As Wright also described, everything that grows and thrives ultimately comprises co-operative networks. An organelle in a human body cell is an ecosystem of co-operating molecules. The cell itself is an ecosystem of organelles. The body is an ecosystem of co-operating cells and bacteria. The early farming culture expanded ecosystems to animals and plants in our environment that we farmed, planted, used and modified. Civilisation binds tribes and cultures together in even larger ecosystems through the use of rules and memes. Free trade agreements, airports and the internet expand it even further. That's what the creative design space does to us, and it's rather natural.

That is roughly how far we came within the preceding chapters, so let's now take it on a stage and try to make a general rule:

SUCCESSFUL CIVILIZATIONS COME ABOUT DUE TO SPONTANEOUS, CREATIVE DEVELOPMENT, WHICH HAPPENS WHEN FIVE ELEMENTS ARE ALL PRESENT IN A SYSTEM: 1) SMALL UNITS 2) CHANGE AGENTS, 3) NETWORKS, 4) SHARED MEMORY SYSTEMS, AND 5) COMPETITION.

Let's start with the units:

1. Small units. Small units are best at dreaming up new ideas, and the smaller the average unit in a network is, the more of them there are, which create better basis for creativity.

In nature, mutations happen in tiny units - they are the small shifts in the strands of DNA which often involve but a single atom. When the ape-men mutated quickly towards becoming human, it was because they frequently got isolated into small units, which then reconnected.

Within human communities, a change is typically derived from a single idea in the head of a single person. The person is typically inspired by others, but it still happens in just one person. While development is all about co-operation, a "collective idea" doesn't really exist.

Human beings are generally herd animals and adapt to each other - so if decisions are taken collectively, they are rarely innovative. In addition, people in large organizations are typically risk-averse – it is safer to swim with the tide than to go against it. Thus, the best way to create maximum creativity is to have a community divided into many small, autonomous groups or individuals.

Next, we need to have:

2. Change agents. Progress requires spontaneous change, even if most of this is negative.

The hominins evolved quickly because of frequent climate change, including frequent local climate shifts and a long over-all trend towards more dry and open landscape. So the climate was a change agent.

In isolated, tribal communities or in countries with censorship and travel restrictions, there are a few change agents, which is why they stagnate or collapse. On the other hand, in open societies with free trade, travel, migrations, media, scientific research and social interaction through urbanization, ideas flourish; mainly through recombination.

So now we have many small units that tend to change and thus become innovative. But we need them to do voluntary win-win transactions with each other, which require:

3. Networks. Units must be connected so that transactions occur, and the more connected they are, the greater and faster the progress. The internet is more effective than a number of small, isolated networks, and a large free trade area is more successful than many self-sufficient regions. In nature, organisms are similarly connected via sex and ecosystems.

Network effects within trade are fascinating. Let us, as a purely arithmetical example, assume that the overall Stone Age population in an area consists of 100 clans, each with 25 people, where each clan has no interaction with other clans. Any person in the whole population will now be associated with 24 others. But let's now imagine that, because of the introduction of trade, there are now a couple of people in every clan who know a member of another clan. This probably means that every person in society is indirectly connected with more than 2,499 people instead of 24!

This means that the use of the social space expands massively, and such a change may be called a "phase shift" by a mathematician, a "community" by a sociologist and an "ecosystem" by a biologist or network economist. And it is a significant business opportunity if you're Mark Zuckerberg, who founded the Facebook network.

Networks enable transactions, exchanges of goods, services and ideas, and movement of people. But they also instantly increase everyone's creative design space massively because when you interact with more people, you also interact with more products and ideas. Once people are changing and have started transacting, they need a means a storing value and exchanging information:

4. Shared memory systems. We need standardized codes to "write down" and memorize the results of successful experiments. The data needs to be in formats that can be shared between the participants in a network. Some of the data can be temporary, like the daily price of a kilo of potatoes, but whenever an experiment has gone well, the information about it should be stored so that the success can be 1) replicated and 2) rewarded. In life, temporary code is chemical transactions between proteins, for example, but the permanent code is the DNA, which replicate and thereby reward successful experiments. In human interaction, we need civilization and many of its institutions to ensure that memory systems are shared and respected.

People who trade a lot tend to become good at making such codes. To study that, the psychologist Peter Gordon of Columbia University made a series of experiments with Pitrahã people. In some of these, he drew a line on the ground between himself and one of the Indians and asked them to put the same number of objects on his side of the line as Gordon did on his. The Indians did this fairly well, placing up to three objects on the line, or more if they could place an object directly next to Gordon's. However, if, for example, they placed their objects orthogonal to his, only 30 - 60% managed to get it right when dealing with between four and eight objects, and no one could count nine objects correctly.[31]

But again, good traders are good code-makers, and their shared memory systems may include property deeds, patents, copyrights, literature, trademarks, accounting systems, measuring units and more. All of these are only of value if they are understood and recognized by all participants.

One of the most important common languages is money. In prehistoric times money didn't exist, but it was developed as soon as people started to trade: amber, seashells, camels, gold - almost anything was used as currency in primitive trade-based economies.

Money is often described as "a unit of accounting, a store of value and a medium of exchange", but is also an essential information technology which describes to us the value of a voluntary win-win transaction. Win-win, yes. But win-win how much? The money provides the answer in a simple, common code. Two camels. 20 seashells. One million dollars. Any blabbermouth can fantasize about how much he did for others, but if he does it in a marketplace, we can make a decent estimate of its value by counting the money people gave him for his effort (of course, there are exceptions to that).

So now we have the small units, the change agents, the network and the shared memory systems, and this creates self-organizing systems which are constantly experimenting and which will spontaneously write down the results of successful experiments in its memory systems and replicate and reward them, just like nature does in its DNA. We should be set for progress.

Great, but remember most mutations are, in fact negative, whether in biology, business or society as a whole. The natural tendency for human organisations is to become increasingly decadent, bureaucratic, self-serving and lazy, and thus stuck-in-a-rut; often to such an extent that they eventually fail completely. This well-known phenomenon reminds somewhat of inbreeding in small, isolated populations in nature, and it applies to private companies with monopoly status as well as to government agencies and charitable and religious institutions; in the book's fifth section we will study in more detail how it can happen.

However, there is a solution to this which is Darwin's competitive pressure, such as in business or natural eco systems, and this shows that our self-organizing creative system absolutely requires its fifth element:

5. Competition. This will usually prevent bad permutations from spreading, whereas the good becomes more widespread. Societies without competitive pressure will eventually (or quite quickly) experience an overall decline, because most changes are actually negative.

So now we have listed the five elements required for spontaneous creativity in a system. When all of these are combined, something truly magical occurs: we start expanding our social networks and co-operating within our entire social space while we also achieve exponential growth in our creative design space.

The people who start such a process are not likely to comprehend the magnitude of what will follow as a consequence of their actions. When a few humans started trading with each other tens of thousands years ago, they could never have known they had set in motion a process that would lead to space travel and discotheques, and nor would they ever understand that what they had started would inevitably evolve exponentially.

This is because exponential processes are very deceptive. IT professionals often tell a short story which illustrates the power of exponential growth. The story is about an artist who performs a play for a Chinese emperor, which the emperor enjoys so much that he asks the artist to state how he would like to be rewarded. "With rice,", the artist answers. "The amount should be calculated so that I receive a grain of rice for the first of the 64 squares on a chessboard, and then the number should double for each of the successive fields."

The emperor is happy with that, because it sounds like nothing, and so they begin to count: 2, 4, 8, 16, 32, 64, etc. However, when they get to field number 15, they get a bit concerned, because this one alone needs 24,576 grains of rice. In field 32, which is in the centre of the chessboard, they have reached 3,221,225,472 grains of rice, at which point the emperor gives an order for the artist to be decapitated. They could never have given him what he asked for, which was 13,835,058,055,282,200,000 grains of rice, equivalent to a rice mountain larger than Mount Everest. That's how exponetiality works.

We don't know exactly when humans started trading, but their creative design space at the time was probably not much more than around 15 things; perhaps controlled fire, stone axes, tents of skin, wooden skewers, cut stones, knives, ropes, serrated blades, domesticated wolves, bone needles, clothing, herbal medicine, boats, flutes and bone spearheads. So the accumulated innovation was tiny, but by trading and exchanging information and products, they had started the exponential process towards evermore diversity, and given around 15 innovations, they would already have recombined previous innovations. Boats, tents and clothes, for instance, would have required recombining elements of previous inventions, and we can easily see that there we quite a few other potential innovations to be developed out of what they had, such as bow and arrow, sails for their boats or fishing equipment.

They were on their way to something spectacular, but we can ask again: if Homo sapiens had existed 200,000 years, and trading started some 40,000 years ago (or even 10,000 or 20,000 thousand years earlier), why did they only start civilization 5,000 years ago?

The answers lies in our chess board story and, to see why, just think about the history of life. After the first self-replicating DNA (and sister molecule RNA) came bacteria. These may seem primitive to us, yet one bacterium may contain some 150 million atoms organized in a non-random structure, and is able to make a perfect copy of itself in, perhaps, 15 minutes – that is almost 17,000 atoms copied into an identical structure per second!

EXAMPLES OF META-IDEAS AND META-TECHNOLOGIES

- Trading
- Postal services
- Free trade agreements
- Logic and the scientific method
- Companies with limited liability
- The electronic computer
- Print media
- Musical notes
- Private companies and private property

- Science-based education
- The protection of patents, copyrights and trademark rights
- Email
- Banks, venture capital and private equity
- Electronic broadcast
- The internet
- Crowdsourcing (mobilizing crowds to solve creative challenges)

No wonder it took nature several billion years to get that sorted out. But afterwards, progress began to accelerate since nature possessed the red-hot combination of small units, change agents, networks, shared memory systems and competition. The creative design space started growing exponentially.

When seen in this light, it is not surprising that the human race spent approx. 120,000 years at pure Stone Age-level, then some 35,000 years creating the precursors of civilization, but took only 5,000 years to reach the industrial revolution and a further 300 years to reach the space age, with the biotech age arriving just 50 years later.

The story with the Chinese emperor assumes simply doubling on every square of the chess board but, in reality, the rate of growth will change periodically. This happens because of phase shifts, where we develop new meta-ideas (the aforementioned ideas about how to get ideas) or significant meta-technologies (technologies for making technologies). Trade was easily - as we have seen - the biggest meta-idea ever to have been conceived, but we have since come up with countless others, such as postal services or the internet.

Aren't there saturation points in this? For instance, with modern social media, we can each connect with millions, but the day only has 24 hours, so we run out of personal bandwith at some point, don t we?

Of course there are, but systems that fulfil our five criteria for creativity get around this as follows: self-organizing, creative systems foster new systems that follow the same simple rules, and this happens in endless cascades. For example, genes made proteins and enabled life, which created organisms which created ecosystems, which created intelligent beings, which created trade, which created culture, which created civilization, which created artificial intelligence. The next in line may include robotic communities and creative computers that can interact spontaneously over the internet.

The gist of this is truly fascinating: At some point in the very distant past, some amino acids linked up in a pattern that could serve as a replicator and then - voila! - started an endless cascade of mutations that created bacteria, dinosaurs, orchids and us. Later, two Stone Age men began to trade with each other and it led to the Roman Empire, Titanic and Pink Floyd. A man invents a transistor, and we end up with the smartphone, satellite TV and robot planes. Another man invents the internet protocol and we now have Facebook, Google and YouTube.

It is fascinating that such simple, basic principles can create such complex results, but this is exactly how creative, self-organizing systems evolve, and we cannot understand the possibilities and the problems of our own civilization if we do not get this phenomenon completely under the skin: our primary resource is the creative design space, which we need to nourish and grow. It is not iron, in the ground or plants on the land. It is primarily the dynamics of creative transaction that make us rich, not natural resources, and we need a very deep understanding of how that works.

Two more things: Intuitively we feel that simple systems are very robust, and that can certainly be true in some cases. However, generally, complex self-organizing systems are far more robust than the simple ones, because the more diverse and de-centralized a system is, the more options it has for adapting to change through new combinations and backup solutions. Its creative design space is larger and it mutates more. That's why the internet is so robust, and why the Soviet Union wasn't. Also, intuitively we may feel that self-sufficiency is most safe. It isn't. After tree generations promoting self-sufficiency, North Korea had several million starved to death, whereas South Korea, which embraced openness to global trade, had none.

Here comes a question: We saw that money is an information technology that informs us about the value of experiments and rewards those who performed them. So, if someone has a good idea, it is obvious that others will copy it, so who gets the spoils? The answer is that the spoils come in two forms, which economists may call "Schumpeter profit" or "alchemist's fallacy".[32]

The former may, for instance, be the profits a pharmaceutical company obtains by inventing and patenting a new product (please note that the patenting is an example of our shared memory system).   Any patent expires, however, and then come all the copy-cats who make very cheap, generic versions of the product at razor thin margins. From this point on, the invention is predominantly to the benefit of society as a whole rather than the original inventors.

The reason the second phase is called the Alchemist's fallacy is that something similar would have happened had the medieval alchemists actually found a way to transform lead into gold: the price of gold would quickly have plunged so the alchemist's gains would have swiftly disappeared.

Let's ask again: who gets what? How are the spoils divided up according to this Schumpeter/alchemist dichotomy? According to studies conducted by Yale economist William Nordhaus, entrepreneurs keep, on average, 4% of the added value they generate – the remaining 96% is shared by society as a whole.[33] These numbers are only averages, of course, and there are cases where the inventor gains more than the 4%, and cases where he or she gains less than that or even nothing or a loss. For example, Johannes Gutenberg, who changed history by inventing the printing press, went bankrupt while society benefitted enormously.

Speaking of money; where does the value come from? When our creative design space was tiny, it surely came largely from ideas. For instance, once a Stone Age man had the idea to combine the bone spearhead and string he had into a bow and arrow, it can't have taken much work to make the first prototype – perhaps a few hours. However, as our technologies grew more complex the time lapse between having the idea and putting it into production must have increased steadily. Before Thomas Edison could file his patent application for the light bulb, he had tested 1,600 different materials - including fibres' from coconuts, fishing line and hair from a friend's beard – and had written 40,000 pages of testing notes. No wonder he later remarked that a "genius consists of 1% inspiration and 99% perspiration." As the creative design space expands, implementation of ideas becomes a greater limiting factor than having ideas in the first place.

We have now covered the core principles of self-organizing creativity and, with this in mind, we just need to address a few other basic concepts to be used in subsequent chapters. Let's start with the fact that we are all born with our genes and a variety of instincts, which give us characteristics:

◆ Action patterns
One can also tame a dog to have action patterns, so they are not unique to humans. However, we are much better than animals at transmitting learning from person-to-person, and when that happens, we develop:
◆ Memes
As good parents will know, it requires a lot of memes to enable a child to function reasonably well in society. If groups of people have roughly the same memes, then we say that they have in common:
◆ Culture
Memes are the yarns with which we knit culture. However, a power-structure will always evolve and the traditional core unit in this is:

◆ Tribes

We have already discussed tribes, but they can be defined as face-to-face social networks organized around genetic relationships and often also religion affiliation. As with tribes among apes, they are typically patrilocal (men stay put; women are exchanged).

Tribal societies may be stable but are rarely creative, and if there is more than one tribe in a tribal nation, you either need a very brutal dictator to keep it together, or there tends to be trouble. Also, tribes often lapse into violent conflict when a leader dies unless there is a son who takes over swiftly, and they tend to suffer from inbreeding. If tribalism occurs within a civilization, it is called nepotism, which goes to say that a tribal society is a nepotistic society.

Much of human history over the past 2,000 years has revolved around attempts to scale back tribal structures and replace them with:

◆ Civilizations

A beehive or an anthill is not a civilization, because we define civilizations as formal systems that have been conceived consciously and are based on devised rules and orders. An anthill or a beehive is based on action patterns and memes, but not on culture or civilization.

Today, many historians agree there are eight major civilizations: Western civilization, Orthodox Christian, Islam, Confucius area, Hindu, Buddhist, non-Islamic Africa and the Indian Latin America, but in reality, many live in the reality of a mixture of Western civilization and something else.[34]

Western civilization is essentially what developed out of Western Europe. Today it clearly includes Western Europe, the USA, Canada, Australia and New Zealand. You can also include parts of Israel, Eastern Europe and Latin America that have an ethnic majority of European immigrants and a Western-oriented culture, i.e. Brazil, Argentina, Uruguay, Chile, Puerto Rico and Costa Rica. Most people from these countries have cultures that are relatively compatible with Western civilization - they share a number of memes and a good deal of culture with other Westerners.

It should be noted that whenever a civilization has formed, the process has involved long, hard struggles to move allegiances from tribes to states. For example, you cannot have a functioning civilization if politicians, policemen, tax collectors or judges favour people from their own tribe over others.

Civilizations require high levels of mutual trust between their inhabitants, high levels of honesty, strong institutions and low levels of tribalism – otherwise they break down.

The concept of civilizations comes with a charming aura of ancient philosophy, elegant oratorical brilliance and deep thinking. The work of philosopher John Locke is one example. He wrote a series of sensational publications in the 17th century; for instance, in 1689, he argued for an emphasis on the individual because it was a natural instinct for people to make their own choices and feel free. The state should therefore respect and protect individual freedom, equality and sovereignty, he said, and, if laws were made correctly, they would protect people's liberty against such violations as criminal action. This, he believed, would increase people's freedom rather than restrict it. Moreover, he argued that it was practically impossible to impose a belief on people against their will, and as this would also be an infringement of their personal sovereignty, all states should practise religious freedom.

Some years earlier - in 1642 - 1651 - England's population had been involved in a nightmare spate of win-lose activity - there was actually a civil war. In the last year of this war, another philosopher named Thomas Hobbes published a book called *Leviathan* after the monster of biblical legend Leviathan. This book proposed that the state (the Leviathan) was needed to prevent people from hurting one another. This compromise required a "social contract", he said, because otherwise people would often abuse each other. In order to prevent such abuse, the Leviathan should, if necessary, use violence and, in consideration for this security, every citizen would have to give up some of his freedom – thus the social contract. Without it, you would have a war of all against all - "bellum omnium contra omnes" as he put it. In such a society, he observed, "there is no place for industry; because the fruit thereof is uncertain" and, as a consequence, he thought that life would be "solitary, poor, nasty, brutish and short."

That sounds unpleasant, but which kind of Leviathan do you need? The traditional sort is what the Chinese call (wáng), which means "king" or "monarch", and virtually every community has started with such a powerful man as their first Leviathan. Anthropologists sometimes refer to his kind as a "Big Man".

In very small clans, such a Big Man was often subject to inherent limitations, in that he could easily be killed or chased away if behaved too badly. As communities expanded, their Big Men, however, were no longer able to cope with it all, and were forced to recruit henchmen. This modified the dynamics, since these sidekicks demanded shares in the Big Man's privileges, in return for acting as his blood brothers and protectors. This was the foundation stone of the aristocratic form of government, but also of the state.

The early states were typically not too pretty, because their Big Men and their henchmen would, in many cases, systematically plunder normal citizens. In other words, the Leviathan was kleptocrat, as we call it today - an institutionalized bandit.

However, in 1748 came an outline for an alternative model of society in a book called *The Spirit of the Laws* from a Frenchman with the pompous name: Charles - Louis de Secondat, Baron de La Brede et de Montesquieu. Fortunately today we just call him Montesquieu and, besides, when he first published the book, it was under an assumed name for fear of reprisals. The most important section of his book dealt with how to prevent abuse of power by separating various state bodies so they could keep each other in check.

The combined ideas of John Locke, Thomas Hobbes and Montesquieu give us a pretty good introduction to what the creation of civilization really is all about. It is about 1) individual rights, such as freedom of speech or equality in the eyes of the law and 2) a social contract bringing with it the obligation upon citizens to pay tax and to obey laws and the right of governments to to enforce this. And 3) it is about the division of powers. Interestingly, the way to put these three arrangements in place comes down to just two processes: promoting the win-win concept and separating things.

First, you set rules that promote win-win transactions and inhibit or forbid win-lose or lose-lose transactions. Tribal societies do the same but, in a civilization, these rules are formalized and equally valid for all, no matter which tribe they come from – they are written down and made public.

Second, you separate functions and identities to avoid tribalism, nepotism, discrimination and power abuse, which could hinder the creative social space. We already saw that trade was an example of de-personalization, which separated it from the limitations of sympathy, family or friendship, making it much bigger. However, as we build civilizations, we separate much, much more. In an advanced civilization, the judicial, legislative and executive branches are separated. The press, the church and the Central Bank are also separated from the state. Personal ties and networks are separated from status under the law. Rights are kept separate from gender, sexuality, religion and race. Boards are separated from directors and shareholders. Auditing is separated from accounting. Food quality control is separated from food production. And so it goes, on and on; separate, separate, separate, and you will have small units and a better civilization. The purpose of all this is to create an ecosystem of entities which act predictably and according to their mandates, so that they have reduced ability to abuse power and whose rights are universally respected.

Although civilizations are formal, they are, curiously, far more open to newcomers than cultures. A German can move to Dubai and function very well in its civilization just as an Emirati can easily integrate into German civilization. But ask the German to adopt Dubain culture and mindsets, and vice versa, and it becomes a lot more challenging.

In order to acquire a culture - or to switch to a new culture - a person must make a great personal effort. They will have to change thousands of memes that they learned as a child or young, and this can be near impossible - they were hardwired into the brain at early age. Even if we want to move from one Western sub-culture to another, it may require much work or be impossible.

The reality is that, because civilizations write down and formalize their rules, you can enjoy the fruits of other people's knowledge and memes without acquiring these yourself and you can transfer aspects of given civilizations to new societies. The Japanese, Chinese and South Koreans, for example, have applied many aspects of Western civilization – and to great effect! - without dropping too much of their own culture.

In fact, Western civilization could eventually be adopted by all those who have a compatible culture at the very time it falls apart in the Western nations that first developed it. For instance, in principle, the Western civilization might, 50 years from now, flourish in China, while disintegrating in parts of Europe. That is not a forecast but it could happen, because memes are not tied to genes.

Perhaps we got a bit sidetracked here, because we were in the process of making definitions, so let's just finish that task with:

◆ International organizations
◆ Empires and supranational organizations, such as the UN or mega religions

We have an empire when a civilization manages other civilizations that are weaker. As mentioned, empires have come and gone over the years, but it seems likely that their era is now largely over; as Adam Smith predicted, voluntary win-win transactions are more economical than enforced centralization. Empires appear to have decreasing marginal returns as they expand. Heads of states, who want an empire of their own, are typically interested in the power and grandeur it can provide for them, but for the empires' citizens, the disadvantages often outweigh the benefits. As already mentioned, this argument was made by Adam Smith as Britain was in the process of building up its empire in the 18th century. What Smith favoured instead was simply to "rule the waves", as the British say; to lead in trade, because that is where the money is.

TO SUMMARIZE WHAT WE HAVE COVERED SO FAR – ALL OF IT:

◆ Spontaneous creativity happens in any system that has a combination of small units, change agents, networks, shared memory systems and competition.
◆ This creates a creative design space, which feeds on itself in an exponential way.
◆ The attraction of the creative design space compels people to expand their social networks and co-operate with strangers within their entire social space.

◆ A creative society (or any creative system such as nature) will spontaneously develop increased diversity, and creative systems will foster new such creative systems

◆ The process of forming a civilization is largely about 1) formalizing rules to promote and protect win-win and 2) separating functions to inhibit tribalism, nepotism, discrimination and power abuse.

◆ Societies that are successful in the very long run are generally not characterized by having many resources, but by being good at nourishing their creative design spaces. They are predominantly idea-based, in other words.

◆ Ideas created by individual units are shared with society at large which, because of the "Alchemist Fallacy", on average, obtain approximately 96% of the benefit.

◆ As the creative design space expands, ideas people have tend to require complex implementation, which means that implementation of ideas becomes a greater limiting factor than having ideas in the first place.

◆ An ideas-based society requires intellectual and financial property rights as well as win-win transaction to be protected by a state.

◆ A civilization based mainly on voluntary win-win transactions will create a more trusting, honest and creative culture and it will also change our genes to become "nicer".

◆ Most spontaneous changes in societies, as well as in nature, are negative, and all systems will therefore decay due to in-breeding or similar processes, unless there is competitive pressure.

That's roughly it, and this should shape our basic mindset in a few ways. First, we should typically focus our minds harder on voluntary facilitating transactions than on extracting resources. Second, beware the dangers of centralisation - small and decentralized is more creative than big and centralized. Third, keep culture in mind. A good civilization provides incentives for creation of a good culture, and the two should be compatible. Fourth: creative systems create diversity. It has been a frequent theme in movies and books that, in future, we will be dominated by a single dictator with media monopoly and a giant mainframe, but that is not the way creative societies develop. Finally, ensure the results of successful experiments are recorded, rewarded and duplicated. That, after all, is the DNA of creativity.

With these thoughts in mind, we shall now proceed to the second section of the book, which considers how the first civilizations developed and why the West became so big and dominant. We shall also dwell on the interactions between cultures and civilizations.

PART 2

THE RISES AND FALLS OF CREATIVITY

Until 1,000 years ago, Western nations were among the worlds poorest. But then their creativity began to sprout, and from the year 1450, it virtually exploded. During the following 250 years, the West established an unprecedented military, economic, cultural and technological global dominance.

But how do its creative processes work?

Other questions: why did this amazing creativity happen in the Middle Ages and not in Roman times or even earlier? And why did it happen in Western Europe, but not in Eastern Europe, the Middle East, China or elsewhere? And how does creativity cease?

4.
THE FIRST
CIVILIZATIONS

We shall now visit China's Shaanxi province.

In the spring of 1974, the people there were suffering the effects of a prolonged drought. One day in late March, six brothers met under some trees on the outskirts of the city to discuss strategies. The eldest of them, Yang Peiyan, pointed to a place which he thought seemed a good place to dig a well.

The next morning, the six brothers arrived with their spades and began digging a hole, four metres square. Everything went as expected until, around the middle of the day, they reached a very hard layer, approximately one metre in. "Maybe it's the top of an old clay oven", said one of them. That was what they hoped, because then they would soon break through its ceiling, and the digging would become much easier again.

It took two brutal days of hard work to break through the hard layer, which turned out to be approximately 30 cm deep – more than you might expect for the top of a clay oven. But after they had broken through, the digging became a lot easier as expected, and soon the hole was so deep they needed a ladder to climb down.

About a week later, the brothers encountered some small terracotta fragments. This didn't surprising them much, since they believed there had been a furnace on the ground before. However, on March 29, one of them hit a piece of pottery that was somewhat larger than before. He threw it away quickly without a second thought but, a few minutes later, one of the others said: "I've found a jar, a big one!" When they began to scrape this one free they saw, to their chagrin, that it was actually the torso of a pottery figure. They threw the disappointing discovery into the basket and pulled it up out of the hole.

A moment later, another of the brothers found a porcelain head. And after, that the artifacts just kept coming; porcelain arms, porcelain legs, procaine heads, arrowheads made of copper. They pulled it all up and threw it on the ground with the soil, while still digging for the water.

Meanwhile, some children had come to watch, and they began to throw stones at the objects and some of them took a few home to play with. Others also created a scarecrow of a porcelain torso, and a few picked up the arrowheads and brought them to a local recycling centre, where they sold them as metal scrap.

This is where this story might very well have ended, had an irrigation specialist from the nearest town not passed by three days later and asked to see the progress of the hitherto fruitless excavation (still no water). Here he noted the scattered remnants of terracotta in the excavated soil. Upon his return home, the specialist reported the discovery to Mr. Zhao Kangmin from the local cultural centre.

On 28 April; a month after the Yang brothers had started their excavation, Zhao came by with his bike, and when he saw pieces of terracotta body parts spread all over the ground, he knew this was something special. Still, he pondered for a while whether to tell anyone because it had proved dangerous, sometimes fatal (especially during Mao's former cultural revolution) to bring to light memories of the past which might be considered anti-revolutionary. He took the chance, went to the recycling centre to buy back the arrowheads, collected the discarded terracotta fragments, glued them together and exhibited it all in his cultural centre.

Nothing further happened over the following two months, until a journalist named Lin Anwen visited the cultural centre. When he saw the new objects exhibited, he became very interested and realised it was an important find. "This is not just anything," he thought. "Perhaps it stems back from China's early civilization."

He was right. It turned out that the figures were created by a civilization that had existed more than 2,000 years earlier. At that time, around the year 200 BC, the Chinese had a civilization that in many ways was far more advanced than the one that existed when the brothers dug their wells in 1974. It was probably this harsh fact that the Maoists wanted kept secret – that they lived in a civilization in steady decline, which had been declining for centuries, if not millenia.

How was it possible that China had a civilization in 1974, which in many ways was less advanced than that of 2,000 years earlier? Or more generally: how is is that some civilizations advance while others decline or collapse? In the previous chapters, we looked at the basic conditions for creativity and growth, but why do these conditions fluctuate in a given civilization?

Let's start from the beginning. Up until approximately 5,000 years ago, the planet was home to lots of cultures within which people traded with one another, but all societies were tribal with none formally organized as real civilizations. Interestingly, when civilizations finally arrived, they developed, curiously enough, in four different areas of the globe that had one trait in common: they all featured flowing water that people were able to to "tame" or manage.[35] Four out of four doesn't sound like a coincidence, and perhaps one reason is that as we all know from our childhood, it can be fascinating to try to control water. But "taming" it on a large scale can also be very useful.

The first of the four sites was in what is now Iraq; in the delta between the rivers Tigris and Euphrates, where there lived a people called the Sumerians.

These people had problems with regular flooding of their (otherwise very fertile and productive) delta, and they therefore (and maybe also because it was fun) began, from about 4,800 BC, to do something about it: they built dams, underground water chambers and drainage. They were creative, in other words, and, from about 3,300 BC, they began to develop the world's first city-state, although "town" may be a better description of what it was.

Similar processes, i.e. first taming of water and then the development of towns, came later by the Nile in Egypt (from approximately 3,200 BC), by the Indus River in India (also from approximately 3,200 BC) and by the Yellow River and Yangtze River in China (from approximately 2,000 BC). It happened later in the Americas, but this was probably for a simple reason. After people left Africa, some walked through Asia, up to Siberia, across to Alaska and then (according to recent genetic studies) all the way down the American West coast to Tierra del Guego in Southern Chile, before spreading inland towards Eastern North-and-South America. As long as these people carried on moving (this obviously took thousands of years), they remained pure extractors. They would not have farmed because they could always keep moving into new land, and they would have had very limited social spaces because the new places were free of people on all sides except where they came from. So self-taming, social interaction, permanent settlements and farming simply came much later to North America than to Euroasia, and it came even later to South America.

Alongside the taming of water and the construction of the first towns in Eurasia came agriculture. Exactly when this started, we do not know, but it's not hard to imagine how it could have happened: a group of hunters captured a large number of goats in one go and realized that if they killed them all, some of them would rot before they could be eaten. So they decided to keep some of them alive in captivity for later use. Then a goat has a kid, and it dawns on the hunters that they have invented an automatic meat machine!

Here's another scenario: while the men are out hunting, the women and children collect fruit, nuts and grass, and one of them realizes that if they sow or plant these just outside their residence, they will be spared a long walk.

These are obvious ideas, so it is no wonder that agriculture developed independently in the Middle East, Mexico, the Andes, China, the Brazilian rain forest, New Guinea and Africa within a few thousand years of one another and, in most of these places, it spread quickly after its start. In the beginning, these early farmers used no crop rotation, so the ground would quickly become depleted. In addition to this, there would eventually appear a high concentration of specific pests around any place in which people cultivated a particular kind of crop. For these two reasons, they became nomadic farmers, moving from place to place, which, of course, stimulated the adaption of their methods among other people.

Farming made it easier to stay closer together, so people could concentrate larger military forces. Also, the higher concentrations of people stimulated trade, which again made specialization feasible, so craftmansship improved. The fact that you did not have to carry all your possessions around anymore made it feasible to have more of them. So people started to work harder to become richer; perhaps because the richest men won the most attractive women, which created genetic selection for strivers.

Complexity grew and, for example, Sumerians developed architecture and city-planning to organize their living spaces and writing systems and simple counting systems to organize their trade and distribution systems. Their largest city, Uruk, was at its peak around 2,900 BC, a six square kilometre extension and, by then, probably contained around 50,000-80,000 inhabitants who lived protected behind a defence wall. Never before had the world seen anything remotely like that, and Uruq was now the centre of the world.

However, Uruk would soon be overtaken by the Chinese, particularly thanks to a man named Qin Shih Huang, who lived from year 260 to 210 BC.[36] Qin's father was the ruler of one of seven rival states in an area that made up a large part of modern China, and when his father died in 246 BC, the young boy replaced him as local ruler. He then managed, through a series of victorious military expeditions, to gather all the seven states under its own leadership. This became the foundation of the Chinese empire, which he named after himself ("China" is derived from Qin). All this happened more than 2,200 years ago.

While before his tenure, China had suffered countless wars, it had actually also been pretty creative with a thriving culture based on the principle of "the hundred schools". This phenomenon, which dates back to 770 BC (2,800 years ago), involved an ongoing process of combining different philosophies in a "melting pot", that led to lots of creativity and innovation. However, Qin ordered the burning of all written texts in year 213 BC and furthermore the live burial of 460 Confucian scholars three years later. Meanwhile he introduced a single philosophy called legalism, which is quite easy to explain: it meant that people should strictly abide by the law.

These laws stated, among other things, that people should participate in public projects and it was through this that Qin managed to build the Great Wall, which is still the world's largest man-made structure. He also built a number of roads that connected his, now gigantic, empire. In 214 BC - four years before his death – he started to design the 36 km long Lingqu channel that would connect two rivers, which meant that you could sail no fewer than 2,000 km through China without ever having to cross land. It still works today.

There was also a very personal, private project. After his death Qin wanted to be buried in an underground tomb with an entire army plus various other delights. According to historian Sima Qian, who lived 145 BC - 90 AD, so was born just 65 years after Qin 's death, 700,000 workers were employed in the construction of this mausoleum. Furthermore, he reported that this amazing tomb contained mercury-filled models of 100 of China's rivers and models of palaces and towers. The ceiling was supposedly decorated with celestial bodies, protected by (Indiana Jones-style) crossbows that would automatically shoot intruders.

This written account was the only reasonably reliable source we had about this Qin's mausoleum - until fairly recently.

And now we must return to the story of the six Yang brothers in Shaanxi Province and their failed attempt to plumb a well. We had reached the point in the story when a reporter from the news agency Xinhua had entered the local cultural centre and sensed that the copper spearheads and terracotta on display were very old and significant.

On 24 June 1974, Lin Anwen reported his observation to central government. The officials sent archaeologists out to the site of the well to take a look, where they found an astonishing quantity of porcelain items and arrow heads. They dug further, and eventually they could form a picture of it all. This find, they now understood, had to be Qin's tomb, and it probably contained some 40,000 copper objects and some 6,000 terracotta soldiers, statuettes of 130 chariots, 520 terracotta draft horses and 150 terracotta cavalry horses had been buried there - most of them life-size.

It is now assumed that the entire underground complex is more than 20,000 square metres in size (200,000 square feet), and there are still large parts of it that haven't been excavated. Most interesting among the areas not yet opened up is an apparent burial mound, which is found above parts of the mausoleum, and which probably contains the remains of the deceased emperor himself .

China under Qin was not just a civilization - it was an empire. As we previously discovered, an empire can be defined as a society in which people from one civilisation rule others. The point at which a specific society can be described as an empire is a matter of definition, but most descriptions of the history of empires put the total number at approximately 200. The following table shows the most important of them.

It is remarkable - and very rich food for thought - that all previous empires have disappeared. Take, for example, the Egyptian Empire which, for a long period of time, constituted the world's most advanced civilization with an extremely advanced division of labour and technical capability. In its third dynasty (2,737-2,717 BC), Egyptian ruler Djoser managed to develop an effi-

Name	Period	Duration in years	Max size in landmass; mio. km2	Max population in percent of world total
The Egyptian Empire	1570-1070 BC.	500	1	4
The Persian Empire	550-330 BC.	220	8	44
The Chinese Qing- Empire	221 BC. - 1912 AD	2133	14,7	37
The Roman Empire	27 BC. - 1453 AD (the Western Roman empire fell in 476 AD)	1480	6,5	36
The Byzantine (Eastern Roman) Empire	330-1453	1123	1,35	5
The Umayyad Caliphate	622-750	138	13	30
The Mongol Empire	1206-1260	54	33	26
The Osmannic Empire	1299-1922	623	5,2	7
The Portuguese Empire	1415-1999	584	10,4	1
The Spanish Empire	1492-1975	483	20	12
The British Empire	1583-1997	414	33,7	23
The Mugal Empire	1526-1857	341	4,6	29
The Russian Empire	1721-1917	196	23,7	10

THE LARGEST EMPIRES IN WORLD HISTORY IN CHRONOLOGICAL ORDER.[37] THE MOST REMARKABLE FIGURES FOR DURATION, SIZE AND POPULATION ARE HIGHLIGHTED IN GREY BACKGROUND. ALL OF THESE EMPIRES, AND ALMOST 200 OTHERS, HAVE FALLEN.

cient bureaucracy and introduce construction with cut stone blocks. When he died, he was buried in a pyramid 62 metres high, which still stands to this day. His successor promoted international trade and began the construction of the largest pyramids, which are also still preserved.

While Egypt arguably remained the most advanced civilization on the planet for more than two millennia, and while it simultaneously ruled the world's oldest empire in 500 years, it is China that takes the prize for being the world's longest-lasting empire of 2,133 years. China was also one of the two empires that held the largest share of the world's contemporary population - approximately 37% (the other being Rome).

The Chinese Empire was, in many ways, fabulous. During China's Song Dynasty, which started approximately 1,200 years after Emperor Qin's death and lasted until 1,279, Hangzhou served as the national capital, which made it the world's most advanced city - an honorary title that previously could have been given to Uruk, Athens, Alexandria and Baghdad.

In Hangzhou, one could then find hundreds of restaurants, hotels and theatres. There were tea houses with landscaped gardens, large-collared lamps, fine porcelain, calligraphy and paintings by famous artists. The night-life was rich and varied, and there were skilled puppeteers, sword-swallowers, theatres with professional actors, acrobats, musicians, snake-charmers, storytellers and more. In addition, those with particular interests could join clubs for food, art, antiques, music, horseback riding and poetry. And all this happened around 800 years ago.[38] In parallel with this cultural extravaganza, the Chinese developed a range of new technologies. For example, they introduced the world's first paper banknotes as well as the first printing machines, gunpowder, matches, toothbrushes and compasses.[39] They also studied biology, botany, zoology, geology, mineralogy, astronomy, medicine, archaeology, mathematics, cartography, optics, and developed social programmes such as nursing homes, public hospitals and cemeteries. They had efficient postal services and constructed public buildings which they maintained with great care. In addition, they took care to further develop China's already extensive road network, and they had thousands of ships that criss-crossed rivers and coastlines, including some which served as floating restaurants.

Because China was successful and well-protected, its population increased rapidly. The best estimates tell us that, in the 1400s, there lived 100 million to 130 million people in China compared with just 50 million to 55 million across Europe.[40] Because of China's population size and creativity, the Chinese were capable of taking on tasks, which were entirely outside of European capability. Let's take an example: We all know the story of Christopher Columbus, who sailed to America in 1492. He had a total crew of 87 men plus three ships which were 18, 17 and 15 metres in length, respectively.

Impressive indeed, and we shall later revisit that story. But by comparison, between 1405 and 1433, a Chinese citizen named Zheng He led seven international expeditions to the African East coast, Saudi Arabia and Indonesia with some 300 ships and a crew of approximately 30,000 men. According to contemporary records, some of these boats were 150 metres long (approximately 450 feet) and had nine masts. Zheng He returned from his trip – which

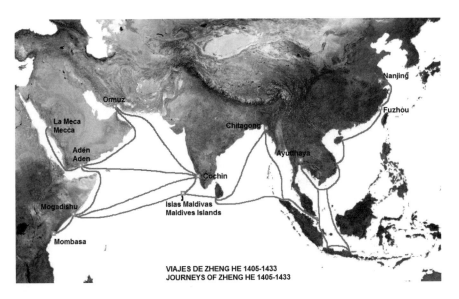

VIAJES DE ZHENG HE 1405-1433
JOURNEYS OF ZHENG HE 1405-1433

ZHENG HE EXPEDITIONS 1405-1433.

took place more than half a century before Columbus' - with a cargo of luxury goods including gold, silver, copper and silk, as well as a collection of exotic animals, all of which were gifts for the emperor.

The reality is that even many hundred of years before the birth of Christ, China had a large middle and upper class society, which cultivated and valued products of exceptional beauty and quality, such as fine pottery (which we still today refer to as "china"), gold, opulent jewellery, refined penmanship, calligraphy, paintings, beads, silver, ivory and of course the famous Ming vases. There were major art collectors, who were advised by art experts. Their ship-building technology was way ahead of Europe's at the time of Columbus, and their boats had watertight compartments.

It was also the Chinese who, between 1403 and 1408, set out to create an encyclopaedia of all known knowledge. To that end, the emperor asked more than 2,000 researchers and authors to read 8,000 sources and extract the information. When this encyclopaedia was finished, it included almost 23,000 hand-written scrolls. In terms of words, it remained the world's biggest encyclopaedia in the 600 years to the 2007, when it was finally surpassed by online encyclopaedia Wikipedia, which no one printed out.[41]

The Chinese had tremendous knowledge, but one thing they apparently did not know. They did not know that there was an almost equally phenomenal empire with an equally large population on the other side of the world: the Roman Empire, which emerged a few hundred years later than the Chinese

Empire. Nor did the Romans apparently know about the Chinese Empire - a peculiarity when you consider that these empires, at one time, together comprised almost three-quarters of the world's population.

Rome was as culturally-fascinating as China and it also introduced a model of society which would later serve as inspiration for many states, including large parts of today's Western world. The precursor for that model came from Greece.

The "Greece" of antiquity was not actually a country, but a scattered cluster of independent mini-states with a shared culture and language. Nor did the people in this culture call their civilization "Greek" at the time, but "Hellenic"; the name "Greece" was coined by the Romans later. Between 700 BC and 350 BC, this area combined all of our criteria for spontaneous creativity: 1) small units 2) change agents, 3) networks, 4) shared memory systems, and 5) competition.

Let's start with the small units. Greek civilization comprised up to 1,000 independent mini-states or "polis", as these were known, most of which were in the area that is now modern Greece, but with some in Greek settleements elsewhere in the Mediterranean. Athens, at its peak, contained approximately 400,000 citizens and slaves; Syrakuse, which was a Greek settlement in Sicily, had 200,000 citizens/slaves and Sparta some 150,000, but many other polis had perhaps 5-10,000 inhabitants, and some were much smaller than that; tiny self-ruling villages.

So Greek civilization was extremely decentralized, and it was also exposed to many change agents, as each of these polis were influenced by the others and also by wide-ranging overseas trade and relationships with Greek settlements elsewhere.

That brings us to networking: The Greeks enjoyed excellent networking due to their sailing culture that was stimulated by Greece's countless islands, curved coastlines, natural harbours and reasonably-calm seas. Networking also happened because groups of mini-states formed loose military alliances around one of the bigger ones. One example was the Delian Leque, which consisted of 150-173 polis under the leadership of Athens, and others included the Spartan League and the Boeotian League.[42] These unions were loose, temporary and shifting, but they did facilitate communication between their members for as long as they lasted.

Fourth, in spite of its decentralization, the Greeks benefitted from speaking a common language and having shared alphabet, numbering system, religion and so on.

And finally, the Greeks had a highly competitive culture, which included commercial competition, staging of frequent drama competitions, fiercely

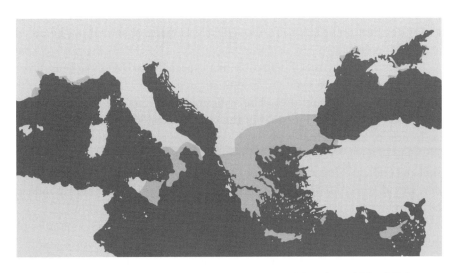

THE GREEK CIVILIZATION 336 BC. AS THE MAP SHOWS, IT IS NO COINCIDENCE THAT THE ROMANS WERE INSPIRED BY THE GREEKS, WHO LIVED IN SOUTHERN ITALY.[43]

competitive sports games (they invented the Olympic Games), and wars.

The Greeks had spread out and settled on the coastal areas of North Africa, around the Black Sea, and in Spain, France, Corsica, Sardinia plus southern Italy, where they established similar small city-states as part of a loose, de-centralized civilization.

Although primitive democracy may well have existed from time-to-time in small Neolithic societies, people today describe some of the Greek city states as the first civilized democracies in world history and, of these, Athens, which introduced its extensive democracy in 453 BC, became the most advanced. Athens was home to great scientists, historians and philosophers such as Aristotle, Plato, Socrates, Euripides, Herodotus and many others who we still admire today.

Athens had become extremely wealthy through shipping and trade, and the city gradually began to attract creative and ambitious people from neighbouring areas. Classical Athens was thus, for a time, extremely dynamic, and it was characterized by freedom, democracy, creativity, individualism and enjoyment of life, although much of this was less true for women, let alone slaves.

Athens was also famous for its philosophers' widespread (and correct) belief, that most complex phenomena in nature could be explained by relatively simple underlying principles. For example, one of Athens' philosophers thought that all matter was in fact composed of different sorts of water (wrong). Another thought it was made up of a combination of earth, fire, air and water (hmmmhh). A third thought it was made of something he called atoms. Bingo!

Art was another Greek fascination that especially thrived in Athens. Over time this evolved into ever-more sophisticated pottery, architecture, paintings, figurines and sculptures. The sculpures were initially inspired by the enormous Egyptian sculptures, but the Greeks learned, over time, to create sculptures of humans that were far more life-like and expressive. They called this kind of work "technología", which was a combination of "technē" for art, skill and craft and "logos", which meant "word" or "expression of an idea". Today, we call it technology, although we sometimes forget that this can indeed be an art.

The Greeks, and in particular the Athenians, also introduced a number of political concepts that the world had not seen before, and the word "politics" even comes from the Greek "politicos". Their word "isegoria" meant freedom to speak in public, "parrhesai" meant the right to say whatever you wished, "demokratia" meant rule by the people, and "eleuteria" meant liberty; it is no coincidence that Athens named three of its warships Demokratia, Eleuteria and Parrhesai, respectively.

They fought for these concepts, and they fought hard. Of course, one might have expected that a disadvantage of decentralization was reduced ability to wage large-scale war, but this wasn't so. This became evident when the Greeks were confronted by attacks from mighty Persian armies between 499 and 449 BC. During the most intense series of these attacks, which took place between 480 and 490 BC, the Persians commanded the largest army and navy in the world, which was under the unified command of the Persian king Xerxes. This force attacked much smaller ones assembled by interim alliances between Hellenic city states such as Athens, Sparta, Corinth, Chalcis and Aegina.

However, even though the Greeks could mobilize far fewer soldiers and ships than the Persians, and even though they often disagreed violently on strategy in what the contemporary historian Herodotus called their "war of words" (their commanders often screamed at each other in public strategy debates), when it came to actual battle, the Greeks beat the Persians again and again. For instance, at the great sea battle at Salamis in 480 BC, a Greek navy destroyed a much larger Persian one sinking approximately 200 Persian ships and killing at least 40,000 Persians; the Greeks only lost 40 ships and a few thousand men at most. At the Battle of Thermopylae in 480 BC, 300 determined Spartans, supported by 5,000 - 20,000 other Greek volunteers, managed to block a pass, holding off 70,000 – 300,000 Persian soldiers for a week and, at the battle of Marathon in 490 BC, some 10,000 Greeks soundly beat a Persian army two-and-a-half times its size. All in all, the Persian king Xerxes, who controlled 70 million people and an area 20 times bigger than Greece, lost 250,000 men in his various failed attempts to conquer two million Greeks.

Despite Greek ideals of freedom, democracy, in 404 BC, Athens was conquered by Sparta, which in many ways was its opposite. Sparta was an authoritarian society based on discipline and ascetic lifestyle. Here, all male citizens worked for the state as full-time soldiers, and Sparta's citizens were, by law, excluded from carrying out trade and craftsmanship and could apparently not own gold or silver or in any way demonstrate signs of prosperity, which is why anyone having a similar lifestyle today is called "Spartan". Most of its inhabitants were slaves who did all the manual work with the women. This nation had no philosophers, historians, writers and architects.

The hyper-creative Greek era of many small city-states lasted for approximately 350 years from around 700 BC to 359 BC, when Phillip II of Macedonia in northern Greece began to conquer the surrounding city states one after the other. At some point in the mid 340s BC, he sent the Spartans a note which, according to one source, said: "If I win this war, you will be slaves forever" and to another "If I bring my army into your land, I will destroy your farms, slay your people, and raze your city." According to both accounts, the Spartans' replied with one of the coolest military bulletins of all times. It contained just one word: "If".

Phillip decided to avoid Sparta, but eventually conquered the rest of the Greek states and united them in a federation. His son Alexander the Great used this as a basis for mobilizing an army that conquered Persia and continued into Pakistan, Syria, Egypt and other countries, where he, for a while, controlled some 5.2 million square kilometres (two million square miles) of land. After his early death, the empire was broken up, and some Greek states such as Rhodes, Dilos, Crete and Chios re-emerged as strong financial centres, but the creative era of hundreds of independent city-states never returned.

While the Greek civilization still comprised hundreds of tiny city-states, Rome had itself been such a miniature nation. Founded during the Etruscan era, it was only one among many others on the Italian peninsula. Like these others, Rome had, at this time, been led by a Big Man - an absolute monarch, who was elected for life by a local Senate. However, probably in the year 509 or 510 BC, there was a rebellion, where this leader was deposed by a number of the city's aristocrats. The city's patriarchs now established a new form of government, which eventually came to delegate responsibility between patriarchs and ordinary citizens, called plebeians.

In the year 494 BC, Rome was involved in a war, but the plebeian army simply refused to fight unless Rome's laws and regulations were written down and applied equally to all free men. This, they hoped, would ensure they always knew where they stood and no longer needed to pander to the powerful. They demanded, in other words, what we today call a constitutional state. At first, the aristocrats refused this, but after years of discord, they agreed to send a commission of three patricians to Greek towns to study how democracy worked there. We don't know if these towns were in Greece or they were Greek settlements in Southern Italy. The latter sounds very likely as, for instance, Naples (Napoli in Italian) just of couple of days travelling from Rome, was of Greek origin. Its original name was Neopolis, which was Greek for Newtown.

To the Romans, it was Athens, which was the inspiration; not Sparta. Many Romans spoke Greek as well as Latin, and it was common among the upper classes either to send their children to Athens or perhaps to Greek settlements in Southern Italy to study or to employ Greek slaves to teach their children Greek. In either case, many of them would know about Greek ideas of politika, isegoria, parrhesai, demokratia and eleuteria. They would know about the freedom some of the Greeks practised.

The Roman interpretation of the Athenian model became wildly successful, because100 years later - in the year 275 BC - Rome had, through a series of military victories and political alliances, taken control of most of the Italian peninsula, and over the subsequent 300 years, the Roman conquests continued. The geographical culmination of the empire came in the year 117 AD, when the empire also encompassed the entire North African coast as well as parts of Great Britain, Iran, Iraq and some other areas.

While the geographical expansion stopped at this point, the Roman culture and civilization continued to flourish. During its golden age under Antonius Pius (138 -161 AD) , the imperial capital had more than 25 public libraries where people could borrow books, and reading was now so popular that Romans had private book collections, even though books were handwritten and therefore very expensive. By this time, many houses in Rome were richly decorated with art and had floors with fine mosaics and walls adorned with frescoes; many even had running water.

Like the Chinese, the Romans evolved as sybarites and advanced connoisseurs of the good things in life. For instance, as they produced large quantities of wine, they also started to write reviews about the best vintages, such as that from the year 121 BC, which was said to be particularly delicate.[44] Roman society was now much better organized than surrounding countries and its postal service could, for example, transport letters and parcels at an average speed of 65 km a day.

Just as we can admire Roman administration, we can enthuse about some of the art and architecture. A visit to the excavated Roman city of Pompeii, for example, is very impressive. This village was buried in ash and pumice in 79 AD, so what we see today is exactly how it was on that devastating day. Here we see countless restaurants and pizza bars and a public sauna built with double walls, so the steam could be trapped between them to create a well-distributed heating effect. The ceilings in the sauna are decorated with paintings and sculptures and boasted trenches to prevent drops of condensation from falling onto the bathers. Life was good!

But beneath the surface, problems began to accumulate. The first was that, since 49 BC, after 500 years of Greek-style democracy the empire had developed an autocratic management style. Getting ahead in Rome now rested either on military merits or flawless rhetoric; being able to express yourself clearly and elegantly. Form was more important than practical experience.

The second and bigger problem was that many of Rome's conquests were constantly on the verge of starvation and provided no returns to the empire - it was perhaps only Egypt that provided the Romans with a stable profit. In addition, more and more practical work was now, as in Sparta , done by slaves. This was not a model to stimulate innovation, because new ideas for managing production will rarely appear if you spend your life in a villa removed from the place of production.

In addition, the army increasingly comprised non-Romans; for example, under, the emperors Trajan and Hadrian (who reigned in 98 -117 and 117-138 respectively) less than 1% of the Roman army was actually made up of Romans.[45]

As the empire reached its maximum geographical extent under these emperors, and as its culture sparkled in that period, the financial tensions began to grow, until they reached breaking point. When Emperor Trajan realized he could not recover sufficient taxes, he introduced forced labour and his successor Hadrian expanded the secret police, hired more internal spies and built a greater layer of bureaucracy in order to collect taxes and keep the ever-more dissatisfied citizens in check.

In his book *The World of Late Antiquity*, historian Peter Brown describes how art and culture blossomed in the later stages of the Roman Empire, but also how people complained that there now seemed to be more tax collectors than tax payers. For example, the state introduced the equivalent of modern VAT but, in practice, this was enormously expensive to collect, as there now had to be a government official present at all business transactions.[46]

The situation deteriorated. In the early fourth century, most industries were forced into the so-called *collegia*, which were mandatory professional associations. To ensure traders did not evade taxation, they were now effectively indentured and could no longer leave their jobs or homeland, and their children were forced to take up the same professions as their parents. Similarly, farmers were forced into large agricultural communities called latifundia and could not leave these again. These labourers were now called coloni, and they were actually, in some ways, even more tied to the spot than the slaves, who, after all, could be sold or purchased free of their owners, if they were lucky.[47] In the year 380, a new law prohibiting young people from marrying outside their own class or industry was introduced, and to prevent the youth from escaping the taxmen, they were branded on their arms with their status. The state was now clearly no longer there to protect win-win transactions between individuals - it was instead engaged in a gigantic win-lose transaction between itself and the majority of the empire's inhabitants.

The rising taxes, the increasing control and surveillance of the population and the ever-harsher restrictions on movement were not the only symptoms of the developing economic crisis. Persecution of the peasants and craftsmen also led to shortages, but to avoid the inflation that usually follows this, a death penalty was introduced for raising prices. However, inflation snuck in through the back door, as the government gradually reduced the silver content of coins from approximately 95% to eventually less than 5%.[48] Soon these coins were considered so worthless that even the state itself would no longer accept them as tax payments. Instead people had to pay in kind through forced labour, or with pure precious metals.

Even that was not sufficient to fill the coffers, and the army began, in parallel, to collect taxes from the people in the areas it passed on its way. It must have been a hellish experience for farmers to have be visited by an army of men collecting taxes and booty.

The increased (regular) tax burden hit farmers especially, which accounted for some 90% of gross domestic product (GDP). Eventually, taxes became so high that more and more left their farms and moved to cities, so that they could get closer to where the tax money was spent, and further away from where taxes were collected. The fields began to lay fallow, which obviously necessitated even higher taxes, which again increased the costs of collecting taxes - a vicious circle that had the added effect of causing food production to fall dramatically.[49] Under Emperor Valens, who reigned 364-378, there were some provinces in which between half and a third of the land was abandoned by peasants, despite the official movement restrictions. The state now tried to discourage further tax avoidance by forcing local communities to pay land tax on rural areas, whether they were cultivated or not.

The entire economic system was thus slowly disintegrating, and when people increasingly lacked a viable currency, they began to focus more on self-sufficiency and barter trade. Peasant revolts were becoming increasingly common and, instead of fighting the regular invading barbarians, peasants would frequently join them; it was no longer unusual for enterprising farmers to run away from Rome and instead work, for example, among the Germanic tribes in the north.

One of the most famous historians of all time, and many historians' first source for analysis of Rome's decline and eventual downfall, is Edward Gibbon, who, between 1776 and 1789, produced a body of work in six parts called *The History of the Decline and Fall of the Roman Empire*.[50] This extends over some 4,000 pages, and Gibbon took advantage, as far as possible, of the original contemporaneous sources.

Very simply put, his overall conclusion is that the Roman Empire fell not only because of over-taxation, but because its original culture, values, morals and virtues had been degraded. The Romans rarely did their own practical (including military) work, but left this to slaves; they themselves became sloppy, pampered, unworldly and unwilling to defend the empire economically or militarily.

Gibbon added another explanation for Rome's demise. He believed that logical and rational thinking inspired by Athens had been one of the main sources of Rome's initial success, but concluded that it began to degrade in the empire's later stages, where people turned away from both rational though and cultural achievement. From the first century AD onwards, this philosophy manifested itself among Roman cynics. Cynicism was a native Greek philosophy, its literal meaning being to live like dogs or "dog people". The cynics rejected material possessions, sex, power and vanity in favour of a simple life without any cultural or personal possessions. Often they even chose to live as beggars and dressed in rags deliberately.[51]

Gibbon also assigned a great part of the responsibility for Rome's decline to the behaviour of the Praetorian Guard. This was originally created by Emperor Augustus as a sort of personal bodyguard. During the first 200 years of its existence, it was mostly a positive and stabilizing factor, and it would remove particularly crazy or incompetent emperors from time-to-time. This could be necessary, as there was no shortage of these. For instance, Emperor Caligula opened a brothel in his palace, raped many women and took pleasure in reporting details of these experiences to their husbands. He also committed incest and appointed his favourite horse as priest (and promised that it should become consul). Elagabalus attended government meetings dressed as a transvestite and tried to castrate himself, while Nero murdered his mother, beat his wife to death accidentally and confiscated senators' property so he could build himself an enormous golden villa.

The Praetorian Guard typically got rid of bad emperors by killing them (for example, they cut off Elagabalus' head off and tossed the rest of the body into the Tiber river). However, over time, their sense of mission started to change, and they now evolved into a sort of armed parasite that predominantly served itself.

THE MOST LIKELY REASONS FOR THE FALL OF ROME

- Conquests became unprofitable after the first raids
- The transition from democracy to dictatorship undermined responsibility and loyalty
- Slaves lacked personal loyalty and motivation to innovate
- Over-taxation led to the abandonment of farms and growing disloyalty
- Increasing superstition, irrationality, cynicism and cultural indifference
- Dilution of the silver content of coins led to partial barter and self-sufficiency rather than trade
- Praetorian Guard became self-serving

As if all these problems were not enough, Rome also suffered from mis-allocation of capital, as savings were primarily used for unproductive land purchase, which didn't contribute to any productivity increases and led to increased concentration of ownership. And finally, it became increasingly intolerant of diversity and dissent. For instance, emperor Theodosius burned the great library in Alexandria, Egypt in 391, and two years later, in 393 he outlawed the pagan rituals at the Olympics, after which they were terminated and remained so for the next 1,503 years (the games were restarted in 1896).

Adding up all these factors, the empire increasingly looked like something that would collapse, and that was indeed what happened. In the year 406, the Romans received alarming reports that Germanic barbarians had crossed the Rhine and begun trespassing on Roman territory. Just four years later, the barbarians attacked and briefly plundered the capital itself, having marched down the Italian peninsula without encountering much resistance.

The barbarians left again, but 15 years later Rome abandoned England, and soon lost much of its Spanish and French lands followed by North Africa. Over the following 50 years, disintegration was complete, and the city of Rome's population declined by three-quarters.

The Western Roman Empire went from total domination to total extinction within just 71 years. The Eastern Roman Empire survived as the dirigiste Byzantine Empire until this was wiped out in 1453 by the Ottoman Muslims. Byzantium, we should add, was the name of a Greek village in present day Turkey, which was later renamed Constantinople as it became the capital of the Eastern Roman emporiums. Today it is called Istanbul.

The stories of the first great civilizations provide general food for thought, because it was not only Rome that fell, but each and every empire that has ever existed. Nowadays, few people speak of the great Mesopotamian, Cretan, Sinitic or Canaanite civilizations and yet, these were very powerful in the past.

From this, it is difficult to conclude anything other than civilizations and empires almost inevitably create something that destroys themselves from within. If you read a very brief history of Rome's rise and fall, one may be led to believe that empire fell because it was overrun by barbarians. Well yes, it fell when it was overrun, but such an interpretation is rather misleading. Before it was overrun it had, as we have seen, been decaying for a very long time. Rome was already about to collapse from within, when the barbarians broke through. The forces that finally brought the empire to its knees were heavily outnumbered by Roman citizens; the Vandals, who conquered North Africa, never numbered more than 80,000 and, even more remarkably, the Ostrogoths, who took over Italy and parts of, inter alia, Switzerland and Croatia, were in a minority of about 5% of the local population that they subdued.

In earlier days, there had always been barbarians harassing Rome at its borders, but it had brushed these off fairly easily and often, subsequently, assimilated them quite successfully. One reason was simply that life in Rome in those days was considered so attractive that many barbarians volunteered for the Roman army or settled on Roman soil. In fact, it was often these barbarians who, after assimilation, conquered new areas for the Romans. In the early stages of the empire, Rome prevailed because people viewed what it offered as very attractive, and because the empire thus was able to mobilize them for its cause.

However, within the later stages of the empire, the common attitude had changed. Now, it was not longer thought attractive to live in the Roman Empire, where the state restricted people's movement and buried them in taxes. Nor was it any longer particularly prestigious or attractive to fight for a Roman army, which had increasing difficulties paying its soldiers. The reality was that if it had not been the Germanic barbarians who had taken Western Rome, it would have been only a matter of time before someone else had done so.

So Rome "committed suicide", and the ironic tragedy is that while the Romans were initially inspired by Athens, over time their society came to resemble Athens' diametric opposite: Sparta. As we will see in the book's fifth section, it is certainly not the first or last time in history that something like that will happen, and we find many elements of the exact same pattern playing out in much of Europe and, to a lesser degree, the US today.

Rome's first expansion was clearly a creative force, as it secured internal peace, opened borders and facilitated trade and emigration through the building of roads and ports, established a vast postal system and implemented practical common standards. If we compare it to modern Europe, the European Union (EU) has, in its early stages, also stimulated creativity by opening borders and facilitating movements of capital, people, goods and services. But what came later in Rome, also has clear parallels in the present: self-serving institutions, over-taxation leading to tax evasion and restricting production, limitations of movements through exit taxes and, finally, increasing irrationality and cultural indifference. We shall examine that more closely in sections five and six.

However, long before we get to that, we must, in the next chapter, delve into the extraordinary and surprising positive consequences the fall of Rome had for Western Europe.

5.
EUROPE'S
REMARKABLE
RE-BOOT

What do most people associate with the phrase "Medieval Age"? Religious fundamentalism? Witch hunts and brutality? Endless wars, plague and cholera? That sounds plausible, because the Medieval Age doesn't strike us as a particular jolly era. However, it was, in a sense, a uniquely useful one, and we shall soon see why.

It all began when the Western Roman Empire fell and, and in many ways, what happened next can be described as a return to an earlier, simpler and more primitive form of civilization. Or perhaps just to less civilization.

Here it must be said that, after the barbarians had destroyed Rome, their intention was typically not to destroy Rome's culture or technology. No, they just wanted to be a part of it. For instance, the Germanic warrior Alaric, whose troops sacked Rome in the year 410, actually seems to have done so because he was upset that he couldn't get a job as a general in the Roman army.

Actually, it seems that a large part of Rome's early conflicts with surrounding tribes were triggered because they had been denied permission to live within Rome's borders. And even as Rome deteriorated from within to the frustration of its citizens, the outsiders saw something in it they wanted a part of. Indeed, when the Western Roman Empire finally collapsed and the Germanic people streamed across its former lands, the Romans were generally surprised to see that they rarely plundered, raped or took slaves as expected. Instead they tended to settle down and live peacefully among the former Roman inhabitants. They even went so far as to initially appoint another Roman (yes, Roman) emperor as their leader, but as none of them was willing to pay tax or be ruled in the sense of being told what to do, and since they all were proficient with their battle axes, the emperor ended up ruling nothing. By the year 476, the illusion that the Roman Empire still existed, albeit under new management, was finally abandoned and the only institution that remained from the former Western Roman Empire was its Catholic church.

Here is why the Medieval Age was so interesting: via a combination of partly random events, Western Europe happened to enter this period with all the criteria for creativity in place: It had plenty of 1) small units, 2) change agents,

3) networks, 4) shared memory systems and 5) competition. For instance, it had an extremely high number of small units in the form of mini-states totalling, at one point, close to 5,000, and while these gradually did amalgamate, much of Western Europe remained a chaotic mix of tiny mini-states for many centuries – the same As was true of Greece during its creative period.

There was also plenty of effective networking, partly due to the roads and port network, which the Romans had built, but also due to a remarkable tradition of sailing, which was facilitated by Western Europe's easy access to seas and rivers. This should not be under-estimated because in the Medieval Ages and antiquity, the countryside was often full of scrub and forests inhabited by wolves, bears and robbers. Trade on a large scale was far easier to conduct over the sea or along rivers and so the fact that the Roman Empire was a shape that followed the rivers and seas was important not because this water provided fish, but because it facilitated trading. In fact, it would typically cost them less to transport goods across the Mediterranean than just a few kilometres over land.

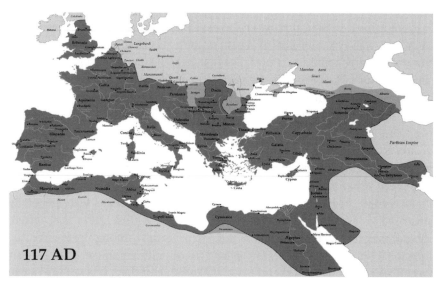

117 AD

THE SHAPE OF THE ROMAN EMPIRE AS IT REACHED ITS PEAK EXTENSION IN THE YEAR 117. AS CAN BE SEEN HERE, THE ROMANS CONCENTRATED THEIR POWER AROUND RIVERS AND CLOSE TO THE SEA - ESPECIALLY THE MEDITERRANEAN, BUT ALSO THE BLACK SEA AND NORTH SEA.[52]

Western Europe also had lots of change agents because its mix of numerous cultures and peoples who intermingled constantly. It maintained the Shared memory systems from the Roman Empire such as a common written language (Latin), common weight and measurement units (such as the amphora), and a common calendar. This was the Julian calendar, where July is called after Julius Caesar and August after Rome's first emperor Augustus (It was modified slightly to the Gregorian calendar in 1582). There was also a shared fundamental legal concept created by Rome. In addition to this, the monks of the Catholic Church copied and re-copied the ancient Roman and Greek writings, so that knowledge was not lost and, due to the Latin language, could be shared easily across borders.

Finally, it had lots of competition between its many mini-states and between the different power centres within these, such as the competing private companies, the church, the landowners, the nobility and so on.

Let's look a bit closer at the importance of sailing. Just as the curved coastline and countless islands had been vital for the early success of Greece, the rivers were incredibly important to Western Europe, and here is why: a significant quantity of Europe's rain falls in the Alps, and from there much of its waters run through European land out to the sea via the Rhine, Seine, Rhone, Elbe, Loire and Po. Also, rainy England has a great river in the Thames. These major rivers were attractive to traders for the following reasons:

◆ Their water flowed slowly and there were no major waterfalls or eddies to inhibit sailing.
◆ They ran out into the oceans, which provided connections to the rest of the world.
◆ They had plenty of water throughout the year to allow for sailing. In Southern Europe, this was facilitated by melting ice in mountains during the summer and in the Thames – well, England always has rainfall.
◆ They generally didn't freeze over in the winter because of the Gulf Stream (although the Thames was an exception during a cold period in medieval times).

In addition to attractive rivers, Western Europe also had a very high number of natural harbours in both the North Sea and the Mediterranean, which further facilitated a sailing culture.

If we look at the world as a whole, there are few areas of the world with as attractive a concentration of sailing opportunities as Western Europe. Africa is far bigger than Europe, but has a much shorter coastline - and remarkably few natural harbours. Also, many of the African rivers have waterfalls and eddies a few kilometres from their outlet into the sea, and many dry out in summer. Furthermore, African access to the Mediterranean is inhibited by the Sahara Desert. It would be more demanding for Africans to start international trade than for Europeans to do so, and it should be noted that the only signifi-

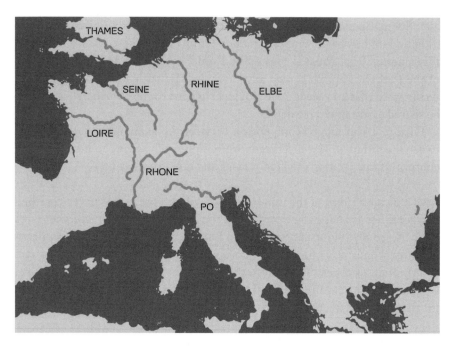

MAIN EUROPEAN MAIN RIVERS THAMES, RHINE, SEINE, RHONE, ELBE, LOIRE AND PO.

cant African civilization throughout history stood along the Nile, which is the continent's most navigable river. Along this natural trade route lived the Egyptians who, as we have seen, were actually very wealthy for a long time.

So yes, the Western Europeans had great access to waterways, and they had learned to use it. This was especially true of the Vikings, who were the first Europeans to navigate all of Europe's surrounding oceans as well as its rivers. It is difficult to pinpoint exactly when pre-Viking Scandinavians began to sail out further afield, but Swedish rock carvings from the Scandinavian Bronze Age (3200 – 600 BC) show at least 15,000 marine motives and, in Denmark, some 800 ship images have been found on more than 400 ornamented bronz-es.[53] In Norway, the Simris Rock Carving Panel, which is dated around 1500 BC, shows carvings of Viking-style ships. It should be noted that this carving was done 3,500 years ago and thus around 1,500 years before the foundation of the Roman Empire and approximately 2,500 years before the beginning of the Viking Age.

The Scandinavians had been into sailing for a very long time, but it was only after the year 800 (or so) that they become really adventurous. Between the years 790 and 800, Danish Vikings began to conduct raids on the northern French coast. In 845, they sailed up the Seine and attacked Paris. The Swed-ish Vikings sailed up the Russian and Ukrainian rivers and, in year 860 AD,

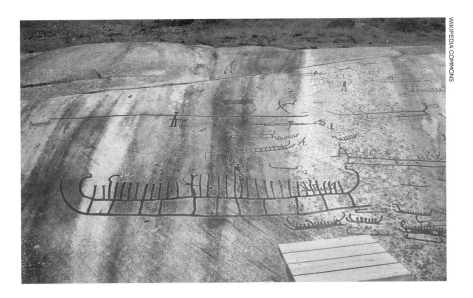

DETAIL FROM TANUM ROCK CARVING PANEL FROM AROUND 3,500 YEARS AGO
DEPICTING SHIPS. CLEARLY, THE SCANDINAVIAN SAILING TRADITION STARTED VERY EARLY.

they attacked the capital of the Byzantine Empire, Constantinople (now Istanbul) with approximately 200 boats. They plundered the suburbs, but failed to climb the city's formidable walls. They did, however, manage to make a significant impression on the local government, which signed a trade agreement with them and later hired some of them as imperial guardsmen. In fact, by the late 10th century, the entire "Varangian Guard" protecting the emperor of Byzantium was made up of Scandinavians, even though they were known for their problematic combinations of huge axes and general drunkenness.[54]

The change from a focus on plunder to a focus on trade was an example of conversion of win-lose strategy to win-win strategy and, after having made peace with Constantinople, the Vikings began to buy furs from Siberia and sell them to the Byzantines for precious metals and other commodities, and they established trading posts along the rivers, of which the city of Kiev in Ukraine was the largest. This must have taken some doing, because to make it from Sweden to Constantinople and back, they needed to row their boats 6,000 kilometres and often drag them over land to cross from one river to the next.

So important was the influence of the Vikings that the name "Russia" probably derives from the words "Ruotsi" or "Rootsi" which are the Finnish and Estonian name for Sweden, and which are both believed to have originated from the word "roðsmenn" or "roðskarlar", which means rowers.

There are many stories of how the Vikings travelled, and some of the best documented examples are found in the Icelanding sagas, which were written in the the 13th and 14th centuries and are both rather detailed and considered reasonably accurate. Another key source is Anglo-Saxon Chronicle, which was written in the ninth century and included details of events that were quite recent, when documented. One illustrative story is that of the Danish Viking King Hastein's southern raids, which took place from 859 to 862 and included 62 ships led by Hastein and Björn Ironside of Sweden. After losing out in skirmishes with Asturians on the Spanish north coast and Muslims on its south coast, they managed to sack Algeciras in Southern Spain after which they raided in Northern Africa, the Balearic Islands (Mallorca, Ibiza and Menorca) and southern France. From there, they continued north where they raided Roussillon, Narbonne, Nimes, Arles and Valence in France, followed by Pisa and Luna in Italy and possibly the Byzantine Empire. On their way home, they bought slaves in Africa. Just after passing Gibraltar, they were badly mauled by an Islamic fleet but managed to escape with 20 remaining ships. Before coming home, they stopped in Ireland to sell their slaves.

So they travelled a lot. It was probably eight years after the return of Hasteins raids that (in 870) Norwegian Vikings settled in Iceland. Just over 40 years later, in 911, Danish Vikings (possibly with Norwegians) forced the French King Charles to give them the northern coast of France, then called Normandy, after these "northern men".[55] During the related negotiations, the French king insisted that their chief Rollo should kiss the French king's feet, which he refused. The king then agreed that one of his people could do it in his place, but instead of bending down to kiss the foot, the chosen Viking grabbed it and lifted it up so that the king fell backwards to the great amusement of the crowd.

In the 980s Norwegians from Iceland migrated to Greenland and, in 985, 26 ships containing 400-700 Norwegian settlers heading from Iceland to Greenland were blown off course, whereby they discovered America; 15 years later, Vikings in Greenland who had heard about this story crossed the Atlantic and made a temporary settlement or trading post at L'Anse aux Meadows on the Canadian island of Newfoundland (their settlement was discovered in 1960). For these trips they were helped by the fact that their boats were light and fast so a crossing from Norway to Greenland under good conditions could be done in less than two weeks.

Meanwhile, the Normans settled in North Africa, the Middle East and Southern Italy and Sicily, and travelled on pilgrimages to Jerusalem. In the year 999, as some of them were on the way home from Jerusalem, they stopped in Sicily where they helped local leaders to oust an African invading force.

Of course, even just two weeks spent in an open boat north of the Polar Circle sounds rather cold and windy. The Viking trips also sound pretty dangerous if you consider that their ships stacked just 50-130 cm under sea level. Of the aforementioned 26 ships that were blown of course and thereby found America, 14 sank. It added to the dangers that the Vikings had very poor maps, if any at all. Here is how the Norwegian Hauksbók describes to fellow sailors how to get to Greenland:

"From Hernam in Norway, head due west towards Hvarf in Greenland, and you will have sailed north of Hjaltland, so that you just glimpse it in clear weather, but south of the Faroe Islands, so that the sea is right in between the distant mountains, and thus also south of Iceland." [56]

Great, let's go! But, of course, you would only see this Hjaltland (Shetland Islands) if indeed the weather was clear, and apparently you probably wouldn't actually see Iceland on your way, but know when you passed it, because you would see birds from it in the sky on your right. That is assuming again that the weather is clear. Sometimes the weather was horribly bad instead, so ships were blown a few thousand kilometres off course, which is how they typically discovered new lands (or perished).

But while the Vikings were clearly the most radical adventurers in Europe (and in the world at the time), they were not the only ones in Europe who could handle boats. Numerous civilisations around the Mediterranean had also been keen sailors for centuries or even millennia; for example, the Semitic Phoenicians sailed widely in the Mediterranean between 1550 BC and 300 BC just as the Greeks did for many centuries.

In the early Medieval Age, absolutely no one in Western Europe seems to have realized that they were in the midst of a cocktail of circumstances which would lead to a creative explosion. At least, there is not a single record of anyone from that age stating that they expecting a creative Big Bang.

But the explosion came, and it was driven by a chain reaction of transformational processes. The first was the Renaissance, which lasted from the late 13th to early 17th century. As the era's name suggests, this was a rediscovery of earlier ideas about art, politics, humanism, individualism and creativity - values that originated in Rome and, before that, actually in the Greek city-states. The Renaissance began in Florence, Italy and was stimulated partly by the Italians' memories of their Roman greatness and also by more recent Greek emigrations following Ottoman occupation of Greece.

One of the key figures of the Renaissance was the monk Thomas Aquinas, who lived from 1225 to 1274. Aquinas argued that man had a natural talent for discovering things without divine guidance and should use this talent, even though the Old Testament had blamed Adam and Eve for eating from the Tree of Knowledge.

The Renaissance led to new publications and translations of classic books by authors such as Plato and Aristotle. Aristotle was an advocate of empiricism, the concept of testing hypotheses thorugh systematic experimention. People became fascinated by these books' thoughts about logical thinking, democracy, pluralism, open discussion of politics and ethics, and also by the Greek belief that not everything is yet known; the need for everybody to seek new information and ask questions constantly, as Socrates had done.

It may be difficult for us today to comprehend how little world knowledge people of the past tended to have. However, it is illustrated by a bizarre episode in the English coastal town of Hartlepool during the Napoleonic wars (after the end of the Medieval Age). Here the local people found a stranded French ship, where the only survivor was a pet monkey dressed in French clothes. As the British had never seen a monkey nor a Frenchman, they assumed the monkey was, in fact, a Frenchman. They held a brief trial in which it failed to defend itself, after which the monkey was hanged as a spy.[57]

Before the Renaissance, people - particularly those who didn't travel much – must predominantly have based their world views on religious texts, unsubstantiated rumours and superstition. Society was then largely static, and most people never encountered any new ways of thinking or saw any new technologies; they only had limited awareness of how other people might live in completely different ways to their own. The concept of change and the idea of thinking for themselves and asking basic questions about the world would have been far from their minds. The closest thing to science that existed were catalogues of observations without any related explanations or hypotheses. So it really wasn't science at all. Because knowledge at that time was not associated with theories, experiments such as there were, were often doomed from the start; alchemy was among the most common, involving random attempts to produce gold out of lead, urine or other stuff.

The free thinking that came with the Renaissance contributed to Europe's second great transformation: the Reformation, which is usually dated to the period 1517-1648. This was a rebellion against the Catholic Church's institutions and its gigantic luxury palaces. These were often financed by "sinners" who had to seek the church's forgiveness by paying up. You could, for instance, buy indulgences to buy your deceased family members out of purgatory or even buy yourself a ticket to spend less time there, after your death.

The Church made sure the common man did not read the Bible by himself because it didn't actually say anything about rich churches collecting taxes and selling indulgences. The method was simple: the Bible was written only in Latin, which only the elite and the clergy could read.

All religions with priests may be tempted to perform a trick that states: "You are under threat, but we can save you. Just submit to the God that I represent." In other words: "Submit to me." This opportunity can create an abuse of power, and it can ensure financing of a huge, self-serving institution and invite corruption. All this happened in the Church, where, for example, it was now possible to purchase certain clerical jobs, which secured lifelong access to power and money. The priests often became rich and began to accumulate wealth that they could pass on to their children, which is the reason why Pope Gregory VII imposed celibacy. By the end of the seventh century, as much as a third of the productive land in France was owned by the Church and, according to records made in Britain in 1086, the Church owned more than a quarter of all land.[58] So the Church seemed, increasingly, to repeat the scenario that had been seen in the Roman Empire - it started as a small, idealistic popular movement, but grew to become a gigantic, extractive organization demanding that citizens were Spartan, while it spent their money.

The rebellion against the church was probably stimulated by urbanization, when people moving to cities saw with their own eyes how rich the church had become with their hard-earned money and were able to discuss exactly that with their peers.

Another contributing factor to the Reformation was the growing trend of individual thought. Europeans began to deny that priests should be better interpreters of religion than themselves, and that gave rise to Protestantism. This movement "dis-intermediated" religion; it cut out the middleman. It started in Central and Northern Europe and, since Protestantism wasn't subject to central authority, it soon split into many variants. Now people had to choose one branch of the church out of many options, so just as Europe had gone from the Roman mega-state power monopoly to medieval city-state decentralization, the central and northern European church now became fragmented and decentralized as well.

The attitude of the Protestants can be summed up roughly like this: "We share the faith of Catholics. But we do not actually need your institution and we want to read the Bible ourselves in a language we can understand." However, there were also differences in the perception of Christian faith, for most Protestants did not think they best qualified for God's love by suffering and submitting, as some Catholics suggested, but rather by contributing something useful on Earth. Work was no longer seen as an annoying necessity best performed by slaves, but as a personal obligation that would qualify you for the love of God.

Since the Catholic Church, after a time, realized that opposition could no longer be prevented, it responded with a counter-reformation, which included better training of priests, more understandable sermons and improved decoration of churches. It also decided to update the official calendar, which seemed to have come to be ten days out of step with the seasons, due to leap years.

One of the astronomers they asked to carry out this project was Nicolaus Copernicus. In 1543, he published his work De revolutionibus orbium coelestium libri VI describing celestial rotation around the sun, and this work became the first of a series of scientific breakthroughs from a growing rank of scientists. The scientific method gradually gained more and more acceptance, and the church gave in.

Now the creativity flourished for real. For example, oxen were often replaced by horses as draft animals and this, combined with the introduction of the

THE SCIENTIFIC METHOD EXPLAINED

The essence of the scientific method is the unbiased, disinterested search for truth. Ideally this takes place roughly as follows:

- Define a question.
- Formulate a logical and reasoned hypothesis about the causes of related observations.
- Define methods to investigate whether the hypothesis is true (verification) or false (falsification).
- Define an analytical universe to be explored.
- Gather information about this through, for example, measurements and statistical analysis.
- Analyse the data and derived conclusions to see if they indicate that the hypothesis is either true or false.
- Describe any derived hypotheses that might be useful to investigate later and comment on any studies made by others that provide results that deviate from your own.
- Publish the results and methods of the analysis (i.e., data and calculations) in a scientifically recognized media, which asks anonymous peers to review and comment on your work (peer reviews).
- When you publish, ensure third parties are equipped with all information necessary to enable them to repeat the experiments and studies.
- Be open and forthcoming to people who critize you.

If other scientists cannot replicate results created as described above, they are rejected. However, if they can replicate them and are unable to prove that the hypothesis is false, the scientist can rightly claim that it is now the best answer available to the original question.

heavy iron plough as well as crop rotation, lead to a marked increase in farm productivity. In fact, some farms became highly profitable, which lead to the systematically clearing of forests, laying of gravity flow pipes and redirecting of streams to increase productivity further. This, in turn, freed up labour for the cities, where urbanites developed innovations such as double-entry book-keeping, new credit instruments, limited liability companies, mercantile laws, stock exchange trading and much more. In parallel, the farmers began selling their surplus production in the open markets, which put pressure to increase quality and competitiveness.

Slaves had now predominantly been replaced by self-employed farmers who had a strong interest in getting the most out of their investment and labour, which encouraged the development in productivity. In the year 1086, the government of England commissioned the *Domesday Book*, which was a very detailed, country-wide inventory of contemporary villages, towns and farms, and one of the most interesting documents that survives from the medieval age.[59] At this time, England had a very small population, estimated at between 1.25 and 2 million, but when we study the details of the book's statements, we see reference to no less than 5,624 water mills, and it is estimated that this number grew to between 10,000 and 13,000 in 1300.

Technologies often developed in cascades where recombinations of ideas led to development of new fields. However, reuse of skills in new ways is also important, and the development of mechanical clocks in Europe meant that there were many skilled instrument makers who could later make other mechanical devices as were needed in the Industrial Revolution.

Between 1000 and 1450, Europeans introduced wheelbarrows, four-wheeled horse-drawn carriages, rudders for boats, paper, spinning wheels, magnetic compasses, glasses and glass-blowing, and much more. Much heavy work which the Romans would have done using thousands of slaves, was now done with treadmill cranes, stationary harbour cranes, floating cranes and slewing cranes. Added to this were practical inventions such as wine presses and clothes with buttons. And for those who were sick, it was a consolation that the local doctor no longer arrived equipped only with a saw plus some opium, but now perhaps also with an illustrated anatomy atlas.

Brave new world! The lives of the richest were now embellished with pianos, fountains, floor heating and beautiful oil paintings, and their best buildings were equipped with rib-vaulted ceilings and fireplaces with chimneys. Ships grew ever larger and sturdier, and the focus shifted from labour-intensive galleys to more economical sailboats, which were tailored to their tasks, including larger boats that were suitable for long distance sea transport.

There were obviously also many military innovations. For example, the use of stirrups, spurs and saddles made an accomplished rider "one" with his horse, which created the basis for cavalry attack - a fearsome technology at the time. And there came crossbows, long bows, trebuchets, gunpowder, guns and even the first simple machine guns.

The result of all the various innovations was that Europe in the mid-15th century was infinitely more advanced in terms of technological and economic innovation than the Roman Empire had ever been, and although no-one seemed to have seen this coming, Europeans were now on the verge of the most stunning development in human history since the ousting of the Neanderthals – a development which would change everything, not just within the Europe, but across the entire globe.

In the next chapter we shall look at how Western civilization thus exploded forward at a time when its two biggest potential rivals, China and the Islamosphere, were stuck in a cultural rut, just has the Romans had been before them.

6.
THE GREAT
TAKE-OFF

U p to the year 1450, all European books had been handwritten, and it had typically taken a monk or a scribe up to a year to produce a single book. For this work they would normally charge a florin per five pages - corresponding to approximately 1,500 dollars today - which meant that a book could easily cost the equivalent of 100,000 dollars or more in modern money.

This changed, however, when, in 1450, German inventor and publisher Johannes Gutenberg launched his printing press. Even though he never made any money out of it (he went bankrupt, as previously mentioned), his invention eventually became a huge success, and was soon copied everywhere (our alchemist's fallacy in action). As an example, the printing house Ripoli would, in year 1483, print no fewer than 1,025 copies of *Plato Dialoges*, an achievement that 33 years earlier would have required at least1,000 man-years of work and cost the equivalent of perhaps $100 million in present money.

In year 1500 - just 50 years after Gutenberg had invented his machine - Europe as a whole had no fewer than 220 book printers, which produced a total of eight million books, ranging from specialist titles to popular pocket-size books.[60]

That we continuously learn theories and information from new books during the course of our lifetimes may seem obvious to any modern person but, in past communities, the prevailing thought would have been that there was only one good ideas system and that all others must therefore be treacherous. However, with the development of cheap books, new ideas started spreading like wildfire.

Other than in China and Korea (which both invented printing presses before Gutenberg) there had not existed reasonably large, popular book markets anywhere else in the world. What was special about the European print book market was, first, that it came at the time of the Renaissance, where people had already become more receptive to free thinking and, second, the book market was subject to fierce competition – book printers could only thrive if they constantly managed to be first with the latest publication. China, on the other hand, had been a centrally-controlled society, where printers largely produced what the state demanded.

European book mania became one of the driving forces behind the Age of Enlightenment.[62] The basic concept of the enlightenment was that science,

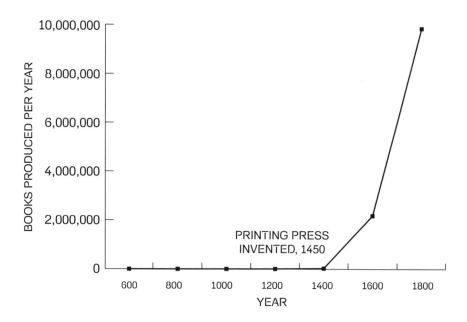

EUROPE'S BOOK PRODUCTION YEAR 600-1800. IT IS EASY TO SPOT THE ENORMOUS CHANGE AS BOOK PRODUCTION CHANGES FROM COPYING-BY-HAND TO PRINTING.[61]

systematic doubt, rationality, cosmopolitanism and individualism should replace superstition, irrationality, theological dogma, insularity and group-think. This movement was partly triggered by Copernicus' aforementioned work from 1543, which, paradoxically, was commissioned by the otherwise conservative Catholic Church.

While the Enlightenment largely grew out of Northern Italy and France, it quickly spread across the Continent and to the US. Its main thinkers in-cluded names we have already heard: Montesquieu (separation of powers), John Locke (personal freedom, equality and protection of private proper-ty), Thomas Hobbes (the social contract), Adam Smith (free trade) and Ed-ward Gibbon (author of the *Decline and Fall of the Roman Empire*). However, there were many others, including Frenchmen Pierre Bayle, Voltaire, Denis Diderot, Anne-Robert-Turgot, René Descartes and Nicolas de Condorcet; Dutchman Baruch Spinoza; Germans Baron d'Holbach, Immanuel Kant and Johann Gottfried von Herder; Britons Francis Bacon, Francis Hutcheson, Da-vid Hume and Isaac Newton; and American Benjamin Franklin. Such famous thinkers were supported by considerable networks of underground pample-theers and printers, who distributed forbidden bestsellers, in which one par-ticularly courageous swiss printing house, Société typographique de Neuchâ-tel, came to play a pivotal role.

As well as making people more open, rational and individualistic, the Enlightenment replaced fatalism with inginuity. Before enlightenment, when people experienced accidents, losses and tragedies such as lost wars or children dying from infections, they would often see the explanation as God's punishent for their sins, which should not be questioned. However, with enlightenment they became more likely to ask questions such as: "What was wrong with our battle strategy?", "What causes these diseases?" or "How can we prevent this problem in the future?" When vaccinations were invented, some religious fundamentalists rejected it as interference in God's ways, but most believed that, while one should not question the ways of the Lord, it was worth noting that he seemed more likely to help those who helped themselves.

Enlightenment did something else: because of its systematic approach to seeking truth, it made it possible to settle discussions simply by testing emperically who was right. It was thus a peace-maker.

There was a final important element of the Enlightenment: it was optimistic. Most of its supporters thought mankind had real scope for making the world better, and many of them envisaged a much improved future. For instance, in 1795, the aforementioned Enlightenment thinker Nicolas de Condorcet predicted that science and technology would bring human progress without limit. He also foresaw that the New World would proclaim independence from Europe and then have tremendous success through introduction of European technologies. Slavery would be abolished, he said, and people would gain contraceptive technology and more free time. Furthermore, like Benjamin Franklin, he predicted that agricultural productivity would soar.[63]

The Enlightenment movement was supported by an increasing number of scientists who,in book after book, described, in parts, how the world worked, and also how people should think about it. These included the physician Andreas Vesalius who published *De Humani Corporis Fabrica Libri Septem* (which translates as "On the fabric of the human body in seven books"), which described the human anatomy – one step of many designed to deconstruct things and study their constituent parts. There was also Kepler, who wrested astronomy out of the hands of the superstitious astrologers and Galileo, who explained why the Earth was not the centre of the universe (and why the sky was not a black ball with holes in, as many had otherwise assumed). And there was Newton, who came up with his laws of gravity and motion as well as the discovery that light comprised the particles we now call photons.

The thoughts that had been revived during the early Renaissance (freedom, rule of law, science, logic and religious tolerance) were now given further tailwind. Likewise, the idea of democracy gained evermore traction. The early interpretation was that those who paid taxes to the state should have a say in how their money was spent. This meant, in practice, that only land-owning men could vote. Later came the argument that if you sent people to war, they should also have a vote, whether or not they were landowners. That sounded fair enough, but some disagreed, because the decisive military technology was the cavalry charge, which tended to be performed by knights, who were either influential and rich landowners or the sons of such landowners. However, the invention of powerful guns and cannons made foot soldiers much more important than previously, so their demands for democracy gained weight. Finally, as rule of law became more common, people began to demand a say in how these laws were written, if they were to be expected to abide by them.

The combination of greater knowledge, democracy and tolerance now made it more common for people to meet in salons, debate clubs and coffee houses to debates the meaning of life, the organization of society or the latest technological and scientific discoveries. It was also during this period that scientists began holding public lectures about, for example, physics and chemistry, and these sessions were often attended by hundreds of listeners of all ages (yes, this was before television). This was also the age where writers and poets such as Goethe and Schiller, as well as musicians including Bach, Haydn and Mozart, stirred people's emotions and where social commentators and philosophers such as Francis Bacon changed their world views. Bacon argued for example, like many of the ancient Greeks, that people should systematically use observation and controlled experiments to gain an understanding of the world.

With the new urge to find better answers to age-old questions came, of course, an increased tendency to ask new questions, and one of these was how the world looked behind the horizon.

Good question. On August 3, 1492, Christopher Columbus sailed out from the small Spanish port of Palos de la Frontera between Gibraltar and Portugal to seek part of the answer.[64] His mission was to circle the Earth to find a shorter trade route across the sea to Asia.

Columbus had long been fascinated by the idea of sailing to Asia. Over the centuries leading up to his adventure, Europe had, in particular, imported silk, spices and porcelain from Asia. These had been transported via the so-called Silk Road, where items were moved laboriously via various combinations of horses, donkeys, camels and boats. When these goods finally reached European markets, they were obviously vastly expensive due to costs accumulated en route. But it had grown even worse; after the Ottoman Empire had conquered the Eastern Roman Empire (Byzantium) the Silk Road had been largely blocked. Columbus, therefore, smelled a huge business opportunity if he could open an alternative route by sailing West.

So the incentive was there, and the idea of visiting the Far East wasn't a new one. For instance, Giovanni de Plano Carpini travelled, in 1241-1247, over land to Mongolia and managed, sensationally, to return alive, as did the Russians Yaroslav, Alexander and Andrey Vladimir later. Frenchman André de Longjumeau and Belgian William of Rubruck had also both travelled to China, but the most famous of the explorers had been Marco Polo, who sailed to Asia between 1264 and 1295, where he visited China and other places.

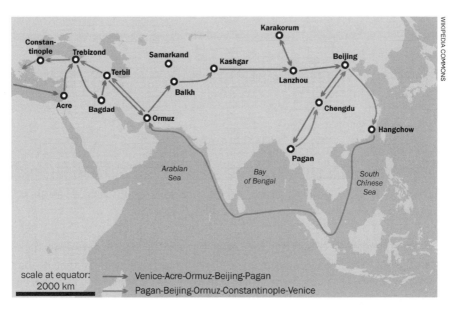

MARCO POLO'S TRAVELS TO CHINA, WHICH PROBABLY TOOK PLACE FROM 1264 TO 1269 AND FROM 1271 TO 1295 RESPECTIVELY.[65]

Columbus' expedition wasn't without its problems and he lost one of his three ships. But he did make it back in 1493 and announced that he had indeed found the sea route to Asia.

Actually he hadn't, because what he discovered was America, but no one knew that at the time and the discovery was exciting anyway. The story soon spread like wildfire across Europe, but the Spanish royal family was the first to pick up the opportunity, so six months later, on September 24th 1493, Columbus again set sail for the new land, this time with no fewer than 17 ships and 1,200 men.[66]

The age in which civilizations set sail and discovered the world could have been led by China and started after Zheng He's expeditions between 1405 and 1433 but they didn't because it was intentionally ceased. Instead, it was Columbus' expeditions that came to mark the beginning of what we now call the Age of Discovery.

This was period of frantic activity. In 1497, four years after the beginning of Columbus' second voyage, Italian Giovanni Caboto was hired by the Brit-

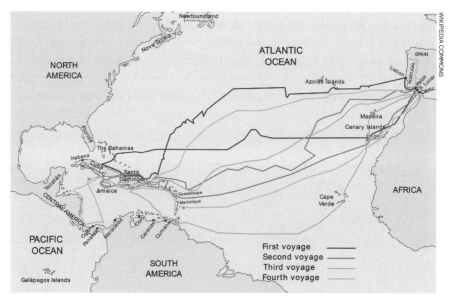

BETWEEN 1492 AND 1500 COLUMBUS MADE FOUR EXPEDITIONS TO AMERICA BUT REMAINED CONVINCED, UNTIL HIS DEATH THAT IT WAS ASIA HE HAD VISITED.[67]

ish king Henry VII to sail out with one ship and 18 men to find a northern passage to Asia. He later returned and reported triumphantly that he had reached Northern Asia via the North Atlantic. This was actually also inaccurate, because it was probably either Newfoundland in Eastern Canada or the state of Maine in the northern US that he had found.

This was now turning into a competitive race and the same year, Portuguese Vasco da Gama set sail in a 27 metre-long ship, accompanied by three other vessels, to find another way to Asia, but this time by going south of Africa. This worked, and he reached India in May 1498.

The key motivation for these people was to enrich themselves, which tended to work fairly well. For instance, da Gamas' fleet returned home with a cargo that financed the cost of the trip 60 times over. (That's what you call a 60x return in modern venture capital lingo, and the internal rate of return, or IRR as the venture capitalists call it, could have been around something like 3,000% (2x return and 10% IRR is now considered fair and 20% IRR is good).

Money, money, money!

The English, who had been behind in the early stages of this land-grab, also liked money. In 1508 they sent an expedition to North America, which led them up the Hudson River and through most of the Northwest Passage north of Canada. Three years later, in 1511, a Portuguese citizen named Fernão Pires de Andrade captured the city of Malacca in Malaysia, after which he

TEN STEPS THAT CREATED
THE MODERN WESTERN WORLD

1. The Renaissance (ca. 1200-1600), which promoted artistic expression, freedom, logic, rule of law, religious tolerance, humanism, empirical experimentation and creativity.
2. The Enlightenment (ca. 1450-1800) , which placed the ideals of science, systematic doubt, rationality, cosmopolitanism and individualism as primary values of society.
3. The Age of Discovery (ca. 1500-1800), involving the European explorations and the ultimate colonization of the majority of the globe.
4. The Reformation (ca. 1520-1650). This is where the traditionally-very-individualistic northerners rejected the perceived over-institutionalization of the Catholic Church and replaced it with a more individualistic and decentralized interpretation of religion, which also emphasised personal achievement over collective obedience.
5. The Scientific Revolution (ca. 1540 to the present). This replaced mysticism with exact, testable knowledge, which formed the basis for the industrial revolution and united people.
6. The Industrial Revolution (ca. 1750-1850). Technical inguinuity brought mass production, which led in part to a wealth explosion and in part to mass urbanization, increased global trade and cultural upheavals.
7. Female Liberation (ca. 1840 – 1930), where women gained access to education and political influence, which greatly increased overall creative output.
8. The Information Revolution (ca. 1997 -). As the internet became available to the public, the quantity of information anyone with a connection could access multiplied by many orders of magnitude.
9. The biotech revolution. (ca. 2000 -). Following the sequencing of the DNA, the coding of life in its finest details started to be known.
10. The crowdsourcing revolution (ca. 2000 -). Building on the internet, anonymous, non-credentialist crowds began to collaborate on countless creative tasks (non-credentialist means that you are not a formally associated co-worker and do not need to have any formal approval in the form of specific education or union membership in order to do the specific work).

headed to China and planted the Portuguese flag close to - or perhaps within – what is currently known as Hong Kong.

Just two years later, in 1513, a Spanish expeditionary force climbed over a mountain range in Colombia and discovered, to their astonishment, another wide ocean, which told them that what they had thought was Asia had been, in fact, an entirely different continent. It turned out that there was plenty of gold and silver there so, six years later in 1519, the Spanish conquest of much of South- and Central America began - an extreme story which we shall re-visit later.

As time passed, more and more Western European nations joined the scene and, from 1602, the Netherlands began colonizing Sri Lanka, parts of India and Indonesia, Taiwan, South Africa, parts of the South American east coast and enclaves on the east coast of Africa and in the US, while Denmark, Germany and Belgium also established colonies.

These Western expeditions and conquests provided a number of new commodities, out of which two probably played a very special role: tea and coffee. It appears, from old records, that Western Europeans well into the Middle Ages, were generally heavy drinkers, and records show, for instance, that, in the 15th century the average English adult, male or female, drank approximately. 4.5 litres of beer a day. That's 9 litres daily for a couple, on average. However, with the introduction of tea and coffee, people probably began to sober up somewhat, which would have made their discussions of politics and science more constructive.[68]

Events took a new turn at the beginning of the 18th century, where an improved melting process was developed for making steel, which was followed by invention of the flying shuttle for textile production (1733), the Bridgewater Channel (1761), the Spinning Jenny (1761), and the steam engine (1769). This was the beginning of the Industrial Age, which began along the Clyde River in Scotland, then spread to England and beyond. It facilitated an acceleration of urbanization while giving Europeans a wealth of mass-produced objects for global trade.[69]

The Industrial Revolution was followed by the Women's Liberation Movement, which demanded equal contract rights, marriage rights, parenting rights, voting rights and property rights for women. After that came the IT revolution, the biotech revolution and the crowdsourcing revolution, all of which we shall study in more detail later.

When you really think about it, there's something utterly bizarre about what happened in Western Europe from 1450 until today, but it is even more amazing to think about the events that took place between 1450 and 1500. During these decades, the lust for learning, the "book bulimia", the race for

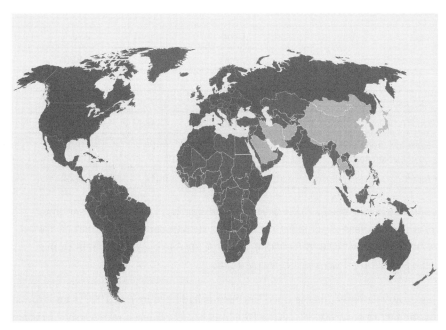

EUROPEAN-DOMINATED AREAS IN 1900. IN ADDITION TO CONTROLLING SOME 85% OF ALL THE WORLDS' LANDMASS AND APPROXIMATELY 85% OF ITS ECONOMY, THE EUROPEANS AND THEIR DESCENDANTS ALSO RULED THE GLOBAL SEAS ALMOST UNCHALLENGED.[70]

space and the grab for gold were all completely frantic, as people suddenly saw countless opportunities for discovery, adventure, development and prosperity everywhere that they hadn't spotted before.

It becomes even more bizarre when we consider the fact that it was not the whole of Europe that was responsible for this gigantic endeavour, but largely Western Europe, whose population had grown from about 20 million when the Roman Empire fell to approximately 45 million in year 1500.[70] This population constituted just 10% of the global population and, before the start of the colonial era, controlled barely 2% of Earth's landmasses. Seen from a global perspective, it was a small population inhabiting a tiny stretch of land. And yet, Western Europeans went out and conquered most of the world's landmasses and gained 100% control of the seas.

It also adds to the story that, in year 1000, the Western European GDP per capita was probably only on par with the South- and Central Americas, which then was only inhabited by Indians. And Western Europeans were probably approximately 5% poorer than the Japanese and, yes, Africans, and (it is assumed) approximately 10% lower than that of non-Japanese Asians. And yet, some 500 years later,these Western Europeans would stream out from their tiny lands and conquer most land in these places.

GDP per capita			
Year	1000	1500	1913
Western Europe	400	771	1.204
Japan	425	500	669
Asia excl. Japan	450	572	550
Latin America	400	416	681
Eastern Europe and the former Soviet Union area	400	498	941
Africa	425	414	500

ESTIMATES OF GDP PER CAPITA IN DIFFERENT PARTS OF THE WORLD IN THE YEAR 1000, YEAR 1500 AND YEAR 1913, RESPECTIVELY (1913 IS THE YEAR IN WHICH THE BRITISH EMPIRE PEAKED). NOTE THAT WESTERN EUROPEANS IN THE YEAR 1000 ARE ESTIMATED TO HAVE BEEN POORER THAN BOTH ASIANS AND AFRICANS.[71]

Just how relatively undeveloped Europeans had been in year 1000 is underlined by the fact that, in 600 BC, Arab Muslims had conquered previously Christian territories in North Africa, Syria, Palestine, Portugal and most of Spain. In the year 732, there had actually been a Muslim army camped just 70 km from Paris, and Muslims possessed a sizeable proportion of Provence and sacked Rome at one point. They had managed to invade parts of Europe, India, China, Africa and China simultaneously and took slaves as far north as Iceland - at this point, they had the mightiest army in the world.[72]

Had someone back then told the Arabs that the primitive Europeans, only 1,000 years later (in 1913) would control approx. 85% of the world's land mass, almost 80% of its population and 85% of its economy, they would, arguably, have split their sides with laughter. But this is exactly what happened.[73] In fact, the West increased its GDP per capita by approximately 300%, between the years 1000 and 1800, whereas, elsewhere in the world GDP rose by only 30%. Already, in 1500, Europe's GDP per capita had surpassed both India's and China's and, in 1600, it was 50 % higher. The Western European nations multiplied their landholdings by a factor of 20 during the Age of Discovery, and the vast majority of this process was conducted within a period of 250 years – within about ten generations.

The fact that the Western European population was very small wasn't a problem. This can be illustrated by the case of Portugal which, in 1450, was a tiny nation with only 1.2 million people, equivalent to approx. 0.26% of world population.[74] And yet, from these humble beginnings, the Portuguese sailed out to build an empire which, for years, was the world's largest, and which would endure for nearly 600 years. This empire reached at its peak with more than 10 million square kilometres (equivalent more than 100 times Portugal's own size) and it included settlements in South America, Africa, Middle East, India and the Far East all the way to Japan and down to the islands just north of Australia. Surely a huge project, but the British historian Charles Boxer has estimated that Portugal, at the end of the 16th century, never had more than 10,000 men deployed to control all this.[75]

One of the theories for this success is that the Renaissance and Enlightenment, combined with individualism, contributed strongly to the enormous achievement of European armies in almost all corners of the world.

The typical Western military commander was not just a superstitious automation, but a fairly creative and rational thinker, and the Western soldier would feel able to bring forwards suggestions to their commanders. The otherwise brutal Spanish conquerer Cortés had studied Latin and worked as a notary, and he was well versed in Greek and Roman literature as well as military history. Many of his men had engineering skills and legal experience, and they were well aware of how different people and civilizations in foreign places could be. Of course, they had no idea what they would meet in South America, but whenever something new turned up, such as armies that outnumbered them massively, they discussed their options freely and ended up using combinations of analysis, engineering and improvisation to find their ways of tackling the problem.

The Indians they confronted were very different and were handicapped by groupism, superstition and insularity. When they encountered the Spanish, they debated whether these were gods or centaurs, whether their ships were floating mountains and whether their guns made thunder. The Aztec emperor Montezuma sent wizards to bewitch the Spanish and, when it came to battle, no one dared to suggest a change of tactics to the emperor.

There are presumably many ways of thinking about this story. One could argue that it was down to a single stroke of luck; for instance, the Western Europeans were just plain lucky that they possessed guns. However, both guns and gunpowder were actually Chinese inventions upon which the Europeans had improved.

Or one could say they were lucky to have invented book printing but the Chinese and Koreans had done the same thing independently - and before the Europeans. Was it their big boats, then? No, the Chinese had been way ahead in ship-building too. Science? Well yes, but the Persians and Arabs had been better at science, at least until around the 12th century.

Here is another narrative: Western Europeans got so far because they were greedy and evil. Sometimes, arguably, they were; but as we shall see later, so were most other people in the world, which was full of slave-traders, rapists, murderers, torturers and warmongers.

No, the key difference was that Western Europeans had become extremely creative in general due to their lucky combination of small units, change agents, networks, shared memory systems, and competition. They had all the conditions in place for developing an amazing creative design space, and other civilizations didn't.

Here's a little experiment to illustrate the point. Ask anyone to write down, on a piece of paper, some important inventions that changed the world; say, 10 things. What would they write? Perhaps aeroplanes, cars, trains and the internal combustion engine? Or radio, television and the internet? The exploration of oil and gas, perhaps? Computers, satellites and smartphones? Genetic engineering? Rockets and satellites?

Some might write rock and jazz music. Or birth control pills, anaesthesia and vaccines. Photography perhaps? Or electric power and electric devices such as air-conditioning, electric lights, refrigeration, electric stoves and vacuum cleaners.

All of these things were invented in the West, and the likely outcome of such an experiment is that most, if not all, of the key innovations listed by anyone in the world would be Western. This would be is no coincidence at all, for as we shall see on the following pages, statistical evidence indicates that the West has been responsible for over 95% of all creative innovation; not only in recent decades, but ever.

Yes, ever, and this in despite the aforementioned fact that Western civilization evolved from just 10% of the world's population inhabiting only 2% of its land surface.

Let's scrutinise that more closely. We can start with music as a good example of staunch creativity. Here, it was actually Westerners who invented nodes and guitars, pianos, microphones, amplifiers, synthesizers and speakers. It was also Westerners who developed the most popular music genres worldwide, from classical and pop to blues, jazz, rock, beat and virtually all their hundreds of sub-genres. By 2014, the 50 most popular music artists or groups in the world ever were all were Western.[76]

That's a big Western dominance, and a survey from 2014 shows, for example, that Western nations throughout history additionally have accounted for:

◆ 96% of the 50 most popular books or book series'
◆ 100% of the 50 most expensive pieces of art painting or sculture
◆ 100% of the 50 highest-grossing film of all time
◆ 100% of the world's 50 leading luxury brands
◆ 82% of the world's 50 highest-ranking restaurants
◆ 88% of the world's 50 top-ranked universities
◆ 100% of the world's 50 largest biotech companies [77]

All these results are global, and when it comes to most expensive or best-selling, it is about all sales ever. These samples indicate a huge Western dominance in art, fashion, luxury and science as well as in biotech, which anyone should recognize as areas that are all largely built on creativity.

The major international auction houses for art, antiques and collector cars are all Western, and the same goes for the largest art fairs. The software companies that have changed people's daily lives worldwide are predominantly Western, whether that's Apple, Google, Microsoft, eBay, Amazon, Facebook, LinkedIn, YouTube, Skype or Twitter. Some of these have since been copied elsewhere, but the ideas came from the West.

Similarly, the West has pioneered many humanistic movements including the Red Cross, Doctors Without Borders, Amnesty International, Human Rights Watch and many other organizations. The phenomenon is also reflected in the awarding of Nobel Prizes, where Western nations have taken 92% of all Nobel Prizes and 94% within the exact sciences.[78]

The immediate impression when you bear in mind all of the above achievements, whether in art, fashion, luxury, science, technology or humanistic endeavours, may be that the West seems to have been responsible for 95% of the world's total creative output since World War II. But this is not very systematic way to measure it, so are there other ways?

There are, but they show a similar picture. Martin Prosperity Institute is headed by renowned creativity expert Richard Florida and is probably the world's leading research institute in the factors that create wealth and stimulate creativity. This institution regularly produces a so-called Global Creativity Index and, in 2011, it showed that 17 out of the 20 most creative nations in the world were Western.[79] Two other very popular indicators are International Innovation Index from Boston Consulting Group and others[80], and Global Innovation Index from Cornell University, INSEAD[81] and the World Intellectual Property Organization. Both of these also placed 17 of the world's 20 most innovative nations in the West. All three studies included Hong Kong and Singapore as two of the top non-Western nations, but both of these are former British colonies with a fairly strong Western influence.

However, all the numbers cited above seem fairly recent, so how does it look if we go further back in time? We have actually a good answer to that, because the reknown social scientist Charles Murray and his associates have performed a massive statistical analysis of who has been responsible for all "human accomplishment", as they call it, from as early as records could be found and until year 1950, and the result is - as we shall see in a moment – quite astonishing.[82]

Murray's objective was to identify all cases in history where 1) a named person had 2) made a creative innovation in art, science or technology that was

3) so important that it was quoted in at least half of the leading modern reference books worldwide.

It was a big project. In fact, it took five years and involved 50 people. The main method was to pore over 163 modern sources of human accomplishment from all over the World and, for each of these, meticulously record the creative people mentioned, as well as how much print space was allocated to each of these. In addition, Murray used a statistical filter as a correction factor where a reference was more often mentioned in reference books from his own country than in other such books.

This work resulted in a list with a total of 4,002 names of generally-respected philosophers, mathematicians, musicians, poets, astronomers, physicists, biologists, technological inventors and so on, who were mentioned in at least half of all the relevant sources. The period covered was approximately 2,750 years (for the reason that, before year 800 BC, no one knows exactly who invented what. For instance, no one knows who invented the stone arrowhead or the bone needle.)

The result showed that the number of new accomplishments had been pretty low and trendless until around year 1000, where they started to pick up, but without accelerating further. It was also scattered around so that, again and again around the globe, there were fairly brief bursts of creativity which then tended to fade or stop abruptly. And although the accumulated human knowledge and abilities overall increased slightly over the first 1,300 years or so, there were long intermittent periods where any upwards momentum in innovation and accomplishment was very difficult to spot.

But then – and here it comes - from approximately 1450, creativity virtually exploded, and that explosion was almost entirely taking place in Western Europe and, subsequently, in the nations that Western Europeans populated.

This does not mean that Europeans had dominated throughout, for as we have already seen, Westerners were actually economic stragglers for a long time. But since the vast majority of all global creativity ever produced happened after 1450, it was Westerners who invented almost any creative invention we can think of. And the consequence of this is that 97% of the total creative thinking from 800 BC to 1950 according to Murrays study was created in the West. And this is indeed astionishing.

So there we have our explanation for why the West came to dominate and we should probably tell children that in school. The West had a unique set of conditions for creativity, and this creativity drove everything else: institutions, work methods, technologies, the arts, everything.

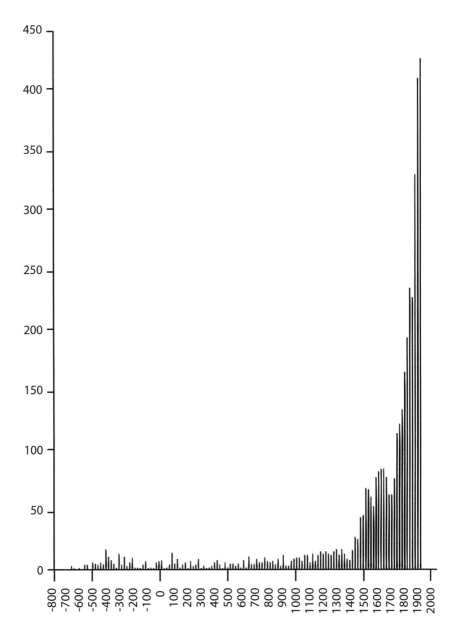

TREND IN HUMAN ACHIEVEMENT (NEW CREATIVITY) FROM 800 BC TO 1950, ACCORDING TO CHARLES MURRAY'S RESEARCH. THE GRAPH DOESN'T SHOW ACCUMULATED CREATIVITY, BUT THE NUMBER OF NEW ACHIEVEMENTS WITHIN EACH PERIOD. UP TO APPROXIMATELY THE YEAR 1000, THERE IS NO CLEAR OVERALL GROWTH TREND, BUT THIS DISGUISES RISING CREATIVE OUTPUT IN WESTERN EUROPA AND DECLINING ELSEWHERE. AFTER APPROXIMATELY 1450, OVERALL CREATIVE OUTPUT EXPLODED, BUT THIS WAS ALMOST ENTIRELY IN THE WEST.[83]

We have now studied the main early drivers of Western creativity, and these explain how a creative explosion in Western Europe led to its global dominance, and also why this creativity evolved in the first place. However, there still remain some questions:

◆ Which were the most important drivers of the Western European creative explosion; the rivers and harbours, cultural factors, decentralization or what?
◆ What are the typical reasons that creativity ceases in societies that have previously been very dynamic?
◆ Why did China and the Islamosphere, which were initially ahead, subsequently fall so far behind?
◆ Why did the areas colonized by England become so much more successful than those colonized by Spain and Portugal?
◆ Why was global development in creativity flat and not exponential between 400 BC and 1400 AD?

We shall address these in the coming chapters.

7.
THE QUESTION
OF THE
CREATIVE CORE

We began the previous chapter with the story of the printing press in Europe and how it contributed to the creative take-off between 1450 and 1500. Fortunately, we know exactly where these first printers were located, and that can help us to identify from where exactly in Western Europe the take-off was driven and why. As the map below shows, most printing activity was concentrated in a wedge running from Northern Italy up through Germany and the eastern part of France and the Netherlands even though there also were a number of printing presses scattered over Spain.

A closer examination of the map shows something else: A significant number of the printers were located along the main rivers, but not all that many along the coastlines. Water access is not really needed for small-scale book printing, so this is probably indicative of where people were most innovative and advanced: along rivers. In the Medieval Age, people needed water access for trade, but they were probably too militarily exposed when they lived on the sea-front.

While these locations seem indicative of creativity concentration between 1450 and 1500, Charles Murray's study provided a far more systematic and long- ranging mapping of creativity, and it showed what he called the "European core" of accomplishment. This is shown on the map below, where it should be noted that this core only constituted approximately 10% of Western Europe which again constituted approx. 2 % of the global landmass. So half of the creativity happened within 0.2 % of the landmass, and only approximately 1% of the global population lived in that tiny area.

One difference between the two maps is that the one with the printing presses only covers that particular innovation, and only between 1450 and 1500, whereas Murrey's map covers all innovation until 1950. Nevertheless, the maps show rather similar patterns with the notable exception that Spain is not included in Murray's creative core, despite that fact that it had a fair number of printers (Spain fell behind during the Spanish Inquisition, which lasted 1478-1834). Conversely, the Scottish area around the Clyde River where the

EUROPEAN PRINT SHOPS IN THE 15TH CENTURY, PER ESTABLISHMENT, DATE AND BOOK
OUTPUT. A CLOSE INSPECTION OF THE MAP SHOWS A VERY HIGH CONCENTRATION OF
PRINTING PRESSES ALONGSIDE RIVERS AND TO A LESSER EXTENT BY SEA PORTS.[84]

Industrial revolution later began had no printers between 1450 and 1500 but
was a creative powerhouse 300 years later.

So which factors have been most important in driving the creative explosion?
While access to good rivers and coastal areas were surely important con-
tributors, they cannot easily explain the timing of the growth in creativity,
since they had been there all along, including when Europe was behind. Nor
can the Roman standards and shared memory systems do it, because, they
were there during the far less creative times of the Roman Empire – even as
it declined and collapsed. Furthermore, the Ottomans and Chinese also had

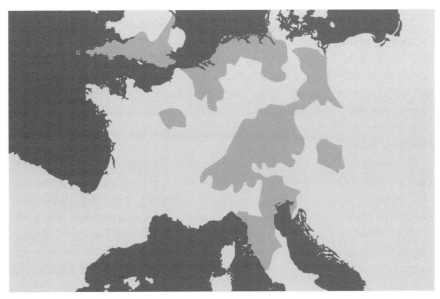

EUROPE'S INNOVATIVE CORE, WHICH CONTRIBUTED APPROXIMATELY HALF OF EUROPE'S CREATIVE OUTPUT UNTIL 1950.[85]

lots of shared memory systems as they entered creative decline, so that cannot do it alone. But here is one factor that can explain the timing: medieval decentralization.

We have already noted that Western Europe was divided into countless mini-states after the fall of the Roman Empire and much of it remained extremely decentralized for many centuries after, as had previously happened in creative Greece. So let's study that phenomenon further.

First we can ask why that de-centralization lasted so long? One reason for this was that the continent had many languages and mountain ranges, which led to the natural fragmentation, but it had also had that under the Roman Empire. A better reason was that Europeans in the Middle Ages had two very strong military concepts that could not overcome one another; namely the knights and the castles. This created a kind of "power stalemate", because castles evidently couldn't attack knights, but knights also had difficulty capturing fortresses; a lord, typically, only had the right to draw on the surrounding farmers for a military campaign for 40 days a year, which wasn't long enough to starve the inhabitants out of a castle.[86]

A third reason for the huge decentralization was that the kings had great difficulty collecting taxes for the simple reason that they did not have standing armies, whereas the local lords had their own armies as well as fortifications. As mentioned before, the Germanic tribesmen were pretty handy with their battle axes.

There was a fourth reason for the lasting decentralization, namely that the Germanic people tended to divide their land between their sons upon death. So it was not, as in some other societies, the eldest son, who inherited it all - no, if there were two or more sons, the land, barony or kingdom would be divided up between them. They could then marry the neighbouring land-owner's daughter and gain some consolidations that way, but because of the inheritage patterns there was no overall trend towards consolidation among Germanic people.

The result of these circumstances was that Western Europe - especially from around 1300 - was divided into several thousand separate communities, including baronies, principalities and other types of mini-state, all of which competed vigorously with one another. Various areas were, from 962 to 1806, connected in a very loose alliance known as the German - Roman Empire (and once as the Holy Roman Empire), but basically it was an enormous chaos of autonomous mini-states similar to Lichtenstein, Luxembourg, Andorra or Monaco.[87]

The Netherlands had a more settled structure than the mini states in the Holy Roman Empire, but it was also highly decentralized and for that reason often the laughing-stock of people from more centralized nations such as France and Spain. After all, its population was a ramshackle mix of Jews, Protestants, Catholics and atheists, it didnt have a king or central leader, it didnt have enough land to feed its population, so it largely lived from trade. Despite all of that, its population was happily flaunting its luxury. As for England, this was, after the so-called Glorious Revolution in 1688, a largely democratic and rational nation which, for a time, led to a sort of "Anglomania" among continental supporters of the Enlightenment.

And this is important: The decentralization was by far most pronounced in a band stretching from northern Italy and Switzerland through Germany, Eastern France and Holland, including England. That band coincides very well with our previous maps of printing presses, of Charles Murray's creative core and the places where modern patents are taken out. As we shall learn later, this decentralization is almost certainly the most important explanation for why Western Europe became particularly creative at the time that it did and in the places it did.

So now that's clear, but we dont get a full picture without examining Anglo-Saxon mentality.

Many people seem to think that Anglo-Saxon means British, but the Anglo-Saxons consisted originally of Juti, Angli and Saxones. The Juti were people from Central and Northern Jutland in Denmark, the Angles were from Schleswig-Holstein, which has historically been either German, Dan-

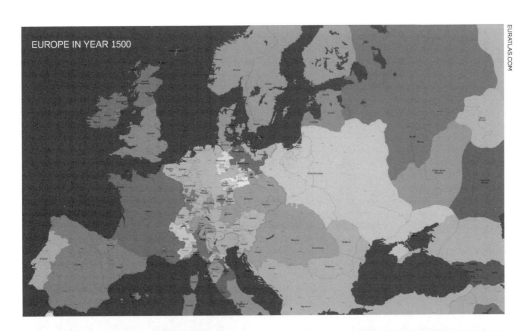

EUROPE IN YEAR 1500

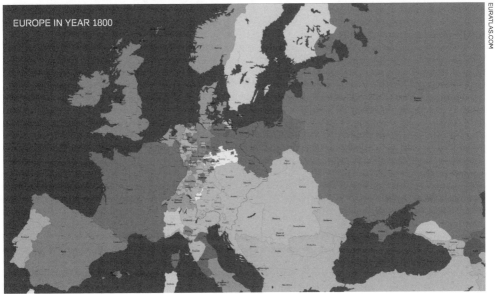

EUROPE IN YEAR 1800

ish or independent, and the Saxons were from northern Germany; perhaps especially from Lower Saxony and from the German north coast just south-west of Schleswig-Holstein. So the Anglo-Saxons were all Danes and North Germans. We know from genetic studies where their descendents in Europe live today:

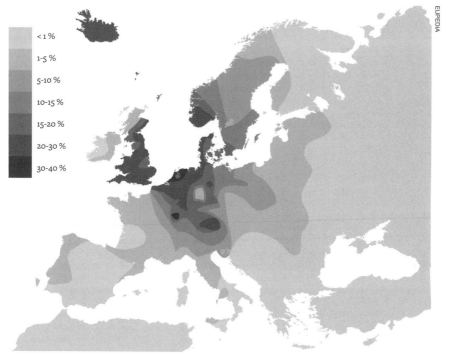

GENETIC MAPPING OF FREQUENCY OF THE R1B-S21 MUTATION, WHICH IS INDICATOR OF ANGLO-SAXON ORIGIN.[87]

Two ancient features of the Anglo-Saxons are striking. The first is their afore-mentioned extremely adventurous sailing tradition (the Vikings), combined with the fact that ancient Germanic tribes (including Vikings) did not tend to build strong fortifications at home. The second is that they had decentralized societies with direct democracy.

When it comes to adventure, we have already seen how the Vikings sailed the European rivers and surrounding oceans. There is a striking con-trast between the energy these people put into their foreign ventures and how little they invested in defending their home bases – almost nothing. The typical Viking village had either no defence walls at all or was surrounded by a small elevation with a simple wood fence. This may have been because few enemies ever bothered or dared to attack them, but the point is that this outwards-focus most have both reflected and shaped their mentality. They would have been accustomed to viewing strangers as opportunities rather than as threats.

As far as the Germanic tribesmen go, these were known, both before and after the Anglo-Saxon settlements in England, for their exceptional work discipline and their sense of time, commitment and tidiness (they are still known for these today). In fact, these traits were already recognised by people in the Roman Empire, whose leaders often hired Germans as bodyguards. They were apparently legendary in Europe during the Middle Ages where, for example, large landowners in Eastern Europe invited Germans to establish local towns on their land, where they were often allowed to govern according to their own, Germanic laws as well as to use German as an official language. For example, in the area called Silesia, which is part of present day Poland and the Czech Republic, there was, in the mid-1300s, more than 1,000 German villages, of which more than 100 were ruled according to German law. Similarly, the Germans established towns in Croatia, Romania and Russia, etc.[88]

Many landowners in Eastern Europe actually considered it so attractive to attract German settlers that they would send for them and offer them money to come. When they actually did come, they would almost always have significantly higher literacy rates than the indigenous inhabitants, and they would bring with them valuable skills in optics, beer brewing, mining, instrument-making and, later, book-printing, for which reason they were often given prominent positions in public administration and armies. In1700, many of these German enclaves started printing their own German language newspapers such as St. Petersburg Zeitung and Odessaer Zeitung.

But why was that so? Why were Germans so incredibly efficient and responsible? The best place to find our answer is in a remarkable book called *De Origine a situ Germanorum*, which was written by the Roman historian Tacitus, in the year 98 – almost 2,000 years ago. This described the Germanic life, as the Romans saw it then, and here you can read that these people lived in small communities, where they decided almost everything by hand vote. Furthermore, their leaders were elected by the local people more based on their "ability to inspire" than on their "ability to persuade", as Tacitus wrote.

We do not know how popular Tacitus' book was in his own time, but it became a best-seller in Germany and France in the 17th and 18th centuries, and our aforementioned writer Montesquieu quoted it often. Perhaps the reason was what one could read between the lines: people develop a responsible culture if they are given responsibility.

And that brings us back to the Vikings and their ancestors, because they also lived in small communities and relied largely on hand vote, where all landowning men, plus landowning widowed women, could vote. They replicated this kind of self-rule (by landowners, which largely meant non-slaves), when they settled abroad, such as when they came to Island and established their parliament in Þingvellir in the year 930.

What we know about the Anglo-Saxons (and the Norwegian and Swedish Vikings) and their ancestors going as far back as 2,000 years ago, clearly suggests that they were extremely adventurous and individualistic with a strong tradition for local self-rule in small communities. Furthermore, their religions encouraged individual performance and suggested that they should be anything but submissive. The Vikings' road to Valhalla was not to show humility and ask forgiveness, but rather to show initiative and bravery; while anyone can debate which is better, it seems obvious that the latter is more economically efficient.

There was one more thing: when the men were out sailing – often the whole summer and sometimes for years - the women would run everything back in the village, and this created a sense of independence and responsibility among them that rarely happened in nations were men were always at home.

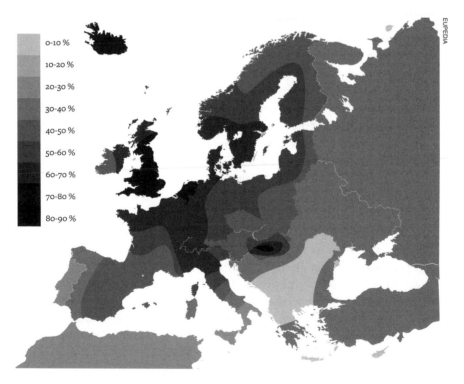

THE PERCENTAGE OF EUROPEANS WHO ARE CATEGORIZED AS HIGHLY INDIVIDUALISTIC. AS CAN BE SEEN, THEY ARE PARTLY CONCENTRATED WHERE THERE ARE MANY ANGLO-SAXONS, AND PARTLY ABOUT WESTERN EUROPE'S MAJOR RIVERS.[89]

As for modern individualism, we can even trace it on a map today, since this is being tested at regular intervals through the extensive World Values Surveys studies. The map below shows the intensity of individualism in Europe, which is generally greatest within Anglo-Saxon areas, although it also elevated around the navigable rivers where the population is not Anglo-Saxon.

So what is the overall conclusion? What were the driving forces behind the Western European creativity and especially the creative core? Was it standards left from the Roman empire? Or sailing culture, religious values, diversity, competition, individualism or decentralizion? At first it might have seemed that these were largely interrelated, but when we look at the 1) timing of the creative development plus the 2) location of the creative core, one factor really stands out: decentralization. It happened when it did and where it did because this particular area at this particular time was extremely decentralized. Therefore , it really does seem that, if a large triangle in the centre of Europe hadn't been complete decentralized for hundreds of years, the creative explosion wouldn't have been nearly the same and the West wouldn't have eneded up dominating the world.

8.
HOW
CREATIVITY
CEASES

As we have already seen, there have been many cases in history, where creative people or nations like Athens, Rome and others were stopped in their tracks. So how does that generally happen? Does every story have its own, unique explanation or are there some general patterns that are frequently repeated?

The answers to both questions is yes. Yes, every story is unique in some ways, but yes, there are also repetitive patterns, and we shall soon look at these.

One element that varies a great deal is the length of time it takes a society to break down. The decay and collapse of Homo floresiensis, some 12,000 years ago, was apparently extremely slow, and while the collapse of the Neanderthals may seem quick on archaeological timescales, it probably still took thousands of years.

Here is a more recent example: thirty years after Europeans first reached Tasmania in 1642, they discovered scattered groups of people, but these people lived largely like animals. For instance, despite the island's cold and often snowy winters, they never lit a fire because they didn't know how to do that. And except for some fur pieces that they wore over their shoulders, they had no clothes but rubbed instead themselves with smelly grease to keep the cold at bay.

Although they often lived close to the coast, they never constructed even the simplest boat. Nor could they fish from the shore, despite the fact that plenty of fish could be seen here; they could neither make a string, a hook nor a net. In fact, these people had almost no tools at all – not even extremely simple bone and stone tools such as those used by the Aboriginal people of Australia or elsewhere in the early Stone Age.

Obviously the Europeans wondered why the locals had completely failed to develop a civilization, not to mention even the most basic Stone Age tools.[90] However, the surprise only grew as they later discovered, through archaeological excavations, that the deeper they dug the more (and better) tools they found. Indeed, the oldest objects showed that the first people who had emigrated from Australia to Tasmania, had indeed known how to sail, fish, make bonfires and much more. So over thousands of years, their culture had been in steady decay until by the arrival of Europeans, virtually nothing was left.

The explanation for the Tasmanian decline was almost certainly that they had been isolated after sea-levels rose. The same was true, to a lesser extent, for the Australian Aboriginals, who had also become cut off from the rest of the world. Their culture had also declined, but less so because they were on a bigger landmass and thus included more people.

THE LAST FOUR FULL-BLOODED TASMANIANS, PHOTOGRAPHED AROUND 1860. THE LAST TASMANIAN TO SURVIVE IS SITTING TO THE RIGHT.

Slow, grinding declines similar to that of the Tasmanians have been seen in many other places that were isolated, and there is every indication that if your social space reduces to below a certain critical mass, decline is inevitable. Such isolation can happen because of religious or political views that isolate small groups of people, but the most common factor is geographical isolation, where there simply aren't any other people within reach. Social isolation happened, for instance, to the Montagnards in Vietnam, the Tierre del Fuego Indians, the Scottish highlanders, the natives in the Canary Islands and, of course, to the Easter Islanders, and the result was, in each case, decline. The Inuit that the Europeans found in Canada had descended from people who had lived in permanent stone houses, had caught the great whales on the open water and had dog sleds, harpoons, toys and boats. But they had entirely forgotten all of this by the time Europeans showed up. What they found were a people who couldn't hunt large animals in the ocean, who lived in primitive snow huts and who no longer managed to store enough food to stay in the same place.[91]

The typical reason for a very slow decline is extreme isolation, but others who were less isolated, but had become highly centralized also decayed from within and then met their nemesis abruptly. When the Spaniards arrived in South America, the Spanish conquistador Hernán Cortés conquered the Aztec empire with just 530 soldiers and Francisco Pizarro took the Incas with 168 men and 62 horses. In reality, the Aztecs were crushed within two years and the Incas within five, despite the fact that these two civilizations had a total of 37 million inhabitants against a combined Spanish invasion force of approximately 1,000 soldiers. On average, each Spaniard overcame 37,000 Indians. When Cortés conquered Mexico, he brought just over 500 soldiers, 100 sailors and 16 horses, who quickly subjugated around 30 million inhabitants. Here, each Spanish invader took on 50,000 locals.

We have already studied the Roman Empire's fall - it was slower and lasted approximately 70 years from the time where barbarians crossed the Rhine in the year 406, to 476, when they took final control of Rome despite being heavily outnumbered. However, most of the empire's dissolution occurred over a period of just 15 years.

And then there's the British Empire which, at its peak in 1913, covered around one-fifth of the planet's surface. Who then could have imagined what Britain would look like in 1975? By then, almost all of the country's empire had disappeared, and UK had over a million unemployed, an inflation rate of 24% and a debt it could not pay. In fact, in 1976 the International Monetary Fund (IMF) had to step in with an emergency loan of £2.3 billion to prevent bankruptcy.

Few collapses have been as speedy as those of the communist regimes. When the Romanian dictator Nicolae Ceauşescu was re-elected as the country's leader in October 1989, he received, literally, an hour-long applause - no one dared to be the first to stop clapping, so it just went on and on. A year later, he had been executed and the Romanian Communist Party dissolved. The rest of the communist regimes collapsed at similar speeds, after which came followed massive crime waves and a number of civil wars.

As these examples show, there are vast differences in the speeds of human decline. However, some of these examples were pre-civilization (and Homo floresiensis were not even humans), but if we focus on how civilizations decline, the recurring patterns become clearer.

One of the people who saw this best is American professor Carroll Quigley, to whom Bill Clinton referred when he announced his first presidential candidacy and when he later gave his inauguration speech. In a nutshell Quigley had taught at Harvard, Princeton and Georgetown universities and focused most of his research on the drivers of civilizations – on why they arise, flourish, go into crisis and disappear.[92]

Quigley found that the basic requirement for a new, viable civilization was strong incentives and distinct possibilities to innovate and accumulate capital (when the UK economy disintegrated in 1975, the marginal tax rate on earned income was 83% and it was 98% on investment profits, so that would explain a good deal). It was also important, he pointed out, and that their population were not stuck in dreams of the past or in excessive attachments to old rules and traditions, and that they had an optimistic culture.

Clinton included specific reference to the latter point (optimism) in his inaugural speech to the Democratic convention in 1992, where he quoted Quigley for highlighting that the US was great because people not only worked for a better future, they also expected one.

Quigley explained how civilizations very often moved through various stages, which he called "mixture, gestation, expansion, age of conflict, universal empire, decay and invasion". Below is a little model which is inspired heavily by him, but somewhat simplified (five steps instead of eight) and with different terms:

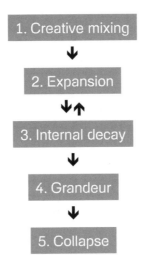

New civilizations typically start because of creative mixing. For instance, England had creative mixing of Celts, Romans, Anglo-Saxons, Jews, Normans and so on and the Romans experienced their take-off after mixing their ideas with Greek ones.

Nest stage is expansion (the Romans and Britons were both really very good at that). Expansion can be military, but it can also simply be economic – you buy assets rather than conquering them. This is what the Chinese have done recently.

All seems fine here, but then comes the inevitable internal decay. Caroll Quigley largely attributed this to what he called "over-institutionalization" but, as we shall discuss in detail is sections four to six, it's a lot more than just that. However, the over-institutionalisation certainly is a big part of the problem, and one of the best known economists to analyse the mechanics of this is Mancur Olson, who is one of the most-cited economists of all time. In his classic book, The Rise and Decline of Nations, he asked why Japan and Germany, both gutterly destroyed during World War II, could have such magnificent booms afterwards.[93]

His answer was in line with Quigleys thinking: that civilization will inevitably over-institutionalize and that a war, terrible as it otherwise is, also liberates nations by destroying excessive institutions.

Olson argued that over-institutionalization largely happened because of accumulation of ever-more special interests and privileges to protect against competition. In addition, to that came endless growth of bureaucracies, which would typically create countless committees and subcommittees, and these would slow each other down. In fact, other economists studying poor countries have shown that overgrown bureaucracy can be a main reason why they never can take off. One study showed, for instance, that if you wanted to buy and register a building permit on a piece of government property in Cairo, it demanded 77 bureaucratic procedures involving 31 government offices and up to 14 years of waiting![94] In Peru, economist Hernando de Soto tried, as an experiment, to open a small clothing shop in the outskirts of Lima in compliance with all statutory provisions. This took 289 days. Later, he tried to gain permission to build on state-owned land, which took six years and 11 months and involved contact with 52 different government agencies.[95]

A third important phenomenon contributed to silting, according to Olson: public organizations were originally created to solve real problems but, over time, their real priority often became to help themselves. They became self-serving and extractive, in other words; they sucked blood out of society and hindered voluntary win-win transactions. And unlike private companies, they seemed to live forever. As US Senator James F. Byrnes once said: "The nearest approach to immortality on Earth is a government bureau."

The overall consequence of such silting is increasing share of involuntary win-lose and even lose-lose transactions. In addition, the process creates an overall cultural change, where more and more citizens become "rent-seekers", specializing in exploiting existing wealth rather than creating it.

Back to Quigley. At some point, he said, a civilization might have its heyday of grandeur without major threat. This phase can easily be deceptive, he said, because this is where the civilization may seem strongest on the surface, but where it may actually be calcifying. The Nazis managed to see their forces march through the Arc de Triomphe in Paris before they were defeated five years later. Similarly, the Roman Empire seemed to be at its peak during the five emperors from 96 AD to 180, where they among, other things, built the

Colosseum and the Pantheon. The Sputnik program was, in a way, the Communist Colosseum and many in the West believed at the time that the Union of Soviet Socialist Republics (USSR) was on track to surpass the West.

Grandeur will often be followed by collapse, which can happen fast, if the ageing civilization collides with another civilization that is the dynamic stage two. If it doesn't, it just withers away slowly. The fall of Rome was fast and the demise of the Incas, Aztecs, Mexicans and Warsaw Pact communists even faster.

Here is another of Quigley's observations: the most dynamic parts of a civilization are typically its outlying areas (those that most recently introduced its ideas). The reason is simple: These areas are typically still in the hyper-dynamic phase two where they enjoy strong growth and enthusiasm, while those who have had civilization for longer, will be more silted and therefore more likely to be in phase three or well on their way to phase five.

Western civilization spread to the US, Canada, Australia and New Zealand, and it has most recently been widely adopted in some Asian markets which are now in phase two. Where European nations are now predominantly in phase three (and some Southern European nations arguably in phase five and only avoiding collapse because of life-support from the EU), one sees higher dynamics in the markets that have recently introduced many elements of Western civilization - countries like Taiwan, South Korea, Chile, Poland and, since 1980, China. Similarly, the younger Western nations like the US, Canada and Australia are today more dynamic than Western Europe. But the threats are the same, and those nations that do not sense all of them now will probably do so in the not-so-distant future. They comprise cults of decline, overinstitutionalization and enemies of enlightenment, and it is these that we shall address in sections four to six. However, long before we get to that, we shall, in the next chapter, study why only Western Europe became hyper-creative, because while this story tells us about how creativity happens in practice, it also shows how it can be halted in real life. That part is a horror story.

9.
WHY ONLY
THE WEST?

If it seems surprising how quickly the Europeans managed to conquer most of the world, it may, at first sight, seem even more strange that China and the Islamic nations did not come first, or at least came along simultaneously. This is actually an important part of the story, because it demonstrates, yet again, how creative societies can commit suicide like the Roman Empire did.

Let's take the Islamosphere first. The Islamic world was, for a long while, very successful. Just four years after the death of Muhammad in 632, Muslim armies conquered Syria, and they took Jerusalem two years after that and then Alexandria in Egypt in 641. By 1715, they had conquered the North African coast and most of Spain. This was clearly a civilization in stage two (expansion) in our aforementioned model of how civilizations develop. It didn't hurt in this connection that the Arab countries enjoyed the advantage of a central location on the threshold between the Mediterranean Sea and the Indian Ocean, which was extended by their access to the Atlantic and control of the strait of Gibraltar. It is thus not surprising that they experienced a 500-years period of enlightenment lasting from the middle of the eighth century until 1258, when the Mongols took Baghdad. This age is now called the Islamic Golden Age (although, it should be said, many inhabitants of what we consider to be Islamic areas didn't actually convert to Islam until the 10th century).

Anyway, this was impressive and affected most of the Islamic nations. Anyone who wants to experience, personally, how far the Islamic nations came, should visit the gorgeous Arabian palace Alhambra in Granada, Southern Spain today; it is arguably one of Spain's five most beautiful buildings and certainly as spectacular as the cathedral of Seville or the best of the more recent works by Antonio Gaudí and Santiago Calatrava. And yet, Alhambra was built between 889 and 1333, which means it was completed almost 700 years ago. Most of Spain was between 929 and 1031 ruled by the Caliphate of Córdoba, during which time the Spanish, in addition to numerous architectural wonders, created the library of Al-Ḥakam II in Cordoba. This is estimated to have contained at least 400,000 volumes, which was probably more literature than you could find in all the rest of Europe put together. Islam was also very tolerant at the time, and much of their construction work was actually made by Jewish stone masons, with whom the intermingled peacefully.

In this age of Islamic enlightenment, Muslims translated all known works of the Greek philosophers, and around the year 800, Baghdad was one of the world's most advanced cities, if not the global leader – perhaps followed by Islamic Cordoba. By this time, the citizens of Bagdad introduced joint-stock companies, palaces, hospitals and schools, and a significant section of the population was literate. It was here that Caliph Harun al-Rashid, who reigned from 786 to 809, founded the House of Wisdom, which, by the middle of the ninth century had evolved into the world's largest library and leading research centre.

During these centuries, the Muslims made a number of breakthroughs in medicine, chemistry, philosophy, geography, astronomy, optics and mathematics. Thus, it was Muslims who invented much of the first algebra and they were also leaders in anatomy and medicine. The physician al-Razi (865-925) identified smallpox and measles and appeared to be the first doctor ever to understand that fever was a defence mechanism. We can read that, and much more besides, in a 23-volume encyclopaedia of medicine, which he wrote. He was also ahead of his time in his systematic implemention of controlled experiments.

Other examples of great Muslim thinkers include Al-Farabi, who became known as "the other thinker", alongside Aristotle. Additionally, there was the polymath Al-Biruni, who wrote 146 technical papers, totalling approximately 13,000 pages on a wide range of topics. In the year 990 this hyperactive gentleman made an estimation of the Earth's circumference, which only deviated from the correct figure by less than 1% - far better than the estimate Columbus made 500 years later.

During this time, Muslims had two alternative conceptions of the Qur'an; that it was dictated directly by God or, alternatively, that it was formulated by the Prophet. From 813 to 833 the empire was ruled by Al- Ma'mun, who held the latter view and enforced a doctrine called Mu'tazilism, which encouraged pursuit of logic and scientific thinking; the same view Thomas Aquinas more than 400 years later introduced to Christianity.

But then something important happened which would eventually change everything. After Al-Ma'mun's death, the prevailing view changed into the anti-rational Ash'ari school, which held the basic assumption that unless science and philosophy arose directly from religious doctrine, it was dangerous, as it could undermine religion and because God controlled everything anyway. In his book from the 11th century, Tahafut al-Falasifa (which translates as "The Incoherence of the Philosophers"), the Persian theologian Al- Ghazali wrote:

"The connection between what is habitually believed to be a cause and what is habitually believed to be an effect is not necessary, according to us (...) Take for instance any two things, such as the quenching of thirst and drinking; satisfaction of hunger and eating; burning and contact with fire; light and the rise of the Sun (...) Their connection is due

to the prior decree of God, who creates them side by side, not to its being necessary in itself, incapable of separation."[96]

So there could be no laws of physics because everything was controlled from above, and some interpretations of the Ash'ari school went even further and regarded man as completely remote-controlled too. When people talked, it was not really them who did it, but the Almighty who made them do it; word-for-word. If they felt as if they had free will, it was because God had given them this illusion. And there were no free will or human virtue; if a person seemed good or bad, it was something that God had caused for a purpose. As the philosopher Ibn Hazm Al Andalusi wrote: "You have no merit from your own virtues, they are only gifts from the Almighty".[97]

Muslims from the Ash'ari school also opposed arts. Music was not allowed, with the possible exception of singing acapella accompanied by a hand-held, one-sided drum on special occasions such as weddings. And paintings were forbidden; especially if they depicted humans.

Rather remarkably, this school would soon be described as "the middle way", as its views were somewhere between those of the Mu'tazilites and the Hanbalites, who exhibited an even more extreme rejection of human ability and the right to think individually.[98] People should never try to assess what was good or bad, because humans were not able to do that, they said. Rather, they should only ever look at what the Qur'an wrote about any situation and then act on that basis alone.

In addition, the movement strictly forbade any attempts to seek laws of nature, for there could be no such laws since God controlled the movements of every single particle in the universe all the time – and God was not subject to any laws. Equally, any man-made legal system was a sin. One could not, therefore, support a democratic idea of "one man, one vote", because the correct view was "one God, one vote", and God had already said, via the Qur'an, everything that needed to be said. The overwhelming objective of education should be to learn the Qur'an by heart; not to learn about philosophy, science and independent thinking, for all of that was blasphemy.

According to the Hanbalites, you could only enter Paradise if you blindly obeyed the imams and failed to consider anything beyond the most convenient necessity yourself. Switch off your brain and obey, and you may be saved. The theologian Ahmad ibn Hanbal, who lived 780-855, made the matter clear: "Any discussion of things that the Prophet did not discuss is a mistake."[99]

In the year 885, it was therefore made punishable by Muslims to copy books on philosophy, and the death penalty was imposed on anyone considered a supporter of Mu'tazilism. Between April 892 and March 893 all bookstore owners were forced to swear that they would not sell books on theology, dialectic and

WHY ONLY THE WEST?

philosophy and, in 1013, the Arabs destroyed their library in Cordoba. The library in Alexandria was burned by the Caliph Omar, and just 16 years later, Sutan Mahmud of Ghazni burned the library in Rayy, Persia. It didn't stop there: in 1151 'Ala ad-Din Husain tourched the library in Ghazna, in 1154 Oghur tyrks burned down the library in Nishapur, and in 1193, Bakhti Khilji took the library of Nalanda down in flames.[100] What did remain was the library in Bagdad, but the Mongols took care of that in 1258, where they burned it down.

No, book had a limited shelf life in the Middle East, and in the 1300s, the Arab historian Ibn Khaldun described how the Arabs, after they had conquered Persia in the seventh century had taken huge amounts of books and scientific articles as booty. General Sa'd ibn Abi Waqqas now requested the reigning Caliph Omar for permission to distribute them to the soldiers, but the Caliph replied:

"Throw them in the water. If what they contain is right guidance, God has given us better guidance. If it is error, God has protected us against it." [101]

The Islamic Ottoman Empire, which ruled most (and at times almost all) of the Muslim world between 1299 and 1922, was not only opposed to books (other than the Qur'an), but also to watches, experimental science, modern philosophy and modern financial systems. For this reason, Muslims did not make much progress within disciplines such as navigation, instrument making, or timekeeping, and they also failed to embark on an industrial revolution.[102]

Furthermore, they did not have a banking system like the West, partly because the Qu'ran prohibited paying interest on loans or deposits. Nor did they have the same rule of law as most Western nations and, in principle, the sultan owned all land in the nation and felt free to confiscate whatever he wanted from whoever he pleased. People did not know how much tax collectors would ask for or when they might turn up. For those reasons, Muslims with assets were reluctant to invest actively and would rather hide their wealth in jewelry or gold coins, which they brought with them. Even when Ottomans went to war, they would often carry all their weath with them; after the Battle of Lepanto in 1571, the Western victors were amazed to find huge treasures in gold in the captured Ottoman battleships. Finally, as the Ottomans were not creative, they could only raise money for imports by selling commodities and by conquering and plundering. Their economic structure became extractive and, when they could not beat the Western armies anymore, the system went into structural decline.

After the Islamic scientific and philosophical curiosity and the desire to invest actively thus had been extinguished, there still remained a tradition of technological innovation within limited areas such medicine and optics, but eventually this also withered away, and the communities became largely static. The only schools children would go to were now so-called madrasses, where they were taught almost exclusively in grammar, religion and Sharia law, and where rote learning and conformity was paramount.

And their problems just grew and grew. The German invention of the printing press in 1450 could, in principle, have contributed to the opening of the Muslim mind, but this was also blocked, as Sultan Selim of the Ottoman Empire in 1515 decreed the death penalty for use of printers in Arabic within his empire, which stretched from, and including, present Greece and around the Mediterranean and even Egypt.

The Ottoman ban on printing was abolished in 1729 and, thereafter, a publisher named Ibrahim Müteferrika was given permission to print books, but only on the condition that all manuscripts received prior approval from a panel of three religious and three legal experts. Between the years 1729 and 1743 he managed to get just 17 books through this needle's eye, after which he abandoned his project.[103] It should be said here, that after Müteferrika gained his initial permission for book-printing, another gentleman with the name Sa'id Efendi also received such a licence, but his production became even more meagre.[104] To put that into perspective, by the middle of the 16th century, so 200 years earlier, the printers in the tiny city of Venice had alone produced approximately 20,000 different titles covering everything from maps to manuals, philosophical titles, debate books and even music reviews.

At that point in time, Europe was, in any case, so far ahead that the Islamic nations couldn't have caught up. In fact, it was by no means attempted, because once the light had been extinguished in the Ottoman Empire, there were great difficulties getting back on track. By 2002, one could read in the Arab Human Development Report of the United Nations that five times as many books were translated to Greek as into Arabic, despite the fact that the Arab population was nearly 30 times as large as the not-particularly-literary Greek population.[105] Similarly, many globetrotters will have noticed how comparatively rare it is to see book shops in malls or markets in the Arab world or, indeed, people reading books (for example, when on public transport), as the average Arab citizen reads just four pages of literature per year (yes, four pages; not four books), which equates to spending five minutes per year or one second a day reading books.[106] By comparison, the average person in the US reads 11 whole books a year.

In 2007 the Pakistani physicist Pervez Hoodbhoy wrote an article in the magazine Physics Today in which he cited some astonishing figures: Less than one percent of the Muslim population are scientists, engineers or technicians, and even though the Muslim nations has 1,800 universities, the staff from just 312 of those have ever published any material in scientific journals. And over the more than 100 years in which Nobel Prizes have been granted, only two Muslims have won such an award in a scientific discipline, he pointed out.[107] (In

2012, Hoodbhoy was fired from his job at Islamabad University, referring to his political opinions.)

In his book The Crisis of Islamic Civilization, the former Iraqi Trade, Finance and Defence Minister Ali Allawi mentioned, in a similar vein, that the 46 Muslim nations produced only 1.17 % of the world's scientific literature, compared to, for example. 1.48% from Spain – Islamic figures that he found so low that he believed that today's 1.5 billion Muslims produce less scientific innovation than 32 million Muslims did in the eighth century.[108]

Fortunately, societies can change and today there are many different interpretations of Islam, some of which are as open, literate and modern as others are closed and antiquated. The former category can be found in countries such as Turkey, Malaysia and United Arab Emirates (UAE); the UAE state of Dubai has, under the leadership of the extremely popular Mohammed bin Rashid Al Maktoum, evolved very rapidly indeed.[109] Afghanistan would be seen at the opposite end of the spectrum.

The overall problem in the Ottoman Empire was that its leaders during the early parts of the Medieval Age deliberately removed the tools for creativity, after which the previously highly-creative culture eroded. This didn't happen in Christianity, partly because a majority of Christians believe in man's free will and because the existence of natural laws was gradually completely accepted, in particular after Aquinas. The prevailing view became that natural laws existed and should be studied. Deviations from natural laws were then called "miracles" and were rare episodes where God as an exception was shown to have intervened directly in world affairs and thereby violated the laws of nature and/or someone's free will.

How strong a position science gained within the European population could be seen when Simon Newton was buried in 1727. He was then put on lit de parade in Westminster Abbey for four days, after which his coffin was carried to his resting place in the church of the prime minister by a group of people that included five of the country's most prominent noblemen. This display of honour towards a writer and scientist came around the same time that the poor Ibrahim Müteferrika was struggling to get a few books published in the Muslim world.

Western Europeans also supported the separation of church and state, so that each had its own leaders, even if the state financed the church, whereas Muslims overwhelmingly supported a union of the two, as we can still see exemplified in Iran today. In addition, the desire for a clear separation of church and state in Europe was strengthened by the many European religious wars, which made many state leaders realize that they could only unite their people if they took a more neutral role in religious affairs. Here it must be said that Christianity has had its own religious tyrants and its Ash'ari-like movements, such as

Millenarisme and Jehovah's Witnesses (arguably), but they remain marginal.

So the divergent evolution of people's ideas explains why it was not the Middle Eastern people who conquered the world. By inhibiting the creative development among their people, they made their societies static, and they did this entirely deliberately. Their killing of creativity was not akin to an accidental manslaughter but rather to premeditated murder aiming to protect the current power structures and interpretation of religion.

But what about China?

The Chinese had, as previously mentioned, been ahead of the Europeans in terms of technology, and it would certainly have looked like they prepared to take over the world around year 1400. But the first indication that something was about to go wrong for them can actually been seen from the story of one of their greatest triumphs: their aforementioned gigantic expedition with 30,000 men on 300 ships between 1405 and 1433rd. To what purpose did they make this expedition? As it turns out, it was not to set up trading posts or find new pastures. No, the expedition simply returned with a lot of gifts to the emperor, and that was pretty much it.

This stood in stark contrast to Western expeditions. In Italy, for example, it was common in the Middle Ages to distribute ownership of newly-built commercial vessels in 24 or 64 shares that were purchased by private businessmen. If the project went well, they were then paid dividends in accordance with their shareholding, and the captains were offered profit-sharing as incentive. Similar commercial structures were common throughout Europe, and it is actually very similar to what is now practised in modern private equity funds, including venture capital funds.

So China was far more centralized than Europe, and from 1424 it all went horribly wrong for the Chinese. At this time, the country had a new emperor named Zhu Gaochi, who immediately put a stop to new maritime expeditions and then burned a number of ships. When he died nine months later (perhaps killed by a captain, one wonders), his successor, Xuande, set out one last expedition between 1432 and 1433 to retrieve Chinese expatriates. Shortly after that he destroyed the sea-faring ships and, in 1500, Emperor Hongzhi issued a decree that simply forbade construction of ships with more than two masts.[110] In 1525, these rules were made even stricter, and vessels of any kind suitable for sea transport now had to be destroyed; in 1551, it was simply made illegal to sail out to sea. In 1644, the government took the restrictions further by forbidding habitation within a coastline of approximately 1,000 km to ensure that no one ever would sail out.[111] By contrast, the tiny state of Venice off the Italian coast had, around the year 1750, more than 800 commercial vessels arriving and departing each year.

So the Chinese closed the door to the world and threw away the key. The highest aspiration of Chinese people was now a job in the state, which required rote learning of the text in a number of old books. The term "Mandarin", which we now use for the Chinese language (and for a hotel chain and a fruit), actually comes from the Chinese expression for government employees, who were the elite of a society, and to whom conformity, tradition, harmony and continuity had become the highest ideals.

Yes, a Mandarain was what you wanted to be, and a conservative Mandarin was a good Mandarin. In order to get such a job, you needed to pass a very difficult exam, which required an excellent memory, but no creative skills. This exam remained largely unchanged from 124 BC until 1368 AD, where it was somewhat modified, after which it hardly changed at all until 1905. Creativity was simply not wanted in this society and, as historian Toby Huff has noted, "Chinese authorities neither created nor tolerated independent institutions of higher learning within which disinterested scholars could pursue their insights."[112] When Europeans first met the Chinese, their extreme conservatism astounded the visitors. An example of their attitude was observed by the British statesman George Macartney, who spent the 1792-1793 trying to establish diplomatic relations with China. He brought with him 600 boxes of gifts from King George III with content that he hoped would show the Chinese how interesting the Europeans were to trade with. These included a planetarium, mathematical instruments, globes, measuring instruments, telescopes, chemical sample collections, works of art and, of course, watches. As this was presented to the local leader in the province, Macartney became astonishing by the response, he received:

"We have never valued ingenious articles, nor do we have the slightest need of your country's manufactures." [113]

If by "we" he ment "the Chinese" then "never" was actually wrong, because they had once valued innovation and been excellent at it. The problem was, therefore, not that the Chinese were incapable of innovating, because they had already demonstrated this ability to the full over many centuries. The problem was that they no longer wanted to.

And they didn't want to trade either. The only harbour where the giant Chinese empire allowed trade was Kanton (now Guangzhou), and Macartney's request to open more harbours and to set up a warehouse in Beijing was rejected.

Societies that stagnate will sooner or later also decay, and this is exactly what happened to China. Slowly, year-after-year, China began to decline. When Marco Polo visited the country in the 1200s, he was very impressed with their deep, ingenious and partially-mechanized coal mines. This was when China was still a very creative nation. In the 1800s, however, such mines were replaced by primitive and manual excavation from the surface without any mechanization. A similar decline in their technological prowess was seen across many fields, and a parallel destruction of their culture also happened, culminating in Mao Zedong's final attempts to wipe out the little that was left (remember the Mao shirts). In parallel with this, their economy declined until at the time of Mao, it had come from being perhaps the richest nation on Earth to being on a par with Somalia; one of the very poorest.[114]

Of course, there had been attempts to reverse the decline. Eventually the Chinese had repealed their sailing restrictions and, in 1851, a Chinese ship arrived for the first time to Europe, but this happened a full 585 years after Marco Polo had visited China in 1266. The race for global dominance was now entirely over since, in the meantime, the Europeans had colonized the Americas, Australia, New Zealand, India, Africa, much of Asia, a large number of small islands between the continents and, for good measure, had also laid claim to the polar regions and taken control of the seas.

The story of how the West became so extremely creative will not be complete unless we investigate the peculiar role that Great Britain and our aforementioned Anglo-Saxons ultimately came to play. Just consider this for a moment: England doesn't really seem to have a national folk costume like most other nations. But it actually did have one once. It was called a jacket and a tie and, today, businessmen, politicians, diplomats or gentlemen around the world will routinely put on this English folk costume, when they have to look presentable.

In 1876, 25 years after the Chinese first arrived in Europe, the British Queen Victoria had just been named the Queen of India, and is was then said, with pride, that the sun never set on her empire, as it had gained possessions on all continents and from the North to the South Pole. In fact, this tiny country now controlled about a fifth of the planet's land masses.

Great Britain could then look back on a remarkable period. In 1785, London had 650 companies that produced or sold books, and it had countless art fairs, theatre plays and concerts that attracted huge crowds.[115] The country had also been home to many of the world's leading thinkers and artists such as Smith, Newton, and Purcell. Likewise, it had caught up with Spain and Portugal in terms of colonization and then overtaken them.

But why was it United Kingdom that ended up as Europe's premier colonial power, and why did the countries that received large migrations from United Kingdom become some of the most successful nations on Earth - countries like the US, Canada, Australia, and New Zealand? Why did the same not happen to countries which other Europeans colonized? Or let's put it more simply: Why did the Spanish colonies become far less successful than the English?

To understand why, we can start by comparing how England colonized its territories in North America to how the Spaniards managed theirs in Latin America. Unlike the mini-states in the creative core, Spain had, after the fall of Rome, quickly become a highly-centralized and authoritarian nation, and the purpose of its ventures were to secure land for the monarchy, which of course offered rewards for the conquistadors; those who did the dirty work. This reward could be gold and silver but was often land with attached right to use the locals living on it as slaves - a system reminiscent of what we saw in the late Roman Empire.

The effect was also the same as in the late Rome. The slaves were sent into the mines and fields while the owners stayed as much as possible in their villas. Since no-one had voting rights, they felt no particular responsibility for the state's well-being, and as they weren't involved in much of the practical work either, they were not particular innovative.

All this was in sharp contrast to the processes of the British colonization of North America. Here the immigrants were offered an opportunity to work, typically for four years for an established farmer family for food and shelter, but without salary, after which they were given their own plot of land plus voting rights. Democracy thus became vibrant and experimental, and since almost everyone soon owned their own land and did their own work, productivity increased dramatically and continuously, driven by dedication and innovation. A study of patents filed between 1820 and 1845 showed, for instance, that a large proportion were filed by people whose parents were neither professionally-trained nor larger landowners, and 40% of patent applicants had only primary school education or less.[116]

It also contributed to the creativity that through the Declaration of Independence, the US's founding fathers built on ideas that led back to Athens rather than to Sparta. And they demonstrated clear understanding of Montesquieu's principles of separation of powers as well as of John Locke's emphasis on personal freedom, equality and sovereignty and therefore on protection of private property. In fact, Locke himself contributed to the drafting of the first Constitution of the state of Ohio, which became a major inspiration for the US's future Constitution. This Constitution was largely written by Thomas Jefferson, who emphasized not only private property and personal freedom, but also equality (except for women and slaves, it must be said), and the right of everyone to seek his own happiness, by which the Constitution implicitly said that individual rights should always be a priority. This protection of the individual was in contrast to typical existing standards elsewhere stressing obligations to others, such as to God, king or country. Indeed, Jefferson was very worried about bringing too much centralization as this would "invite the public agents to corruption, plunder and waste." And he also feared the consequences of democracy, even though he wrote it into the constitution, because, as he said, "Democracy is nothing but mob rule, where 51% of the people may take away the rights of the 49%. Benjamin Franklin, another of the founding fathers raised the same concern, when he said that "Democracy is two wolves and a lamb voting about what they are going to have for lunch."

So respect for the individual was a high priority (Franklin continued his statement with the words: "Liberty is a well-armed lamb contesting the vote."), and it should be noted in this connection that the Anglo-Saxon nations and former Anglo-Saxon colonies such as the US, Canada, South Africa, Australia, Malaysia, and India were all structured as federations and intended to remain decentralized and with respect for individuals, even though many of them have since consolidated. In fact, the only exceptions to the pattern of federalism are New Zealand and the (partly) the UK. The Spanish colonies, in contrast, were centralized.

So here is food for thought: The Anglo-Saxons who came from Scandinavia and England have, in modern times, never been particularly attracted by totalitarian regimes such as communism, fascism or Nazism. In the middle decades of the 1900s, Germany, Russia, Austria, Bulgaria, Greece, Hungary, Latvia , Lithuania, Poland, Portugal, Spain and Romania all had totalitarian regimes, but none of the Scandinavian countries, nor the UK, US, Canada, Australia or New Zealand has ever had strong fascist or communist movements – not even during severe recessions or depressions. Out of the 600 MPs who have been elected to the UK Parliament's House of Commons through its history, for example, only six revolutionary socialists were ever elected. The tradition for individualism and freedom is simply too ingrained.

Another difference is between what scientists Daron Acemoglu and James Robinson have called "inclusive" and "extractive" organisations, respectively. The former are pluralistic and ensure the rule of law, property rights, and individual rewards, whereas the latter are elitist and focused on extracting economic assets through monopoly, coercion, expropriation and taxation.   The Anglo-Saxon nations tended to have more inclusive institutions whereas the Spanish had more extractive institutions. The latter was also illustrated by the infamous Spanish Inquisition, where 150,000 people between the years 1478 and 1834 were arrested, interrogated and often tortured, and probably 3,000-5,000 were executed. When not killed, the victims' fortunes were often confiscated, and many contemporary sources reported that the Church, as far as they could see, overwhelmingly pursued people with money and for their money. This meant that many of Spain's most enterprising people left the country for fear of having their assets seized.

The Spanish government also managed to enforce centralized tax collection, which had previously been decentralized. Given that the royal family thereby controlled massive cash-flows, they could also centralize power, which gave them a free hand to increase extractive power structures and enforce even more taxes. The local communities had previously been subject to competition and thus the risk of people voting with their feet and moving out, which had restrained their abuses, but the central government did not face the same limitations once tax collection had been centralized. The predictable result was - as had been the case in late Roman Empire – that farmers abandoned their land, which led to falling food production and a declining tax base.

However, even this tax evasion did not prevent the state from engaging in a wide range of extremely expensive wars and, on several occasions, the Spanish government resorted to seizing private gold shipments and replacing them with government bonds to finance the bill. These bonds would often turn out to be worthless, because despite its large gold and silver revenue from Latin America, the country went bankrupt in 1557, 1576, 1607, 1627, 1647, 1652, 1660, 1662 and 1739.

Things grew particularly bad in Spain under King Charles II, who reigned from 1665 to 1700. Charles was the product of 100 years of close inbreeding in the Spanish Royal Family. His jaw thrust so far that he could not chew; his tongue was so great that he had difficulty speaking and often drooled, and he was known to be rather dim-witted. His leadership brought Spain a series of military defeats, intellectual decline and famine, although it must be said that it actually didn't go bankrupt during his reign; perhaps because no one wanted to lend him money in the first place.

Why was the British approach so different from the Spanish? In a way it goes back to who they were, and here, funnily enough, we find that about 85% of the British were of Spanish origin.

Yes, Spanish, but that was from way back. Recent genetic studies have shown that the vast majority of the British today are Celtic, descendants of Basques, who walked from Spain to England and Ireland after the end of the last Ice Age. They could do this because the sea level then was approximately 130 metres lower than it is today, so the current British Isles at the time were only peninsulas on top of Europe. After these Basques (now called Celts) had arrived, sea levels rose and they became somewhat isolated, even though they eventually developed boats. They now lived in relative isolation for millennia until they were invaded by the Romans in the year 43. The Romans had great difficulty governing the country and described, with disdain, how they were attacked by disorganized bands of naked men and women with painted bodies - the so-called picts (picts meant painted). In around 410, they left the country which had never brought them much benefit, but rather a whole lot of rain and trouble.

We have only one source providing insight into what happened during the following 130 years: the monk Gildas who, around the year 540, wrote about it. According to him, after the Roman withdrawal, the Celtic tribes started fighting each other and, in particular, the southern tribes were attacked from the north. The southerners therefore hired Anglo-Saxon mercenaries, but this soon backfired as these brutes soon took over control of everything except Scotland, Ireland and Wales.

The Anglo-Saxon Jutes and Angles (Danes) now settled predominantly in Kent, whereas the Saxons (Germans) settled further towards the southwest. In fact, the word "England" descends from the words "Agnlorum ", "Angelcynn" and "Engelcynn" which all means the place of the Angli– the Romans had called it the islands Provincia Britannia. However, county names, that currently ends in "sex", are all originally Saxon. Sussex, for example, means "South Saxony", "Wessex" (which no longer exists) was "West Saxony", "Essex" is "East Saxony" and "Middlesex" is...well, you guessed it. The reason that there isn't a "Nossex" is probably that the Danes further up north got in the way.

We can be pretty sure that Gildas was right when he wrote that the Anglo-Saxons bullied the Celts, because recent DNA studies show that British Y-chromosomes are disproportionately from Anglo-Saxon men, while the DNA of the mitochondria are disproportionately from Celtic women. Indeed, a study from University College in 2011 showed that half of all British men have an Anglo-Saxon segment of their Y - chromosome, which is also shared by almost all men in Denmark and northern Germany.[118] So a lot of Anglo-Saxon men took Celtic women, and not the other way around, and if this isn't bullying, what is?

There were many more migrations and invasions after the early Anglo-Saxon take-over. For instance, in the year 886 the Danish Viking king Gorm won a war with England's King Alfred, after which he imposed Danelagh (Danish law) in the Anglo-Saxon-dominated area. In 1015, England was attacked again, this time by the Danish King "Canute", or Knut in Danish, who came to rule much of England until 1035.

Again, in 1066, the British Isles was attacked twice and almost simultaneously from two sides. From the northeast came a party of Norwegian Vikings, while the Normans attacked from the south. The locals (which were now Celts mixed with a minority of Anglo-Saxons from earlier emigrations) defeated the Norwegian invading force at the Battle of Stamford Bridge, but lost shortly after to the Normans at the Battle of Hastings. After this, the Normans took complete power in all the previous Anglo-Saxon areas. And they would soon use this base to expand their international trading culture by building larger ships and sailing still further afield.

It is the combination of all this that created the Anglo-Saxon mentality; the combination of sailing tradition, individualism, Germanic effectiveness, Viking lust for adventure, pagan religions emphasizing achievement and the very old shared tradition for small communities and direct democracy. All this evolved into what German sociologist Max Weber in 1905 called "the Protestant work ethic".[119] A very simplified summary of Weber's hypothesis may sound like this:

◆ The Catholic Church had guaranteed access to Paradise if believers submitted themselves to its leadership (and perhaps paid indulgences).
◆ Protestants were not offered similar guarantees, but nor were they required to submit to an institution. Instead, they believed they would qualify for God's love through individual achievement (as with the previous road to Valhalla).
◆ They wouldn't give money away to charity as they thought it would make the beneficiaries weak, and they didn't give cash to the Church either, as it didn't need it. So they invested it in farms, workshops and factories.

Going back in time, many writers and thinkers visited the US and were amazed by the Protestant work ethic. In fact, many of them described how Protestants looked down on people who didn't work hard and start a family. For instance, the Frenchman Michael Chevalier visited the US in the 1830s and wrote:

"The American is educated with the idea that he will have some particular occupation, that he is to be a farmer, artisan, manufacturer, merchant, speculator, lawyer, physician, or minister, perhaps all in succession, and that, if he is active and intelligent, he will make his fortune. He has no conception of living without a profession, even when his family is rich, for he sees nobody about him not engaged in business."[31]

Their individualism was important. Already in 1384, before Martin Luther founded Protestantism, the English theologian John Wycliffe wrote that: "This Bible is for the government of the people, for the people and by the people". When the US. Constitution was written in 1787, it contained the following sentence: "Government of the people, by the people, for the people shall not perish from the Earth."

So the idea of giving priority to the individual over institutions was repeated here almost 400 years later, but probably stretched back to the aforementioned phenomenon that Germanic people had ruled themselves in small communities for at least 1,500 years and possibly much longer.

Not many other people in the world had that experience and culture. The closest comparison is the decentralized Greeks from approximately 700 BC until it consolidated from 359 BC; after this, it was centrally ruled by first Alexander the Great, then by the Roman Empire, which, however, initially gave some self-rule to a few Greek city states such as Rhodes, Dilos, Crete and Chios until at least 30 BC. This was followed by rule by the static Byzantine Empire, then the even more static Ottomans, and finally, from 1839 until today, by kings, military dictators and (only since 1973) by a democratically-elected parliament. Greece invented many of the ideas that inspired democracy, enlightenment and more in the West, but the Greek democracy, we know today, is only two generations old, which explains a lot.

We have now studied which of the creative drivers seemed most important for Western Europe (the answer was decentralization); why China and the Islamic nations fell behind (they closed the door to travelling and knowledge,) and why England and its colonies became so disproportionally successful (adventurous, individualistic and democratic culture going thousands of years back). Our last big question is this: why was the increase in creativity not exponential between 400 BC and 1400 AD? After all, we have previously seen that the natural development of a creative design space is hyper-exponential, so why didnt Charles Myrray's curve of human accomplishment look exponential all the way?

The answer to this is simple and scary: Creativity in a civilization tends not to last for long because it is destroyed from within. The natural process of a creative design space is exponential development, but someone tends to step in to stop it, and while it was accelerating in Western Europe, it was decelerating in China and the Islamic nations, which explains the lack of overall acceleration from year 400 to 1400 AD.

This is a general pattern. There was intense creativity during Djoser in ancient Egypt in the third dynasty 2737-2717 BC. The same was true at the beginning of the Mesopotamian civilization and among Incas, Aztecs and Mughals. But all of those societies then stagnated. Similarly, creativity prevailed in the early Roman Empire, but was suffocated in its latter days. The fact is that virtually all civilizations that previously were creative, only maintained their dynamism for a limited time.

And within Western Europe after Rome? Here it triumphed in Spain, but was then choked by the consolidation of power and the Inquisition. Florence had its golden age in the 1400s and especially during the Lorenzo de Medici, who was the city-state's leader from 1469 to 1492, where art, philosophy, science and technology flourished. In fact, the Medici family sent people out in the world to buy books which they copied, and it was under them that we saw artists such as Michelangelo, Leonardo da Vinci and Botticelli shine.

However, this golden period lasted only one generation (yes, one). In 1494 the power was taken over by the monk Girolamo Savonarola, who immediately introduced a series of prohibitions and restrictions to impose austere demeanour. You were then only allowed to wear simple clothes, and bully gangs of so-called vigilantes patrolled the streets to find unnecessary items such as mirrors, cosmetics, books and other items that were now forbidden. Music and modern literature was also banned, and Savonarola arranged a huge burning of books and symbols of vanity aptly known as Bonfire of the Vanities.

Similarly, Venice's heyday ended abruptly when its government, in 1314, began to nationalize some foreign trade activities and from year 1324 began collecting heavy taxes for citizens who would took part in private foreign trade. The city never really recovered again.[120]

So lots of people tried to stop the party, but the crucial advantage Europe had was that its decentralized structure resulted in fierce competition and gave residents the opportunity to move from their own community to another, if they felt suffocated or persecuted. With so many small states, the next one was rarely far away. Consequently, there were constant migrations back and forth, and for example, when Constantinople and the Byzantine Empire fell in 1453, it triggered a massive migration of Greeks, especially to Italy.

In 1993, the US National Bureau of Economic Research completed a comprehensive analysis of the development of various city-states of medieval Europe and their migration patterns, and it showed something interesting:

"As measured by the pace of city growth in Western Europe from 1000 to 1800, absolutist monarchs stunted the growth of commerce and industry. A region ruled by an absolutist prince saw its total urban population shrink by one hundred thousand people per century relative to a region without absolutist government. This might be explained by higher rates of taxation under revenue-maximizing, absolutist governments than under non-absolutist governments, which care more about general economic prosperity and less about State revenue." [121]

So people voted with their feet, and they consistently voted for freedom. If the West had been centralized, its creativity would probably have stopped long ago.

PART 3

HOW CREATIVITY CHANGES PEOPLE

"You are what you eat."
"Tell me who your friends are, and I'll tell you who you are."
"Clothes make the man. "

With such sayings we suggest, that people are strongly influenced by their surroundings.

And they are. In fact, the cultures and civilizations in which we grow up equip us with thousands of ideas and memes from the earliest age, many of which are extremely difficult to change later in life. It is as if they are hard-wired into our brains - often unconsciously. "Fish do not see the water they swim in," says another proverb.
So what effect has Western ideas and Western creativity had on its people? Did it make them better individuals or worse? More peaceful or aggressive? Did it create cultures that were particularly effective? Might it even have changed our genes?

CHAPTER 10:
How we learned to co-operate

CHAPTER 11:
Creativity and culture

10.
HOW WE
LEARNED
TO CO-OPERATE

Erika Simon and her husband Helmut puffed and panted, because it was a tough uphill hike, on which they had embarked. They were heading for the summit of Similaun, Austria's sixth-highest mountain and one of the country's Oetztal Alps. This was on September 18th, 1991, and these two German hikers had no idea that this trip would lead them to an historic discovery.[122]

They had now reached the edge of the glacier, and before them was a mass of ice and snow that led up to the 3,606 meter high peak. At this point, they had already been walking for six hours, so they were pretty tired, but their aim had been to reach the summit that day, if at all possible. So they added crampons under their boots to provide sure footing on the ice. Then they set out on the last, but also toughest, part of the trip.

Eventually they reached their goal and, afterwards, they spent the night in a mountain hut with an Austrian couple who they had met at the top. The next day, they climbed to another peak with this couple, then started to head downwards on their own. Shortly after, at 13:30, Helmut and Erika reached a recess filled with snow and melted ice, with a natural rock barrier to one side. As they walked along it, Helmut was annoyed to see something resembling litter in the snow ahead. However, just moments later, Erika cried out, "Look, it's a human being!" It was a corpse!

Helmut dragged out his camera to take a picture, but Erika protested, as she thought it was disrespectful. However, Helmut argued that if there were relatives, these had a right to see what had happened, and so he took the picture.

But why was there even a corpse here so high in the mountains? It was a strange place to find one, wasn't it? Had there been a murder? Or was it a hiker, who had become lost or stuck on the mountain in bad weather and died? They did not know, but when they came down to their hotel, they immediately notified the police.

The next day a policeman with a mountain guide arrived at the place where the body had been found and more experts came later. The corpse was then taken to the Forensic Institute in Innsbruck, where the Attorney General immediately opened a file for "criminal case 619/91 against unknown perpetrator".

However, it didn't take long before various studies made it clear that the body - which is now known as "Ötzi " after where it had been found - was a man who had died more than 5,000 years earlier. So the police dropped the criminal case and archaeologists took over.

Their initial investigations showed that, when he died, the man had been approx. 45 years of age and was wearing waterproof shoes of bear fur and a coat, loincloth, hat, trousers made of leather and, outside this, a cloak made of straw. Instead of socks, he had grass in his shoes. He also wore a flint knife, a longbow which was (oddly enough) unfinished (why carry an unfinished bow to the mountain?), a quiver, a goatskin with 14 arrows and a copper axe. His stomach contents showed that his last meal had been deer and that he had previously eaten meat from an Alpine Ibex (a type of goat) and some plants and bread made of einkorn wheat.

The initial assessment of his health before death wasn't too good. He lacked teeth in his upper jaw but, before the invention of dentistry and given his age, this was hardly surprising. Further studies showed he had broken a rib and nose bone, and light frostbite in one toe. Finally, it was found that he had two pieces of Birch on him, which might have been used to treat intestinal worms.

The cause of death? He had probably been surprised by a sudden snowstorm and then died of hunger and cold. And with that, what started out as the criminal proceedings 619/91 had been brought to a conclusion by the archaeologists.

Five years after the discovery of Ötzi, Oxford University Press published a book that turned the archaeological world on its head. The title was *War Before Civilization*, and its author was an archaeology professor named Lawrence H. Keeley. As the book's name indicated, this was about the world before civilization, and Keeley surprised many by clearly demonstrating that this had been far more brutal than many laymen and scientists had previously thought.

Really? A very common view in the West – also among archaeologists – had, for a long time, been inspired by the so-called romantic movement that emerged in Germany in the early 1800s as a reaction against the Enlightenment, the Industrial Revolution and the scientific rationalization of nature. This romanticism was a somewhat modified version of the so-called "Sturm und Drang" movement in the 1760s to 1780s, which were Germans opposed to aestecism, enlightenment, empiricism (the concept of testing and observing nature systematically) and universalism (the belief that some ideas have universal value, irrespective of their origin). Although Romanticism's strongest foothold had remained Germany, it had spread to the whole of the West, and had continued to capture people's emotions, as they imagined the simpler life in the past as peaceful. Although the Romantic movement in itself isn't religious, it uses a narrative that resembles the Genesis narrative of the Old

Testament, where people originally lived in happy harmony in the Garden of Eden until Adam and Eve ate from the Tree of Knowledge, after which they were expelled and everything went haywire.

The romantic view of early life was, in modern times, reflected in various Disney movies, children's books and in parts of the environmental movement. Philosophers such as Rousseau, and especially many of the modern-age archaeologists, had eagerly described the unspoiled past before civilization as far more harmonious and peaceful than the present. For example, in 1989, amateur anthropologist Elizabeth Marshall Thomas published a book called *The Harmless People*, which was about the African !kung-people (the previously mentioned people talking partly with clicking sounds). This book described how friendly and peaceful they always were.[123]

But they weren't harmless. The Canadian anthropologist Richard Borshay Lee, who studied the same people, had a conversation one day with four men in the tribe during which he asked one of them how many giraffes and deer he had killed. Suddenly it occurred to him to ask also how many people he had killed. The answer came promptly: "I killed Debe from Namchoha and Now and Neisi from Gam." When he asked the next, the reply sounded: "I shot Kushe in the back, but she survived." The third said, "I shot Kana in the foot, but he lived."And finally, he turned to the fourth man who said that he had never killed anyone. When Lee then asked, if he had then shot someone, he replied with obvious regret, that he had always missed his shots at people.

So were these "harmless people"?[124]

Hardly. But this is what many wanted to believe about life before civilization. When anthropologist Karl G. Heider visited the Dani tribe in New Guinea for the first time in 1961, he wrote a book called *Grand Valley Dani: Peaceful Warriors*.[125] However, having visited them many times later and tried to reconstruct their family histories and causes of death, he had changed his view. His own statistics showed that 29% of tribesmen had been killed by others; typically in war. For comparison, 3-4 % of the world population was killed in World War II, including 8-10 % of Germans and about 4% of the Japanese.

In his book *Before the Dawn*, Nicholas Wade shows similar examples of how naive some archaeologists have been. For instance, when some found large pebble piles, they were sure it was paraphernalia for boiling water; not armour for slingshots. Other archaeologists who found a significant collection of weapons at a site suggested they were used as decoration; not for warfare. In fact, many claimed that copper and bronze axes were simply a sort of money.

Christy Turner of Arizona State University found the burned, cut bones from 30 Anasazi Indians who he thought were the remains of a cannibal feast. However, this story was rejected by many colleagues who instead suggested other explanations such as the roof having collapsed on their heads. Since then, clear traces of cannibalism have been found in 25 archaeological sites in the American Southwest as well as in Africa, Latin America, Fiji and New Zealand.

In fact, Keeley (the aforementioned author of *War Before Civilization*) had also held a romantic view of prehistoric life, just like Elisabeth Thomas, Karl Heider and others, but this had gradually changed, as, during repeated excavations, he discovered that residences were protected by large military bulwarks. For example, he noted that the first inhabitants of Jericho had built formidable defences; their first defence wall was at least four metre high (13 feet) and 1.8 meters thick at the base. Inside that was a stone tower, which was at least eight meters high (27 feet). But most remarkable, they had cut a ditch into the rock outside which was nine meters wide (30 feet) wide, and three meters deep (nine feet). They had cut that without metal tools, so by hacking rock away with rock - a quite enormous amount of work which you would only do for a good reason.

Keeley began a systematic reading of archaeological reports from around the world, and especially the analysis of likely causes of death for prehistoric corpses. What he discovered opened his eyes. An example: studies of a 12,000 year old Nubian burial site showed that about half of the dead were killed by other people. In many cases, tribes or entire peoples had been totally eradicated by others in acts of ethnic cleansing or clan vendettas such as among Eskimos and Canadian Indians.

Several reports recounted mass murder scenes that were frozen in time. In a cave in Germany scientists discovered 34 skulls, most of which had been beaten with stone axes, after which the heads had been cut from the body. Keeley also studied reports from meetings between Western residents' and tribal peoples in recent times, where they discovered young men often were not considered worthy of marriage before they had killed at least one enemy (or simply a member of another tribe).

And then there was an Indian village in Colorado in the US, whose defence wall was almost burned down. Here, the physical objects had been systematically destroyed, and corpses lay scattered in the various rooms of the ruins. Of the total population of about 600, approximately 60% had been killed in a single attack. What were conspicuously missing among the corpses were remains of young women. Why had they not been killed, and what subsequently happened to them? One can imagine only too easily.

Keeley did not only base his studies on archaeology, but also on anthropological observations of contemporary tribal populations. In many cases he could find modern studies that put quite accurate figures on how many killings took place in such communities and how these were done. The conclusion was that 65% of all primitive tribes that had been observed in recent times had been in a constant state of war, and a higher proportion had been at war at least once a year. On average, Keeley found that the death rate in tribal war was about 20 times higher than that in modern warfare. Archaeologist Steven LeBlanc of Harvard University has found similar figures through his own independent study of the same issue.[126]

A study in Arnhem Land in Australia conducted in the late 19th century followed a tribe of Aborigines over a 20-year period. Of approximately 800 men, some 200 were killed over those 20 years.[127] In another study, this time of Indians on the border between Brazil and Venezuela, missionaries observed that every third man was killed in the war - often in attempts to take slaves.[128]

When Westerners arrived in the current US, they found that local Indians often made wars and raids. For instance, in 1847, Chief Seattle, about whom we will hear more later, organized a surprise attack on neighbouring tribe the Chimakums in an attempt to wipe it out. Together with approximately 150 members of an allied tribe, Seattle and his men waited in hiding outside the village of the chimakums. As a Chimakum family unsuspectingly passed by Seattle's army, his men fired a series of shots. As this brought many Chimakums to run out to see what had happened, Seattle's people ran into the Chimakums village and mowed most of them down in a quick hail of bullets. The survivors were taken as slaves.[129]

It was pretty brutal, and statistics indicate that approximately 87% of the Indian tribes in North America regularly engaged in war, and many had traditions of prolonged torture of prisoners, scalping and cannibalism.

In Europe, many of the oldest finds show signs that people had frequently been hanged, tortured, stabbed or beaten to death. Archaeologists have found an incredibly well-preserved corpse of the 2,000 year old so-called "Lindow man" in England. The man had a fractured skull from a massive blow to the head and had also had his spine broken and his throat cut. In another find, from 2009, archaeologists found, in Alken Enge in Denmark, several hundred bodies that had been hacked to pieces 2,000 years ago.

A significant proportion of violence-related deaths in pre-civilized society came from raids, where a group from one community snuck into another group and killed the men, raped the women and perhaps took slaves from any survivors – similar to what the Vikings later did in Europe. Often they also took souvenirs with them by slicing off scalps, head, genitals or other body parts from victims. It was also popular to take a few prisoners home to the tribe where they could be tortured to death slowly for general amusement.

So what was Keeleys overall conclusion? It was that before civilization, people lived to an average age of 20 years old and approximately one in every three was killed by another human being. This is strong stuff, and it brings us back to the reconstruction of what happened to Ötzi, because it turned out that both the first assumption (that he had died recently) was wrong, as was the second (that he died 5,000 years ago by an accident). Now comes the real version of criminal case 619 /91, and yes, crime was involved.

In 2001- ten years after the discovery of Ötzi and five years after the release of Keeleys groundbreaking book - some archaeologists decided to study Ötzi case again, this time using the newly-developed DNA analysis techniques and X-rays. Their X-ray revealed, to their surprise, an arrowhead wedged in Ötzis left shoulder blade, and they quickly found a matching hole in his coat. The man had been shot!

They also examined his knife, as well as an axe and arrowhead that had been found next to him, for DNA traces. The arrowhead had blood traces from two people, and the knife contained blood from a third person. They also found evidence of fresh wounds on his hand, wrists, chest and head as he died, and they noted that he had a firm grip on his knife to the last, as if feared for his life. On his jacket, they found even more traces of human blood, which was from a fourth person. Further studies of food traces in his stomach and intestines in 2012 showed that he died some distance from his home.

And with all these observations, we can now reconstruct reasonably well what happened in the last days of Ötzi's extremely harsh life, and it wasn't pretty: Ötzi had, with an unknown number of others, ventured out to take part in a raid against another tribe. As the blood on his arrowhead and knife indicates, he had managed to kill or wound three tribe members, and he had pulled out his valuable arrow from his victims so it could be reused. But something had gone wrong and there had probably been a fierce battle in which at least one of his friends had been hurt. At the same time, his bow either been destroyed, or he had lost it.

His group had now taken flight, and Ötzi had carried a wounded comrade over his shoulders, hence the blood traces. Maybe he stopped along the way to find a branch to make a new bow, but he had not had time to finish it before new fighting broke out. Here, he had been hit by an arrow in the shoulder and wounded in the hand, wrist, chest and head. He was now slumped and his friends had turned him over to remove the arrows butt sticking out from the back of his shoulder, but the tip was broken off and remained seated. They left him like that, where he died after suffering alone for several days. He was subsequently covered in many layers of snow and stayed there until his body was discovered 5,000 years later – on September 18, 1991.

What do ancient documents tell us about life in ancient times? We can start with the Old Testament, which is a collection of old reports and documents, probably written over a long period presumably beginning around 1400 BC, but based on older oral reports. Here we read the story of Adam and Eve who, after being banished from Paradise, had sons Cain and Abel, which increased Earth's total population to four people. However, it quickly dropped to three after Cain murdered Abel, bringing the global murder rate to 25 %, (just below the aforementioned ancient average of 30%).

Admittedly, this is a very small statistical sample, but it grows as the tale proceeds. We have, for instance, the story of how Abraham and his nephew, Lot, move to a town called Sodom, where people have rather lively sex lives. This angers God, who burns all men, women and children. When Lot's wife, who is in the process of fleeing from all of this, makes the mistake of looking back, she is punished with death as well. Later, God asks Abraham to take his son to a mountain, where he shall tie him and then cut his throat and burn him as a gift to his creator.

And so it continues. According to priest and Bible historian Raymund Schwager, the Old Testament contains 600 reports of nations, kings and individuals engaged in brutal violence, including extreme cases of what we would today call terrorism or crimes against humanity.[130] In short, the whole thing is one giant bloodbath. The librarian Matthew White has calculated how many people are apparently killed in this old tale, and he reached about 1.2 million. This number even excludes the war between Judah and Israel, which itself cost half a million lives. His number evidently also excludes the flood story, where God wiped out all life on Earth except for the eight people who were in Noah's ark.[131]

The tone of this and other early religious stories says a lot about how many people previously perceived their God: namely as a sovereign who demanded complete surrender and that people had few pleasures in life other than revering Him. As history Professor David Fromkin writes, the earlier Sumerians, Egyptians and Greeks viewed their gods as "vain, jealous, foolish, ill-tempered and unfaithful."[132] Ancient gods also tended to expect, regardless of religious suit, that their believers should kill non-believers. You should fear gods and constantly ask for forgiveness and make sacrifices, or else.

We should note, in this context, that religion has not always been perceived as a moral movement. The Gods of the Vikings or the Greeks were definitely not moralists who told people that they should be peaceful - quite the contrary. Perhaps Hinduism in India is the first example of a moralistic religion, but many religions, which today are perceived as moral by the followers, did not, in their originally interpretations, inspire similar moral concerns. In early interpretations of Christianity, for example, it seemed perfectly acceptable to engage in religious wars, where counterparties were tortured to death or slaughtered in their thousands. It is only subsequent interpretations of Christianity that changed it into the peace-loving religion that the majority of its contemporary followers consider it to be now.

People's actual life on Earth was perhaps later more peaceful than described in the Old Testament, but not much. We have already discussed how the Vikings plundered and killed, and the Mongol ruler Genghis Khan, who ruled and conquered in the 1200s, encapsulated the joy of spreading misery with this line: "The greatest happiness is to scatter your enemy, to drive him before you, to see his towns reduced to ashes, to see those who love him shrouded in tears, and to gather into your bosom his wives and daughters."[133]

A cultural relativist may note that it sounds like a modern slasher film. The difference is, it wasn't a film: Genghis Khan really did what he said, and the blood wasn't tomato sauce.

And that was how it was, all the time and throughout the world. Murder, killings and torture were extremely common, and considered great entertainment; think of the Romans holding gladiatorial games, where people fought to their deaths in front of cheering crowds. After the Romans had been beaten a few times by the Goths, they showed their discontent by catching a lot of their children and driving them into different Gothic villages, where they murdered them in front of people. When Julius Caesar put down a rebellion in Gaul (France), contemporary authors reported that he killed approximately a third of the population and enslaved another third. The Roman Emperor Titus celebrated his brother's birthday by forcing 2,500 Jews to fight against wild animals in the arenas.[134]

Throughout the history of the mighty Roman Empire, 131 of its emperors, more than a third (33%) were assassinated while in office. Of the rest, 25% abdicated and many of this group were later tortured, executed, imprisoned or had their eyes gouged out. Overall, 58% were killed, while or after they were in this apparently quite dangerous job.[135]

If we compare to life in the Stone Age or in Rome, Europe's early middle Ages actually appear somewhat more peaceful, even though this was the age of Vikings and, yes, of Genghis Khan attacking from the East.

The world became more peaceful still as the concept of chivalry evolved. Chivalry can perhaps best be described as a pragmatic fusion between the ideals of Christian faith ("Though shall not kill") and memes of the Nordic warriors ("Though shall kill"). The compromise was that knights could kill enemies of the Church, and the result was the tamed Tetons, if you will, who were called Templers.

However, we should really not overstate how positive chivalry was. We can get an idea by reading the entertaining story Lancelot, which was written somewhere between the 11th and 13th centuries, and recounting events that occurred in the sixth century. Here, one of the knights promises a beautiful princess that he, as a kind of symbolic tribute to her, will rape the most beautiful woman he can find. How sweet! Another knight tells the woman he adores that he will send her the severed heads of other knights he kills in jousting tournaments. That has to beat flowers.

Tournaments and other forms of duels form a story in its own right. If a knight felt offended, and if you were, the only suitable answer was a duel. However, kings, didn't take part in duels, they just ordered killings. Going forward in history, we all know the story of the English King Henry VIII, who had two of his wives beheaded. At one point, he became jealous because he discovered that one of his wives, Catherine, had apparently previously had a juvenile love. The young man in question was now arrested, and sentenced to be 'hanged, drawn and quartered'. He was hanged, but not for long enough to die, then his stomach was cut open, while his was still alive. He was then castrated, beheaded, and finally dismembered.

When Henry's eldest daughter, Mary, became queen, she was soon nicknamed Bloody Mary (now a cocktail made with vodka and tomato juice), due to her mass killings of Protestants, often through burning. Her half-sister, Elisabeth, was imprisoned for a year and their common cousin Lady Jane Grey was executed. When Elizabeth became Queen Elizabeth 1 after Mary's death, she executed another cousin, Queen Mary Stuart of Scotland (known as Mary Queen of Scots), whose own father had also been executed.

This was quite typical. Criminologist Manuel Eisner from Cambridge University has calculated that one-sixth of all European monarchs were killed between the years 600 - 1800. Awful, but please note that around a quarter of the former Roman emperors were killed, as were those in tribal communities. By the way, after the murders of leaders, in a third of cases the killer took over the throne, which gives us a motive.

Public executions were also popular in times past; so much so, in fact, that French villages in the 16th century bought doomed prisoners from the neighbouring villages so that they could entertain people with the executions. But again, this was nothing compared to the mass killings in the arenas the Romans had enjoyed.

Religious mass murder has been just as common as religion. One of the most brutal examples we know is found in the history of the Aztecs. The Aztecs (based in Central America in the 14th to 16th centuries) enjoyed catching people from other tribes, whom they dragged up to their temples and dismembered alive with sharpened flints, pulling out their hearts while they were still beating. Often, they lowered these people over flames before doing this, but raised them again before they died to maximize their pain. During these ceremonies, the dead bodies were, one-by-one, flung down the temple steps. To round of the ceremony, the heads of the victims were cut off and mounted in neat rows on large racks in the middle of the town in plain sight of men, women and children As a celebration of their rebuilt Tenochtitlan pyramid in 1487 alone, the Aztecs later claimed proudly that they slaughtered 80,400 prisoners in this way - a figure, however, that archaeologists believe is somewhat exaggerated. Excavations have also shown that both the Aztecs (and the Peruvian Inca people before them) regularly sacrificed their own children.

The Europeans have also been responsible for an abundant contribution to these statistics. In the period 1095-1208 the religious Crusades from Europe to the Middle East led to the deaths of approximately one million Muslims and Jews. Correspondingly, Muslims dispatched millions of Christians, primarily during the development of the Ottoman Empire and with the killing of 1-1.5 million Armenians; a mass murder which culminated between 1914 and 1918.

Slavery has also been a regular feature of countless early societies. Specifically, it was common in Africa, where, for example, Nigerians captured slaves and sold them off to Arab buyers. This went on for more than 1,000 years, and the French historian and slave researcher Olivier Petre-Grenouilleau has estimated that the Arabs between the seventh century and the 1920s bought approximately 17 million slaves, of which about 1.5 million died (or were castrated) en route to market - often when they were travelling through the Sahara Desert. The Arabs also took slaves from Portugal, Spain, France, Italy, Ireland and the British Isles and, when Europeans powers later grew, the English, Dutch, Danes, Portuguese, Spanish and others started doing the same, exporting them to South America or Africa.

Is there a common feature in all of this? To find the answer, we should look to scientist Steven Pinker, a psychology professor at the Massachusetts Institute of Technology (MIT), and later Harvard University, who has achieved academic superstar status. In 2011, Pinker published his book *The Better Angels of Our Nature: Why Violence Has Declined* which, over more than about 800 pages filled with charts, tables, and references, provides extensive documentation to show that the human tendency to engage in violence has been declining for several thousand years and that this decline is extreme. One of Pinker's main conclusions - which he supported by a gigantic body of statistics - is that as civilization progresses, its propensity for violence declines, and this phenomenon is seen in a variety of forms of violence, in all cultures and among all races, and it has been persistent throughout history.[136]

But why?

One of Pinker's explanations for the decline in violent tendency is so ordinary that it could easily be overlooked, namely that people in times past would often have been quite repulsive. Like Ötzi, they would often be missing teeth, they often smelled pretty horribly, and they would very often have fungus, lice, fleas and worms. In such a situation, it is perhaps not surprising that people did not feel much empathy for others unless they knew them personally, as friends or family members. In his book, Pinker gives an example of how a manual of manners from medieval times described the standards of performance:

"Don't foul the staircases, corridors, closets, or wall hangings with urine or other filth. • Don't relieve yourself in front of ladies, or before doors or windows of court chambers. • Don't slide back and forth on your chair as if you're trying to pass gas. • Don't touch your private parts under your clothes with your bare hands. • Don't greet someone while they are urinating or defecating. • Don't make noise when you pass gas. • Don't undo your clothes in front of other people in preparation for defecating, or do them up afterwards."

Certainly, this is not bad advice, but the fact that it was necessary to voice it provides a clue about how people often behaved at the time.

Boredom could also have been a factor. Unless you were a soldier or participated in marauding gangs like the Vikings, you would perhaps, over your whole lifetime, never travel more than a few miles from your birthplace. Every day would have been almost identical to the last and, in the evenings, all but the richest people lacked light except, possibly, a fireplace, which is why they may have been bored stiff. But if they did venture out, there were no hotels and no tourist industry or banks to change your money. No, you lived off the land, which easily gets violent, if that land is somebody else's.

A third possible explanation for our ancestors' extreme violence may simply be that most of them experienced a lot of misfortune in their lives. To start with, the majority of their children died during childhood and there were regular epidemics that wiped out half the inhabitants of villages. If children left home, parents would very likely never see them again and, add to that, regular famine, wars, pain and and hardship. All this was brutal, and violence and suffering hardens the soul.

Superstition also had an effect. Between the years 1450 and 1750 somewhere between 40,000 and 60,000 alleged witches were executed in Europe and the US - most of them by public hanging or burning.

A fifth explanation could be the role of early religions. Given the many terrible experiences most people had during their lives, it could appear as if the gods regularly demanded sacrifice, so the best solution was to sacrifice others rather than yourself. If somebody has to do it, needn't be you!

Widow-burning was also common. As the British colonized India, they spent many years battling the local traditions of burning dead men's wives alive with the corpses of their dead husbands.

We can imagine many more explanations, including so-called "democide": demonstrating personal power through murder. A description of the British colonial life in India says the following:

"A party given by the Mogul governor of Surat, the very first British settlement, was rudely interrupted when the host fell into a sudden rage and ordered all the dancing girls to be decapitated on the spot, to the stupefaction of his English guests." [137]

Perhaps the guy was simply mad, but to assassinate your subjects in front of prominent guests has been a strategy used throughout history - it is the ultimate demonstration of power.

One last important explanation of violence from the past is presumably that the most violent members of some primitive societies often had more children, as we previously saw in Yanomami tribe in Brazil, where murderers had many more children than non-murderers. So there was a genetic selection pressure in favour of sociopaths and sadists. Even after farming had arrived, the richest people would have been the biggest landowners, and they or their ancestors would typically have gained this land through violent battle. These people would have the most surviving children and they passed on their aggressive genes in this way. However, as trade gained ground and provided more riches, it was traders who had most surviving children, and this supported genes for abilities in co-operation.

These elements can explain past violence, but why has the trend been downwards as Western civilization developed and spread? The obvious partial explanation is, of course, that people have become more attractive, experience fewer personal tragedies, are less bored, less superstitious and have more peaceful interpretations of their religions. And murderers no longer have the most children.

Something else has also been important: the shift from hunting to farming means that people became stationary rather than nomadic. In 2000, the US economist Mancur Lloyd Olson introduced a theoretical framework of government, which he divided into anarchy, tyranny and democracy.[138] Anarchy was the worst, because there you had roving bandits such a Genghis Kahn or the early Vikings, who would steal rape and ravage without any inhibitions whatsoever. A tyrant would also steal and perhaps more than that, but since he was a "stationary bandit" he had an incentive to encourage some degree of economic success, just like a farmer eats most of his corn but leaves a bit to sow for next year. A stationary bandit does not like that his subjects fight each other, as this hurts the economy and may escalate and bring himself in danger. So there is less violence in stationary societies than among nomads, and it should be added to this that it is also easier for a nomad to run away after committing a crime than for a farmer to do this as he loses his farm if he runs. Having something to lose can be a make people more peaceful and the more they have, the more peaceful they will be.

Furtunately, the stationary bandit tends to evolve as Thomas Hobbes hoped, so that states develop better systems to prevent crime. Steven Pinker calculated some amazing statistics around this link: When tribal societies unite to form primitive states, violence falls to approximately. 1/5 of its former level, and when these states again developed into modern nations, it falls once again to 1/30 of that, so the overall decrease from the primitive society to modern, fully civilized state involves a decline in violence to 1/150 of what it was originally.[139] So the citizens give up some of their freedom to the state, but violence falls by more than 99% as a consequence, and being free from violence is presumably freedom at its very best.

However, while dictators seek to maintain inner peace, they often feel little or no personal concern about starting a an external war, and the concept of maintaining a constant threat from external enemies is a great internal power tool - just think of North Korea or Saddam Hussein's Iraq.

When there is a further shift to democracy, things get better still. In a democracy, it is the ordinary people who ultimately make decisions and they rarely see personal benefit in participating in war; rather the contrary.

Other explanations must also be included: When society grows richer, people have fewer children, and the fewer children you have, the less willing you are to send a son to war. People also grow older, and older people are more peaceful. And women gain more power, which again leads to greater peace.

We should not ignore the fact that war has actually, to some degree, played a role in creating peace, since winners of wars typically create peace within the area they have conquered, similar to Pax Romana. In other words, while empires may be rough at the edges (acting as roving bandits), they are typically peaceful inside, where the bandits are stationary.[140]

The final reason why people have become more peaceful is the introduction of rationality and science. As previously mention, with science you can resolve disputes about what is truth simply by testing it scientifically.

The phenomenon whereby people become more peaceful is a part of what is often called the *The Civilizing Process* after a book written about it in 1939 by German sociologist Norbert Elias.[141] The timing of his book was beond awful, because a very uncivilized World War broke out shortly after the book's release, but the message is very relevant anyway.

As Elias pointed out, when civilization evolved, violent, self-important, ego-defensive and violent people fared worse, while co-operative people fared better. So the ancestors of wild and uninhibited Vikings and Teutons were (sometimes) knights (think Lancelot); and perhaps their ancestors were gentlemen (think James Bond), who again may have been replaced by modern office workers. Without otherwise comparing, this process does have clear parallels to the way wolves, through co-operation, with humans have turned into dogs.

We have previously discussed how the process of creating a civilization largely consists of separating things. Now here is another example: Elias argued convincingly that Europe's prevailing culture of chivalry (which lasted from approximately 1000 to 1500) was dominated by a self-image, centered on personal honour and dignity. If you were contradicted, this was not just seen as an attack on your ideas, but on you as a person. It was an insult, in other words, and it therefore had to be avenged with violence. And this again leads to vendettas, sometimes endlessly, over generations and between families, tribes, nations and religions.

In the Middle Ages, some of these vendettas translated into formal duels, which was actually a step towards greater civilization, as it could break endless revenge cycles. But duels still represented personification of reasoning which, apart from leading to violence, also prevented dialogue and creativity.

However, eventually the culture changed so that arguments became more de-personalized. This meant that the previous honour/shame/revenge complex was gradually replaced with peaceful dialogue and often humour. Already the citizens of Athens had, as an early example of this separation process, developed the concept of "politics" whereby one could discuss society and its management without necessarily discussing the leaders themselves. Each idea then had to stand or fall on its own merits.

This was an extremely useful meta-idea, as it facilitated debate and thus creativity. The gradual dismantling of the honour culture during the Mediaeval Age inspired more humour. In the West today, it is strictly forbidden to discriminate against people because of religion, sexuality or race, but there is a clear exception to these rules; you can say more or less anything, if it is delivered in the form of humour.

Humour is often the pressure relief valve that can be used to deal with defeat and weakness in a peaceful manner, but it also makes it more difficult for people to be fanatics. Because of its immense cultural usefulness and the free joy it brings (laughing is even healthy), it has therefore gradually developed into a higher art form with styles such as sarcasm, irony, farce, gallows humour and so on. Irony is a good way of preventing fanaticism, self-irony is an effective vaccine against shame, and humour can generally replace hatred and anxiety that may otherwise block innovation.

Many other phenomena were separated. Today, in the West, you can discuss almost anything without thinking about whether it is accepted by the

State, the Church, your boss or family elders, because opinions are separated from authority.

This cultural trait is probably more unusual than many of the West's inhabitants fully understand. In many other cultures, Western humour is often perceived as incomprehensible or offensive if it insults authorities or deals with taboo subjects. In countries with cultures without a tradition of irony it is impossible to admit publicly that you have made a mistake or do not have the answer to a question, as it would cast shame upon oneself and perhaps even on one's family, tribe, religion or country. Ayatollah Khomeini, for instance, was strongly against laughter and explained why: "Allah did not create man so that he could have fun. The aim of creation was for mankind to be put to the test through hardship and prayer. An Islamic regime must be serious in every field. There are no jokes in Islam. There is no humor in Islam. There is no fun in Islam. There can be no fun and joy in whatever is serious."[142] For this reason, there are still societies in Islam where it is frowned upon if people laugh out loud, and that may especially go for women.

It should mentioned that some early interpretations of Christianity held similar views, which are described in Umberto Eco's book *The Name of The Rose*, where munks are searching in secret for Aristole's allegedly lost treatise on comedy. The Christian view in some corners was that you should not laugh at anything, since it all was Gods creation and thus not funny.

Evidently, the Western concept of de-personalization is not always adhered to and, especially if people have weak arguments in a debate, you may see them "get personal". But generally people accept that the proper way is to "play the ball, not the man", and that is why we often start a critique with the phrase "With all due respect ..." .The implication here is: "I respect you, but not your ideas." Furthermore, we might add "disarming" humour, as we often call it.

So we have developed a set of highly-effective memes for the peaceful and respectful exchange of ideas that stimulate innovation without involving duels or axe murders. In reality, this is a clear parallel to the depersonalization that happened much earlier with the introduction of trade. Once the personal issues were separated out, the number of win-win transactions exploded and creativity blossomed.

It is very likely that the start of the 21st century is the most peaceful point so far in human history. And the century before it was - even in spite of its two World Wars and Mao and Stalin's mass killings - far more peaceful than the Middle Ages. They were even more peaceful than the century before, which involved the Napoleonic wars, countless colonial wars, the American Civil War, the horrifying Taiping rebellion, and much more. The Taiping rebellion alone killed at least 20 million people which, adjusted for the world's much smaller population, makes it comparable to World War II, whereas the Napoleonic Wars alone matches WWI, when adjusted.

Now, as Pinker points out, war and raids are not the only forms of violence. There are also, for example, piracy, honour killings, ritual executions, ethnic cleansings, civilian murders, fights, rape, slavery, conscious cruelty and discrimination against people because of their race, gender or sexual orientation that can be viewed as emotional violence.

But all of this has declined as civilizing processes progressed. In Europe, for example, virtually all previous dictatorships from after World War II, such as in Spain, Greece, Portugal and Eastern Europe, have now been replaced by democracies, and the same is true of many countries in Latin America, Africa and Asia. Furthermore, racial hatred has become increasingly rare, e.g. fewer and fewer whites in the U.S. express reluctance to have black neighbours, and the country has even elected a black president (Obama) - twice!

Here are two important correlations: we grow more peaceful when we trade more and also when we get richer. As previously mentioned, the predominant way of getting rich in past times was extractive and based on win-loose transactions. It was to take other people's land, buildings or women by force. This would normally involve hiring mercenaries, but these would often live partially from looting after conquests, so once you had them, they expected action.[143]

In modern society, success comes predominantly from being able to offer people something they are willing to pay for or which somebody else will sponsor. We have all heard about concerts for peace, and that's great, but surely global investment and trade is the biggest peacemaker, because it requires co-operation and it gives you something to lose if you attack others. In fact, studies show that the nations that take part in a lot of foreign trade are less likely to engage in war than isolationist nations.[144] Demonstrating for world peace is unlikely to achieve it, but negotiating free trade agreements might.

Nations that trade a lot tend to become richest, and Benjamin M. Friedman of Harvard University has, in studies of the US, UK, France and Germany, identified that when there was economic growth in these nations, they became more open, tolerant, fair, rational, moral and democratic, and they tolerated more social and geographical mobility. For example, it was in such boom times that Germany was united, that the US introduced many civil rights, and that the UK launched university educations and introduced women's suffrage. It was also in boom-times that we have seen taboo-breaking movements focused on freedom, such as the "hippie", "yuppie" and "geek"movements.[145] When we grow richer we become more fun, more experimental, more tolerant and more peaceful.

Corresponding trends can be seen in developing countries. Development expert and Oxford economics professor Paul Collier has shown that the incidence of war and civil war in poor countries falls when they enjoy economic growth. People become increasingly intolerant and unpleasant to one another when an economy stagnates or starts to decline. If a poor country experiences declining incomes, it will typically attract dictatorial regimes and rising corruption, crime and superstition.[146] It was in bad economic times that the richer countries saw the beginning of Ku Klux Klan, the growth of protectionism, organized anti-Semitism, Nazism and fascism.

As for the poor countries, Collier tried to find statistical correlations that could explain the frequency of civil wars. He studied political repression, colonial history, internal income gaps and many other reasons for civil war that are often given in the political debate. He could not find any correlation with any of those variables. Nor was ethnic diversity a statistically-valid explanation. For example, there has been an almost constant civil war-like situation in Somalia, which has one of the world's most ethnically homogeneous populations.

However, what he did find was a very clear correlation between civil war and economic growth: The richer a country is and the faster its wealth grows, the lower its risk of civil war. The statistics are simple: a doubling of the level of income halves the risk of civil war. As an example, it is those Muslim nations that have had the greatest absolute or relative economic decline, that have seen growing trends of violence and terror, if not outbreaks of civil wars such as in Iraq, Afghanistan, Palestine, Sudan, Pakistan, Lebanon, Syria, Libya, Egypt and Somalia. Similarly, there is a clear negative correlation with the economic growth rates. Statistically, Collier has found that the average poor country has a 14% chance of starting a new civil war over a given five-year period. If the country has an economic growth rate of 3%, however, this risk is 12%. If the growth rate is 10%, the risk of civil war falls to 3%. But when, instead of growth, the economy declines by 3%, the risk of civil war rises to a horrifying 17%. Since most developing countries after the 1980s has shifted to market economic systems, their income levels and growth rates increased significantly, and therefore there are fewer civil wars.

There is another statistical method for predicting the risk of an outbreak of war or civil war; the proportion of the population which is made up of young men and, especially, young unemployed men – the so-called "youth bulge". If the latter is more than 30% of a country's population, the risk of an outbreak of some kind of war has historically been almost 90%.

However, the civilizing process following economic growth is also a cure here, as one of the most predictable effects of wealth growth is declining birth rates, and this counteracts - with some delay - youth unemployment among men.

Let us conclude: Western civilization has many opponents who argue that it has made the world more violent and dangerous. For this reason, they think like the German Sturm und Drang romantics and yearn for a more primitive, pre-civilized society with less technology, wealth and globalisation. But they are wrong, and this is important. Life before civilization was really "solitary, poor, nasty, brutish and short", as Hobbes put it so well, and life without civilization today is not much better. The West's creativity has made life safer and more peaceful; not vice versa. It has taught us how to co-operate. It has done this because it has:

◆ Stimulated genetic self-domestication
◆ Made people healthier and more attractive to look at (and better smelling), which increases respect for the lives of strangers
◆ Given people more contentment in life, reducing their boredom
◆ Reduced the amount of horror people experience in their lives, which has made them less hardened to violence
◆ Moved from dominance by roving bandits to the more peaceful stationary bandits and finally to the even more peaceful democracy
◆ Reduced the prevalence of dogmatic religion and superstition
◆ Lead to falling birth rates, which stimulated increased reluctance to send children to war
◆ Resulted in a greater proportion of older people, who are naturally less violent.
◆ Given more power to women, who are also less violent
◆ Introduced the scientific method for solving conflictingviews on truth
◆ Enabled more international trade and global investments, which make people more peaceful
◆ Genetically selected peaceful and co-operate people
◆ Replaced the concepts of honour and revenge with respectful debate and disarming humour
◆ Endowed higher economic growth and prosperity which make people more satisfied with their lives and therefore also more peaceful
◆ In general, caused less population growth, thus reducing excess of aggressive and unemployed young men

All this is because of a combination of Robert Wright's competitive advantage of being co-operative, Thomas Hobbes' Leviathan as protector of peace, Norbert Elias' civilizing process and Adam Smith's egoistic pursuits of peaceful win-win transactions. Co-operation taught us to become creative, and creativity tought us to co-operate.

11.
CREATIVITY
AND CULTURE

It is frequently assumed in economic models that people are all the same. They are all, to put it in techno-speak, "rational agents", who make logical choices like Adams Smith's rational butcher, brewer and baker. It is then assumed that if you stuff that into a computer, it can spit out decent predictions for prices, production and more. Of course, you also have enter assumptions about capital input, savings and other variables, but if it's all there, the models should tell you what will happen.

The problem is this that people's cultures are incredibly different, and what might work in one culture, say South Korea, may work completely differently in another, say, Bolivia. We shall now look at some reasons why such differences have developed, and as we will discover, creativity changes people's culture in many and often rather surprising ways, apart from making them more peaceful, as we saw in the previous chapter.

A good starting point for anyone studying cultural differences is World Values Surveys. This is a recurring, global study based on the sociologist Gert Hofstede's theory of cultural dimensions. It involves approximately 250 questions, given to close to 100,000 respondents in 60-70 countries at regular intervals, which means about 25 million questions asked each time. As scientists have studied the responses given, they have found very clear statistic clusters that show what different mindsets people actually have. Within this they have identified two particularly important dimensions that distinguish different cultures:

◆ Traditional values versus rational values
◆ Survival values versus self-realization values

How so? Well, people with "traditional" values are often nationalists and very religious, and they usually have clear ideas about what is good ("us"), and evil ("others") and they do not believe that other people can be trusted, for which reason they favour strong authorities to enforce disipline; even if these authorities might also be dishonest. They are not very tolerant; homosexuality, divorce are rarely tolerated and are often prohibited, having divergent religious views is frowned upon or even illegal and women should not have too much responsibility, but they must produce many children. For this reason, and because of low mutual trust, they have a limited social network and are not good at co-operating with people in their bigger social space or with women. The limitations to social networking and voluntary win-win transactions mean that their creative design space doesn't grow much, if at all.

Conversely, the people deemed "rational" according to World Values Surveys are more guided by data, logics, objectivity and science, and they are more trusting and tolerant. This mindset is most widespread in Protestant Europe and parts of Eastern Europe as well as China, Japan and Korea.

The other aforementioned important dimension is "survival" versus "self-realization". Survival here relates to obtaining basic material goods like food, shelter and safety, and in countries where this is difficult, people often cheat each other a lot. Conversely, high degree of self-realization means that people take survival for given and give priority to democracy, freedom, adventure and an emotionally-rich life. These typically live in Western countries and, in particular, in Protestant Europe. These are areas with lower corruption, higher inter-cultural trust and solid democracies.

This also has a clear economic correlation, because in rich societies people are more rational and prioritize self-realization higher. They have much more confidence in each other, exhibit more positive interest in other cultures and show higher respect for women and tolerance for minorities such as homosexuals. They are good at utilizing their social space and developing their creative design space.

The high degree of self-realization here also means prioritizing environmental protection and having a personal influence within the workplace and society in general. Freedom to choose a personal lifestyle (punk, banker, nerd, yuppie) is high here, and orthodoxy is low.

The map overleaf illustrates where different cultures are placed on the cultural map, where we see maximum rates of rationality and self-realization in Protestant Europe and minimal rates in some African and/or Muslim countries. People in Confucian areas are equally rational, but have self-realization as a lower priority.

How can we explain this? The high rationality in northern European countries can perhaps be explained by the ancient Anglo-Saxon valuesets plus the fact that Protestantism, from its inception, has tended to accept science and often pioneered it. It should be noted here that the top-scoring countries on rationality and self-expression correlate very well with Charles Murray's aforementioned European creativity maps.

As for the people in the most rational Asian countries, these are typically not religious in the sense that they believe in a creator and a strict body of

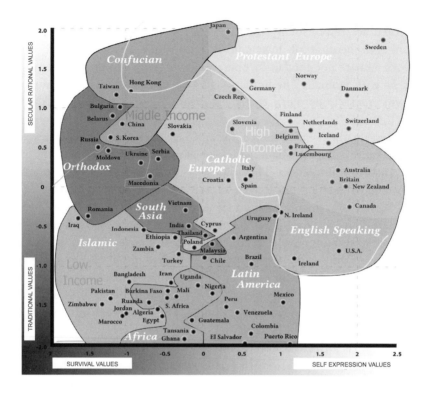

GRADING OF DIFFERENT CIVILIZATIONS AND CULTURES IN A SO-CALLED INGLEHART-WELZEL
WORLD VALUES SURVEY VALUE MAP. IT IS SEEN THAT THE PROTESTANT NATIONS ARE AT THE
UPPER RIGHT END OF THE SPECTRUM, AND AFRICAN AND MUSLIM ONES ARE PREDOMINANTLY IN
THE OPPOSITE END.[147]

dogma. Buddhism is arguably just as much a philosophy and set of ethical norms as it is a religion and Confucinism is definitely a philosophy.

When it comes to self-realization, this is lower in Europe's Catholic community and in former communist states than in Protestant northern Europe, which may be largely because the economies in many of these countries are struggling. Furthermore, because they have age-old tradition of authoritarian government rather than decentralized self-rule, they have far lower mutual trust between people, more corruption and weaker democracies. In former East Germany the mutual trust between people is lower than in former West Germany, which suggests that something fundamental in society's culture was damaged under communism.

Harward economics Professor Benjamin Friedmann has analyzed correlations between GDP per capita, human rights and freedom and found that the richer a society is the greater freedom and the more human rights its inhabitants have. He then examined whether there was a similar correlation in terms of the economic growth rate, and indeed there was.[148] Similarly, in 1966, a group of scientists found a clear correlation between income and democracy: "A democracy can expect to last an average of about 8.5 years in a country with per capita income below $1,000 per annum, 16 years in one with income between $1,000 and $2,000, 33 years between $2,000 and $4,000, and 100 years between $ 4,000 and $ 6,000."[149] Because of these correlations, it is not surprising that, as nations get richer, they will initially see a particularly high increase in rationality World Values Survey value map, but that at some point, further riches start to have a bigger effect on self-realization.

So as people in creative nations get richer they tend to become rational and to give higher priority to freedom, human rights, democracy, the environment and other non-material objectives. But does it also make them happier?

It does, and quite lot, in fact. The world's most famous happiness research source is arguably Ruut Veenhoven, who in 1984 founded the so-called World Database of Happiness which summarizes the results of thousands of happiness studies and has become an ever-evolving meta-study of the subject. The database uses a happiness scale that goes from 0 to 10, with 10 meaning most happiness. So here is what it shows: pretty much all the happiest countries in the world are Western and wealthy. If we go to the opposite end of the scale and study the least happy nations, these are predominantly African and extremely poor - there is not a single wealthy country among those with a very low degree of happiness and not a single poor one among the happiest nations.

The database also shows whether a nation's happiness changes over time. In the 14 nations for which there is enough data to track the progress of happiness, it is seen that during 1973-2008 happiness increased in nine countries, was largely unchanged for three, and had only declined in two. So Western happiness is highest and has been growing, albeit slowly.

The relationship between income and happiness is also confirmed by the OECD (Organisation for Economic Co-operation and Development), which calculates the correlation between its Better Life Index and a number of other variables. This statement shows a clear correlation between income and the perception of having a good life, and this is without any known income-related ceiling. Perhaps we like to say that money can't buy you happiness but, on average, it clearly can.[150] In 2003, Veenhoven published an article with Michael Hagerty called Wealth and Happiness Revisited which showed that happiness increases significantly up to an income level of approximately $15,000 a year, while income beyond that level has declining marginal benefit. However, once you passed the $15,000 barrier (the number should be higher today due to inflation), what most influenced your happiness was freedom – the more free people were, the happier they became, without any apparent upper limit. If you feel very free to choose your line of work, sexual orientation, life-style, spouse, faith and residence, you will be much happier than otherwise.

The most important freedom-related driver of happiness is the sub-cat-egory called economic freedom, which includes variables such as living in a society which guarantees property rights and fights corruption, where you can dispose freely of most of your money, where there is business and labour freedom, free trade and freedom to invest or move around your money, as you like. Western nations generally score high on these variables even though property rights and corruption is a significant problem in many Latin nations and over-taxation a problem in some Protestant countries.

The previous chapter was about how and why the Western population has be-come much more peaceful. In this chapter, we have further seen that the devel-opment of Western civilization has made people much more rational, trusting, tolerant, freedom-seeking, individualistic, democratic and, yes, happy.

That's not bad! However, we have not finished examining the human con-sequences of our creative development until we have studied broader aspects of culture– the sum of all our memes and its effects on human cooperation.

Cultures are vastly different and this is hugely important, so let's look at some concrete examples of what it may mean, starting with the Chinese. In Malaysia in 1960, 400 young people from the Chinese minority completed an engineering degree, while the corresponding figure for the Malaysian majori-ty was only four.[151] So the Chinese are very efficient in Malaysia, and the same has seen for the Chinese Diaspora in Singapore, the US and elsewhere.

Another example of efficient people are Christian Lebanese emigrants and their children and grandchildren who include a former holder of the "world's richest man" title (Carlos Slim), the founder of Swatch (Nicolas Hayek), the musician Shakira, the actress Salma Hayek, an impressive number of Latin American presidents and vice presidents and the director of Renault and Nis-san (Carlos Ghosn) .

The Japanese make a third classic example of effective emigrants. In the early 1900s there was great poverty in rural Japan and to give people a chance to escape this, in 1907 the government forged an emigration agreement with Brazil. Since then, a quarter of a million mostly pennyless Japanese people have emigrated there. Initially, the natives perceived these small, skinny Jap-anese people as relatively spineless and slow-witted, and they were subjected to discrimination. But today, the children and grandchildren of these pover-ty-stricken Japanese emigrants constitute approximately 1% of Brazil's pop-ulation, but are now clearly over-represented in management positions, and account for 17% of students at the elite University of São Paulo. Combined, they now own about as much land in Brazil as all the land there is in Japan.

The US offers, in its own way, many interesting demonstrations of the effects of cultural disparity; perhaps the most interesting of these stories concern the roles of Celts versus Anglo-Saxons. The US. was originally predominantly colonized by Great Britain, but the way it happened is interesting. Today, it is hard to detect big very big differences between people with Celtic and Anglo-Saxon roots in Britain (except in voting preferences), but the differences were still very pronounced when the British began to settle in America from the year 1607.

As we have already seen, Anglo-Saxons had, over many generations, dominated the Celts in the UK.[152] This divergence had an effect on America, because, as is often the case with mass migrations, the inhabitants of a given region would typically emigrate to roughly the same place in America, which made entire areas cultural copies of local areas in Britain, and they frequently even named them after the places they came from, but perhaps starting with "New", as in "New Hampshire". Hampshire was an Anglo-Saxon area in Britain, and New Hampshire is in the American northern states, which is symptomatic, because the British Anglo-Saxons overwhelmingly went to the northern states, whereas the British Celts (mainly from Ireland, Scotland and Wales), predominantly went to the southern states (the Confederacy). This created a clear cultural divide in USA, where southerners often called northern state people "yankees" whereas these would refer to southerners as "rednecks" and "hillbillies". "Redneck" was a native English phrase to describe Scottish bulkheads in the 1640s who refused to be ruled by bishops, because they often wrote protest letters with their own blood, and sometimes wore red neckerchiefs in protest – thus the red necks. Hillbillies were people in the South who marched down from the hills and mountains every year on July 12th to celebrate the Scottish King William III, also known as "King Billy". The reason they celebrated him of all royals was because he had conquered Anglo-Saxon England. There was no love lost between them.

Many past visitors to the US would describe the culture of rednecks and hillbillies as being very different from that of the yankee people in the north states. For example, Frenchman Alexis de Tocqueville travelled in the early 1800s around in US and described afterwards his experiences in his book Democracy in America, where he explained that even the poorest of the southern whites had slaves which had the effect that:

"The first notion he acquires in life is that he is born to command, and the first habit which he contracts is that of ruling without resistance. His education tends, then, to give him the character of a haughty and hasty man, — irascible, violent, ardent in his desires, impatient of obstacles, but easily discouraged if he cannot succeed upon his first attempt."

Torqueville described further the rednecks as relatively ignorant, easy to irritate, violent and without much initiative or enterprise."[153] Others made similar descriptions, and the combined impression of the southerners was of a people who were often comparatively lazy, violent, drunken, lacking initiative, irresponsible, boastful and loud; they often had excessive personal pride and were very easily offended, after which they regularly sought violent revenge. Southerners were later known to lynch criminals and eventually black people.

In addition, southerners were notorious for being reckless and irresponsible; boatmen on the Mississippi River would sometimes, for fun, compete in races with their paddle steamers, where they blocked relief valves for extra speed, which at times led to boiler explosions and killed passengers – in fact, it happened so often that it was said that it was more dangerous to take a paddle steamer on the Mississippi than to cross the Atlantic.

Another difference between the southern and northern state people lay in their work discipline. Northerners, who cleared a forest to make fields, would typically remove the roots of the felled trees, so you could plough the soil more easily. Southerners, however, would often let the roots stay in and just plough around them forever after.

The common lack of initiative in Confederate nations was also reflected in the limited innovation and creativity. A study of the US citizens who have contributed most to the country's scientific and cultural development in the first half of the 1800s showed, for instance, that the Confederacy, with the exception of Virginia, had very large areas from which not a single leading innovator or artist had come. Almost all the innovation, creativity and inspiration came from the north, and even though a third of the population lived in the Confederacy, they only took out 8% of the patents.[154]

All this, plus different attitudes to slavery, contributed to the American Civil War, which seemed like a repetition of the countless battles between the Celts and Anglo-Saxons in the British Isles over the preceeding 1,200 years. This is an example of how the civilizing process can have roots that stretch centuries if not millennia back in time. Just think about it: The Anglo-Saxons arrived on the British Isles approximately 1,600 years ago but, if you study the typical results of British elections, it is clear that Anglo-Saxons vote differently than Celts: The original Anglo-Saxon areas have, in recent elections, had large majority of Conservative voters (right-wing), and the Celtic areas have had majority of Labour (left-wing) or Liberal Democrats (centre) voters.

Stanford Professor Thomas Sowell describes in his two books Intellectuals and Society and Black Rednecks, White Liberals what the confederate redneck culture did to the US black population. First, as he points out, due to slavery in the southern states, 90% of the country's black population lived there rather than in the northern states and, as they were freed after the civil war, many had adopted the redneck culture. In schools, it is still quite common among black children to mock those who do well, on the grounds that they are "acting white". Thus, studies have shown that among black students there is a negative correlation between academic achievement and their popularity among classmates - the brightest are the least popular. The opposite is true among white and Asian students. Sowell's point is that the effect of the redneck culture in the southern states penalizes blacks, who come from there.[155]

Actually, cultural differences among otherwise quite similar people may even be reflected in measured intelligence. This was revealed, for instance, during World War I, when army recruits had to undergo mandatory intelligence tests, and it turned out, that black people from the northern states had, on average, higher IQs than whites (and blacks) from the southern states.[156]

This brings us to the whole discussion of intelligence. In 1984, James Flynn of the University of Otago studied the results of some Dutch intelligence tests, which were performed on 18-year-olds in the early 1950s and later in the 1980s. Something in these numbers surprised him: The measured levels of intelligence from the 1980s showed higher IQ numbers (intelligence quotient) than those from the 1950s.[157]

To examine whether this could really be true, he now gathered new and old intelligence tests from 30 civilized countries worldwide, and he found the same pattern here: people had become smarter and this seemed to have happened in a fairly linearly manner over many decades. Furthermore, they had actually become much smarter - average intelligence had increased by 0.3% per year, equivalent to 3% per decade.[158] An increase of 3% per decade corresponds, in pure arithmetical terms, to more than 30 points in 100 years, and that is a lot. Such an increase can - as seen below - move a person from the category called "definite feeble-mindedness" to the more comfortable "normal" or even superior category on a standard scale for intelligence:[159]

Classification of human intelligence (IQ)	
+140	"Near" genius or genius
120-140	Very superior intelligence
110-120	Superior intelligence
90-110	Normal, or average, intelligence
80-90	Dullness or feeble-mindedness
70-80	Border-line deficiency
Under 70	Definite feeble-mindedness

This discovery of an increase in people's intelligence - now known as "the Flynn effect" - was followed by an emotional, and often aggressive, discussion, since intelligence is always a hot potato (so hot that Jared Diamond has claimed that we are all equally intelligent except for people in New Guinea, who are smarter).

In 1995, the American Psychological Association instituted a working group led by the psychologist Ulric Neisser to conduct a meta-study of intelligence studies. We shall look a quite a number of meta-studies in this book, and what it means is a process during which scientists examine all previous scientific studies of the subject and essentially turn each of their conclusions into a single data point. They can thereby reach an overall conclusion from all these studies. Regarding the aforementioned study of intelligence, 11 scientists nominated by various organizations participated in this work, and their conclusions were clear and radical. For instance, if US children born in 1932 were to take a standard, modern day intelligence test at that time, their average IQ would only be around 80 (dull and bordering on outright deficiency; the global scale is always calibrated so that the average becomes 100). That's how (un)intelligent average Americans were in 1932!

There are a number of possible explanations for the rapid increase in intelligence since then. One is this: Norbert's civilizing process creates greater tolerance and human interaction across borders as well as through migration, and this stimulates more outbreeding and less inbreeding which, over many generations, will raise intelligence.[160] Conversely, systematic inbreeding such as cousin marriages reduces intelligence.

Another likely contributor is the known fact that first-born children are, on average, slightly more intelligent than their siblings - perhaps partly because they spend more time with very enthusiastic parents, and partly because they will be held responsible for looking after their younger siblings.[161] The latter is indicated by the fact that only-children are less intelligent than first-born siblings.

However, a much more important contributing factor is probably that people in civilized societies have far better nutrition and contract less serious illnesses, which is especially important for the brain during the first year of life. Malaria, for instance, can lead to anaemia in children's brains just at the time where it is supposed to grow quickly, which hampers development.[162] Many who visit poor countries may be annoyed that some people seem lethargic, apathetic and perhaps stupid, but they may not consider that many of these individuals may be sick or weakened from malnutrition and diseases such as malaria. This is also relevant to the recent history of Western average intelligence, as malaria was widespread in Europe, the US, and even as far north as Siberia up until and including World War II. Actually, in the years just before World War II, between one and six million Americans were infected with malaria each year. Then they began to spraying with the insecticide DDT against it and, in 1952, they only identified two cases. Not two million. Two.

The massive decrease in the number of serious infectious diseases in the West must have contributed to increased intelligence, which also applies to the Netherlands, where Flynn first discovered his indication of increasing intelligence. The Netherlands was plagued by malaria until its last major outbreak in 1947 – only three years before the date of Lynn's first Dutch IQ tests.

Flynn himself has suggested that cultural diferences could be important. Intelligence tests are designed to be independent of specific knowledge.[163] However, they are not entirely neutral in terms of whether people have a grasp of basic concepts such as logical, abstract and hypothetical thinking, reasoned assumption, statistics and separation of ideas from the authorities or impartial search for truth. Some people are brought up with these memes and others not, and this might make big differences in measured intelligence, even if their brains were physically identical.[164]

Let's finish the discussion of the effects of creativity and culture (and intelligence) with one last example: the Ashkenazi Jews. The Jewish religion evolved among Arabs in the Middle East approximately 3,000 years ago, which goes to say that Jews at that time were simply Arabs with a special faith. Because of increasing strife (a very long story) these Arabs turned Jews began emigrating, and some settled among the Anglo-Saxons in Western Europe, (which means within what became the world's creative centre). Some of these emigrants are called Ashkenazi Jews, and these were the ones who settled within modern day Austria, Switzerland, Germany, Eastern France and Holland, which means smack in the middle of Europe's creative centre. There, they developed a hybrid language combining German, Hebrew and Slavic called Yiddish. Unlike other Jews, the descendents of the Ashkenazi Jews now have average IQ of approximately 112-115 (overall US and European averages are both in the region of 100).

Why are they so effective? Recent studies have explained that, due to persecution they were unable to own land and possibly also too scared to be tied to any specific area. So, instead, they lived primarily from trade and finance, where intelligence and creativity was more important than brute strength and power. Furthermore, records have shown that the richest Jews, on average, had most surviving children, and here we have our explanation: they grew intelligent because they needed to be creative.[165] This must obviously mean they contributed greatly to the success of Europe's creative core, but it doesn't mean that this core became creative because of them alone, as we should recall that their intelligence increased relative to that of other Jews because only the Ashkenazi Jews lived in a creative area.

The story continues; because many of these emigrated to the US due large-ly to further persecution, and while their descendants there now only con-stitute approximately 3% of the US population,[166] they constitute 27% of US Nobel prize winners in the 20th century and 25% of ACM Turing Award winners, 32% of chess champions and a quarter of Westinghouse Science Talent Search winners[167]. Furthermore, Jews constitute a completely dispro-portionate percentage of chief executive officers (CEOs) in large companies in Europe and especially the US and, according to Forbes Magazine, in 2013 Jews constituted 11.6% of the world's billionaires, even though only approx. 0.2% of the world's population is Jewish (there are approximately 14 million Jews). In the US, no less than 48% of all billionaires in 2013 were Jews and these included Larry Ellison (founder of Oracle), Michael Bloomberg (found-er of Bloomberg), George Soros (Founder of Quantum Fund), Sergey Brin and Larry Page (founders of Google), Mark Zuckerberg (founder of Face-book) and Michael Dell (Founder of Dell).

What does all this mean? First, it basically means this: people in the West did not get richer because they were smarter, but over a period they actually did get a good deal smarter, because they grew richer.

And second: culture matters a lot. People with a productive culture can arrive empty-handed almost anywhere and will, on average, be successful within a few generations or less. Creating incentives for hard work, personal responsibility and innovation does pay off.

Many scientists downplay culture and ideas when they try to describe what shaped the world. Instead, they focus on a resource-based approach, such as was promoted by Marxist thinker Friedrich Engels. Just listen to what he wrote in 1884: "Now the Eastern continent, the so-called Old World, contained almost all the animals suitable for domestication and all the cultivable cereals with one exception, while America contained only one domesticable mammal, the llama, and this only in a part of the South; and only one cereal fit for cultivation, but that the best, maize."[168] The basic idea is thus that Stone Age Europe overtook America due to the natural distribution of fauna and flora.

The scientist Jared Diamond popularized and expanded this idea in his book *Guns, Germs and Steel*, published in 1997, in which he elaborated that the European head-start enabled Europeans to make powerful weapons before others. When Europeans acclimatised to living with animals via farming they also developed a much stronger genetic immune system than the Indians and, when they arrived in America, European diseases killed many Indians. Dia-mond's starting point was therefore largely based on the availability of natural resources and, throughout the book, which is more than 500 pages long, he only mentions "ideas" 31 times and does not refer to memes at all.

He was correct in saying that the Europeans had a better immune system than the Indians because of farming, but otherwise the story makes little sense. It is, for instance, difficult to argue that Scandinavia, northern Germany or the British Isles offered especially attractive natural resources to a Neolithic or Bronze Age man. It was often bitterly cold and windy, and winter was long, dark and barren. And how do you explain the economic differences between Albania and Switzerland, North-and-South Korea or Zimbabwe and Botswana? Why was Australia among the poorest nations on Earth when the Aboriginal peoples ruled there but became one of the richest, after Anglo-Saxons arrived? If natural resources are more important than ideas, why was China initially ahead of Europe and later way behind? Why did Venezuela which, like Argentina, was neck-to- neck with Germany between 1900 and 1950, drop down the ranks to 93 in terms of GDP per capita in 2013, even though it was sitting on some of the world's largest energy reserves?

Engels, Diamond and many others were looking for their explanations in the wrong place. While resources have certainly helped or hindered here and there (as they helped people in the UAE and hindered those in the North Pole), the main explanation for differences come from how well people make transactions with one another, and this translates into cultural characteristics that can either be highly conducive to the development of dynamic societies or a massive hindrance. For example, well-situated harbours, decentralization, free markets and open minds have been far more influential than weather, indigenous grains, rich soil or mineral resources. So here is an important distinction to consider, and it may sound harsh: if your grandparents, or even far more distant ancestors were active traders in an open society, the statistical (yes, statistical!) likelihood increases, that you are a fairly honest, trustworthy, trusting, meticulous, tolerant, and creative person. However, if you come from a closed tyranny, you are statistically less likely to be trusting of others, less trustworthy yourself, less tolerant and less creative.

What happened to our ancestors also contributes to our cultural attitudes to change. To traditional sailors like the Anglo-Saxons and, before them, the Romans, Greeks and Phoenicians, foreigners would primarily have offered opportunity. The antithesis of such a dynamic mentality is peoples who shielded themselves behind fortresses and believed in self-sufficiency and isolation. Such people would predominantly see limits and set limits.

While Western history has included a constant battle between these two mindsets since medieval times, and especially from 1450, it has mostly been those who embraced change and openness who had the upper-hand in the debate. However, the opposite has, nevertheless,never been very far from the surface - just think of the huge bestselling book Limits to Growth (we shall return to that) or, even worse, the communists, fascists and Nazis, who actually ruled almost all of Europe a couple of generations ago. There has always been, and there will surely also in the future remain, lots of people who are far more inclined to see limits and suggest limitations than to see opportunities and promote creativity.

People wishing for a static society may not know, or may not want to know, that Western civilisation has made people far better and happier, and that it has shaped people and cultures that are far more creative and co-operative than before. Or they may lack imagination to see how creativity can solve our problems. Or perhaps they are simply, psychologically, afraid of change.

The next section is largely written for these people (and about them), because it will address their four main specific objections; namely that 1) we are approaching the end of what is possible or desirable, so we must prepare ourself for a more static society; 2) free and creative societies will automatically concentrate power and money in fewer and fewer hands, so we should rein them in; 3) economic growth will consume all the world's resources, so it should be halted; and 4) modern technologies and increased wealth will destroy our environment, so we should hit the brakes.

PART 4

THE RISE
OF THE
NAYSAYERS

Most would probably agree that the creative explosion we have experienced so far has been a great ride in many ways, even if it has had its problems. However, many people believe that it now must - or should – end, wherefore we should prepare for a more sustainable society without further growth.

And they have reasons for thinking that. Some people note, for instance, that many of our technologies seem to be approaching the limits of what is physically possible, so won't that halt our growth? Or haven't we already invented almost everything that can possibly be imagined?

Another question: won't our market economies lead to ever bigger concentrations of money and power, which will kill the system in the end unless we stop it?

There is also this concern: is growth positive? After all, aren't we well on our way to depleting the world's resources and destroying the environment? Don't we poison ourselves with all sorts of artificial stuff? In this section we shall examine these questions, and find answers that are often surprising and contrary to what common sense might tell us.

CHAPTER 12:
Won't the ideas soon run out?

CHAPTER 13:
Are free markets self-defeating?

CHAPTER 14:
Are we draining the last resources?

CHAPTER 15:
Growth and the environment

12.
WON'T THE
IDEAS SOON
RUN OUT?

In 1953, NASA held some planning meetings to select projects for the coming years. For preparation, they asked the Air Force Office of Scientific Research to make a graph of the top speeds of vehicles throughout history, since this could give them an idea of what would be expected of them in the future.

The resulting graph contained an exponential vertical axis showing fractions of the speed of light. On the horizontal axis were given years 1750 - 2050. Furthermore, there was an indication of what speed was required for a satellite to reach orbit or to leave the Earth entirely. The latter was 40,320 km/h (25,000 mph). The graph started with the Pony Express of 1750, and then came the trains, cars, aircraft and rockets. Faster and faster it went, and a curve matched the exponentially-growing top speeds and extended this into the future.

When the planning team saw the shape of this curve and how it projected forward, they received a big surprise, because it suggested that mankind was only four years away from being able to send a rocket into orbit. Four years! But NASA was not working with any such plans at all. However, as it later turned out, the Russians were, and four years later, on October 4th, 1957, they sent a rocket into orbit.

Horror! NASA was behind!

The US now started a crash course to catch up. On 6 December of that same year, they attempted to send a satellite into orbit, but it blew up two seconds after ignition. The following year, the Soviet Union made five new attempts to send satellites into orbit, of which, one succeeded, and the Americans made 23 attempts and sent five satellites into orbit. The US was now taking over the lead in the space race and put the first people on the Moon in 1969. Two years later, our friend Alan Sheppard arrived there too, where, to the surprise of many, he pulled out a golf club and three golf balls. His first swing didn't go well; he buried the ball. The second only brought the ball a metre or so forward, which made Houston space control comment: "It looks like a slice to me, Al." But his final shot was clean and the ball flew for what was probably more than a minute due to the low gravity. The Americans were back on top, and they definitely enjoyed it.

The space race had enormous implications for mankind, as it soon led to development of communications satellites, which today helps us with satellite TV, weather forecasts, telephone communications, GPS navigation, surveillance and much more.

In 1959, something happened on the technology front that was not about millions of kilometres or giant rocket engines, but about technological adventure on a microscopic scale. On December 29,1959, the (incoming) Nobel Laureate Richard Feynman held a speech at the California Institute of Technology, during which he astonished his audience with wild fantasies about how much information one could, in principle, compress onto a single computing device.[169]

Technically speaking, he said, just considering the limitations of physics, maybe one day it would be possible to make a physical representation of a data unit, (a "bit"), with a maximum of only 100 atoms. If you did that, he continued, it would also be possible to store the full text of all books ever published (which he estimated to be 24 million titles), on a single computer chip with a diameter of 100,000 nanometres. To put that in perspective, a hair is approximately 50,000 nanometres wide, so what he really claimed was that you could, in principle, store the contents of all the world's books in an almost invisible speck of dust that was only twice as wide as a hair!

At the end of his speech, he offered two prizes of $1,000 each - one for developing an electric motor not exceeding 0.4 mm in each dimension, and another one for scaling down letters 25,000 times, so that the entire Encyclopaedia Britannica could be stored on the head of a pin.

These tasks were supposed to be very difficult, but the following year (1960), an electrical engineer claimed the first prize. However, it would take all of 26 years before the second prize was given to a student from Stanford University. He had, with an ingenious laser machine, engraved the first page of Charles Dickens' A Tale of Two Cities on the head of a pin.

This was impressive, but how do you read it afterwards? Newman was struggling with this himself, as he had great problems finding his own text with a microscope; the letters were just so tiny compared to the pin head. No, it is far more practical to make compact data storage by using transistors.

What's a transistor? These have, in a sense, a kinship with cogwheels in clocks. In a complicated watch, there will be large and small cogwheels that mesh with each other and each of them represents a small mathematical algorithm, such that there is 60 seconds to one minute and 24 hours in a day. When you write basic software code ("machine code"), you also use simple algorithms, and the basic one is an equation that says "if ... then ... otherwise...". Let's say you are driving your car and reach a traffic light: If the light is green, then we continue, otherwise we stop. It's that sort of thing.

This concept was first patented in Canada in 1925, but its technical break-through came in 1947, when engineers at Bell Labs learned to make them by sending electric current through germanium. This was smart because, with-out a power field, this crystal was a very poor conductor of electricity, but when you switched on a power field, it suddenly became a good conductor. It was, in other words, a "semi-conductor".

The transistors in a computer chip can nowadays be switched on and off billions of times per second, and the signals within them move at speeds cor-responding to travelling around Earth at equator-level 7.5 times in a single second. So we have made these ultra tiny machines that just run unbelievably fast and, if you inter-connect a myriad of such transistors, you have endless creative possibilities. Since this invention was developed, the industry has beaten one record after another. For example, the production of transistors reached close to 1.4 billion per capita worldwide in 2010.

The stories about the increases in maximum speeds of human travel or of performance improvements in IT are both about exponential growth. In 1965, the co-founder of Intel, Gordon Moore, described how the number of transistors on computer chips had doubled every 18 months between 1958 and 1965. He ventured that this exponential trend could probably be main-tained for at least another ten years. Since then, others have dubbed this rule "Moore's Law."

How on earth was that achieved? Via good, solid, engineering. For exam-ple, by making the entire electronic maze ever smaller, so the distances the electrons had to travel were minimized and more and more transistors could fit on a chip. Also, by optimizing the structure of the maze and even by mak-ing it three-dimentional, learning to turn the power on and off faster and faster, thus increasing the so-called "clock rate"; and by making multi-core chips to reduce heat problems.

It's amazing how long Moore's Law has been in force and, since the 1950s, the average performance of the chips has grown more than 10,000 billion times.[170] In 1996, the US military ran the world's fastest super-computer ASCI Red, which cost $55 million, used 800,000 watts and took up approximately 150 square metres (1,600 square feet). Ten years leter, in 2006, it was taken out of service because you could achieve the same performance with, for in-stance, the Sony Playstation, which cost in the region of $500, took up less space than a desk-top computer and used 200 watts.

Moore's observation started with looking at data going back to 1958 and his original forecast was only good until 1975. However, American author, serial entrepreneur and computer scientist Ray Kurzweil has calculated that the law has actually been in operation for close to 200 years. As long as this law remains valid, it means that the improvements in performance at any time over the next 18-24 months will be as great as they were the preceeding 200 years. However, we know that if the size of the current gates in the chip falls below what corresponds to the width of approximately 50 hydrogen atoms, the electrons can jump spontaneously over them, even if they are supposed to be in a shot position. Many experts expect that we will reach this limit around 2020-2025, but further efficiency can then be obtained by connecting many chips and computers into virtual super-computers, and also by introducing other materials and concepts such as quantum and optical computing (using electron spin to represent bits and light to move them).[171]

Rules similar to Moore's Law apply to most forms of information technology, and Kurzweil, for example, has documented similar laws concerning prices of chips, annual sales of chips and the performance of super-computers. Oh yes, and also for the sequencing speeds for DNA, the price drop of DNA sequencing, the total amount of decoded genetic material, the resolution of three-dimensional brain scans and much, much more. It is also evident in some parts of the software's effectiveness – for instance, scientist Martin Grötschel found that computers' ability to solve certain computational problems were improved 43 million times between 1988 and 2003, although the computer's hardware had only been made 1,000 times faster during the same period.[172]

In 2009, Kevin Kelly, founding executive editor of Wired Magazine, made a list of 22 different variations of Moore's Law, where he found the historical doubling times ranging from nine months for optical network performance and price reductions; over 12 months for price of pixels in cameras; and 36 months in computer clock rates.[173] As Kelly noted, it is in the small things that you see these extreme doubling rates. The work of these scales requires much thought, but these are far easier to exchange than physical products, and they rarely require much energy to replicate.

All of this means that Moore's Law can be generalized - it applies to information technology in general. Information technologies tend to increase their performance exponentially, with typical doubling times of one to two years.

That's all very well, but it's also very much history by now, and this raises an obvious question: for how long can such intense creativity continue? Aren't we, for instance, closing in on some limits in the laws of physics? After all, when the gates in transistors cannot get any smaller, when the crystals that drive clock speeds cannot vibrate any faster, when speeds of rockets approach the speed of light, what then? There is also another concern: are we simply approaching the bottom of the well of possible ideas?

It is true that the limitations set by the laws of physics are real, but the resource-view of innovation is, nevertheless, quite wrong for a whole lot of reasons. First, we can see from history that not only has our innovation grown exponentially, but the doubling time of our knowledge has become shorter – the growth process has, in other words, been hyper-exponential since around 1450. According to some estimates, at the start of the 22nd century our knowledge doubled roughly every eight to nine years, which is a far faster doubling rate than that of, for example, 100, 10,000 or 500,000 years earlier.[174] Just look again at how it began:

- 400,000 –1,500,000 BC: Control of fire
- 700,000 BC: Stone axe
- 500,000 BC: Tents of skin
- 400,000 BC: Wooden skewers
- 250,000 BC: Fine stone cutting
- 230,000 BC: Funerals
- 200,000 BC: Knives and rope
- 100,000 BC: Serrated blades and domestication of wolves
- 90,000 BC: The needle made of bone
- 70,000 BC: Art and clothing
- 60,000 BC: Herbal medicine
- 50,000 BC: Boats, flutes, bone spearheads

This is roughly exponential, but the doubling time was evidently not eight to nine years, so yes, it has become hyper-exponential.

But why does this happen? A lot of the explanation can simply be found in the logics of an expanding creative design space which, as we saw earlier, creates more opportunities for new combinations as it grows. As per our earlier example, if we double the number of existing products in a creative design space from two to four, the number of possible simple re-combinations rises from three to 14. The mechanics of a creative design space's growth is inherently hyper-exponential.

However, there are other important explanations to the acceleration, and one is very simple: the growing population. The greater the number of people who live in a dynamic society, the more people there are to come up with ideas. Today, there are approximately 30,000 times as many people on the planet than there were at the end of the last Ice Age. The effect of having 30,000 times more people is much more than a factor of 30,000, because today we are much better connected to one another than people were during the Stone Age, and the creative design space we have at our disposal is infinitely bigger.

Now, one might think that, similarly, ideas need longer to cascade and spread in a much larger population, but it is not so. Good ideas spread exponentially the same way that viruses do, and if the population becomes, for example,1,000 times larger, it only takes twice as long for a good idea to spread widely. As people grew richer and therefore had more money to travel, communicate and study, the processes just became faster and faster.

The third reason is emerging market switch to market economies. Until 1980, China, the Warsaw Pact countries and many other emerging markets had socialist governments and were largely static and had very little innovation except perhaps within military/space programmes. Now, they have almost all become market-driven and are far more creative; China and India alone can massively improve global creativity, as they are clearly ramping up their creativity-levels very quickly now.

In addition, there are more people who are educated, and, in particular, there are more females in higher education. We also conduct far more win-win transactions and exchanges of ideas than we used to, and we constantly invent new meta-ideas and meta-technologies that facilitate such transactions.

Urbanization plays a major role. An increasing percentage of the world's population lives in cities and, an analysis from 2007 showed that innovation intensity increases in a super-linear proportion to the size of cities.[175] To be more specific, if city size increases by 100% it will, on average, increase its production by 115 %, while its resource efficiency also improves. The effect of concentrating people in cities is akin to developing a more compact architecture in a semi-conductor chip and, interestingly, the clock frequency in cities is higher than in towns or villagers: It has been proved that people in cities walk faster on the street, probably because their lives offer more opportunities.[176] And there is more: the denser the cities, the more patents are filed inproportion to the population.[177]

So there is an underlying hyper-exponential growth in our overall creativity, and while we do run into the limits of physics in specific technologies all the time (and also will with micro-processors and rocket speeds), something new in other areas keeps coming up, and the typical pattern is this: 1) A new core technology is invented from combinations of previous ones; 2) this creates its own creative design space, where applications pop up; 3) fashion trends enter the picture; 4) the technology or the derived application combines with other technologies to create another new core technology after which the process starts all over again.

Overall, the following looks like a good bet for some simple basic assumptions about creativity in the future:

◆ If something is desirable and doesn't violate the laws of physics, it will probably be invented and launched commercially. We do not know, in advance, how this will be achieved, but we know that, in a free market economy, people will not stop trying, until they have succeeded.

◆ It can happen, even if it sounds magic. Many new technologies seem "magical" when we first encounter them, just as glass, mirrors, anaesthesia, aeroplanes, computers and television would have appeared incredible the first time they were encountered.

◆ Perhaps the development is already well underway. The mere fact that someone thinks that a technology cannot be implemented probably means that there are others who think about how it could be done.

◆ It often starts later than you think but then grows bigger than you ever imagined. Those who are good at designing a new core technology often overestimate how fast they can get it launched, but underestimate the ultimate size of the market, because they do not envisage the creative design space that will evolve around it.

It is one thing to conclude that, in theory, we should keep inventing evermore amazing developments, but another is to imagine what it may be like. Let's try for a moment.

We can start with (arguably) the weirdest material ever discovered: graphene. In 2010, Andre Geim and Konstantin Novoselov received the Nobel Prize in Physics for experiments with this odd material, which are grids of carbon atoms that are only one atom thick. This is the best heat conducting material ever discovered and is also an excellent electric conductor, which means that we may use it in semi-conductors. And more than that: It is so strong, that if you put an elephant on a (very strong) pencil, the edge of that pencil would not be able to penetrate this ultra thin layer of graphene.

There are many other things going on in materials research, but let's now look at computers. Somewhere between 2020 and 2030, the biggest computer will probably reach the same data capacity as the human brain (at least, if they work together in clusters), and we will also have made software that enables them to be intuitive and creative. We gained an early sense of this in a "Jeopardy" competition in 2011. Normally, this television show involves competition between three exceptionally intelligent people who compete to provide fast, accurate answers to questions that are read aloud to them. However, in this particular event, one of the competitors was an IBM computer called Watson, which was the size of a bedroom and able to speak and understand speech. It won the competition and thus a million dollars. Watson was not allowed to be connected to any external network, but had saved 200 million pages of information, including all of Wikipedia in its memory, and it was able to read and understand roughly about a million books per second. Two years later, IBM made a new version with three times the capacity that was only the size of a regular desk-top computer. This could read and understand three million books per second and was later put to use to diagnose cancer while its services were also offered online over the web. However, one of the most interesting future applications may be to make automated search for scientific hyphothesis. In an intriguing experiment, IBM let the Watson compuer study 186,879 scientific papers written up until 2003 with the purpose of identifying possible proteins that could trigger another protein called P53 to curb cancer. Watson suggested a number of candidates, and of the top nine on its list, seven had actually been found to have that effect after the cut-off date on Watsons reading list. This gave strong indication that Watson can predict what will be successful future areas in research and development, and it is a new meta-technology called "automated hyphothesis generation".

Artificial intelligence has disappointed for decades, but many scientists now believe we are close to creative and intuitive computers. For example, in June 2014 a computer programme convinced 33% of a panel of judges at the University Reading that it was a 13-year-old Ukrainian boy.[178]

Such progress is the result of faster chips, better programming and a better understanding of how the human intuition and creativity work. The latter comes from a number of public or semi-public brain research and simulation projects, including the Swiss Blue Brain Project, the EU's Human Brain Project, Paul Allen's Allen Brain Atlas and, since 2013, the American BRAIN project.

IBM's Watson computer uses so-called "deep learning" technology, which is a form of artificial intelligence, and it is now offered as an open platform. A specific use is as "Doctor Watson", assisting doctors in making diagnoses of patients' conditions. This shows that IBM is good at names, but also that human experts soon will be second-guessed by AI-based computer assistants. Perhaps the next will be Sherlock Holmes; a computer that can solve crime mysteries.

When computers begin to think independently and act creatively, they will not only exhibit great ability to answer our questions, they will even ask intelligent questions of each other.

Creative computers will also be able to write newspapers independently, news reports and books, make music and computer animations, design houses and write software for themselves and each other. Websites will be able to design themselves. You will be able to ask computers to explain a scientific problem, and they will instantly read all the science-based analysis on the topic and produce a meta report summarizing the best and most reliable information - all within seconds. Perhaps they will also take over a myriad of control functions for the service industry, such as reading licence plates to check if they match passing cars.

We may also use smarter computers to navigate the regulatory mazes for us. Especially in the US, it has already become common among large law firms to use computers to sift through huge numbers of previous trials to find precedent for this and that - a task that would otherwise require legions of paralegals. In the future, we can develop more and more opportunities to test the legality of the activities envisaged by letting computers talk directly to one another. To have acted in "good faith" may mean, legally, to have trusted a leading legal analysis program.

Computers will also be able to help with school and university tuition. If a pupil has lagged behind in maths or chemistry, the computer programmes may, for example, offer interactive tutoring based on a dialogue, where the computer really understands the student's problems and addresses them well. For the same reason, it will be very effective to take a higher education course online via interactive computer instruction combined with video broadcasts of lectures at elite universities.

With such computers, we shall enter the robot age. The first and one of the most important breakthroughs will here be driver-less vehicles. When these materialize in scale, a taxi might be something you call via a click on your smartphone. The phone will tell the taxi where you are and tell you where the taxi currently is. As is already available in cities such as London through the service Uber, you will not call a specific taxi company, but simply a taxi. The software will then identify the closest taxi and tell you how its previous users have rated it. You will be able to use a filter so that you will only use cars that have been rated, for instance, at least four stars out of five. In addition, the smartphone will, of course, also take care of the payment for the trip, as it already does on Uber. Because taxis will then no longer require drivers, they will be far cheaper than they are today and, accordingly, we will also have driverless ships, aircraft, tractors and other vehicles.

In addition to driverless vehicles, we will have robots that have what is known as "telepresence", which means that the owner can move them around by remote control while using their sensors to see and hear what goes on around them. An early example is the so-called "Double Robot", which is essentially a remote-controlled iPad on a Segway. Such robots can represent an expert doctor visiting patients at a hospital, or help us monitor our homes while we are away, shop for us in retail shops, help in factories and with cleaning and cooking. There may also be telepresence robots in spacecraft, or they will be used to clean sewers, fight in wars and do other things that are impractical, dangerous, unpleasant or just physically remote.

Other robots will be autonomous and may, in certain cases, have taught themselves tenacity after they have been taught by the owner via telepresence. In fact, parts of society may become so automated that robots could "live" on even if all people disappeared (do we have a disaster movie theme here?).

Some of these robots will be pre-programmed to solve specific tasks, while others will be adaptable and able to learn anything from experience. At the same time, there will be application (app) stores for robots, where you can download hundreds of thousands of software applications for them, such as ability to monitor a carpark for thieves and vandals or to clear weeds in the garden, wash dishes, serve cocktails, or whatever is required.

There will also be endless physical robotic gadgets such as custom-built components for specific purposes. It will be possible to buy their designs online or find them free online, so you can print them out at home or in a corner shop with a 3D printer. Eventually, the robots will take over so many tasks that people will laugh at previous predictions of coming labour shortages due to falling birth rates.

In the future we will have transparent mobile phones and smart glasses that can annotate anything in the world around us with explanations. If you look at a bottle of wine, you will immediately receive reviews and a narration about the manufacturer. Focus on some food, and you will receive nutritional content information and a calorie count. View a building, and you will be told its history. With smart glasses, you may see simulations of potential changes to a building, as you walk through it. You will see how it would appear with different wallpaper, mirrors or other features. Take a walk down a street in a big city and small arrows will point out where there are companies seeking labour, or where to buy milk. Listen to someone speaking a foreign language, and you will see subtitles in your own language.

There will also be an explosion in so-called M2M (machine-to-machine) communication, whereby all sorts of things will be online and talking with one another over the internet – the "internet of things". In parallel, there will be evermore analytical use of "data exhaust" which is collection of statistical data for analytical purposes. For instance, a study of how mobile phones connect to transmitters along highways will tell computers where there is traffic congestion, and studies of search terms on the internet can be highly-efficient predictors of fluctuations in house prices in local areas or sales of specific cars. There is already impressive software such as R and Amazon Web Services available for such analysis.

Additionally, you will have access to the Semantic Web which, instead of answering a question with reference to relevant links, simply gives us the direct answer, as IBM's Watson already can. Try typing "How high is the Eiffel Tower?" on Google and see what happens - we are already moving towards the "magic mirror on the wall" from the fairy tale Snow White and the Seven Dwarves.

In parallel with the IT revolution, we are now in the early stages of a revolution in biotechnology, which will also have huge impact.

The cost of full DNA sequencing of human DNA started at about $3 billion between 1990 and 2003. Ten years after this project, in 2013, that cost had dropped to about $1,000 and the predicted length of time it would take had simultaneously dropped from 12 years (or many hundred years in 1990) to a single day; scientists are working on methods that might take as little as two hours or even 20 minutes (Ion Torrent sequencing and Sanger sequencing are examples).

Genetic engineering and microbiology can, of course, be used for medical purposes. One of the main issues would be to do what the insulin industry does today: You insert a gene into a micro-organism, plant or animal, which is enabled to secrete a desired compound such as aircraft fuel or medicine.

Virtually all medications cause side-effects in a small minority of users but, with low-cost genetic testing, it will become easier to pre-determine which drugs best serve a person. Medication can also come in the form of nanoparticles, which are only able to adhere to specific cell types by hatching on to a specific protein that only this cell-type has on its surface. They will thereby act as "smart bombs" rather than the "carpet bombs" almost all medicine resembles today. One of the goals is to replace standard chemotherapy with smart bombs that do not provide discomfort and collateral damage.

Another significant area of development is development of vaccines. With outbreaks of new infectious diseases, such as annual strains of influenza, we aim to develop an effective vaccine as soon as possible, but it may still take two-to-three months, currently. With computer analysis and synthetic production processes, this may be reduced to 24 hours - a technique that could protect us against a future outbreak of a devastating infectious disease such as the Spanish Flu that hit last century or Ebola, that hit in this one.

In addition to flu, scientists hope, in future, to be able to vaccinate against malaria, asthma, food allergies, multiple sclerosis, leukaemia, arthritis, high blood pressure and even alcohol and drug abuse. Furthermore, one could produce injections of virus-containing plasmids, which are small separate DNA strands. These will compensate for any individual DNA error in a way that is similar to when your software downloads a "patch" from the internet.

One of the most interesting opportunities is this: you make a genetic analysis of a person to determine which forms of cancer they have highest risk of developing in their lifetime. You then develop a vaccine against these forms of cancer, after which your own body will immediately attack the cancer, should it ever appear. The only way you might ever know you had had cancer is if a blood test revealed a spike in your cancer specific anti-bodies.

Stem cell technology will also be revolutionary. These are cells that have not yet determined any particular function in the body so that they can be used as building blocks almost anywhere. With these cells you can, in laboratories, grow copies of people's skin, blood, blood vessels, heart valves, bones, noses, veins, and much more by using their own stem cells. First, you may make an ultrasound scan of the relevant body part, then you use a 3D printer, directed by a computer, to build a porous mould wherein the artificial part will be cultivated out of stem cells. Note, by the way, how this illustrates the effect of an expanding creative design space: we combine 1) genetic analysis, 2) ultrasound scanning, 3) computing and 4) 3D printing to create a new technology.

Other interesting areas include bio-engineering of modified yeasts, algae and bacteria to make new foods, pharmaceuticals, fibre materials and chemical agents; or to extract raw materials; or to combat pollution caused by oil spills at sea via oil-eating bacteria.

Once we reach and surpass the middle of our aforementioned chessboard (from the anecdote about the emperor and the artist), we may have developed accurate bio-computation software to the level where we can fairly easily computer-design simple new life forms with desired properties. This would necessitate computer simulation of whole-cell behaviour, including the DNA, proteins, organelles and totality of it all. Proteins, it should be said, are long and often extremely complex chains that fold themselves into three-dimensional spaghettis, where both their molecular structure and 3D folding patterns determine function. Such programmes will simulate millions of biochemical combinations to find opportunities and explain problems, and one of the first out of the gates is the Openworm project which, in 2014, raised money via the internet to simulate all the 959 cells of the worm C. elegans.

In 2012, genetic engineer Craig Venter expressed his expectations for bio-computation in an interview in Wired Magazine:

"What's needed is an automated way to discover what they do. And then we can actually make substitutions starting with the digital world and converting that into these analogy DNA molecules, then transplant them automatically and get cells out. It's a matter of scoring the cells based on knowing what the input information is, to work out what that gene does, what impact it has. Do you get a living cell or not? I think we can make a robot that learns 10,000 times faster than a scientist can. And then all bets are off on the rate of new discovery." [179]

A robot that learns 10,000 times faster? That may perhaps sound absurd, but when we consider that DNA sequencing speeds have improved by roughly that magnitude within 25 years, why is that not feasible? But if we really do improve the speed of biochemical and genetic discovery like that we then will have yet another phase shift in development of our creative design space – our hyper-exponentiallity gets even more hyper.

Such prospects have led some to speak of a future "singularity" - a point in time during which development is so fast-paced that we can no longer make forecasts about the future. However, perhaps a better way of looking at it is that we already have passed through many such singularities, including the invention of trade, farming, the electronic computer and the internet.

These were all wild technologies, but it can get even wilder. Let's go crazy for a moment and imagine really weird stuff that might happen. We can start by taking a deep breath and then asking ourselves: "What if we really begin to change our own genes?" As we have already seen, this is actually not as strange as it may sound, because we have already, inadvertently, done this ever since we started civilization. But the process can accelerate dramatically if we start doing it consciously.

The first steps towards genetic manipulation of people could be cloning of beloved dogs and cats. In fact, this has already begun; in 2004, the company Genetic Savings & Clone cloned a cat for a woman in Texas, USA[180] and, in 2007, three clones were made of a dead dog as part of the Missyplicity project.[181] The next step could be to genetically-engineer pets so they live longer. Scientists have actually already extended life-spans dramatically in some animals. This can be done by extending the telomeres. These are inactive codes that sit at the end of each chromosome in our DNA. Each time a cell divides, a piece of the telomeres break off, until there is nothing left. After that, the cells will lose active DNA each time it divides and, which creates trouble. Extending the telomeres would postpone this problem, and possibly by a lot, and you can do it by modifying the single DNA string in the zygote (the very first cell of an organism). Experiments with mice have thus extended their life expectancy by 24%. Other successful attempts at life extension have, for example, used incorporation of genetic material of blueberries into an insect's DNA to form a steady flow of life-prolonging antioxidants that slows its ageing process.[183]

Genetic self-modification could involve people asking to have a number of eggs and sperm screened for about 4,000 different genetic diseases prior to in vitro fertilization (IVF) so they can choose those of highest quality. At a later stage, people would be able to ask for screening of some of their embryos to select those who have the most attractive properties. For instance, perfect pitch is the rare ability to identify or re-create a given musical note without the benefit of a reference tone. It turns out that the position of a single atom on an individual's DNA string decides whether or not you have that.

The highest IQ measured, to date, was that of a Korean boy, Kim Ung-Yong, who could read German, Japanese, Korean and English when he was two years old. He began studying physics at university when he was aged three. Twelve years later, he completed a postgraduate degree in physics in the US, having previously worked in NASA. His IQ was measured at 210.

So what if people decide to modify their unborn children's genes to make them as smart as Kim Ung-Yong, but perhaps also healthier, happier and more beautiful for good measure, or to enable them to live for much longer than normal? Much of this is already starting to work at laboratory-level, but there is a potential market for it? "No!" many will cry, "We will never do any such things. We don't modify people artificially."

But we already do. People are already having fillings in their teeth, contact lenses, artificial knees, hips and heart valves, heart transplants, plastic surgery, Botulinum toxin facial treatments, pacemakers, hearing aids, artificial corneas and liposuction. In 2007, it was possible, for the first time, to cultivate an artificial bladder and, in 2009, an artificial windpipe; since then, our ability to grow body parts has gone exponential. We already perform amniocentesis to screen for defective genes and, to date, we have created more than half a million test-tube babies - two technologies which sparked outrage when they were introduced, just like contraceptive pills. We have also, after initial difficulties and some accidents, learned how to cure some genetic diseases by infecting the patients with viruses containing corrected versions of the defect genes.[184]

If genetic manipulation of embryonic cells occurs, it may well start in Asia. In 1993, Darryl Macer, from Eubios Ethics Institute in Japan, found that a large majority of Asian people are in favour of using genetic manipulation and genetic screening to improve children's physical and mental abilities.[185]

Would you be willing to use genetic engineering to...	Austra-lia	Japan	India	Thai-land	Russia	USA
...reduce the risk of life-threatening genetic disease in later life?	81 %	75 %	83 %	82 %	79 %	77 %
...prevent your children from getting non-life-threatening diseases, such as diabetes?	79 %	62 %	73 %	91 %	71 %	77 %
...increase your children's innate intelligence?	27 %	26 %	70 %	72 %	35 %	44 %

SHARE OF POPULATION IN DIFFERENT COUNTRIES THAT ARE IN FAVOUR OF USING GENETIC MANIPULATION OF UNBORN CHILDREN FOR VARIOUS PURPOSES.

Even a very simple strategy based, in each case, on screening ten embryos for the one with best potential for high intelligence is estimated, in itself, to be able to raise each generation's IQ by five points. Within a 100-year period, that would multiply the proportion of individuals who have an IQ of 145 by a factor of 40. In mice, scientists have already managed to improve memory significantly by providing them with an extra copy of the gene NR2B.[186]

Could it be that the next epic power struggle in humanity will not be traditional wars, but brains wars? China's leading gene research institute in early 2013 had approximately 4,000 employees and was beginning to decode and analyze the complete genomes of 1,000 people with extremely high intelligence to find reasons why they were so bright. One of the genes that have been found to matter is called KL-VS and this is associated with an increase in IQ by 6 points. In a random sample of 220 people, approximately 20% were shown to have this gene variant.[187]

We can now imagine that, one day, we hear about rich men without heirs who put a clone of themselves as the beneficiary of their testament. Or we may hear of parents who lose a beloved child and have it revived (sort of) in the form of a clone. Or there may be people who recreate famous dead people or even Neanderthals. In fact, genetics professor George Church of Harvard Medical School has stated that he believes the latter could be done today for 30 million dollars. By the way, recreation of an extinct species is called de-extinction, and this is definitely on its way, as we shall see later. It won't be Jurassic Park, but expect to see extinct species return.

What about causing deliberate extinction? We have, so far, managed to eradicate smallpox and rinderpest and are close to eliminating polio, guinea worm and Yaws as well, and this is done with combinations of isolation, vaccines, and environmental improvements. Next in line may be rubella, hookworm, measles, river blindness, and Creutzfeldt–Jakob disease (commonly known as mad cow disease). While some of this may be achievable by traditional means, scientists have proposed using genetic engineering to eliminate some of the more troublesome diseases such as malaria. For instance, biologist Olivia Judson has proposed to use introduction of knock-out genes to eliminate 30 mosquito species as follows:

"...put itself into the middle of an essential gene and thereby render it useless, creating what geneticists call a 'knockout'. If the knockout is recessive (with one copy of it you're alive and well, but with two you're dead), it could spread through, and then extinguish, a species in fewer than 20 generations." [189]

The 30 species she had in mind constitute approximately 1% of the world's 2,500 mosquito species, whose disappearance would eliminate dengue and yellow fever plus malaria. It would take in the region of 10 years to eradicate these mosquitos after the release of the gene. In 2014, scientists at Imperial College in London announced that they had developed a genetic modification so that malaria-carrying mosquitoes produce 95% male offspring, which means the the population will crash over approx six generations.[190] An alternative approach, suggested by the Gates Foundation, is to make the mosquitoes carrying deng fever immune to the viruses causing it, which may be done by infecting them with the bacterium Wolbacia.[191]

Each of us is entitled to our own opinions about all the possibilities described above, but the key is that much, or all, of it probably will happen and some of it is already happening at laboratory-level.

If we take the helicopter view for a moment, we can say that there are two compelling, but different, ways of describing our technological development. The first is to see it as a tale of human creativity, and this is the most entertaining – at least you can include the great anadectotes.

The other is to see it as a self-organizing creative design space, which means that it follows a roughly pre-determined path. Why? Because each technology or combination of technologies will, almost inevitably, lead to the next, according to a simple logic of combinations in a creative design space.

An example: Ernest Rutherford developed ideas about atomic structures, and Max Planck developed quantum theory. It was therefore only a matter of time before someone (it was Niels Bohr) combined their thoughts into a single atomic theory. Or another example: Someone invented a steam engine and others the stagecoach Ergo, it was inevitably that someone else would combine the two into a car or a train, because it was the adjacent possibilty at the edge of the creative design space.

When you think about it, it has to be like that – our scientific and technological development is like a self-organizing creative design space that inevitably must expand roughly in a somewhat pre-determined sequence - and therefore the same products will often be invented at approximately the same time by different people, which is why patent offices often receive almost identical patent applications every few months or even on the same day. For example, Alexander Bell filed a patent application for the telephone on February 14, 1876, which was exactly the same day that Elisha Grey filed a patent application for a telephone. In fact, Ian Morris explained in his book Why the West Rules for Now, that 20 out of humanity's first 15 major inventions arose independently in the same sequence in the West and the East, but only by 2,000 years of displacement.

When people think we are approaching the end of innovation and thus growth, it may be because there is something basic in our psychology causing us to believe that the development has reached its end point right here and now. Of course, we may know from history about the endless, and even accelerating, number of inventions that came before us, but we can't imagine how this should continue. We fail to see that it is in the basic trait of inventions that you normally do not know about them in advance. Could people in, say, year 1900, have imagined genetic manipulation, when DNA's chemical components were only (and quite wrongly) proposed in 1919? Or could they have thought of nuclear power, when Niels Bohr's atomic theory was first put forward in 1922 and when Einstein, 10 years later, stated that: "There is not the slightest indication that nuclear energy will ever be obtainable. It would mean that the atom would have to be shattered at will."

Not only have we often been very reluctant to accept new technologies, we are also frequently very sceptical about how much more can be learned and discovered. In Roman times, shortly before the birth of Christ, the eminent engineer Sextus Julius Frontinus said: "Inventions reached their limit long ago, and I see no hope for further development." And so it has been ever since.

"What? You would make a ship sail against the wind and currents by lighting a bonfire under its deck? I ask you to excuse me. I do not have time to listen to such nonsense. "

So said Napoleon Bonaparte to Robert Fulton's idea of a steamship in 1803. (That was not a year in which he made good decisions since he also sold a third of the current US. to the US. government for 68 million Francs, equivalent to less than $300 million in today's money. He wanted the money to rule Haiti, which he found more promising.)

And what about this one: "Rail travel at high speed is not possible, because passengers, unable to breathe, would die of asphyxia." This was said by Professor Dionysius Lardner in 1830.

"It's an empty dream to imagine that the cars will take the place of railways for long trips." This was the pronouncement, in 1913, by the American Railroad Congress (who else?). In 1837, medicine Professor Alfred Velpeau said: "The elimination of pain during surgery is a figment of the imagination. It is absurd to apply it today." It was anaesthetics he had in mind.

One can go on and on. When, in 1859, Edwin L. Drake tried to recruit workers to drill oil, he had a very hard time finding someone willing to do it. "Drill for oil?" they asked. "You mean drill into the ground to try and find oil? You're crazy."

The aeroplane was obviously no exception to this rule. Today, there are more than half-a-million people flying in plances at any given time but, in 1903, The Times wrote that it was a waste of time to try to develop flying machines. This was poor timing, because just a few weeks later the Wright brothers managed to make a machine fly. When Boeing later introduced its B247, one of its engineers said: "There will never be a bigger plane built." It carried 10 passengers. Later, Ferdinand Foch from Ecole Superieure de Guerre said that "aircraft are interesting toys but of no military value." That was before the Battle of Britain in 1940.

In 1920, the New York Times reported that it would be a physical impossibility to make a rocket as its exhaust would have nothing to push against. When, 49 years later, Americans were about to land on the Moon, they printed the following humorous correction: "It is now definitely established that a rocket can function in a vacuum as well as in an atmosphere. The New York Times regrets the error."

Our lack of imagination does not only apply to what is technically possible, but also what has commercial potential, and the reason for this is that we do not foresee that each new core innovation, which in itself may seem rather useless, will stimulate its own creative design space of applications, which will later be followed by increasing fashion shifts. When David Sarnoff tried to encourage his colleagues to invest in the newly-invented radio, they replied: "The wireless music box has no imaginable commercial value. Who would pay for a message sent to no one in particular?" Yes, who indeed, if there are no applications for it?

The same scepticism is echoed in the earlier history of technology. In 1878, Erasmus Wilson from Oxford University said the following about electric power: "When the Paris Exhibition closes, electric light will close with it and no more will be heard of it."

The lack of imagination seems particularly prevalent when people comment on their own field. In 1995, British Telecom futurologist Ian Pearson made a speech in which he predicted that IBM's Big Blue computer would, within a few years, beat reigning champion Kasparov in chess. After the lecture, a member of the audience came up to him and said that he was sure the Deep Blues chess programme could never beat Kasparov, as he himself had written that programme and knew its limitations. Just 18 months later, it happened. Astronomy has also been the subject of our scepticism. In 1888, astronomer Simon Newcomb stated that: "We are probably nearing the limit of all we can know about astronomy."

However, there are scientists and engineers who gradually learn from their experiences. As the co-inventor of the electronic computer John von Neumann in 1949 commented on this invention's future, he left the door ajar for future surprises:

"It would appear that we have reached the limits of what it is possible to achieve with computer technology, although one should be careful with such statements, as they tend to sound pretty silly in five years."

Yes, you may say that, and the reason is that ideas are not finite resources, but rather parts of an expanding, self-organizing creative design space, which feeds on itself without end. Unless, of course, we decide to halt it, like the Ottomans and Chinese did.

13.
ARE FREE MARKETS SELF-DEFEATING?

In 1903, the American Wright brothers were the first people ever to fly in an aeroplane. Four years later, on December 23rd, 1907, the US military issued a sensational call for proposals for an aircraft that could lift two passengers with a total weight of 350 pounds (160 kilos), contain sufficient fuel for a flight of 125 miles (200 km) and achieve a speed of at least 36 mph (58 km/h)[192] And so the era of mass aviation had begun.

Exactly 100 years later, on a sunny Friday afternoon in March 2007, the editor of Wired Magazine, Chris Anderson, was looking forward to his weekend. His publication always received lots of test specimens of technical gadgets that people hoped it would cover. And for this weekend, Anderson had decided to take two of these home, namely a LEGO Mindstorm kit to build robots and a remote-controlled model aeroplane. The idea was to play with the two together with his children.

The weekend arrived, and the children first created a LEGO vehicle, but they soon tired of it, as it couldn't do much. Then they went to a park to launch the plane, which headed straight for a tree-top.[193]

Later that day, as Chris went jogging, he suddenly had the idea to combine the two systems. He would use the LEGO operating system to provide better control of the model aircraft by turning it into a drone. The difference between a drone and a remote-controlled model airplane is that the drone can receive pre-programmed instructions and then run on autopilot. This could work because the LEGO set included an accelerometer, a compass, a gyroscope and a Bluetooth transmitter that could be connected to a wireless GPS sensor (this is yet another example of the creative design space in action).

A few weeks later, he and his family made the first drone test flight. At this time, the cheapest drone in the world was the Raven, which you could buy from AeroVironment for $35,000, and Anderson's experiment gave him an idea: try to make a mass produced drone that had 90% of the Ravens functionality, but which was cheaper, because it used cheap standard parts.

Much cheaper.

But this required a creative social space. He therefore registered the internet domain www.diydrones.com (diy stood for "do it yourself"), which became an online forum where people interested in drones wrote blogs, created discussion forums and uploaded images, videos and software codes for drone software. Soon the website was humming with activity and it became clear that these hobbyists, by helping each other, could accomplish the most incredible developments with free, shared software and ultra-cheap sensors from microchips, mobile phones and so on. Meanwhile, Anderson founded the company 3DRobotics, which had soon sold more operating systems (software) for drones than were used by the entire US military.

Three years after its launch, this forum had 26,000 members, who built approximately 1,000 new drones a month, and Anderson's own company was now selling a Quadcopter - a mini helicopter - for $300 - less than one percent of the price of the aforementioned Raven. What Anderson had really done was to create a social environment that could create products. He institutionalized creativity.

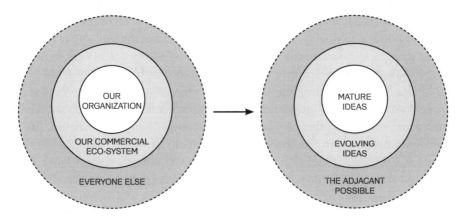

This story demonstrates how Western creativity works, when it works best and as we shall see, this tends to involve our five basic conditions for creativity: the small units, change agents, networks, shared memory systems and competition.

The specific process that Anderson used is what is known as crowdsourcing. This is a special kind of de-personalization - a network phenomenon in which many people, who do not know one another or work in the same organization, (many lacking formal qualifying credentials) spontaneously find themselves working together to solve tasks. The internet encyclopedia Wikipedia is written in this way – as co-operation between strangers - and there are now crowdsourcing projects for numerous applications - from writing Linux software to solving problems with a given brand of camera.

Wikipedia is itself a fascinating story. The idea for it came from a economist and former university professor named Jimmy Wales. Originally, his aspiration was to make an internet encyclopaedia called Nupedia, where various experts would write each section, which would be checked and corrected by other experts. But it progressed at a snails' pace and, in frustration, he developed a small side project called Wikipedia, where anyone could write about any topic without formal controls. This website launched in January 2001, and after only a month, it contained approximately 1,000 articles. It surpassed 40,000 entries in August of that year, and in the spring of 2012 it had reached an incredible 22 million articles. Like Anderson, he had harnassed the creativity he needed.

The amazing thing about Wikipedia is the collective working spirit and morale it illustrates. If someone writes an inaccurate or defective article on a topic, it will often only take a few hours for someone else to correct the deficiencies, until the article is good and rich. To test this, the journalist AJ Jacobs of Esquire Magazine wrote an article about Wikipedia itself, on Wikipedia. This was not only deliberately poor and incomplete, but full of intended misspellings. In the following 24 hours, Jacobs watched in amazement as others went in and improved on the article 224 times; an additional 149 corrections were made by various people, turning his post into an high-quality article.

Wales was a big fan of the ultra-liberal writer Ayn Rand, the Russian/American novelist, philosopher, playright and screenwriter, who has shocked many and delighted others by advocating strongly that people should, first and foremost, focus on their own interests. Initially, it would seem that Wikipedia is a significant violation of this principle, because its writers work for free and often put in huge effort which is not acknowledged or attributed to them. However, what actually occurs is a voluntary win-win transaction, because most people apparently gain great satisfaction from contributing in this way, as long as they can do so voluntarily. In this case, no-one coerced anyone; it was a win-win scenario.

Today there are myriads of other "wikis" on more specialized topics, and lots of companies use internal versions of this model to share information among employees and external crowdsourcing systems to boost their creative output. The site InnoCentive has created a network of 300,000 registered problem solvers from 200 countries that by 2014 had received more than 1,500 awards ranging from USD 5,000 to one million each. Recently, two scientists studied 166 scientific problems posted there and found that 49 of these were solved, mostly by people who had expertise that was very different from that of the people who had posted the problem.[194] For instance, NASA had, for years, tracked solar flares (a sudden flash of brightness observed over the Sun's surface), but could not figure out an accurate way of forecasting when they would occur. So it posted its data and outlined the problem on InnoCentive in 2010, and a retired radio frequency engineer called Bruce Cragin responded. Cragin knew nothing about solar flares but a whole lot about something called magnetic reconnection. Using this knowledge, he quickly came up with a model that could forecast the solar flares rather well.

This is the power of crowdsourcing – a stranger who has no role or credendials assumed relevant to a particular problem, and who – in this example – knows nothing about solar flares, figures out how to solve the problem anyway because he knows something else that you don't. This is a variation on the "social space" concept, where the inner circle typically comprises people working in your organization; the next layer is made up of other people with relevant credentials and the outer circle is everyone else, who you acces via crowdsourcing techniques.

There are many other crowdsourcing types, some of them relating to the exchange or aggregation of technological information over the internet, such as in the example of the website www.diydrones.com.

Another variant of crowdsourcing is offering public inducement prizes for the solving of important social or technical problems. The advantage of inducement prizes compared to, for example, Nobel prizes (awarded on the basis of results), is that the former encourages future achievement and is awarded only if defined objectives are met, rather than past achievement, which may be less effective.

Inducement prizes are especially effective when you can clearly define the problem you want solved or the task to be undertaken, but where it is not clear how this can be achieved. It also works well where there is extreme imbalance between "Schumpeter profit" and "alchemist fallacy" (defined earlier) – in other words: where society may benefit significantly from a solution, compared with the gain made by an innovator solving it in a commercial market.

The classic example of the inducement prize is innovation awards. One specific example is the famous Longitude Competition, which was organized by the British government in 1714.[195] The motive for this was the need to solve the problem of sailors being unable to determine, reliably, their east-west position (their position in longitude), as the Earth revolved around its axis towards the east. Their position to the south or north (latitudes) could be calculated from positions of the stars in the night sky.

To find their longitude, they had to know exactly what time it was and then compare the visible stars with a star map. This problem was very important, because a ship that does not know its position on the sea can encounter serious difficulties. Competitors were offered the chance to win £10,000 if they could come up with a method of determining the location of longitude with a precision of 60 miles, £15,000 if the accuracy was 40 miles, and £20,000 with a precision of 30 miles. The £20,000 corresponds to about £2-3 million (or $3-5 million) today, so it was big money.

Despite the incentive, it took 59 years for anyone to come up with a solution. This came from a carpenter named John Harrison, who during all these years - throughout his career – had worked intensely on the development of a watch that could work with sufficient precision in high seas, in order to win the competition. More specifically, his goal was that the timepiece should not lose or gain more than 150 seconds per day, even if it moved a lot. In total, Harrison received £15,000 pounds for his work, paid out to him at various times, and he died wealthy.

Later, the British and the French governments initiated many other innovation competitions which led to the invention of, for example, the steam turbines and various chemical processes. When Napoleon needed to find a way of preservng food rations for his soldiers, a pastry baker won an innovation prize of 12,000 Francs in 1810 by inventing the airtight tin can.

Many individuals have since launched similar awards to encourage innovation. For example, in 1919, French New York City hotel owner Raymond Orteig promised $25,000 to the first person who could fly directly from New York to Paris - a prize which was won by pilot Charles Lindbergh in 1927.

Since then, many companies – mostly in the US - have used crowdsourcing to solve specific problems as well as to seek general inspiration: IBM has launched several international crowdsourcing projects since 2001, where the best-known was its "Innovation Jam" in 2006, which involved 150,000 participants from 104 countries. Over a period of 72 hours, many of IBM's own employees and their families, its customers and business partners, as well as some universities, attended. Via a website, participants watched presentations about a number of IBM's core technologies and were then invited to make suggestions for how these could be applied in practice. This resulted in 46,000 individual ideas that a team of IBM executives turned into 312 more general ideas. Since then, IBM has helped several of its clients develop similar idea competitions to harnass knowledge.

US military research institute DARPA has also run a number of crowdsourcing competitions concerning drones, versatile robots, driverless vehicles and much more. The first competition regarding the vehicles was held in 2004 and involved private firms, individuals, and student teams from different universities competing with driverless cars that should automatically run through a desert stretch of 240 km.

It did not go well because two of the selected cars never made it to the starting line,one flipped over at the start, and none of the remaining 12 made it further than 12 kilometres (5% of the intended stretch). However, the following year the same competition was repeated with 23 participating cars, and this time they all made it past 12 km, and five completed the full distance. In 2007 came the much more demanding DARPA Urban Challenge, where 11 selected teams' cars had to drive 96 km through an urban environment in a military base, while respecting all public traffic rules. Six out of the 11 cars achieved this. In 2011, the leader of the winning team in the DARPA competition in 2005, German computer scientist Sebastian Thrun, introduced Google driverless cars in a real urban environment in Nevada, after that state made it legal to use such vehicles in June of that year.

Isn't it amazing that you can go from not being able to drive a single driver-less car more than 12 kilometres in a desert, to having them operate safely in a city environment within just seven years? That's what crowd-sourcing can achieve, and we should note how it happened: there was no central plan for how it should be done, but there was a clear incentive to get it done and a crowdsourcing platform to organize the process.

Innovation awards represent an effective way of inspiring creativity and identifying talent. The awards can help create new, creative social networks and raise awareness of social or technological problems, while pinpointing a range of possible solutions. Finally, they can motivate students by offering them real tasks to solve. What a fun way to study!

These are excellent examples of how creativity can arise when one completely abstains from central planning and instead focuses simply on motivating people deeply to get things done. According to consulting firm McKinsey, the use of such prizes tripled between 1970 and 2007, growing by 18% annually, on average, over the last ten years. A number of companies such as Idea Crossing, Nine Sigma, Spigiot, BigCarrot and InnoCentive now offer ready-made platforms and system solutions for running such contests.

Companies have used innovation awards to complete a wide range of tasks from identifying ways of sourcing more gold in a gold mine to improving a software application that helps people find movies on Netflix, and developing ways to make mice live longer. Google has launched annual "code jams", where anyone could help solve difficult math problems and the FIRST Robotics Competition in the US in 2008-2009 involved 175,000 students, 16,000 robots, 58,000 teachers and 33,000 volunteer assistants. This competition is repeated each year; thousands of teams compete to build the best robots to solve specific tasks. Another example of crowdsourcing is the International Genetically Engineered Machine (iGEM), a series of global competitions among teams of students to create biological systems from standard components called BioBricks. In another competition programme, called iGEM, participants were, in one case, challenged with creating a strain of the bacterium E. coli, which eminated a luminous green colour. Some teams actually managed to fulfill this bizarre brief. Another task involved the creation of a vaccine against the bacterium Helicobacter pylori. An amateur team from Slovenia won this award. In yet another programme, called DIYbio, various institutions have, since 2005, offered "biohackers" access to their resources in order to create their own bio-experiments with DNA and non-pathogenic microorganisms.

A similar example is the robot PR2, which is based on open software systems known as ROS, OpenCV and PCL. People have written these applications with gusto, and as anyone has been able to follow on YouTube, the robot has through this crowd-sourcing learned to fold clothes, play billiards and do many other things.

Some of the best known competitions are the X-Prizes, which are sponsored by private companies and donors. The organization behind it has, for instance, offered a reward for making a private spaceship that can fly in-and-out of the atmosphere twice in two weeks. In addition, there have been prizes offered for placing a robot on the Moon; for developing small, inexpensive and accurate rockets; for creating a super-cheap mini-lab for home diagnosis of diseases; for technology that can clean up oil spills at sea; for finding ways of reducing poverty and for developing far more environmentally-friendly cars.

Crowdsourcing can also be used to enable closer, virtual on clearly-defined tasks. An example is the crowdsourced computing task project SETI (Search for Extra-Terrestrial Intelligence), where people make their computers available to a large data-intensive project involving the interception of radio waves from the universe in search for signs of alien civilizations, when they are not using their machines themselves. Similarly, you often see examples of people who, via the internet, share a task of reviewing large quantities of published material in order to pinpoint spedific areas of interest.

One of the most fascinating creative phenomena in crowdsourcing is the observation that members of large crowds are often very good at jointly estimating a numerical value or at choosing between different solutions to a problem. This is especially the case in situations in which individuals cite an opinion without knowing the views of others. The explanation is partly a statistical phenomenon known as Condorcet Jury Theorem (after the previously mentioned "enlightenment" writer, the Marquis de Condorcet). This is about the relative probability of a given group of individuals arriving at a correct decision. In its simplest form, it says that the more people who guess the correct answer to a question out of two options, the more likely it is that their average guess will lean in the right direction. If each person, for example, has a 55% probability of guessing the correct solution to a problem, the probability that the guess is wrong will of course be 45%, if there is only one person involved. But when you increase the number of people guessing independently and take the average of their guesses, the risk of a collective error falls amazingly quickly.

This phenomenon is very relevant to so-called prediction markets. These typically operate like stock markets, so that people bet on the outcome of a future event. The world's leading expert and pioneer in this area is probably Oxford Professor Robin D. Hanson; he and others have shown that betting contracts predicting who will win a general election are more accurate, on average, than opinion polls.[197] One of the benefits of such markets is that those who participate tend to be knowledgeable about the subject. With the Hollywood Stock Exchange, for instance, one can bet how much revenue a given movie will achieve, or on who will be nominated for an Oscar. Collectively, people do that very well.

Stock exchanges are obviously also prediction markets, and here, economists have discovered that even though stock markets are sometimes/often mistaken, they are better at predicting large turning points in the economy than almost any other indicator. This is true even though they suffer from the problem that participants can see each other's predictions via the stock prices, which create group-think problems.[198]

A number of multinational companies such as Eli Lilly, HP, Deutsche Bank, Google, Goldman Sachs and Microsoft have been using prediction markets as tools for forecasting important events. For example, in August 2004, Microsoft launched an internal market for assessing the number of cars that would successfully complete the aforementioned DARPA 2004 Challenge; participants correctly predicted that the result would be "none". That same year, it made a prediction on when a specific internal software project would be completed. The project leaders said "November", but just three minutes after the betting contract was opened, the prices traded at levels indicating only a 1.2% chance that this target would be reached. Although this crowdsourced assessment later increased to 3%, the betting contract's behaviour persuaded management to postpone the release date. The programme was finally released in February 2005.[199]

Incidentally, crowdsourcing is also used to create a phenomenon known as collaboratory filtering. Anyone who has used Amazon or iTunes (or many similar online shopping services) will have experienced the phenomenon. These websites register what each user is clicking on and buying. They use this to create a database of people's preferences, deducing what each user might like from what similar users have liked. They have thus created virtual collaboration between lots of people who learned from each other without ever knowing each other. It is a variant of the same mechanism which helps to make Google so efficient at predicting searches.

Speaking of the internet, we must also mention blogs. Here you have amateurs acting as web authors, and quite often they do this skillfully and with an enthusiasm that even professional journalists, writers or scientists can find hard to better. Some bloggers earn revenue from advertisement sales, whereas many simply do it fun, as an intellectual indulgence.

It works. There have now been numerous famous instances, where bloggers have revealed mistakes made in traditional media or among established scientists. One of the more notable examples came about in 2004, when CBS journalist Dan Rather published some apparently very revealing documents about George Bush's military service. However, soon after the story was featured on television, a blogger pointed out that the documents were written using a proportionally spaced font, so that some letters took up more space than others. In 1972, when the documents were alleged to have been written, people used typewriters for documents of this kind, using a monospaced font, meaning that the documents had to be fake. CBS then fired a number of those responsible for making the television programme and issued an apology to viewers.

A fairly recent example of crowdsourcing is "social impact bonds". Various countries, including the US, UK and Australia, have started to finance certain social activities via private no-cure; no-pay contracts, where you only get paid for actual results. The principle is to reward institutions according to the measurable social utility of their solutions. For example, you pay a private or charitable organization an amount to provide social services to former prisoners, but the final payment depends entirely on how often they are convicted of further crimes. Full payment happens only if this never happens.

This principle has two major advantages. First, no one signs up for the job if the allocated amount is disproportional to the magnitude of the task. Society will therefore automatically avoid spending money on hopeless projects, as it otherwise often does. Second, there will be great diligence and creativity among institutions that actually volunteer to undertake such activities.

We should also mention another example of crowdsourcing, which may change many sectors: online sharing service such as Uber, Airbnb and many others, which have brought us the voluntary sharing community. We previously saw that you can use Uber to hail a taxi, but the funny thing is that it isn't really a taxi you hail. It's anyone with a car. So anyone who wants to be a driver for other people using his own car can just register with Uber, and then they will be hailed. After the journey is over, the client is asked to rate the experience, and so is the driver. Any driver who doesn't provide a clean car and good service and thus receives poor average ratings, is thus kicked out of business, and any client who doesn't behave decently cannot use it anymore. Relay Riders does something similar, but where you get the car without the chauffeur. And Airbnb does it for short-term accommodation – you can use it for an overnight stay or to rent holiday homes, but again, bad behaviour by either party sees them kicked out of the network.

A final example of crowdsourcing is crowdfunding, where start-up companies and projects are presented online to potential investors without having to go through a long-winded, complicated process. As an example of this, the Crowdfunding platform Kickstarter funded between 2009 and 2014 more than 50,000 projects with a total of 900 million dollars.

Evidently, crowdsourcing can mobilize huge creative energy. For example, innovation prizes often stimulate a co-operative effort among the participants that are of much greater value than the promised prize award sum. Since X - Prizes promised a prize for flying in space, 26 teams invested a total approximately $100 million in attempts to win the $10 million that were promised as a reward for the winner. Similarly, nine teams spent, between them, around $400,000 trying to win the bounty of $25,000 for flying from New York to Paris. In the 1920s, people were so eager to win this that many pilots and navigators ended up sacrificing life and limb in the process. In the spring and summer of 1927 alone, 40 pilots tried to make long-distance flights over the ocean, and 21 of them died in the attempt. This was obviously tragic, but it indicates, once again, the enormous untapped potential creative resource a society has available to it if it opens up its social space by inviting people to come forward with their own contributions to joint projects.

All this brings us to the interesting underlying phenomenon in creativity that we already discussed with our case of the grey wolf, which turned into 160 kinds of dogs: voluntary co-operation creates diversity.

Just think of this: In the 1970s, computer people were considered, by many others, to be the very manifestation of conformity and centralism. Back then, most computer people worked with mainframes, or what they sometimes called "master-slave computing", where a central computer provided information to the terminals. Then came "client-server computing", where local terminals also had their own processing power, which meant delegation of power. The next step was "personal computing", where everyone had their own PC. And then came the internet, whereby everyone was connected to everyone else. This was sometimes called "networked computing". Around the same time came "ubiquitous computing", where computers were built into all sorts of other things that also were interconnected. Then we got our smartphones, tablets and other mobile devices, as a part of "mobile computing". So computing has spontaneously become evermore diverse and friendly, similar to how one wolf became 160 dogs. Today we have userfriendly computers - large and small - on our desktops, in our pockets and hidden inside many of the things we use, and we can call this the "I movement".

Developments in the media is another example of spontaneous decentralization. In the 1970s, most countries had a single state television channel, or perhaps two, and maybe two or three state radio channels. But then came terrestrial private channels, followed by cable and satellite radio and TV. After this, along came YouTube and eventually hundreds of millions of individual websites, blogs, chat forums and social media networks such as Facebook and LinkedIn. Media became diverse and decentralized; just like computing.

Such trends towards decentralization – yes, de-centralization - are a logical consequence of spontaneous creativity. It is simply our creative design spaces and social spaces that are expanding. It happens everywhere, and for instance, the new so-called "maker movement" is a new social phenomenon, where people manufacture locally and in small scale. How? With open, compact fabrication tools such as 3D printing, desktop programmable manufacturing tools and crowdsouring to produce physical products at home or in shared "hackerspaces", "Fab Labs" and other "maker spaces". These phenomena are now also popping up in educational institutions.[200]

Decentralization and diversity is actually also reflected in the number of nations. From 1945 to 2015, the number of nations in the world recognized by the UN rose from 50 to 193; typically in alignment with transitions from dictatorship to democracy. For instance, when the Soviet Union and Yugoslavia became democratic, they each divided into a number of smaller nations, as might also happen should China or various Arab nations become democratic. Interestingly, a recent Credit Suisse study showed that small nations (defined as those with fewer than 10 million inhabitants) score, on average, considerably higher on the Human Development Index and Country Strength Indicator than larger countries.[201] Furthermore, Credit Suisse found that small nations that had emerged out of larger ones, such as Croatia, Lithuania and Kazakstan, had tended to improve their relative standing in the global Human Development Index rankings subsequently.

The point of crowd-sourcing, diversity, decentralization of products, the sharing society and the maker movement is that they all bring us closer to what we can call a true "participation society" - a society where more and more doors are opened so that people can participate to the limits of their personal abilities. Another example is that ever more women receive tertiary education - in fact, in many countries, they have already surpassed men in this respect.

It is also happening due to a new phenomenon called "massive open online courses", or "MOOCs". An example was seen when Professor Peter Norvig of Stanford University introduced online transmissions from a class in artificial intelligence on 29 July, 2011. After two weeks, to his astonishment, 50,000 students had signed up for this free course, and even before classes had started, the number of subscribers had risen to 160,000. This was for lectures that would normally be attended by a few dozen people, up to perhaps a maximum of 150. So this was a quick productivity increase in a private university by a factor of approximately 100-fold, but it was also a new opportunity open to anyone, across the globe, with access to a connected computer.

Free online training has since spread like wildfire. Harvard University and Massachusetts Institute of Technology (MIT) collaborate, for example, on the edX program, where they offer single courses free of charge, online, and, by April 2013, the online education network EDU video on YouTube surpassed 100 contributing universities.[202] Other international programmes appear in Coursera, which was started in May 2012 and topped its first million students just four months later, and two million by year end.[203] Similar explosive growth has been seen in the online-based learning organizations Udacity and Udemy.[204] In Brazil, Kroton Educational has become possibly the world's largest private educational company partly by emphasizing computerized learning and online courses that can be followed even by students living in the remotest jungle villages. Brazil had approximately six million students following distance- learning programmes in 2014.

The growth of cheap online education offers countless opportunities, and Professor Anant Agarwal, CEO of edX, has proposed a new higher education structure combining online and on-campus study plus work experience as follows: First year is pure online education. Those who can pass this have two years on campus focused largely on case-work. In the fourth year, they are given a job but while doing some final online courses.[205]

This educational trend towards decentralized, none-exclusive participation societies is not only for university courses. Former hedge fund analyst Salman Khan began in 2005 helping his cousin Nadia with her homework over the internet while using Doodle notepad software. Since then, he has produced thousands of learning videos on YouTube, which together have had several hundred thousand downloads and, in 2009, he founded his own e-learning company that, in late 2012, had more than half-a-million subscribers.[206] By analysing the use of his videos, he and his team now see very clearly where students have problems.

Furthermore, in the information society the pace of innovation has become so fast that even medium-sized companies may find it difficult to keep pace, and this is also reflected in decentralization; the average size of firms in OECD countries has fallen steadily for years, and among US companies, it has decreased from 25 to 10 employees over 25 years.[207] There is also a rise in the number of so-called micro-multinationals which comprise very few staff, or even a single employee, who manages purchasing, manufacturing and marketing worldwide.

This development has gone hand-in-hand with a typical development within different product categories. There is a steady trend from cheap, mass-produced industrial goods toward premium and luxury (mass-to-class). Premium calls for more decentralized production with more elements of fine crafts and handwork – just think how cars, coffee, sporting goods, clothing, handbags, bread, and other products seem to become evermore diverse. The same goes for production where, for example, we have seen recent growth in the number of mini–breweries in many countries. Indeed, many marketing strategies are now based on mass-customarization targeting; what the marketers call "the segment of one", where every single client has to have his or her indivuidualized version of a product.

Meanwhile, management of companies has become far more multi-cultural, and in many smaller nations a substantial number of the most iconic companies are now run by foreigners. (something that is not reflected in the public sector at all). Ownership of larger companies has also become far more diverse. Originally, all private companies were owned by a single person, a family or a closed partnership of a handful of partners. Today, the largest companies have millions of owners, including private investors, pensions funds (which again have millions of members) university endownments and sovereign wealth funds (which are owned by entire populations). Furthermore, since the late 1990s, the use of stock options has contributed to a further spread of ownership.

The decentralization phenomenon is also reflected in how physical products tend to develop. Initially, townsmen would typically draw their water from a common well. Then water came to every house (tap water), and later into both the kitchen and bathrooms, where we gained sinks, showers and bathtubs. These were then turned into style objects and were produced in more and more variants. So we recognise decentralization and diversity again, and something similar is now happening with aircraft, as we saw with the case Chris Andersen and his diydrones.com. What is important in all this is that the emerging participation society is based on *voluntary* sharing of products, services and opportunities, but not coercion or centralization.

The fact that increased diversity and decentralization occurs spontaneously in a market economy is actually not that surprising when we consider that exactly the same happens in nature, where the number of species has grown continuosly for billions of years. It is, in both cases, simply an expression of the inner logic of creative design spaces, including the aforementioned character displacement and co-evolution phenomena.

Increasing product diversity and commercial decentralization in product markets goes hand-in-hand with lower prices and more compact designs, which means that items that are initially bulky and expensive, over time, become cheaper and small enough to have at home. Today, for instance, we have our own printing in the form of printers and, increasingly, 3D printers.

We also have our own personal church clocks to wake us in the morning (alarm clocks), locomotives (cars), movie studios (video recording and editing software), concert halls (stereo), cinemas and theatres (television), etc.

Generally it is the case that, if something can, in principle, be made on a reasonably small scale, it is only a matter of time before it becomes decentralized and personalized. This, together with ever-increasing crowdsourcing, shows that a market economy is essentially inclusive, rather than extracting, and it will not place more and more power in fewer and fewer hands, as many have feared, but rather delegate more and more power to individuals. The participation society is evolving all around us.

However, here is another concern: will decentralized market economies concentrate more and more money in ever fewer hands?

This is what economist David Ricardo said in 1817, where he claimed that land-owners would accumulate an ever-greater share of the world's wealth since you could increase the number of factories, but not the quantity of farmland.[208] What he didn't foresee was the enormous growth in farm productivity, which had the same economic effect as if the landmass had expanded.

In *Das Kapital* (written between 1867 and 1894), Karl Marx also predicted an inevitable collapse of liberal democracies because they would create ever-widening gaps between the "haves" and the "have-nots". Workers should thus seize power, he said, and so, indeed, they did. "We are poor because they are rich", was the belief and so they went on to slaughter the rich people and their supporters. All in all, Lenin, Stalin, Mao, Pol Pot and others murdered in the region of 94 million people such as bankers, Kulaks, traders, "rootless cosmopolitans" and others so they could enforce redistribution. Hitler's national socialists had a similar mindset, but here the "rich crooks" were the Jews, of whom they killed approximately six million. So the combined murders committed by the Nazis and communists amounted to some 100 million people.

The persecution of the rich elite also occurred in democratic Western countries. For instance, in 1966, Paul Baran and Paul Sweezy released their influential book *Monopoly Capitalism*, which claimed that capitalism would exhibit a continuous concentration of mega-companies, until a "military-industrial complex" would largely run the world, paying off politician cronies to go along with their plans.[209] So instead of Kulaks or Jews, it was now multinationals and global trade and investments that should be stopped, a mission with which terrorist groups such as the Baader-Meinhof group, Revolutionäre Zellen and Brigate Rosse soon engaged.

However, this was only in Europe. In Indonesia, locals were violently jealous of the rich Chinese upper class, which accounted for 3-5% of the population, so thousands of this demographic were raped or murdered, especially in

1998. Elsewhere, it was the rich Japanese, Lebanese, Indian, Jewish or Koreans emigrants that people hunted down.

Ugandans were also concerned about concentration of capital among the elite. In their case, it concerned approximately 1% of the population of Asian origin mainly Indian, which controlled some 20% of the economy. In 1972, the possessions of these people, which amounted to 5,655 companies, commercial real estate and agriculture, cars, houses and furniture, was confiscated and redistributed, while the Asians were given 90 days to leave. Unfortunately, this had disastrous economic consequences, which is why, 20 years later, they were invited back and offered partial compensation (which most declined). Once bitten, twice shy.

In Zimbabwe, it was the Whites who constituted the rich 1%, which is why the government began confiscating and redistributing their land and other property. This triggered the country's aforementioned economic downturn, during which unemployment rose to 80% and inflation to 489 billion %, and both living standards and life expectancy almost halved.

Of course, there are also more moderate methods of redistributing the wealth of the rich. In the UK in 1974, for example, the marginal tax rate on earned income was rasied to 83% and to 98% on capital gains tax. Two years later, the country had to seek emergency loans from IMF to avoid bankruptcy.

None of these experiments went well, but the rich will always be a proverbial stone in the shoe to some, and, in 2013, the French economist Thomas Piketty gave their persecution yet another go with his bestselling book *Capital in the Twenty-First Century*. This time, the target wasn't Kulaks, Jews, Indians, Whites or multinationals, but the wealthiest 1%, who he considered too rich.

The book contained a very thorough examination of inequality in income and wealth between 1810 and 2010. Piketty didn't claim that global inequality was rising, because it was, in fact, declining, and the decline was especially significant when adjusting for the fact that there were more children in the poorest countries (income and wealth peak around middle age, so nations with a very young average age can have deceptively low average income).[210] No, Piketti examined only the inequality in four countries: the US, UK, France and Sweden; and he actually showed that inequality had been unchanged or falling over these 200 years in these countries as well. What he did say was that the inequality gap had, in particular, shrunk in the first 70 years of the 20th century, but after that had widened. He argued that the initial reduction had been due to temporary factors such as war, whereas the subsequent widening in inequality was because capital gave a return that exceeded economic growth.

Let's consider that for a while. Economic inequality can increase due to a combination of factors that help the rich. First, technical innovation has evolved, so that today, many innovators, especially in IT, can develop multinational giants within just a few years and with the use of very little capital compared to what is needed in industry and farming. As modern IT entrepreneurs' businesses are based more on ideas than on capital, they don't become too financially diluted, so they still own a large part of their company, when it matures. The founders of such companies are typically young and often single and childless when they hit the jackpot, and this is new. In times past, it typically took two to three generations or longer to build up an international industrial group, and when its value peaked, the founder would be long gone and the assets shared between his countless grandchildren and spouses from divorces in the extended family - plus possibly between children and spouses of those as well.

A second factor that may have led to greater capital concentration is that more women now benefit from a higher education, which means that young men and women meet at university and get married.[211] This leads to polarization, so that those who are about to get rich are more likely to marry each other.

A third factor is population growth, which has put upward pressure on property prices, since supply of land is flat. As property constitutes about half of global wealth, this has boosted the return on capital, as the world's population roughly doubled during the time that concerned Piketty.

Global ageing together with the IT revolution and globalization has also put downward pressure on inflation and interest rates during the exact period (from 1970) during which Piketty believed the inequality widened. When interest rates fall, the discount factor of future earnings on investment assets goes up, and this drives up their prices. For example, the exact same house or share may double in value if interest rates fall by half, so that the owner appears twice as rich, even if what he owns is exactly the same.

A final factor that can drive up asset prices is an excessive global credit expansion, which is also exactly what happened between the late 1970s and 2010.

The other type of inequality drivers are obviously those that can put downward pressure on low earners. The first of these is the frequent statistical mistake of measuring income per household, because as there are more single households, the average "household income" falls, even as "personal median income" actually rises. This makes the poor seem poorer in statistics.

Increased pursuit of tertiary education has also had a more direct statistical effect in as much as approximately a third of those registered as "poor" in many developed nations are university students (another third tends to be small-scale private businessmen going through a rough patch).

Globalization has also been important, because while it has stimulated a huge increase in wealth among poor people in nations like China and India and thus global decline in inequality, it has also put downward pressure on low earners in rich countries.

A final factor that should be mentioned, is, as American political scientist Charles Murray has pointed out: welfare states create rapid increases in the number of latent poor, which may be followed by an increase in the number of actual poor, after a delay. The rise of welfare in the four countries Piketty investigated happened precisely during the period in which he believed the inequality gap had widened, so this may also be a contributing factor.

All in all, there have certainly been developments that could be said to have contributed to greater inequality since the 1970s. However, when we scrutinise the story, we are in for some surprising finds.

Admirably, Piketty published all his figures and equations on the Internet for everyone to see, and, soon after, UK business newspaper, *The Financial Times* (FT), uncovered what it thought were a number of oddities and mistakes. "There is little evidence in Professor Piketty's original sources to bear out the thesis that an increasing share of total wealth is held by the richest few," it concluded, adding: "There seems to be little consistent evidence of any upward trend in wealth inequality of the top 1%."[212] The FT also noted that Piketty had incorporated inaccurate British data into figures for Europe as a whole and given it the same weight as data from France and Sweden, which had smaller economies. If you corrected for that, they concluded: "There is no sign that wealth inequality in Europe is rising again."

Whether or not it had risen, it remains the fact that it is almost unavoidable for wealth concentration in a market economy to fluctuate around an equilibrium instead of ever-increasing. Occasionally, there will be over-investment in the quantity of production equipment (due to so-called competitive overinvestment), and then the relative bargaining power of the workers in these factories increase, while profits decrease, due to oversupply. That reduces inequality, but it cannot last, because business then stops investing, which hurts workers but boost profits for a while. A curious example of this effect was seen in the years 1346-53 when the Black Death killed approximately half the European population, which meant the ratio of capital to population doubled. This scenario leads to a speedy improvement in rights and incomes of common folks.

Fluctuation in productive investments is a natural part of business cycles and self-correcting, also driven by equally self-correcting fluctuations in property prices and more. Furthermore, the price of assets that make rich people rich fluctuate with interest rates, credit formation and countless other cyclical factors, but again, this is self-correcting.

Most of the other factors mentioned above, such as population increases, global aging, globalization, increased uptake of higher education among females and the growth of welfare states are also likely to peak or fall, and the

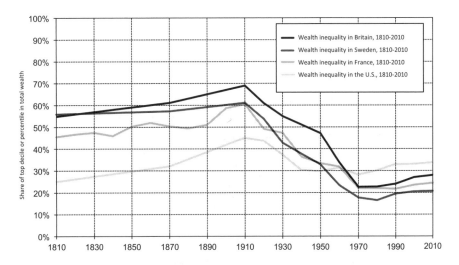

THOMAS PIKETTYS DATA FOR WEALTH SHARED AMONG THE TOP 1% IN THE US, BRITAIN, FRANCE AND SWEDEN 1810 – 2010. AS THE DATA SHOW, THE OVERALL TREND HAS BEEN TOWARDS FAR LESS INEQUALITY IN THREE OF THE FOUR NATIONS OVER THE PERIOD. THE EXPECTION IS THE US, WHERE THERE HAS BEEN A SLIGHT INCREASE.

greatest effects, when this happens, will come from rising interest rates and reverse globalization.

A quick look at the GINI co-efficient, which measures inequality nation-by-nation, shows that this is generally far lowest in countries that have embraced free market economies for a long period of time – Western nations, in other words.

But there are also problems in the concept of "the rich" (of "the 1%", as it is often called), because this group is far more volatile today than in the past, when the same families kept vast fortunes tied up in land or factories throughout many centuries.

To look at some numbers: A statement about incomes, from the US Department of the Treasury, showed that those people who, in 1996, were among the poorest 20%, saw their income rise by an average of 91% in the following nine years, while the richest 20%, over the same period, only experienced income growth of 10%. The wealthiest 5% in 1996 actually had a subsequent average decline over the same period. What about the richest 0.1%? Their income also declined afterwards, and, in this case, by a mind-boggling average of 50%.[213] In other words: if you follow the destinies of individual people rather than comparing statistical snapshots, you find the poor tend to grow a lot richer and the rich tend to become significantly poorer.

10 DRIVERS OF THE PARTICIPATION SOCIETY

1. Less centralized, more devolved, manufacturing and individualized products due to mass-customerization; "segment of one" manufacturing techniques, including the maker movement, the Do-it-yourself (DIY) communities, plus "mass-to-class" and luxury products, which are largely hand-made to individual specifications.
2. Trend toward smaller companies, including micro-multinationals.
3. Higher income volatility over people's life-times, where the poor tend to grow richer and the rich become poorer.
4. Increase in crowd media, such as blogs and YouTube instead of mass media such as TV and newspapers.
5. Broader shareholder base in larger companies due to investments from mass-owned funds plus use of stock options.
6. The I-movement: Trend towards home version of products that previously were available only in larger companies. For example home video editing, 3D printing, home cinemas and change from centralized mainframe computing to personal and mobile computing.
7. The sharing society such as Uber, Airbnb and cloud computing
8. Trend towards creative crowdsourcing phenomena such as collaborator-filtering, mass ratings, prediction markets, crowdfunding, mass-edited wikis, Social impact bonds, open innovation contests, crowdvoting, collaborator filtering.
9. Trend towards mass access to online university education via Massive Open Online Courses and more female education.
10. More migrations and intermarriages between people of different nationality, race or culture, where people vote on an issue over the internet

Why are income and wealth so highly volatile among the very richest? It's usually because you only grow very rich by doing things that are very demanding, risky and volatile. Companies today pay more for their absolute top-level executives than ever before, but tolerance is also much lower. As in elite sport, the rewards are huge if you deliver absolute top performance, but the moment you stop doing it, dismissal notice comes far more promptly than it used to. Also, share prices fluctuate, technologies change, fashions shift and other factors influence who is sought after at the top.

This explains some remarkable observations. Looking at *Fortune Magazine's* list of the US's wealthiest "Fortunate 400", between 1992 and 2008 a total of 3,672 different people made it to that list, but only four (yes , 4!) of these remained on the list throughout the period.[214] In fact, a survey of these 400 richest people from 1992 to 2000 showed that fewer than a quarter remained in this category for more than a year, and less than 13% remained there for longer than two years. Similarly, more than 75 % of Americans who were among the poorest 20% in 1975 were among the 40 % richest in 1991. And in a sizeable longitudinal study (where you follow the same people for many years), two scientists found that:

◆ 12% of Americans had, at least once in their lifetime, experienced being among the 1% in the US with the highest incomes
◆ 39% had been among the wealthiest 5%
◆ 56% experienced time among the top10 %
◆ 73% had been among the richest 20 %
◆ 54% had tried to be officially poor or close to poor

This confirms again that, in modern times, the rotation between rich and poor is very significant indeed, and a lot of the poor will later become rich, and vice versa. This means the narrative that you have with a small group of people – the 1% - who become ever-richer in comparison with the rest, is misleading not only because global wealth inequality has in fact been falling recently and inequality in wealthy nations has fallen over the last two centuries, but also because there is widespread-and-growing creative destruction taking place around the top, which means faster exchange in who constitute the richest 1%.

For the past couple of centuries, market economies have been subject to repeated conspiracy-style theories claiming that information, money and power will grow increasingly concentrated. Somebody – the Kulaks, the bankers, the Jews, the Chinese, the Japanese, the Koreans, the Indians, the multinational companies or the top 1% are leading a conspiracy against the rest. Karl Marx and Piketty believed this would lead to the collapse of free markets, Baran and Sweezy believed it created tyranny via big companies, various Hollywood producers and authors have envisioned future scenarious in which people are run by computer-aided dictatorship, and Piketty thought the richest 1% would dominate evermore.

Actually, the feared concentration of power and money in very few hands was widespread before liberal democracies, and thus before Karl Marx. This can be seen from the records in the *Domesday Book* from 1086 (a manuscript record of the Great Survey of England and parts of Wales); or sensed by any visitor to the opulent the Palace of Versailles in France (a symbol of of the system of absolute monarchy, pre French Revolution). According to the *Domesday Book*, a handful of families, plus the Church, owned the vast majority of England and Wales, while the French kings could essentially take whatever they wanted from anyone in their country. In 2014, Celebrity Network published an estimate of the inflation-corrected maximum wealth of the 25 richest people of all time.[215] Only three of these people lived after World War II, even though world population and average income has a great deal larger since World War II than ever before.

When you think more deeply about it, it would actually have been fairly surprising if free markets had created increasing concentration of anything, because the natural tendency of any creative system is to create greater diversity and pluralism. Therefore, we are not, by now, all controlled by a single, evil mainframe computer (think HAL in 2001: A Space Odyssey), but instead use our own many small computing devices, from smartphones to PCs and tablets. We are not indoctrinated by a single branch of the media or central institution (think Aldous Huxley's novel Brave New World; George Orwell's 1984 or – a more recent example – Suzanne Collin's Hunger Games). By contrast, we have become individual publishers via our own blogs and social media platforms. Furthermore, we can now all take online courses at the world's top universities, virtually for free, and will soon be able to print out our own products using home 3D printers. We have not seen monopoly capitalism play out as Karl Marx and others expected, but have instead seen average company sizes decline considerably while shareholder bases have broadened. Social mobility has not declined, but has rather increased to the point where being among the super-rich now tends to be a very temporary affair. And, as Piketty's own figures actually demonstrated, wealth concentration is not a long-term rising trend.

The recurrent persecution of "the elites" across the world has, as we have seen, led to mass-murder and economic melt-down again and again, but, in a clear example of the civilization process in progress, the persecuters are now far more likely to call for higher taxes than to shed blood. Piketty, for instance, proposed a 10% annual wealth tax and 80% marginal tax. This was radical stuff, because if capital yielded 4% profit but was taxed at 10% (both annually), the taxation would equal 250% of the profit. If this was combined with 80% income tax, the effective marginal tax would easily equate to more than 300 %, not even counting VAT and other taxes. So, in order to implement Piketty's system, you would need a global, centralized government, or the rich would surely flee to wherever his draconian taxes were not implemented. Furthermore, no one would have any financial incentive to take risks or postpone gratification; they would spend any money earned straight away or they would hide it from authorities in the guise of jewellery, gold bars or by making undeclared improvements on their homes (for tax-dodging pur-posees), all of which would leave no capital for investment in new business. Society would, almost immediately, stagnate and fairly quickly collapse.

So the summary is this: many people have, over the past several centuries, ex-pressed concern that free market economies will be self-defeating because they will lead to more conformity and greater concentration of information, wealth and power among ever fewer people. But when we study realities, it is the op-posite pattern we detect; a pattern where free market economies create greater diversity, mobility, mass participation, pluralism, decentralization and change.

No, if you should look to any sector of society that has actually concentrated evermore power and money, look to the state:

Government spending as percentage of GDP, developed nations[216]							
1870	1920	1960	1970	1980	1990	2000	2010
10 %	18 %	27 %	33 %	43 %	46 %	43 %	49 %

14.
ARE WE DRAINING THE WORLD'S LAST RESOURCES?

In the morning of 13 May 1908, several hundred of the US's leaders and opinion-makers were gathered in the East Room of the White House in Washington DC. In fact, the room was packed, and among those present were governors from each of the nation's 44 states and selected members of Congress. There were also members of the Supreme Court and the cabinet, as well as experts in natural resources. It was a fantastic turnout, but for a good reason, for the day's topic was a looming national crisis: the US' imminent depletion of natural resources.[217]

The atmosphere was very hopeful now, because attendees were due to hear a speech by President Roosevelt himself - a man whom many of the participants had never seen. Everyone knew that protection of natural resources was a key issue for the president, for he had talked about it before, but, so far, without generating the desired interest. This time, however, he had decided to do everything possible to grab people's attention; he had sent extensive advance briefings to all mainstream media, some of which had already begun to write about the conference in advance. So it was hardly surprising that a considerable number of journalists had shown up from near and far.

Shortly before 11 o'clock, the Senate chaplain, Dr Edward Hale, rose and said a short blessing, after which the assembly prayed together. Then there was a brief, expectant silence, until a trumpet fanfare resounded through the room at exactly 11 o'clock, as the president strode in and walked to the podium. The governors now stood up and applauded, and there were supportive shouts. The whole assembly then stood up, and the scene became almost tumultuous until the president succeeded in quietening people down so he could begin his speech.[218]

The US was still a young nation, he explained, and the country's mentality was characterized by the many years during which men could simply wander further west and find new land and resources. He warned that now the country was about to be filled up, and the resources might swiftly run out. "We began with an unapproached heritage of forests; more than half of the timber is gone,", he said. "We began with coal fields more extensive than those of any other nation and with iron ores regarded as inexhaustible, and many experts now declare that the end of both iron and coal is in sight." He added: "The mere increase in our consumption of coal during 1907 over 1906 exceeded the total consumption in 1876, the Centennial year." So coal consumption was completely unsustainable, and it was even worse with gas and oil. As Roosevelt said: "The enormous stores of mineral oil and gas are largely gone."

Soil quality also worried him: "We began with soils of unexampled fertility, and we have so impoverished them by injudicious use and by failing to check erosion that their crop-producing power is diminishing instead of increasing" he said.

His message seemed to hit home this time, as he was interrupted by applause no less than 18 times, but although the subject matter was deadly serious, he also managed to elicit smiles and laughter among audience members. "That is like providing for the farmer's family to live sumptuously on the flesh of the milk cow", he said at one point, after which he was interrupted by laughter. "Any farmer can live pretty well for a year if he is content not to live at all the year after." That brought even more mirth, followed by lengthy applause.

All in all, Roosevelt's talk lasted some 50 minutes, and if you they had not known it beforehand, it should be clear to everyone afterwards that the US was running out of water, timber, metals, coal, oil, gas and good soil – a disaster was approaching, and soon.

Everyone embraced the message, and journalists opined afterwards that it had been one of the most important initiatives in Roosevelt's political career. The industrialists agreed with the message too. For example, industry magnate Andrew Carnegie commented after the conference: "By 1938, about half the original supply of iron will be gone, and only the lower grades of ore will remain, and all the ore now deemed workable will be used long before the end of the present century."[219]

You can only have sympathy for Roosevelt's concerns, and doubtless something good came out of his initiative. But neither he, nor his technical experts, nor Carnegie got any of their predictions even remotely right. Instead, the US production of energy, iron, timber and food continued to accelerate after the speech was made, and that increase has never slowed. In fact, since the meeting, on several fronts, this increase is even now – more than 100 years later - accelerating. Who would have expected it?

Not many people, because we always seem to think that we are about to run out of resources. Just listen to the words of Bishop Cyprianus from Carthage, writing in the third century: "The layers of marble are dug out in less quantity from the disembowelled and wearied mountains; the diminished quantities of gold and silver suggest the early exhaustion of the metals, and the impoverished veins are straitened and decreased day by day." The depressed bishop wrote these words approximately 1,700 years before Roosevelt's conference took place.[220]

In the late Middle Ages, famine was a recurring problem in Europe, partly because of a phenomenon known as the Little Ice Age, which lasted from 1250 to 1830 (approximately), during which growing glaciers wiped out entire villages, while people held markets on the frozen waters of the River Thames in London.[221] In this chilling period, harvests often failed, leading to recurrent famine. So at that time, they really did seem to run out from time to time, as they also did when bishop Cyprianus lived and moaned.

In 1798, when the Little Ice Age was still not over, and where grain prices were increasing rapidly due to poor harvests, reverend Thomas Malthus famously wrote that population growth inevitably would lead to eventual global famine. Population growth was exponential, he pointed out, while growth in food production, in the best case, was linear. To solve this problem, he proposed to exterminate the poor in the most practical way, which he described as follows:

"Instead of recommending cleanliness to the poor, we should encourage contrary habits. In our towns we should make the streets narrower, crowd more people into the houses, and court the return of the plague. In the country, we should build our villages near stagnant pools, and particularly encourage settlements in all marshy and unwholesome situations. But above all, we should reprobate specific remedies for ravaging diseases; and those benevolent, but much mistaken men, who have thought they were doing a service to mankind by projecting schemes for the total extirpation of particular disorders." [222]

Harsh words from a reverend's mouth, because few priests would recommend killing the poor. However, as the Mini Ice Age began to retreat from approximately the year 1830, the harvests improved, but attention turned to coal. In 1865, the economist William Stanley Jevons predicted that Britain was on the verge of running out of coal, which would grind the entire country's industry to a halt.[223] The following year, this evolved into a full-fledged coal panic, which led the then finance minister, William Gladstone, to promise to repay Britain's foreign debt quickly, while the country still had some coal left.

In 1926 - 18 years after Roosevelt's speech - the US Federal Oil Conservation Board announced, to great public concern, that the country only had enough oil for another seven years.

However, when these seven years had passed, there was still oil. Two years after it should have run out, the US Department of State issued another report which predicted (as they clearly hadn't learned from the past) that the US would run out of oil within 13 years – that is, in 1948.

There was still oil in 1948, but in this year the American conservationist Fairfield Osborn published a book called *Our Plundered Planet*, in which he predicted imminent acute resource shortages and famine.[224] That same year, ecologist and ornithologist William Vogt published *Our Road to Survival*, in which he warned about the lack of farmland and minerals, which would force the US to go to war to gain access to zinc.[225] Luckily they didn't do this, but on September 15 - again in 1948 – you could read an article in New York Times describing "the dark outlook for the human race" because of "overpopulation and dwindling of natural resources."

In 1951 – three years after the US should, yet again, have run out of oil - the US Department of State predicted the supply would run out in 1964, 13 years later. There was still oil in 1964, but, at that point, a new forecast was issued, according to which the oil would run out... within 13 years. So, by 1977 there should have been no more oil.

No, really, the end of oil was very near, and gas was also a problem. In 1974 the US. Geological Survey (USGS) issued an analysis, which indicated that "by 1974 technology and the 1974 Prize", the US had only enough gas for another ten years, so it should run out by 1984 unless something surprising came up. The following year, The Environment Fund took out full-page adverts in several magazines in which they wrote: "The world as we know it will be destroyed in 2000."

Although all previous predictions of impending shortages of raw materials had been found to be incorrect, the fear of running out developed into veritable panic from the mid-1960s and early 1970s, at which point US president Jimmy Carter joined the fray and stated that there was a great risk that they would run out of oil within ten years.

One of the driving forces behind this never-ending resource panic was the biologist Paul Ehrlich, who must be one of the worst public forecasters of all time. In 1968, he published the book *The Population Bomb*, in which he wrote that the population explosion would be stopped by a combination of disease, war and famine.[226] "I don't see how India could possibly feed two hundred million more people by 1980", was one of his many odd forecasts. But he was wrong, because there are more than 1.2 billion people living in India today. The very first sentence in the forword, written by environmentalist David Brower, sounded: "The battle to feed humanity is over. In the 1970s and 1980s hundreds of millions of people will starve to death in spite of any crash program embarked on now." And on page 3, Paul Erlich elaborated "a minimum of ten million people, most of them children, will starve to death during each year of the 1970s. But this is a mere handful compared to the numbers that will be starving before the end of the century. And it is now too late to take action to save many of those people."

As for the US, he provided in an article a scenario of what it would be like in year 2000: 65 million Americans would have starved to death between 1980 and 2000, and the population would have fallen to 22.6 million due to resource shortage and pollution (In actual fact, the population increased to 273 million, and there was no famine, but significant problems with obesity).[227] Later in the same article he predicted four billion deaths globally due to famine within the 20 years.

Ehrlich had many other Domesday predictions. As for England, he wrote: "I would take even money that England will not exist in the year 2000." Good for him that he didn't, because in year 2000, England's population and gross domestic product had both reached all times highs.

But lots of people really believed what he and other doomsday preachers predicted, and the resource panics came, wave after wave. In 1968, William and Paul Paddock published their bestseller *Famine 1975!*, in which they predicted confidently that there would be global famine in 1975, where basically only the US would have surplus food.[228] The US should, then, ideally only distribute food to nations that imposed harsh birth control; people in other nations should be left to starve. Denis Hayes, who was the leader of the first environmental protection event, Earth Day, had a similar view. "It is already too late to avoid mass starvation," he said in 1970. The world was doomed. Billions would die!

By contrast, the world's average life expectancy has increased by approximately ten years since Ehrlich and others came with their doomsday predictions, and the proportion of people who are undernourished has fallen from around 30% in 1970 to 10% today - all this, despite the fact that the world's population has, simultaneousy roughly doubled. In fact, we have increased the daily caloric intake per capita in developing countries from an average of 2,054 in 1964-66 to an estimated 2,850 in 2015.[229] This is an increase in average (per person) food consumption among the poor of almost 39% over a period during which the world population doubled.

It is no less impressive when you consider that, in the US - where Ehrlich and others had predicted famine - a growing percentage of the farmland was no longer used to produce food, but instead to produce biofuels. In the EU - one of the world's most densely-populated regions – authorities struggled with the so-called butter mountains and wine lakes, where excess production piled up; the EU even paid farmers to stop farming and local governments introduced campaigns to counteract the growing trend of obesity.

As regards Paul Ehrlich's forecast of more than a hundred million starvation deaths in the 1970s, the actual figure was around 3.5 to 4 million, of which around half were due to the Khmer Rouge's genocidal policies in Cambodia during the period 1975-1979.

Later, in the 1980s, it is estimated that between 1.22 and 1.63 million people died of starvation worldwide, and in 1990s, the number was approximately 400,000-600,000, if you exclude North Korea, where 2.8 to 3.5 million people died (but again not due to lack of soil but because of Marxist policies). In comparison, between 30 million and 33 million people died in China between 1958 and 1962 due to forced collectivisations in agriculture – yet again not because lack of natural resources, but due to Marxism.[230] So the number of famines has declined significantly since Ehrlich and others made their doomsday predictions, and they would have fallen even faster, had it not been for the harmful politics of China, North Korea, Cambodia and elsewhere.

Perhaps the worst thing about all this is not the irrational fear and pessimism that the Domesday forecasters made roused in people, but the mentality that Ehrlich and others displayed; a world view that has since been described as anti-humanism, and which is still very much alive, if not increasing. These views are following directly in Malthus' tracks and have often come unpleasantly close to what various dictators have expressed, not too long ago. Paul Ehrlich described, for example, the planet's growing population as a "cancer" (exactly the same term that Hitler often used about the Jews), and explained what needed to be done about it:

"We must shift our efforts from the treatment of the symptoms to the cutting out of the cancer. The operation will demand many apparently brutal and heartless decisions. The pain may be intense. But the disease is so far advanced that only with radical surgery does the patient have a chance of survival." [231]

Among his suggestions were mandatory sterilization and forced abortions. This message was exceedingly popular, and *The Population Bomb* sold more than three million copies, while Ehrlich probably became the only author ever to be interviewed for the a full hour of US television programme *The Tonight Show*.

Six years after this book's publication, he wrote another publication with his wife, *The End of Affluence*, where he predicted that "before 1985, mankind will enter an era of real shortage", where "available resources of many key minerals will be close to being exhausted."

This had now become a widespread opinion in much of academia and the general public. On 4 May 1969 the Nobel laureate George Wald made a speech at MIT, during which he said:

"There is every indication that the world population will double before the year 2000; and there is a widespread expectation of famine on an unprecedented scale in many parts of the world. The experts tend to differ only in their estimates of when those famines will begin. Some think by 1980, others think they can be staved off until 1990, very few expect that they will not occur by the year 2000."[232]

This speech was later reprinted in numerous newspapers and Canadian newspaper *The Globe* published it in 87,000 copies. In 1970, Harrison Brown, a member of the US National Academy of Sciences, predicted in an article in *Scientific American*, that the world would run out of lead, zinc, tin, gold and silver in 1990. The same year (1970) aforementioned Earth Day founder Denis Hayes told the magazine *Living Wilderness* that "civilization will end within 15 or 30 years unless immediate action is taken against problems facing mankind."

One could go on and on, but let's just add Lester Brown of environmental research group Worldwatch Institute. In his book *The Skeptical Environmentalist*, statistician Bjørn Lomborg explains how Brown, incessantly, throughout his a life-long career, has made similar, if not almost identical, "doom sermons" about how we will soon have acute shortages of this and that. As one example among countless, Brown predicted, in 1981, that the world's available oil reserves would very soon be gone: "Yet, most of the readily accessible reserves of oil formed over hundreds of millions of years will be consumed within a single generation, spanning the years from 1960 to 1995."[233]

The message was clear: Western civilization and relentless technological development and economic growth was a Domesday machine, which should immediately be halted. In 1971, journalist Gordon Taylor launched his book *The Doomsday Book*, where he extrapolated, from the fact that the US used half of all the world's resources, that in 2000 the US would use all global resources, unless it was stopped by the world!

The following year saw the publication of aforementioned book *Limits to Growth*, based on an extensive computer analysis from MIT, which showed that the world would run out of gold in 1983, silver and mercury in 1987, tin in 1989, zinc in 1992, lead and copper in 1995 and aluminium in 2005. Somewhat comfortingly, the book contained an alternative forecast, which was far more optimistic as it assumed that reserves of limited resources were five times larger than in the worst case. If this was true, we would have enough metals for a few decades longer. This book also became a global bestseller as it was translated into 30 languages and sold 12 million copies.

The whole problem could actually be summed up simply, and none made it simpler than Paul Ehrlich, who launched the so-called "IPAT equation" to explain it. It read as follows:

$$I = P \times A \times T$$

"I" stood for the impact, "P" for population, "A" for affluence and "T" for technology. It meant this: the more people there were, and the more technology and wealth they produced, the worse the impact on the environment and resources would be. Therefore, we should enforce a reduction of the world population and living standards for the protection of the environment and resources, and we should limit the use of new technologies. The creative society should be put on hold, for it was simply too dangerous.

Of course, all these Doomsday sermons were not unopposed. For instance, after USGS's dramatic analysis in 1974 predicting that the US would have enough natural gas for only a further ten years, the American Gas Association issued a rebuttal, claiming that it had sufficient resources for between 1,000 and 2,500 years of consumption.[234]

And then there was Julian Simon, an economist with a Doctorate from the University of Chicago, who had specialized in population growth, economic development and resources. Just like most of his peers, Simon had been, in his younger days, concerned about the increasing world overpopulation, but he had then come across studies which showed, first, that commodity prices had fallen in absolute or inflation-adjusted terms for hundreds of years and, second, that the most densely-populated countries often did best economically.[235]

This discovery had made him think and had caused him to trawl through countless other statistics on population and resources, and these had constantly confirmed the same astonishing picture of, yes, increasing resource abundance. How odd was that?

Very strange, but numbers are numbers, and over time, he came to the conclusion that the ultimate resources on the globe weren't any particular raw materials, but simply human creativity. And this explained why densely-populated areas often grew richest: the greater the number of people living close together in an area, the higher the number of ideas they would come up with, by combining their thoughts.

Most people would credit at least part of this theory. But Simon's views differed from the majority in that he claimed that our creativity is so great, mankind, given a dynamic economic system, will never suffer from lack of resources.

Never? Many couldn't agree on that and Ehrlich was obviously one of them. It wasn't long before there was an ongoing debate between Simon and Ehrlich, which eventually attracted wider attention. After all, it was an entertaining story, because here you had two professors, peers, who funnily enough, had both grown up in a suburb of Newark, New Jersey, and were both ready to argue their case loudly, even though Ehrlich always refused Simon's offer to meet and discuss the subject directly in public; the debate took place through articles.[236] The two combatants had, in particular, a sharp exchange of views via articles in the journal Social Science Quarterly, and in September 1980, Simon took it to a new level, as he challenged anyone to a bet:

"I'll put my money where my mouth is. This is a public offer to stake $10,000, in separate transactions of $1,000 or $100 each, on my belief that the cost of non-government-controlled raw materials (including grain and oil) will not rise in the long run. If you will pay me the current market price of $1000 or $100 worth of any standard mineral or other extractive product you name, and specify any date more than a year away, I will contract to pay you the then-current market price of the material. How about it, doomsayers and catastrophists? First come, first served." [237]

Ehrlich announced, almost immediately, that he would "accept Simon's astonishing offer before other greedy people jump in". He now formed a consortium with two resource experts from the University of California at Berkeley, and, together, they selected those five commodities, which they believed would rise very much in price: chromium, copper, nickel, tin and tungsten.

However, over the next ten years, the price of these five metals didn't rise. In fact, they all fell dramatically, despite the world population increasing more than ever, and that the cumulative inflation for the same period being 50%. At the end of the period, Ehrlich had to send a cheque to Simon for $576.07.

One of the important tasks of a scientist who makes predictions is to compare these with the actual statistical outcome. You will typically undertake "back-testing", i.e. check if your model could have predicted the past accurately. And, of course, as time passes, you pay attention to whether what you predicted actually comes true. If models and reality do not match, you must change your models. However, none of this seems to happen among the doomsayers who constantly, year in and year out, make the same kind of failed forecasts about coming resource shortages. Apparently, they find the logic of their models so obvious, that there is no need to examine the actual facts.

But as we have seen, such models are clearly making systematic errors, so what is it really going on here? How, for example, could the prices of all five metals in the Simon and Ehrlich bet, fall in a time of high inflation, economic growth and population growth? In fact, the same five metals actually declined in terms of inflation-adjusted prices over the 100 years from 1900 to 2000?[238] So again: how come?

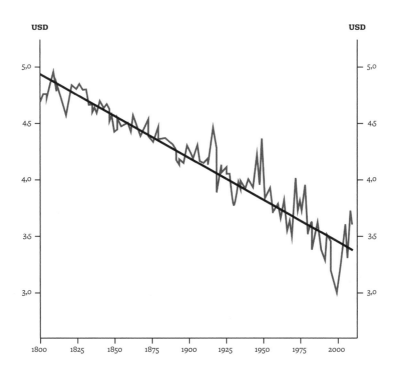

INDUSTRIAL COMMODITY PRICES; 1800 TO 2014, ADJUSTED FOR US INFLATION. THE LONG TERM TREND FOR INDUSTRIAL COMMODITIES CORRECTED FOR INFLATION HAS BEEN DOWN FOR SEVERAL HUNDRED YEARS IN SPITE OF REPEATED WARNINGS OF SHORTAGE THROUGHOUT THE PERIOD.

Let's start with the concept of reserves. One might easily assume this means the available amount of material. It doesn't; it is the quantity that can be extracted profitably at current prices given the current technology. So, if technology improves, or if prices increase, so do the reserves.

If people misread the concept of reserves, they may also completely misjudge the size of mineral resources that are actually available. Wilfred Beckerman, a leading commodity economics expert from Cambridge University and the University of London, explains it like this:

"At no point is it worth prospecting for enough to last to the end of eternity, or even some compromise period, such as a hundred million years, or even 1,000 years. New reserves are found, on the whole, as they are needed, and needs do not always rise exponentially at past rates. In fact, given the natural concentrations of the key metals in the Earth's crust, as indicated by a large number of random samples, the total natural occurrence of most metals in the top mile of the Earth's crust has been estimated to be about a million times as great as present known reserves. Since the latter amount to about 100

years' supplies, this means we have enough to last about one hundred million years." [239]
In other words, we have so far defined only in the region of 0.0001% of the
actual metals in the upper kilometre of the Earth's crust as reserves.

What about fossil fuels? To date, we have extracted approximately one
trillion barrels of oil, and it is estimated that there is a similar amount left in
so-called conventional oil fields, which very simply put, are fields where you
stick a tube into the ground and pump it out. Actually, the fact that we still
have so much left is quite remarkable, given all the aforementioned predictions of imminent oil depletion. However, apart from this trillion, there are
huge discoveries of other types of oil deposits in the form of shale and tar oil,
which is why known oil reserves now are massively higher than in the 1970s
or when Roosevelt addressed his conference more than 100 years ago. We
know, for instance, that US shale oil reserves alone now are higher than all
conventional oil reserves worldwide. The American Green River Formation
alone, which stretches through Colorado, Wyoming, and Utah, is assumed to
have approximately three trillion barrels (480 billion cubic metres) of shale
oil, of which $1-1.5 trillion is assumed to be recoverable. That is at least as
much as all the oil that has been consumed, worldwide, over the past 200
years in that formation alone.

It does not end there. After 2000, giant gas fields in the shale oil deposits
have been discovered in many places, and due to new so-called fracking technology, much of this is now commercial reserves. Even before this technique
was developed, the world's natural gas reserves had increased steadily, but
global reserves had in 2014 reached approximately 250 years of consumption
and were still climbing. [240] And while they should continue to do so for a long
time, scientists are beginning to investigate methods for extracting methane
hydrate, a flammable hydrocarbon that is believed to be two to ten times as
prevalent as natural gas, so that it could potentially extend to centuries or
millennia of consumption.

Now, of course there is the issue of global warming (we will address that
later), so we shall have to stop burning fossil fuels before too long. However,
many other sources and technologies are evolving rapidly.

One of these areas is biofuels. The so-called first generation of this is only
profitable in limited areas such as parts of Brazil, but the second generation
is potentially two to three times more efficient because it will use not only
plant sugars, but also their cellulose, hemicelluloses and lignin, which make
up a much larger proportion of the biomass. However, perhaps this stage will
be largely bypassed to focus instead on third generation biofuels, which is
produced in water tanks with genetically modified algae. These will extract
CO_2 from the air and convert it into oil. This requires very high capital in-

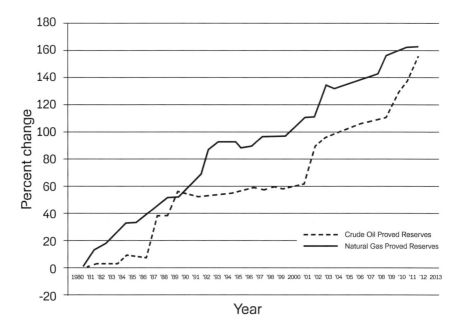

CHANGE IN PROVED OIL AND NATURAL GAS RESERVES 1980 – 2013 [241]

vestments but give yields per land unit that are 15-300 times higher than for first-generation biofuels.[242]

Other interesting energy technologies include so-called photovoltaic solar panels, which generate electric power from sunshine. Due to new technologies and price wars, these have reached so-called grid parity in many sunny areas (grid parity is reached when the electricity costs the same as if produced locally by conventional sources such as coal).

There is also growth and development in geothermal energy, where fluid is pumped into the ground and back via closed pipes, whereby it can be used for heating purposes. This is already competitive in areas with especially warm underground, but can be further developed into much larger installations elsewhere. In Switzerland and Sweden, approximately 75% of all new houses use geothermal energy.

Other technologies are focused on energy savings. For instance, cars have become far more efficient due to combinations of cylinder deactivations, cruise control, turbo-charging, hybrid technology and the use of lightweight materials such as aluminium, titanium, ceramics and carbon fibre. Similarly, the new light bulbs (diodes) are often eight to ten times as energy-efficient as the ones they replace. Aircraft have also become more efficient.

According to Airbus, global air traffic increased by 45% between 2000 and 2010, while their total fuel consumption increased by only 3% due to improved fuel efficiency. [243]

And then there is nuclear power which could (and probably will) become the ultimate energy source. In 2012, there were about 440 nuclear reactors around the world, which together supplied some 7% of total world energy use and 17% of the electric power. A significant portion of the fuel used came from the recycling of fuel in the Russian nuclear bombs in disarmament agreements.

Nuclear power is a compact technology, since a kilogram of uranium delivers as much energy as two to three million kilograms of coal.[244]

Most nuclear systems in use today belong to the second generation of reactors, and they are typically individually designed, which has made them very expensive. However, a number of new designs have been developed, including pebble bed technology. Such reactors are based on placing heat-generating uranium balls into a large tank from which they are tapped out from the bottom when worn, in the same way that gumball machines work. Helium, which cannot become radioactive, is circulated between these balls (we will look at the problem of waste in a later chapter). With this technology, one obtains an endless and continuous process, which is cheap to run and where meltdowns are impossible.[245]

Given current technologies and resources, we have enough uranium for about 280 years of consumption, but if we re-use the waste, resources stretch to several thousand years, and if we further extracted uranium from seawater, it could stretch for several hundred thousand years. That is longer than the human race has existed.

So uranium is a huge source of energy that can be made much safer, and a number of new technologies for its use are in the pipeline or testing phases. An example is the company Terra Power, which is financially supported by Bill Gates and Nathan Myhrvold, who are, respectively, cofounder and former chief technology officer of Microsoft. This company is working on "travelling wave" technology which, through transmutation, may be able to utilize much of the remaining energy in nuclear waste (currently, approximately 99% of the energy potential is typically wasted). Making a transmutation means transforming one element into another, like medieval alchemists dreamed of doing.

With travelling wave you would, to state it very simply, place nuclear waste in a tube that may stick into the ground. Then it may gradually degrade itself from one end to the other in a process that should take at least 40 years, and it would release the remaining 98-99 % of its energy potential in the process. If this worked, it could deliver the entire world's energy supply for 16,000 years with the current global energy consumption based alone on the current waste.

Nuclear power gets better still, though, because one kilogram of thorium has the same practical energy potential as 200 kilograms of uranium (without using travelling wave or breeder technology). It also has the same energy potential as 400-600 million kilograms of coal, and a modern man's total lifetime supply of energy for all purposes could be accommodated in a thorium ball the size of a golf ball, which, in mass production, would not cost more than a few dollars – perhaps $2.

Thorium itself is not radioactive and is a common metal alloy – you prepare it for nuclear power use by bombarding it with neutrinos. It is very clean: thorium only creates 1% to less than 0.1% of the nuclear waste components you currently get from similar power generation with uranium – and this waste could be transmutated. If it isn't, it would be largely harmless after approximately 300 years.

Unlike conventional uranium reactors, thorium reactors work without high pressure and are technically unable to explode or melt down, if you use a molten, liquid salt configuration. If one cuts off the power to such a thorium reactor, the process just stops by itself. And because the process is relatively safe and simple, the thorium reactors can be made very compact and installed in ships, trains and even rockets - where a nuclear thermal rocket might, in principle, accelerate to up to perhaps 20% of the speed of light (that equates to travelling around the Earth in less than one second). However, the obvious first use is to replace coal-burning chambers in coal-based powers stations with thorium reactors. There is currently ongoing work on thorium reactors being undertaken in Norway, China, U.S., Israel, Russia and especially India.

So how big is the energy potential from this? With molten, liquid salt configuration thorium reactor technology, we have potentially enough thorium to supply the world with energy for several hundred thousand years.[246]

Nuclear power based on uranium or thorium are both based on nuclear fission, which means splitting atoms. However, the ultimate alternative is to create nuclear fusion. Potentially, the most effective forms of fuel for this are deuterium and tritium. The fusion happens if you can slam atoms together with such a force that their cores merge. This requires either extreme heat or a massive compression (or both, as in the centre of the sun, where it happens), and it releases vast quantities of energy.

For many years, scientists have been working to create and sustain this, but progress here has been painfully slow. However, in recent years, there have been significant achievements in many places. One such is in the National Ignition Facility in California, and there is ongoing work to create the 30-metre-high, internationally-funded ITER reactor in France. In parallel with that, many of US's brightest venture capitalists and others, including Paul Allen (co-founder of Microsoft) and Jeff Bezos (founder of Amazon) plus banking group Goldman Sachs, have invested in alternative projects that seek to achieve nuclear fusion with much simpler, smaller machines. Companies involved include Focus Fusion, General Fusion, Polywell, LENR, Lawrenceville Plasma Physics and Tri Alpha Energy.

Larger companies are also on the task, and one of the newer initiatives by aerospace giant Lockheed Martin is called High Beta Fusion Project. Its hope is to develop mass-produced reactors with dimensions of approximately 2*2*4 metres that can be installed almost anywhere.

If any of this works (obviously still a big "if"), what is the size of our reserves? A study in 2001 concluded that only the known mine-based lithium reserves could provide the Earth with nuclear power for approx. 3,000 years, and lithium from sea water for 60 million years (yes, million). That is approx. 300 times as long as humans have existed. If you went a step further and used deuterium from sea water, there would be enough to supply the world with energy for 150 billion years - ten times as long as the universe has existed.[247] So if that works, we're done, and sooner or later it should work, since it doesn't violate the laws of physics (the sun does it).

And it will be vastly cleaner and safer than any existing energy technology today, including wind turbines and solar panels. The waste products will only be quite small quantities of helium, which cannot become radioactive and which can be sold commercially for industrial use or even to fill up gas balloons for children's parties. Even the core shield may be harmless once a reactor is decommissioned, if it is made of carbon fibre. In addition, a fusion reactor will automatically come to a halt if, for example, you disconnect its power supply. It would be similar to when you stop the power supply to a car engine: it doesn't explode, it just stops, and there is no waste that can leak out.

Given access to such infinite, cheap and clean power, we would readily make artificial liquid fuel by combining atmospheric CO_2 with hydrogen over the catalysts of copper and zinc or in some other synthetic way. The result would be methanol, which burns cleanly and does not alter the atmospheric CO_2 content. Of course, we wouldn't have much need of that as everyone could drive electric cars, but internal combustion machines do sound good in sports cars, and life should be fun.

As mentioned, in the distant past, humans suffered frequently from acute lack of resources, and we have, for example, seen that many of the Roman colonies constantly hovered on the edge of starvation.

In the West, scarcity is now completely over and in 2015, farmers amounted to approximately 1% of the British population, 2% of the US population and 3% of the French population; the US and France were, in fact, net food exporters. If it wasn't for farm subsidies to keep farmers afloat in mountain areas, for example, 2% of the population of Western civilization could easily feed all its citizens.[248] The reason for this is simply the West's fast-paced creativity.

So here is the basic mechanism which the catastrophists and panic mongers do not understand: in a dynamic society we will, on average, develop or find new resources faster than we use them, and eventually we will approach solutions without practical limitations. The methods we use are mainly combinations of efficiency, recycling, compression, substitution, digitization, virtualization, biological cultivation, synthesizing and sharing, as shown in the box below.

WHY WE DON'T RUN OUT OF RESOURCES

The resource paradoxes happen primarily because of the following nine processes:

- Efficiency: As technologies mature, they become more efficient at all levels, as demonstrated in cars, planes and houses. Likewise, we get better at searching for resources.
- Recycling: As societies become richer, their recycling of many resources approaches 100%. For example, the e-commerce site (and recycling service) eBay had, by early 2012, sold more than 170 million items consumer-to-consumer, representing close to one item every two seconds since its inception.
- Compression: We learn to make the same products with less and less input of critical raw materials, whether for the structure of the product or for its operation. A good example is mobile phones which initially weighed 25 kilograms, but today weign closer to 100 grams. Correspondingly, factories, machinery and agriculture become increasingly compact. For instance, modern efficient farming may use 20% of the land previously needed to produce the same amount of food and we are now launching modern satellites that weigh down to a kilo or less. Some ("sprites") are even the size of stamps and build entirely of standard parts that cost $25 in total per satellite.[249]
- Substitution: We replace one commodity for another that is better, cheaper, or can be synthesized without end. One example is the use of carbon fibre rather than metal for many purposes. It should be mentioned here that a quarter of the Earth's crust consists of silicon, which is a semi-metal and which, like carbon fibre, could be used to provide many of the features that today we are doing with traditional metals. The reason that we do not, is that it is not necessary.

- Digitization: Sooner or later, many products and production methods become information technologies. Productivity increases within information technology is often significantly faster than analogue technologies. For example, the use of gene-splicing for genetic evolution of plants is much faster than improvement through selective breeding based on random mutations.

- Virtualization: Technology often makes it possible to reduce or eliminate the need for physical products. For instance, cloud computing servers in countless homes and businesses eliminate the need for local servers, and internet commerce eliminates physical stores. Smartphones can replace alarm clocks, calculators, compasses, cameras, radios and remote controls. Other technologies eliminate objects such as coins and credit cards, CDs, printed catalogues and directories. Email replaces physical letters, and video conferencing reduces the need for face-to-face meetings.

- Biological cultivation: Instead of extracting commodities from nature, we begin to cultivate them, such as when we switched from hunting to animal husbandry in agriculture or from extracting insulin from cow's stomachs to making artificial insulin with genes spliced into micro-organisms. Similarly, more than half of all fish for human consumption have come from fish farms since 2013.

- Synthesizing: We learn to create materials completely synthetically; for example, making artificial diamonds by compressing gas and artificial brains (computers).

- Sharing: We use online services to share houses (Airbnb), cars (uber), computers (cloud services), tools, bicycles, home appliances and much more.

The observation that we gain more resources as we use more could be called the resource paradox. Obviously, this phenomenon is as counter-intuitive as anything can be, and this is probably why countless thinkers and laymen consistently ignored or denied it for centuries, even though the statistics are clear. It is one of the most radical implications of Western creativity, and few have described it as well as the American economist and politician Henry George, as he explained the reason for the increasing abundance of food in the US:

"There is more food, simply because there are more men. Here is a difference between the animal and the man. Both the jay-hawk and the man eat chickens, but the more jay-hawks the fewer chickens, while the more men the more chickens." [250]

The remarkable point about this quote is that it is from 1879, which is 29 years before Roosevelt held his conference about dwindlng resources, and almost 100 years before the great panic over resources during the 1970s. His message was just ignored, and it largely still is.

But this quotation brings us back to the issue of food, which concerned Paul Erlich and others so much. Between 1970 and 2010, 80% of the growth in farm production came from productivity increases and only 20% from the cultivation of new land. If we take a longer perspective, the world population increased approximately 400% from 1900 to 2000, and its agricultural production increased by 600%, while agricultural land use increased only by approximately 30% , which meant that farm productivity grew approximately five times, why the inflation-adjusted food prices decreased by 90%.[251] This productivity growth in agriculture came from a wide range of creative ideas, including the so-called Green Revolution, launched by American biologist, humanitarian and Nobel laureate Norman Borlaug, which included more efficient watering, fertilizing and spraying.[252]

One of the main effects, however, came from the development of new crop varieties. An example: Since 1901, the Japanese sprayed plants with a bacterium called Bacillus thuringiensis that kept larvae and insects away. This worked because when these bacteria entered the insects' stomachs, they made crystals that cut holes in their intestines and killed them. But they could only do it in the stomach with alkaline liquid (which insects have), so they were completely harmless to other species which had acidic stomach contents (non-insects). This technology is now widely-used in organic farming worldwide, but it has the disadvantage that some of the spray can get carried by the wind to areas outside the farms, where it causes unintentional killing of butterflies and other insects.

To solve this problem, and to boost efficiency, scientists have incorporated a small part of the responsible bacterial genes into plant DNA, so that these could protect themselves without being sprayed by the pesticides. This was attractive, since about 40% of global agricultural production is lost to weeds and pests – the environmental and economic benefits of reducing this loss are enormous.[253]

Later, another idea was generated. In the 1970s, US company Monsanto developed a herbicide named Roundup, which destroyed all the plants and then very quickly decomposed. They now developed modified plants that could tolerate Roundup, and the result of these "Roundup Ready" plants was that farmers no longer needed to plough or spray as often. For instance, trials in Mississippi and Alabama showed that farmers using such crops could go from an average of spraying eight times a season to only one and half times.

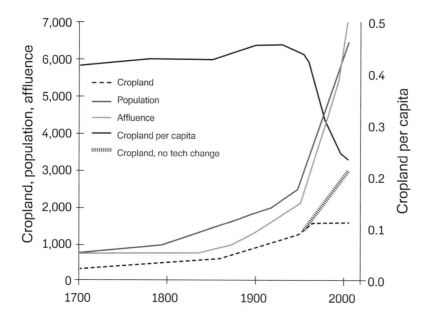

GOKLANY, I.M.: HAVE INCREASES IN POPULATION, AFFLUENCE AND TECHNOLOGY WORSENED HUMAN AND ENVIRONMENTAL WELL-BEING? THE ELECTRONIC JOURNAL OF SUSTAINABLE DEVELOPMENT, VOLUME 1, ISSUE 3, SUMMER 2009

GLOBAL CROPLAND AND CROPLAND PER CAPITA, 1700-2005. AS THE ILLUSTRATION SHOWS, SINCE THE GREEN REVOLUTION AND THE INTRODUCTION OF GM CROPS, WE HAVE KEPT TOTAL FARMLAND ROUGHLY UNCHANGED IN SPITE OF A RAPIDLY GROWING POPULATION. THIS CORRESPONDS WITH APPROXIMATELY HALVING OF THE CROPLAND PER CAPITA.

The result was less energy use, less need for agricultural land, less soil erosion and less need for spraying with herbicides.[254]

Technological developments in agriculture continue unabated, and while, in 1996, just 1.7 million hectares of agricultural land had GM (genetically modified) crops, by 2010 this number had grown to 147 million hectares. For the same reason, well over two trillion meals based on GM crops have been served, without any indication of adverse health effects.[255] If anything, it is the other way around; GM food can be healthier, as it may be deliberately enhanced with more vitamins or minerals and have fewer natural toxins.

A good example of how quickly progress can be made can be seen in US corn production. Since World War II, the average yield per hectare has increased by 400%. This trend is expected to continue, and one of the new contributing technologies is machines for what is known as seed chipping. This technology enables seed producers to take DNA samples from each seed without destroying its ability to grow. Each of these machines can undertake one DNA test per second or more. Based on this technology, the producers maintain a database of the seeds with various genetic traits, and each customer can now order seeds that will satisfy the most relevant requirements for local conditions.

Genetically modified plants may require less water, fertilizer and pesticides, be more resistant to wind and endure more rain, frost or salt water in the soil they grow in, and they may grow faster, become bigger and often be substantially healthier. An example of the latter is ongoing attempts to make a variant of the cassava fruit, which contains more protein, iron and zinc as well as vitamins A and E. In addition, an effort is being made to remove the poison cyanide from it, which it produces. Finally, the aim is to make these plants resistant to certain infections, so that they keep for two weeks after being harvested, rather than just for a single day, which is not long enough to take them to market and sell them. Such a project has the potential to make a huge economic and nutritional difference to some 250 million people in poverty.

Another example of healthier crops is the rice variety known as "golden rice", which was originally developed by two Swiss scientists. In contrast to conventional rice, this provides significant amounts of beta-carotene (which turns into vitamin A upon digestion), because it has incorporated a gene from maize that creates beta-carotene. It is estimated that using it could save up to two million lives annually in developing countries and it could prevent 250,000 to 500,000 new cases of chronic blindness and millions of annual cases of Xerophthalmia. Overall, it could mean a significant improvement in the lives of 200 million people in developing countries and also help them to find a way out of general poverty.

To help such people, scientists are also working to develop plants that immunize children against herpes, hepatitis, severe diarrhoea and even cystic fibrosis. These diseases (especially diarrhoea) kill up to four million people a year in developing countries, mainly children.

While bearing all this in mind, consider what is happening to the world population. The global population growth rate peaked in 1963 and has declined ever since. The world population grew 20% from 1970 to 1980, then 19% until 1990, 15% from 1990 to 2000 and 14% from 2000 to 2010. The UN expects it to grow 11%, 8%, 6%, and 4% respectively over the following decades and we may go below replacement fertility between 2020 and 2025 or at least before 2030, which would signal a coming population decline. And yet, as this happens, we have the tools to accelerate the productivity growth in farming due to significant breakthroughs in genetic engineering since 2000. For example, due to the the Monsanto seed chipping technology, the company expects to be able to accelerate productivity increases in corn fields by approximately 3.5% per year, equivalent to more than 40% per decade.[256] This means we have the means of decreasing substantially the amount of farmland required, so that we can, instead, create natural parks.

All this comes about, quite clearly, because we live in a creative society; a society that often comes up with extremely elegant solutions to our problems.

And although we cannot always describe exactly how the solutions of the future will work in practice, our experience, so far, tells us very clearly that as long as we believe in creativity and experimentation, there will be new technologies again and again, and many of them will surprise us completely.

That's all very well, but what about water? We cannot produce water via genetic engineering, can we?

Perhaps we could, but it would hardly make sense, because the issue with water is not that we lack it or are running out in the strictest sense, since it is not a chemical that is broken down by application. But many countries are experiencing problems such as declining water tables or groundwater contamination or drying rivers due to contamination, and others simply have too little water easily available. Farming, for instance, often requires approximately 1,000 litres of water to produce just one kilo of food.

Consequently, there have been, for decades, forecasts of future catastrophic water shortages or even "water wars". The astonishing fact about this is that access to clean water has actually been improving constantly, as we have become richer. By 1970, only about 30% of the population in developing countries had access to clean water, but despite the large intermediate population growth, this number had been increased to nearer 80% in 2010.[257] Obviously this does not imply that everything now is ideal, since nearly 900 million people still lack adequate access to clean water, so the problem is there, it is big and, in China, its very big. But while many people continue to predict that the issue will grow even more problematic, it actually continues to get ever-smaller.

Let's consider some figures. The average daily rainfall in the world is equal to approximately 40,000 litres per capita.[258] Typically, you can expect people to need about 100 litres of clean water every day to use as drinking water and for washing and personal hygiene. And yet only 8% of the world's water consumption is down to personal use. Almost three times as much - approximately 22% - is used for industrial purposes, and 70% for agriculture. If we add up all of this, we need about 2,000 litres per person, per day.

In practice, this is obtained by a combination of pumping up groundwater, draining from lakes and rivers, collecting rain water from roofs and so on. In more and more cases you would also use desalination of sea water, which costs $0.045 to $1 per 1000 litre, or from another perspective, filling up a pool of, say, 10*5*2 metres would cost $4.5 – $100.

Other solutions are focused on reducing water use, for instance with computer-controlled drip irrigation and genetically-modified plants that are better at utilizing and holding water. A large part of the solution is simply to place more farming where there is an abundance of water, and that is precisely what the Chinese and others do by buying and renting farmland in Africa - it can be easier to transport food than to transport the water needed for its production.

However, one of the ultimate technologies to alleviate the shortage of water is what is used in Singapore, Namibia, San Diego and Fairfax, Virginia, and, for that matter, in spaceships. It is what was, in its early days, called toilet-to-tap technology, which involves filtering and reusing all wastewater - including from lavatories - so that it can be reused indefinitely. It doesn't sound too appetizing, but this water is actually cleaner than the purest bottled mineral water.

As Singapore illustrates so well, the solution to water shortages always comes down to money, and anyone can check out for themselves by visiting Dubai. This desert city has almost no natural fresh water, but today it has not only thousands of swimming pools, but even an indoor ski resort.

All this must not be construed as meaning that the necessary resources will come automatically or, for that matter, that it is an environmentally-sound idea to create a ski resort in a desert, if it is driven by gas (nuclear fusion would be another matter). But it does mean that we can achieve what we need through creative innovation.

The enthusiastic participants at Roosevelt's 1908 conference about resources were absolutely correct that we must safeguard our resources. For example, in the early 1930s, the US confronted the "dust bowl phenomenon", where strong dust storms emerged in the Midwest and parts of Canada during an exceptional drought. These were so intense that visibility could drop to one metre or less. President Franklin Roosevelt (not Theodore) then ordered the planting of more than 200 million trees from Canada to Texas to break the wind and protect the water and soil. Farmers were taught anti-erosion techniques such as contour farming, crop rotation, use of terraces and various other techniques - and thus the problem was eventually solved.

But they were not correct in assuming that the US would experience a shortage of wood. Since the conference was held, the country's annual production of timber has increased by approximately 15% and, as people now use very little firewood for heating, this has been enough to turn the country into a major net exporter of timber.[259] The US didn't run out of iron or any other metals either – its annual steel production is now seven times is big as it was then.[260]

Nor did the nation run out of coal, because the annual production from coal mines is approximately five times as great now as then. And even if it had run out of coal, the demand for power could have been fully met with gas and nuclear power. As for overall US energy production, it is now soaring, and the price of natural gas has fallen sharply due to an ever-increasing abundance. Furthermore, the US's known energy reserves are at an all-time high and still rising.

Let us, once again, take the example of the five commodities Ehrlich and his partners choose for their bet with Julian Simon: chromium, copper, nickel, tin and tungsten. Obviously they believed there would be particularly acute shortage of these, but if we look at the total quantities of them in the Earth's crust, there is actually enough for approximately 55, 15, 165, 59 and 4.14 million years of consumption.[261]

Yes, million.

However, there are many other explanations to why they lost the bet. Instead of sending signals via copper wires, for example, people started using fibre optics, based on glass, which is primarily based on silicon. Approximately a quarter of the Earth's crust is made of silicon. In addition, people began to transmit electronic signals via satellite, which again didn't need copper wires. They also started substituting cutting metal with tungsten and ceramics. Tin prices fell because people had begun to manaufacture aluminium cans instead of tin cans. Aluminium, it should be added, represents 8.3 % of the Earth's crust, and, if we could extract it all, there would be enough to cover all the continents with a several-kilometres-thick cap of pure aluminium (bad idea, but still).

So the concept on which Paul Ehrlich and his partners really gambled was that people would not find ways of extracting a fraction of a millionth of the Earth's crust deposits of these metals and/or find substitutes for them because they were creative.

This again illustrates the point that you cannot know how we will move forward, but you can almost certainly assume that it will happen, if the community is creative. At Theodore Roosevelt's conference no one could possibly have known that, before the end of the century, humanity would invent carbon fibre, genetic engineering , nuclear power, hyper filtration , LEDs and more. Even in 2006, nobody had heard of the concepts of the smartphone and fracking which, by 2010 - just four years later - had drastically changed economic forecasts and many people's everyday lives. Nor can we now predict all the amazing technologies that mankind will have at its disposal 5, 10, 50 or 100 years from now. But we can assume that some of them will be awesome, because our creative design space is expanding hyper-exponentially.

If history is any guidance, what we should really expect is a world where the reserves and performance of our available resources a 100 years from now will exceed most people's wildest imagination today, and where the cost of resources will have continued to decline in real terms as they have done in the previous centuries. And we should also expect that energy will become abundant, cheap and very clean.

The resource paradox is very real, and we will never run out, as long as we choose to maintain a dynamic and creative civilization. Since the *book Limits to Growth* (authored by Donatella H Meadows et al and funded by the Volkswagen Foundation) was published in 1972, the world population has doubled and the world economy has increased five-fold, while our proven reserves and production capabilities for most commodities have risen even faster; and no, we haven't run out of anything.

So the ultimate resource is really - as Julian Simon put it so well - our creativity. And here is an strange fact: over the long term, the price of human labour is rising faster than inflation, whereas the price of commodities is rising slower than inflation (if at all). To an economist, the conclusion to make is that we have a growing abundance of raw materials and a growing shortage of people. That doesn't mean that we should hope for many more people, but it does mean that we must not, as is often suggested, bring Western civilization to a halt because it is will soon run out of resources. It is the opposite: if we stifle creativity and instead create a static society, we will actually run dry.

15.
DOES GROWTH DESTROY THE ENVIRONMENT?

On 17 March 1722 three Dutch ships sailed out from the Juan Fernández Islands west of the Chilean coast. They were on a mission to find a large area of land called Davis' Land after the English buccaneer Edward Davis, who had allegedly spotted this land in 1687. Over the subsequent 19 days, the three Dutch ships sailed almost due West toward the unknown.

On April 5, they saw a small island in the distance, and as they approached, a strange sight met them: the island was teeming with hundreds of virtually-identical sculptures, typically four metres high. The ships now dropped anchor, and the expedition's leader, Admiral Jacob Roggeveen, named their discovery "Easter Island". For precautionary reasons, no one went ashore.

The next morning, they saw smoke rising from different places on the island, but the Dutch opted to stay on their ships while they continued to observe the island.[262]

On the third day, the weather was mixed, with scattered thunderstorms, lightning and rain, and the sailors were still biding their time when they suddenly spotted a small kayak, containing a solitary man, rowing towards them. As this arrived, the sailors welcomed him and offered him something to eat and a glass of wine, which, to their amazement, he poured over his head. He progressed through the whole ship with great curiosity. Then he left.

On the fourth day, the same man returned with his kayak, and later that day, 134 heavily-armed Dutchmen boarded five smaller vessels and headed ashore. After a while, the locals appeared and soon gathered around them and as some of the locals wanted to touch the Dutch sailors and their weapons, a few of the latter panicked, and they shot 13 locals. Shortly after this event, the Dutch left the island and sailed on.

What a bizarre experience this must have been for the locals, especially because they apparently had thought, until the Dutchmen arrived, that they were the only people in the world. And it must have been stranger still that no-one else visited them for another 48 years after they had been discovered. But then came Spaniard Don Felipe González de Haedo with two ships, and he immediately drafted a document which stated that the island now belonged to the Spanish crown.[263] After this visit, only four years passed until

1774, when another expedition passed by, this time led by the famous English explorer James Cook. As his men went ashore in search of fresh water and food, they found surprisingly little of either, and quickly left again.

So it continued. As time passed, more and more European expeditions passed by the small island, and they had this in common: they did not reflect very deeply on what they found there, other than making the observation that it seemed very poor and barren. In 1786 came a French expedition led by J F G de la Perouse, and since he had heard about the poverty beforehand, he brought the islanders sheep, goats, pigs and a variety of crops such as vegetables and citrus, so they could begin farming and have a better quality life. However, later expeditions did not find any traces of these; the natives had apparently just eaten everything brought to them.

No, this was a rather miserable place, and as James Cook had previously written in his logbook: "No Nation will ever contend for the honour of the discovery of Easter Island as there is hardly an Island in this sea which affords less refreshments, and conveniences for Shipping than it does."[264]

It was only much later that scientists learned the tragic story that had played out on Easter Island - or Rapa Nui, as it is known locally. When settlers had originally arrived on the island, it had had a rich vegetation of trees, of which at least three species could grow to more than 15 metres in height. No fewer than 21 species had later become extinct, so the only remaining tree vegetation when Europeans first found the island were a few trees of about three metres high.

Because of the loss of large trees soil erosion had occurred. Excavations revealed how the natives had fought this by planting seeds in caves where there were openings in the ceiling, just as they had put stones on top of the soil after planting to prevent the seeds or plants from blowing away.

As the big trees had disappeared, it had also become more difficult to make sizeable boats, and the islanders' diet had changed from predominantly fish to birds, which had led to yet another environmental disaster, because this led to the eradication of all land-based bird species, and the population of seabirds was decimated. In fact, the islanders had destroyed in the region of half of the original species. To complete the disaster, the deforestation had exposed the natives to water shortages.

The consequences were terrible, and islanders had begun to produce art showing people with distinct ribs and sunken stomachs, suggesting that they were starving. This had probably contributed to violent wars between the clans, in which most sculptures had been toppled. There were even signs of cannibalism.

For all these reasons, the population had fallen from some 15,000-30,000 a hundred years before the arrival of Europeans to the approximately 2,000-

3,000 when the island was discovered in the 1700s - a population that Europeans then reduced further by infecting the natives with new diseases and taking many of the survivors as slaves.

This is a horrible story and it is no wonder that Easter Island now is perhaps the strongest symbol of how human civilization can destroy the environment and thereby itself. Imagine if we did the same with the entire globe?

In his book *Collapse*, the aforementioned author Jared Diamond described this and other examples of how earlier cultures have destroyed their environment and then collapsed. These stand as a clear warning to modern civilizations, and Diamond described the Easter Island tragedy as follows:

"I have often asked myself 'What did the Easter Islander who cut down the last palm tree say while he was doing it?' Like modern loggers, did he shout 'Jobs, not trees!'or: 'Technology will solve our problems, never fear, we'll find a substitute for wood?' " [265]

People destroyed the trees to use them to transport their giant sculptures to their destinations, explained Diamond, and it led to a chain reaction of problems culminating in the natives eating one another out of desperation. He explained the analogy to the rest of the world as follows:

"The parallels between Easter Island and the whole modern world are chillingly obvious. Thanks to globalisation, international trade, jet planes, and the internet, all countries on Earth today share resources and affect each other, just as did Easter's dozen clans."

He therefore concluded that the Easter Island's downfall constituted a flashing warning light for the wider world:

"Those are the reasons why people see the collapse of Easter Island society as a metaphor, a worst-case scenario, for what may lie ahead of us in our own future."

It is stories of these kind that contribute to a widespread fear that Western civilization will do irreparable damage to the planet if it keeps growing and developing its technologies. But, as we shall see, in the following section, there is something about this narrative that is a bit... odd.

Environmental concerns similar to those expressed by Diamond are not a new phenomenon. In her book *Silent Spring*, published in 1962, marine biologist Rachel Carson predicted that the use of pesticide DDT would cause an enormous increase in cancers:

"In the spring of 1961 an epidemic of liver cancer appeared among rainbow trout in many federal, state, and private hatcheries. Trout in both eastern and western parts of the US were affected; in some areas practically 100 per cent of the trout over three years of age developed cancer (...) Dr. Hueper has described this epidemic as a serious warning that greatly increased attention must be given to controlling the number and variety of environmental carcinogens. 'If such preventive measures are not taken,' says Dr. Hueper, 'the stage will be set at a progressive rate for the future occurrence of a similar disaster to the human population.'" [266]

So the scene was apparently set for cancer to afflict close to 100% of the human population.

However, the human species was not the only one in danger. In 1970, the former senator and governor, Gaylord Nelson, founded the annual environmental event Earth Day, and in this connection, he gave an interview to Look Magazine, where he referred to the ornithologist Dillon Ripley as having predicted that between 75% and 85% of all species on Earth would be wiped out by 1995.

In 1979, ecologist Norman Myers published The Sinking Ark, in which he pointed out that if we lost some 2% of the world's forest land each year - as he expected and feared - we would lose about 40,000 species annually, which meant that 50% of the world's species would be gone by 2000. [267]

The following year, the biologist Thomas Lovejoy from Mason University submitted a report to the then US president, Jimmy Carter, containing the following scientific assessment:

"What then is a reasonable estimate of global extinctions by 2000? In the low deforestation case, approximately 15 per cent of the planet's species can be expected to be lost. In the high deforestation case, perhaps as much as 20 per cent will be lost. This means that of 3-10 million species now present on the Earth, at least 500,000 – 600,000, will be extinguished during the next two decades." [268]

The source of this estimate was Myers' report from the year before, and in which you can read a complete description of his scientific approach:

"In 1974 a gathering of scientists concerned with the problem hazarded a guess that the overall extinction rate among all species, whether known to science or not, could now have reached 100 species per year. Let us suppose that, as a consequence of this man-handling of natural environments, the final one-quarter of this century witnesses the elimination of one million species - a far from unlikely prospect. This would work out, during the course of 25 years, at an average extinction rate of 40,000 species per year, or rather over 100 species per day." [269]

This estimate of 40,000 extinct species annually is among the most-cited by environmentalists ever since, but as shown, it is just a wild guess with no evidence behind it whatsoever.

Lovejoy estimated a loss of 25,000-30,000 species per year, which was somewhat lower than Myers. Some years later, in 1988, botanist Peter Raven came forward with a third estimate, which claimed that 25 % of all species would become extinct between 1980 and 2015.[270] Four years after that, biologist E.O. Wilson published his global bestseller *The Diversity of Life*, in which he estimated that we lost between 27,000 and 100,000 species a year. The following year, Paul Ehrlich joined the debate by making his own estimate, and he did not disappoint his enthuisiastic followers. He believed that, if, at that time we lost 250,000 species a year, half of all species would be gone by 2000. Moreover, he predicted, somewhat radically, even for him, that all species would be gone in 2015.

The typical estimate that we see cited on environmental organizations websites are that around 40,000-60,000 species are lost every year. Since this is such a large number, there are countless press references to the assumption that mankind is now conducting "the sixth mass extinction", which sounds very scary. The most famous of the five extinctions happened some 65 million years ago and destroyed the dinosaurs, and probably half of all species' in the sea.

Now, time passes, and it has been quite a few years since these predictions were made, so let us see what actually happened. We can start with Rachel Carson's book *Silent Spring*. Her motive for writing the book was that she thought the pesticide DDT would kill off birds and decimate or destroy mankind by causing a cancer epidemic.

Both claims were speculative and not based on hard evidence. People had previously used DDT to eradicate malaria in the US for years, and many neighbourhoods had tankers driving down the street regularly to spray. As one person described it: "Every summer the DDT truck would drive throughout my neighbourhood spraying a fine fog of pesticide that us kids ran behind and played in for blocks at a time. You couldn't even see the kid standing three feet next to you, and yet after all that, we didn't drop dead like the flies it was killing."[271] Another wrote: "My mom would feed us early enough that we were done with dinner in time to run after the trucks as they sprayed our neighborhood several times per week, sometimes every night, with the thick and exciting bank of fog. Much like waiting for the ice cream truck, we couldn't wait for the sound of the fogger motors as they rounded the corner to our street. Kids would ride bikes, skate, and run behind them."[272]

In spite of this, no one has identified any clear consequences from that other than the disappearance of deadly malaria. Clinical trials were conducted by the US Public Health Service, in which human volunteers ate up to 35 milligrams of DDT every day for 18 months, approximately 1,000 times as much as people would normally be exposed to.[273] No adverse effects could be observed during the test period or over the next 10 years where they were still checked. The workers in the DDT-producing Montrose Chemical Company operated without any protective clothing and had, for years, inhaled so much DDT dust that it amounted, in one case, to what a normal person would experience in 1,300 years, and yet, as a study of them by the American Medical Association concluded: "It is noteworthy that (after 10 to 20 years on the job) no cases of cancer developed among these workers, in some 1,300 man-years of exposure, a statistically improbable event."[274] So they actually contracted less cancer than average (none at all was recorded). In fact, other studies found that DTT seemed to be a quite powerful inhibitor of cancer, and one team of scientists even concluded that it should be used actively to combat human cancers: "The proposed mechanism for DDT's protective effect in rats may also apply to man."[275] One of the world's leading experts on the toxicity of DDT, Professor J Gordon Edwards of San Jose State University, used to start his lectures on DDT by eating a spoonful of it in front of his students, and he appeared in the media doing the same. In 2004, he died at the age of 84 of a heart attack while climbing a mountain.

What about the birds? Later studies have shown that DDT can lead to thinner eggshells in certain species of birds. But the striking fact was that the birds population in the US actually seemed to have increased significantly in the years before the publication of Carson's book. The most prominent source of bird-counts in the US is the Audubon Society; an organization of bird-watchers which, every Christmas, launches its "Christmas Bird Counts". This activity consists of sending thousands of members out into the countryside to count birds. In 1941 - just before the introduction of DDT – on average, each of these observers counted 1,480 birds. In 1960, the observers counted, on average, 5,860 birds. So the bird population seemed to have almost quadrupled, after the introduction of DDT.

In 1967, the Virginia Department of Agriculture made an analysis which concluded that the use of DDT had indeed increased bird populations, partly because mosquitoes also spread diseases among birds, and also because their food was less damaged by insects, and finally because DDT stimulated the birds' natural defence against toxins.[276] Others pointed out that it also seemed to facilitate the breakdown of aflatoxins, which are very strong carcinogens, which might explain why it inhibited cancer.[277]

However, all this was ignored by environmentalists, who had now shifted the focus from what could happen in the air to the potential effects of the substance when it reached the sea. This altered focus became widespread primarily in 1968 when Charles Wurster – who became co-founder of the Environmental Defence Fund – demonstrated that a resolution of 500 ppm (parts per million) DDT in seawater reduced plankton photosynthesis.[278] That sounded very worrying until people pointed out that you actually cannot dissolve that much DDT in sea water – it saturates at 1.2 ppm. In addition, they also noted that the actual concentrations of DDT in the oceans were less than 0.1 % of the lowest concentration he had tested and that his tests had shown that concentrations below the 1.2 ppm saturation actually had been beneficial for photosynthesis. But how had he made a maximum concentration that was 400 times the saturation point? He had dissolved large amounts of alcohol in the saltwater, so that the concentration of DDT could be brought up to 400 times the natural saturation point.[279] To replicate this in nature, one would have to turn the world's oceans into alcoholic drinks and then mix in approximately 660 cubic kilometres of DDT. And then you would have to keep mixing more in rather frantically, because tests conducted at EPA's Gulf Breeze Laboratory in Louisiana showed that 92% of the DDT disappeared from the seawater within 38 days.[280]

In 1970, the American Academy of Sciences published a report in which they argued that DDT used for malaria had probably already saved the lives of some 500 million people worldwide. Therefore, they pointed out, banning the use of this substance would lead to millions of deaths and disablings, and it would also induce people to fight malaria with other, more toxic, agents.

The following year the Environmental Protection Agency in the US staged a seven-month-long consultation during which 125 experts and 365 papers on the effects of DDT were presented to a judge. After this investigation and examination of witnesses, the judge concluded that DDT was beneficial, harmless and should remain legal.[281]

However, the environmentalists ignored all of this and kept up their political pressure, after which use of DDT was banned via a combination of laws and international political pressure tactics. By 2001, because of this campaign, there was just one DDT factory was left in the world, in Kochi in India. Environmental campaigning organisation Greenpeace now began an intense campaign to get this factory closed too and, on December 15 2003, issued a press release that stated: "Greenpeace calls on Indian Authorities to Phase Out and Substitute DDT Immediately. It is clear that the Indian government should phase-out and substitute DDT immediately as required by the POPs convention."[282]

The consequence of the banning of DDT was that an unknown number of millions of people who could have been saved, through use of DDT, became ill or died of malaria. How many exactly is impossible to say, but if the previous estimate that DDT had saved 500 million people before the ban was realistic, the number of deaths caused by this ban has been the greatest man-made disaster ever.

On 15 September 2006 the nightmare finally ended, when the UN issued a press release stating: "Nearly 30 years after safety concerns led to the phasing out of indoor spraying with DDT and other insecticides to control malaria, the United Nations health agency said today it will start promoting this method again to fight the global scourge that kills more than one million people every year, including around 3,000 children every day."[283] Greenpeace and WWF, two of the main driving forces behind the ban, have since softened their language about DDT, but never apologized.

Let's get back to the extinction of species. Have we killed 40,000 species per year, as Myers thought we would? Or 25,000-30,000, as Lovejoy guessed? Or is it nearer Ehrlich's 250,000? Are we, in other words, doing as the natives did on Easter Island?

Overall, scientists have given estimates of the planet's total number of plant and animal species that vary between (roughly) 2 and 80 million, where 1.6 million species have actually been catalogued. One prominent study in 2011 suggested 8.7 million species plus/minus 1.3 million (so 7.4-10 million)[284], whereas many previous estimates had centred around 3.5 million. Such estimates do not include bacteria, the total number of which is totally unknown, but estimates typically range from 10,000 to more than 10 million species. Some experts are actually talking about billions of bacterial species, and argue that these come and go constantly.

It is estimated with some uncertainty that a given species typically survives between one and 10 million years (during which time it might have mutated beyond recognition). *Encyclopædia Britannica* indicates, with reference to a number of sources, - and a very long explanation - that the natural extinction rate probably varies from one species a year to a species per decade. If we, for example, study the period 1980 - 2000, as Lovejoy's report to US president Jimmy Carter covered, one would therefore expect a natural loss of 2 to 20 species during this period, according to *Britannica's* estimate.

All scientific reports of endangered and presumed-extinct species are meticulously recorded by two international organizations. One is International Union for Conservation of Nature (IUCN), whose members include a number of government institutions and international organizations. This produces the so-called "Red List". The second organization is the Committee on Recently Extinct Organisms (CREO) under the American Museum of Natural History, which publishes the CREO List. The statements made by these two organizations are very similar and they refer to each other.

The former's statement showed in 2012 that, globally, almost 800 known species had been eradicated between 1600 and 2012. Most scientific sources put the actual number of known extinct species over these 400 years a bit higher – at just around 1,000 – or equivalent to 0.066 % of known species. For instance, the standard textbook for genetic studies in conservation *A Primer of Conservation Genetics* and *Introduction to Conservation Genetics* from 2007 and 2010 list both 917 extinct species since the year 1600. The following is an estimate of how they are distributed, based on key categories and this time assuming 1,059 extinctions.

Category	Number of known species	Known species extinctions since 1600	Proportion of known species extinct since 1600
Mammals	4,500	110	2.444 %
Birds	9,500	103	1.084 %
Reptiles	6,300	21	0.333 %
Amphibians	4,200	5	0.119 %
Fish	24,000	82	0.342 %
Mollusks	100,000	235	0.235 %
Crustaceans	4,000	9	0.225 %
Vascular plants			
	250,000	396	0.158 %
Insects and other	1,200,000	98	0.008 %
Total	1,602,500	1,059	0.066 %

ESTIMATES OF THE PROPORTION OF SPECIES THAT HAVE BECOME EXTINCT IN THE PAST 400 YEARS. AS THE TABLE SHOWS, THE LARGER SPECIES ARE FAR MORE THREATENED THAN THE SMALLER ONES.[285]

The reason why estimates of actual extinction differ slightly is that, after you can no longer locate a species, you deliberately wait some years or decades before you declare it extinct, as quite a number have reappeared after having been declared extinct (for example, one study found that more than a third of mammals reappeared after having officially been declared extinct).[286] In any event, the numbers in the table above indicate that approximately 0.0001625 % of the 1.6 million known species have been lost annually.

These numbers are completely out of line with the forecasts we mentioned previously; rather than all or half of all species becoming extinct between 1980 and 2000, we see that, in reality, less than 0.1 % were lost – and that was not over a period of 20 years, but over more than 400 years. While popular environmentalists who appeared regularly in the media spoke of 40,000 or more species lost annually, what scientists actually found was that approximately 2.6 species died out annually. This means the environmentalists' number was 15,000 times too high, which is how they reached their "sixth mass extinction" prediction.

But what about species becoming extinct without us ever discovering that they existed? If, for example, there were 8.7 million species plus or minus 1.3 million, where would that get us? Here we should first note that large species are far more prone to extinction than small ones. As the table above shows, we have lost 2.4% of our known mammals over the past 400 years, but well below 0.4 % of reptiles, amphibians, fish, molluscs and crustaceans. Looking at the insects that are either small or extremely small, we have, over 400 years, lost only 0.008% of known species.

Obviously, it is also large species such as mammals that are easiest to observe, so if there are many uncatalogued species, these are probably, overwhelmingly, of the smaller kinds.

If we use the relatively common estimate that there are 3.5 million species in total, then there are 1.9 million of these that are not catalogued, and they must predominantly be insects, plankton, horn leaves, liverworts and mosses, green algae and charophytes. If we extrapolate known extermination data from these kinds of species, and if we use the aforementioned even greater numbers of 8.7 million species plus or minus 1.3 million, the number of unknown species rises to between 5.8 and 8.4 million, and an estimate of the number of extinctions rises to in the order of 1,500-1,750 species, or a total of approximately 0.02 % within 400 years or 0.00005 % annually. That is 3.8-4.4 species per year, which reduces the popular environmentalist overstatement factor from in the region of 15,000 to 3.400-3.900 times the real numbers.

Although it doesn't move the dial much, we should mention that, while species disappear, they also evolve. How quickly something like this can happen is indicated by the assumption made by some scientists that 300-500 new cichlid species might have developed in Lake Victoria, East Africa, over the past 14,000 years, and that such a species can in fact develop over just 20 generations.[287] A new species develops, it should be mentioned, when it can no longer breed with its ancestral species. Experiments with fruit flies have demonstrated that new speciation can develop within just 25 generations (which takes about half a year) just by giving two groups different growth conditions. Currently, biologists have observed how new species seem to be emerging naturally, including among finches, maggots, guppies, thale cress, goatee, ragweed, cabbage and the bird species monk. In addition, new species arise because of human activity. When Europeans arrived in Madeira, they brought mice which have since evolved into at least six new species.

Among the more absurd examples is England's London Underground mosquito. This insect lives in London's underground train network and is now completely separated, genetically, from its ancestor species, which lives above ground and feeds on birds rather than people. This speciation has happened over 150 years.

There is no doubt, however, that the loss of species in recent centuries has far exceeded the creation of new species, and the net loss is probably more than 1,000 species since 1600.

In *Keeping Options Alive: The Scientific Basis for Conserving Biodiversity* Walter Reid and Kenton Miller provide an estimate of the number of mammal and bird species to have become extinct in every 50-year period from 1600 to 1950. Between 1600 and 1850 it was 10-20 species per 50-year period, but it increased to 50-70 per species per 50-year period while peaking in around 1850. In the same book are estimates of the distribution of extinctions by 2000, and it appears that the number of extinctions among birds and mammals has fallen by three-quarters share from 1900-1950 to the period 1950-2000.

That was a lot of numbers, but we needed to consider them before we could discuss what happens with the environment, when we change from static to dynamic societies, as the West has done. Does the environmental impact grow ever worse, and are we about to repeat what happened on Easter Island? Or does it get worst initially, but then better? Or something else?

A common romantic view is that ancient people had much higher respect for the environment than modern man in Western society. For instance, former US vice president Al Gore wrote in his book *Earth in the Balance* that "native American religion, for instance, offers a rich tapestry of ideas about our relationship to the Earth. One of the most moving and frequently quoted explanations was attributed two Chief Seattle in 1855... ". He then quoted North American Indian Chief Seattle making the following in a speech in 1855:

"How can you buy or sell the sky, the warmth of the land? The idea is strange to us. If we do not own the freshness of the air and the sparkle of the water, how can you buy them from us? (...) Every part of this Earth is sacred to my people. Every shining pine needle, every sandy shore, every mist in the dark woods, every clearing, and humming insect is holy in the memory and experience of my people."

This touching speech has also been referenced in numerous environmental activist websites, for it resembles a clear testimony of how we, in Western civilization, have lost the respect for nature that native people find natural. It has also been reported in such diverse publications as Northwest Airlines' magazine *Passages*, the Canadian government's Green Plan and NASA's *Mis-*

sion to Earth. In 1991, an immensely popular children's book about Chief Se-attle and his beautiful message was published. Its title was *Brother Eagle, Sister Sky: A Message from Chief Seattle* and, in 1992, it reached number five on the *New York Times* bestseller list. It outlined Seattle's messages of peace and har-mony, and how he was "a respected and peaceful man", who could teach us a lot about decent behaviour. No wonder they all admired this man, because his message was moving and lyrical, continuing like this:

"But if we sell our land, you must remember that the air is precious to us, that the air shares its spirit with all the life it supports. The wind that gave our grandfather his first breath also receives his last sigh. And the wind must also give our children the spirit of life. (...) This we know. The earth does not belong to man; man belongs to the earth. This we know. All things are connected like the blood which unites one family."

However, there are several problems here. The first is the belief that primitive people typically had, or have, a particularly deep respect for nature. If one recalls our earlier observation about the enormous rates of violence among most tribal people, one can have one's doubts. What we know about ancient environmental damage can only increase those concerns, so let's take a brief look at that.

It isn't pretty, because historically, ancient people have, relatively quickly, driven countless species to extinction, when arriving in a new area. The first human migration in Australia, for instance, happened 48,000-50,000 years ago, and the local mega fauna (defined as species with body weight above 44 kg) became extinct there about 46,000 years ago. Meanwhile, those same spe-cies survived on the island of Tasmania south of Australia, which had not yet been populated by man. But man arrived there 43,000 years ago as sea levels fell and enabled them to walk across. Et voilà: the mega fauna also disappeared there.[288]

That should probably tell us something, and we see the same story every-where. When the first immigrants crossed over to North America approxi-mately 11,500 years ago, three quarters of the area's large mammals died out quickly. Some 7,000 years later, when people also populated South America, this continent quickly lost most of its largest mammals. That is one reason why Engels' and Diamonds' aforementioned narrative about the differences in nat-ural fauna explaining the differences in human development isn't very compel-ling; but it also tells us how Stone Age folk treated nature. If we take North and South America together, after human emigration, the Americas lost such wild animals as wild horses (which were later replaced by European species) mast-odons, (elephant-like animals with trunks), mammoths, lions, sabre-toothed cats and various species of musk, llama, bison, bear and wolf, giant condors, wild pigs, giant armadillos, camels, giant beavers and 2.7 metre-long salmon with sabre teeth plus anteaters the size of horses. So, for all we know, the early Indians killed off all these species fairly soon after they arrived.

Shortly after the immigration in the Americas, the first people showed up in Hawaii, and studies of fossils showed what happened there next: 50 of the island's original 98 species were wiped out by the local tribes - long before Europeans arrived in 1778. In fact, a typical pattern was, as Charles Darwin discovered, that a multitude of new species would easily have developed through inbreeding on islands, but also, as archeological records and more recent experiences show, that island species are far more sensitive to eradication threats than those living on main lands.

So it continues. Shortly after people first appeared on Madagascar off the African coast around 2,500 years ago, 17 species of lemur died out. And 600 years ago, when people arrived to New Zealand, they swiftly managed to eliminate 29 species of bird - including all flightless birds – again, long before Europeans arrived.[289]

From an archaeological discovery near Otago, scientists found the remains of approximately 30,000 Moa birds that had been slaughtered within a relatively short time. On average, about a third of the meat from the birds was left uneaten, and there were ovens full of roasted birds that had not even been touched. What a great parties there must have been, but no wonder the Moa became extinct.

If we look at North and South America and Australia combined, we see a total decimation of between 74% and 86% of the local megafauna since the Stone Age people arrived in these areas (but again; before Europeans arrived in the Age of Discovery).[290] This is signficant, and biologist and ornithologist Storrs Olson from the Smithsonian Institution has estimated that a quarter of all bird species on sea islands were wiped out by tribesmen before Western civilization was established.[291] In other words: very small populations of tribal people destroyed far more species than the much larger group of civilized nations later did. So perhaps that is where we have our "sixth extinction".

Contemporary non-civilized tribes often behave the same way, and studies of isolated tribes in Brazil today revealed that these people frequently hunted in areas where the game was already under pressure, and they fished a single species of fish by pouring poison into ponds, whereby they killed everything else.[292] They also consciously sought out pregnant monkeys or apes with infants, because these were easier to kill. Furthermore, they would gladly fell a whole tree to get a few fruits from the top; and they regularly exhibited indifference or cruelty to wounded animals.

Past burning of forests has probably contributed a lot. After humans arrived in Australia, there seems to have been a change in the vegetation, where species that were particularly resistant to burning became more widespread.[293] In America, the Indians also burned forests periodically, and the prairies that the Europeans found on arrival had previously largely been forested areas, which the Indians had destroyed. In Africa, the Masais systematically burned forests to create grazing land for their cattle and to combat the tsetse fly. When they were forced to move out the Kruger National Park, bush quickly began to spread. Another indication of the extent of people's natural burning of forests was seen after Spaniards murdered countless Indians of Panama. After these Indians were gone, rainforests began to grow in what had previously been savannah.[294]

So the basic pattern is this: when Stone Age people arrived for the first time to a new area, they would typically quickly eradicate most, or all, of the mega fauna there, plus any wingless bird species. If they were on islands, they would also wipe out a substantial proportion of flying bird species. And they regularly torched the forests and created savannah or prairie instead.

So the common perception of primitive tribes as being peace-loving environmentalists is, to put it mildly, very questionable, and it is therefore not surprising that Chief Seattle, on closer examination, never really made the touching speech that Al Gore and others like to quote. Instead, it was written in the winter of 1971/72 by a media man named Ted Perry, who was hired as text writer for an environmentalist movie called Home, where he was asked to weave-in an Indian who defended environment.[295]

To Perry's consternation, the finished movie never attributed the text to him, and this is why so many thought it was authentic. It could not, in any case, have been authentic; because it included the sentence "I have seen a thousand rotting buffalo on the prairie, left by the White Man who shot them from a passing train." These events took place more than 1,500 kilometres from where the chief lived, and they began 20 years after his death. Whether the chief ever made any speech on the subject Ted Perry addressed, we do not know, because the first mention of this appeared in a newspaper column written by an amateur poet 33 years after the speech allegedly occurred.[296] That sounds unlikely, partly because they didn't understand each other's languages, and partly because the Indians never used a form of poetic speech which sounded even remotely like that used in Perry's narrative.[297] And finally we should not forget the aforementioned fact (in chapter eight) that it was the very same Chief Seattle who, in 1847, organized a notorious ambush attack on his neighbouring tribe, where some 150 men were mown down in a hail of bullets, after which he took all the surviving women and children as slaves.[298] In general, primitive tribal people have hardly been particularly respectful of nature nor stranger, but their ability to destroy the environment was, of course, somewhat limited by their very small numbers. This restriction disappeared when the world's population began to grow, and when the West began to industrialize there was major damage to the environment such as we see, for instance, in China today as they go through the same process.

As an example of how it was in the West, we can take England. Its first settlers had begun the destruction by burning wood to start farming, but when industrialization and largescale urbanization began, it grew really rough. Kitchen waste and the contents of latrines was now regularly emptied out of upper windows (it was advisable to look up), and faeces piled up in city streets, alleys and backyards together with layer-upon-layer of horse manure creating an unbearable stench, to the delight of flys and rats. Furthermore, as people began to burn coal and coke, black smoke soon poured from tens of thousands, perhaps eventually millions, of chimneys, creating the notorious "pea soup fog".[299]

It was truly dreadful. For example, in 1257, Queen Eleanor visited the northern English city of Nottingham, but found the smoke from its many ovens so overwhelming that she feared for the live and health and left the place immediately.[300] Around this time, London was popularly called "The Big Smoke" (a nickname that still exists today), and in 1272 it had become so problematic that King Edward I introduced a not very effective law to reduce air pollution.

Later, in the 1700s, we can read this contemporary complaint about the English capital's air quality: "By reason likewise of this smoak, that the air of the city, especially in the winter time, is rendered very unwholesome: for in case there be no wind, and especially in frosty weather, the city is cover'd with a thick brovillard or cloud, which the force of the winter sun is not able to scatter, so that the inhabitants thereby suffer under a dead benumbing cold..."[301] So the air was so polluted that the sun couldn't shine through and people were freezing in the permanent shadow.

The water wasn't any cleaner. Sewage was discharged untreated directly into the River Thames, which in the early 1800's went by the nickname "The Great Stink". Soon the fish disappeared, and the permanent stench from the waters grew so bad that, in parliament, it became necessary to soak the curtains with calcium chloride to counter it.[302] On 7 July 1855, the famous physicist Michael Faraday wrote an indignant letter to the editor of *The Times*, where he described his observation after having sailed on the Thames:

"The appearance and the smell of the water forced themselves at once on my attention. The whole of the river was an opaque pale brown fluid. In order to test the degree of opacity, I tore up some white cards into pieces, moistened them so as to make them sink easily below the surface, and then dropped some of these pieces into the water at every pier the boat came to; before they had sunk an inch below the surface they were indistin-

guishable, though the sun shone brightly at the time; and when the pieces fell edgeways the lower part was hidden from sight before the upper part was under water." [303]

In addition to stench, flys and rats, the filthy water gave rise to thousands of cholera deaths. When a steamer capsized in the River Thames in 1878, 600 people died - most of them due to effects of acute infections caught from the fermenting soup.

As cars and trains were later invented, these brought with them new sources of pollution. Air pollution in the 20th century was sometimes so bad that the occupants in the streets of London could not spot the curb, and pedestrians sometimes had to use flashlights to detect where the pavement ended and the road began. In a particularly glaring incident in 1952, where visibility decreased to about 10 cm, about 3,900 people died within a few days due to this air pollution, especially because the burning of coal and coke gave a very high concentration of sulphuric acid content in the air.

But then the trend turned. We cannot say exactly when air and water pollution in the UK peaked, but it was probably somewhere between 50 and 200 years ago, and especially since the 1960s, the improvements have been very swift. A modern car on UK roads spews forth less than 5% of the pollution it used to in the 1960s, which was again far less than the pollution caused by cars in the 1940s, which was less than that of the 1920s.

As a consequence of this and other clean-up efforts, particle pollution in British air has dropped to a tiny fraction of what it was before, and this should continue. According to the EU's "Euro 6", the 2014 standard cars emission of NO and NO2 should be 84% lower than in 2000, and the emission of soot should be 96% lower. Similarly, CO_2 emissions, per kilometre, have fallen dramatically and are expected to drop by half again between 2013 and 2025. [304]

The reality is that there have been amazing improvements in air quality, and London water quality has also improved massively. If we turn again to the Thames, the London Evening Standard newspaper reported the following in 2009:

"The Thames is packed full of fish and cleaner than it has been for 200 years, fishing experts say. More than 125 species, including wild salmon, trout, Dover sole, plaice, haddock and bass, now live in the 215-mile waterway which was declared biologically dead in 1957. The stocks are attracting predators including porpoise, seals and dolphins which have been spotted as far upstream as London Bridge." [305]

So the sea- and water pollution in the UK got worse at first, but then it got better - and then a lot better.

Similar trends have been seen anywhere in the West, as its civilization modernized itself. For example, the number of species in the Rhine sediments rose from 27 in 1971 to 97 in 1997.[306] Between 1970 and 2010, the number of cars and trucks in the US more than doubled, but at the same time their total emissions of carbon monoxide and sulphur dioxide dropped by more than half, and their combined emissions of particulate emissions fell by 80% and of lead by 98% while the release per car of these substances fell by approximately 75, 90 and 99%, respectively.[307]

However, people worried about more than the effects of air particle pollution on our health. In January1970, US magazine Newsweek reported that a new Ice Age was coming because of air pollution. On 19 April the same year, ecologist Kenneth Watt predicted, in a speech at Swarthmore College, Pennsylvania, that the world's average temperature would drop 11 degrees by the year 2000, which is twice as much as is needed to trigger a new Ice Age. This threat of a man-made ice-age was so alarming in the eyes of Professor Arnold Reize from Case Western Reserve University, that he stated in a newspaper interview that "We will be forced to sacrifice democracy by the laws that will protect us from further pollution."[308]

The following year (1971), climate scientist Stephen Schneider wrote a widely-quoted study that contained the following conclusion: "Our calculations suggest a decrease in global temperature by as much as 3.5 °C. Such a large decrease in the average temperature of Earth, sustained over a period of few years, is believed to be sufficient to trigger an Ice Age."[309]

In1972, a number of climate scientists held a climate conference about the upcoming cooling, which resulted in a letter sent to President Nixon dated 3 December in which they warned that this future global cooling would lead to "increased frequency and amplitude of extreme weather anomalies such as those bringing floods, snowstorms, killing frosts, etc."[310] The government subsequently set up the "Working Group Ad Hoc Panel on the Present Interglacial", which predicted annual temperature drops of 0.15 degrees up until 2015, equivalent to an aggregate temperature drop of almost 4 degrees.

One of the consequences of this anthropogenic (man-made) cooling about which many scientists warned was a catastrophic decline in crop yields. And on 29 December 1974, the *New York Times* commented:

"A number of climatologists, whose job it is to keep an eye on long-term weather changes, have lately been predicting deterioration of the benign climate to which we have grown accustomed....Various climatologists issued a statement that 'the facts of the present climate change are such that the most optimistic experts would assign near certainty to major crop failure in a decade.' If policy makers do not account for this oncoming doom, 'mass deaths by starvation and probably in anarchy and violence' will result."

Increased weather extremes was another concern, and an article in News-week from 1975 gave examples: "Last April in the most devastating outbreak of tornadoes ever recorded, 148 twisters killed more than 300 people and caused a half billion dollars worth of damage in 13 states." On 5 January the same year the *New York Times* reported that "an international team of special-ists has concluded from eight indexes of climate that there is no end in sight to the cooling trend of the last 30 years, at least in the Northern Hemisphere."

The cooling trend was clearly a killer, and the year after the reporter Low-ell Ponte explained in his scary book *The Cooling*:

"This cooling has already killed hundreds of thousands of people. If it continues and no strong action is taken, it will cause world famine, world chaos and world war, and this could all come about before the year 2000." [311]

Schneider, who was one of the people who had started the panic, was partic-ularly concerned about the increased number of extreme weather events that would follow as the world cooled. In his book *The Genesis Strategy* from 1976 he consequently dedicated an entire chapter to explaining how and why the climate would become evermore unstable as it grew colder. Here he wrote, for example: "Now, where we appear to have entered a cooler period in high latitudes, there have been suggestions that we will suffer more droughts, floods, temperature extremes, or other manifestations of climate variability." This and a possible man-made ice age could, he explained, be counteracted if you were to detonate "clean" thermonuclear devices in the Arctic Ocean or spreading black soot particles by aircraft in order to reduce the reflexion of sun light.

As the signs of an impending Ice Age started to vanish in the 1980s, the focus shifted to the so-called "acid rain", and in 1982, Canada's Environment Minister, John Roberts described this problem as follows: "Acid rain is one of the most devastating forms of pollution imaginable, an insidious malaria of the biosphere."

In 1984, the well-known German magazine *Stern* reported that a third of German forests was already dead or dying because of acid rain. At the same time, the German Interior Ministry expressed the expectation that all German forests would be gone in 2002, and the biologist Bernd Ulrich from Göttingen Universi-ty caused a furore by stating in 1981 that large forests would be "dead within five years. They cannot be saved." [312] In November 1981, leading magazine *Der Spiegel* brought a headline screaming "Acid Rain over Germany. The Forests Die." [313] Other media brought similar sensational stories about the disaster.

However, an extremely large study in the US involving approx. 700 scien-tists with a budget of more than half a billion dollars concluded in 1990 that, actually, only between 1 and 4% of lakes in different regions of the nation had excessively low pH levels and that this did not cause significant problems.[314] A follow-up study by the same organisation (called NAPAP) published in 2011 noted that emissions of SO_2 had fallen by 64 % from 1990 to 2009 while NOx emissions fell by 67% and SO_2 emissions by 59%.[315]

In Europe, it turned out, on closer examination, that only 0.5% of the forests were affected by this problem at any one time, and the forests didn't die as expected.[316] In fact, it turned out later that, even as the acid rain debate had been raging, the biomass of the European forests had grown rapidly. As ecology professor Han van Dobben wrote: "During the last few decades, forest growth has strongly increased over large parts of Europe." He added that "survey studies on tree ring analysis indicate a 20-50 % increase of forest production since c. 1950."[317] Furthermore, it was determined, through experiments, that if you irrigated trees with different concentrations of acid, they actually grew faster than usual when acid concentrations were slightly above the actual measured.[318]

After acid rain came the ozone crises, which was actually a genuine threat. As it turned out, some substances from refrigerators and spray bottles degraded the vital ozone layer in the high atmosphere, so a global ban of these was soon implemented. Meanwhile, the fear of a new Ice Age was replaced by a fear of global warming.

Before we delve a little into this new panic, we can start by looking at the factors scientists think affect our climate. Among the most long-term is movement in the tectonic plates that creates mountain ranges affecting wind and water currents. In addition, there is a cycle of approximately 143 million years, driven by the solar system through the Milky Way's spiral arms, which leads to varying exposure to "cosmic rays" from stars. These rays are actually "storms" of atoms and subatomic particles emitted from stars that create cascades of tiny nuclear reactions when they enter the atmosphere at incredible speeds. These reactions create charged particles that can stimulate the formation of water drops (H_2O are like small magnets that get attracted to charged particles). This may stimulate cloud formation and cooling. (More about that in a minute.)

Moving to the somewhat shorter-term, the climate is affected by what are known as geomagnetic reversals, whereby the Earth's magnetic field reverses its polarity at irregular and, so far unpredictable, intervals but, on average, every 450,000 years. It actually happened about 41,000 years ago and then flipped back within just 440 years. As the reversal takes place, the magnetic field drops towards zero for a time, which means the Earth becomes more exposed to cosmic rays and thus probably more cloud cover and perhaps lower temperatures.

Another variable is Milankovitch climate cycles, which relate to 1) changes in the Earth's rotational axis relative to the sun; 2) the fact that this axis also wobbles; and 3) the fact that the Earth's orbit around the sun fluctuates between being more or less elliptical. These cycles interact in a complicated pattern, but seen in isolation, they create quite powerful cycles of approximately 21,000 - 41,000 years' duration. Collectively, they seem to play major roles in creation of ice ages, which over the past 2.5 million years have started every 40,000-100,000 years.

In periods such as now, where we are not in an Ice Age, we say that we are in an "interglacial period". The previous four of these lasted 23,000, 12,000, 4,000 and 16,000 years, respectively, and the current has now lasted approximately 12.300 years.

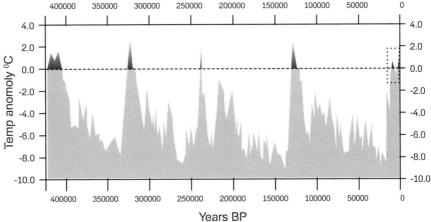

Years BP
RECONSTRUCTION OF GLOBAL TEMPERATURES OVER THE PAST 420,000 YEARS BASED ON DRILLING OF THE VOSTOK ICE CORE FROM THE ANTARCTICA (IT'S CALLED VOSTOC BECAUSE IT THE RESEARCH STATION IS RUSSIAN).[319]

If we zoom into what has happened within our recent 12,300 interglacial years, it appears that the natural warming contribution of Milankovitch cycles culminated between 7000 BC and 500 BC, and that actual temperatures had a culmination around 7000 BC to 5000 BC. We call this the Holocene Climatic Optimum. During this optimum almost all the ice in the Alps melted and the North African territories became rainy and lush (on average it rains more when it gets warmer, due to increased evaporation). In fact, all this rain accumulated in vast underground pools of water, which today are pumped up and used for irrigation and drinking water in Northern Africa.

As for the Milankovitch cycles, we now seem to be in a slow slide towards more cooling. However, in the shorter-term scientists assume there are other natural variables called the Schwabe, Hale, Gleissberg, Suess/de Vries, Eddy and Hallstatt cycles, respectively.

Assuming these are real, what drives them? The proposed explanations include rotation of the sun's magnetic field (Schwabe cycle) and cyclical fluctuations in how planets pull in the sun (the other cycles). For instance, the Hallstatt cycle correlates with periods during which four large planets are aligned and therefore exhibit increased gravity pull in the sun, which displaces it away from its average position. Apart from displacing it, it is also speculated that gravitational pull can change the inner dynamics within the sun.[320]

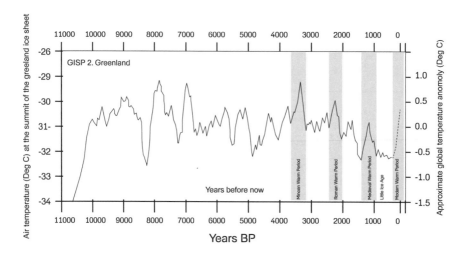

RECONSTRUCTION OF THE CLIMATE OVER THE LAST APPROX. 11,000 YEARS; STARTING WITH THE END OF LAST ICE AGE. THE DATA SERIES IS BASED ON GREENLAND ICE SHEET DRILLINGS AND END AROUND YEAR 1865. THE DOTTED LINE SHOWS HAS BEEN ADDED TO THE GRAPH TO SHOW THE SUBSEQUENT TEMPERATURE RISE OF APPROXIMATELY 0.8 CENTIGRADE.[321]

The sun is evidently important for our climate, and total solar radiation fluctuates approximately plus or minus 0.1 %, but for certain ultraviolet spectrums, the fluctuation can be as much as plus or minus 70 %. However, what may have a bigger effect is the fact that fluctuations in solar activity involve sunspots and solar flares, which influence the sun's magnetic field. This seems to cause fluctuations in the Earth's exposure to cosmic radiation of about 10-15%.

Is cosmic radiation important? It may very well be. The Danish climate scientist Henning Svensmark and others have, for years, worked with a theory that long-term fluctuations in cosmic rays due to sun spot cycles constituted the main driver of the smaller historical climate fluctuations, including the recent Little Ice Age. He and others have in CERN in Switzerland successfully simulated how increased cosmic radiation can stimulate formation of water droplets in the atmosphere. This is an interesting theory because the sunspot activity almost stopped during the Little Ice Age, but during the warming period 1975-2000, it was about as strong as it had ever been over the last 11,000 years.[322]

So far, so complicated, but we aren't through yet. For instance, we also have a lunar cycle of 18.6 years plus cyclical shifts in ocean currents called Pacific Decadal Oscillation and Pacific Decadal Oscillation, which both oscillate every 20 to 30 years. And we have the sea currents called El Niño and its counter phase La Niña. El Niño is the warming phase, which comes every two to seven years, and persists for nine months to two years. Like the other sea oscillations, these alternate between bringing hot and cold water to the surface.

And there is more, because climate is also affected by random disasters such as meteor impacts, volcanic eruptions above and below the water or natural methane release episodes such as one that seem to have happened around 55 million years where a sudden release of a trillion tons ago methane lead raised temperatures by eight degrees for a while.

And then there is CO_2 and other greenhouse gases, which allow entry of ultraviolet sunlight, but limit outgoing radiation of infrared light from the Earth to space. Since we started industrialization in the West, the atmospheric concentration of CO_2 has increased from approximately 0028% to 0.04%, and if we do not make a big transition to nuclear power and/or other non-fossil technologies, it can increase to about 0.05%-0.1% by 2100. The marginal direct effect of more CO_2 is, in itself, exponentially decreasing, but indirect effects, such as results of increased evaporation and therefore greater cloud cover, are very difficult to calculate and may either enhance or inhibit the greenhouse effect.

So just think about it; this was a very simplified summary of some of the likely natural drivers of our climate, and yet it included the following 20 variables:

1. Continental drift, changing mountain ranges and so on
2. Milky Way Spiral Arm Passages (every 143 million years)
3. Geomagnetic reversals (random, but on average every 450,000 years)
4. Milankovitch Axial tilt (41,000 years)
5. Milankovitch Axial precession (26,000 years)
6. Milankovitch Apsidal precession (22,000 – 26,000 years)
7. Hallstatt cycle (2,300 years)
8. Eddy cycle (1,000 years)
9. Suess / de Vries cycle (210 years)
10. Gleissberg cycle (87 years)
11. Hale cycle (22 years)

12. Pacific Decadal Oscillation (20-30 years)
13. Pacific Decadal Oszillation (20-30 years)
14. Moon cycle (18.6 years)
15. El Niño/ La Niña (2-7 years)
16. Vulcanic eruptions above water
17. Vulcanic eruptions below water
18. Meteor impacts
19. Natural methane releases
20. Greenhouse gases

As mentioned, we are now probably in the declining stage of the natural interglacial period as driven by the natural Milankovitch-temperature. On top of this comes natural cycles created by solar activity and ocean currents.

The most prominent is the aforementioned Eddy cycle of approximately 1,000 years (or rather 800-1,100 years), so where are we in that? If we look back, one of its peaks was the Minoan Warm Period 3,300-3,450 years ago. This was followed by a significant cooling, and then we had a new temperature rise, which created the Roman Warm Period approximately 2,100 to 2,250 years ago. This was fairly warm, as olive trees grew further north than today, and we know that many of the current glaciers in the Alps at the time were completely gone.[323] New archaeological finds, for example, have shown that, in Roman times, people often crossed over the pass at Schnidejoch in Switzerland, which today is covered by glaciers.[324]

The next Eddy-warming was the Medieval Warm Period approximately 1,000-1,200 years ago, when we know from the aforementioned *Domesday Book*, written in 1086, that there were wine farms in the UK. The distance between each peak in this cycle has thus been around 1,000 years, and each warming plateau has lasted 150-200 years.

If we believe this pattern is no coincidence, then we should once again be in a culmination phase of this cycle, which could last until the middle of this century. At the same time, the shorter Gleissberg and Suess/de Vries cycles may have contributed to warming in the last decades of the last century, but could exhibit the opposite effect in the coming decades, as may the Pacific Decadal Oscillation.

The Little Ice Age ended in 1830, and a dedicated heating can be said to have begun around 1860. If we expect the Eddy Cycle to keep us on a plateau for 50-200 years, then it would start cooling somewhere around the middle of the century.

That was a lot of "may" and "could", but that is how it is. However, one thing that we know is that, since the current warming started after 1830, we have seen three longer warming periods: 1860-1880, 1910-1940 and 1975-2000, in which the latter two were almost identical in intensity. In the first of these two periods, CO_2 emissions were minimal; why they seem to be completely natural. The third heating phase may be due to a combination of greenhouse gas emissions, a rather strong solar activity in this particular period, cyclical changes in ocean currents and the phases of the Eddy, Gleissberg and Suess/ de Vries cycles.

During this warming period we have seen a reduction in sea ice around the North Pole of around 20 %, although it varies significantly from year-to-year. In contrast, the intensity of ice on Greenland's mainland as well as ice cover at the South Pole have been relatively stable, with the latter even increasing. Particularly at the South Pole, it follows that higher sea temperatures lead to a melting of the edges of the ice, but at the same time to an increase in snowfall of the land-based ice cream, which roughly balances out.

Furthermore, there has been a very linear sea level rise of about three mil-limetres per year (equivalent to 30 cm in 100 years) from approximately 1880 until today, of which it is estimated that 13-25% came from pumping up and discharging of groundwater, and the rest from the melting of land ice and vol-ume expansion due to heating.[325] The Intergovernmental Panel on Climate Change (the IPCC) expect in their 2013 report expected increases in sea levels of approx. 26-97 cm over 100 years.

It is obvious that our civilization, through the burning of fossil fuels, contrib-utes to global warming. However, a recurring criticism of the IPCC assess-ments is that they downplay natural climate variations such as those men-tioned above. At one point, they even almost eliminated the Little Ice Age and the Medieval Warm Period through a so-called "hockey stick graph"- we will revisit that episode in section five.

Overall, it is clearly possible that natural phenomena such as variations in solar activity, the Eddy cycle and other cyclic currents have contributed significantly to the observed process from 1970 to 2000 as the events before and after this episode are not consistent with the prevailing climate models' projections. As NASA climatologist Roy Spencer noted in 2013, 87 out of 90 leading climate models from 1983 projected higher temperature increases than have actually occurred, and these over-estimations were significant.[326]

While science may underestimate natural and cyclical climate phenomena, much of the media tends to deliver sensationalist horror scenarios without scientific basis. Some examples:

◆ It is true that summer ice in Greenland has dwindled in recent decades, but the same thing happened in the 1930s where it actually occurred faster.[327]

◆ Coral reefs will not necessarily disappear if sea levels continue to rise, as the coral can grow up to a centimetre a year – actually, coral formations can be over a kilometre high.[328] If this was it not the case, all coral reefs would now be far below the surface, as the sea has already risen about 130 meters since the last Ice Age.

◆ It is not new that boats have occasionally, in recent years, been able to sail through the Northwest Passage north of Canada or through the Northeast Passage north of Siberia, because the ice has opened. The former was done, in part, by Sebastian Cabot in 1508 and completed by Roald Amundsen in his ship Gjoa in 1903-1906. It was also done repeatedly during World War II. The Northeast Passage north of Siberia was used by Vitus Bering in 1733 to 1743.

◆ There is no statistical evidence that we are getting more extreme storm episodes in a warmer climate. Historically, it has actually been the opposite.[329]

◆ It is not true that malaria will spread to the north because of global warming. During the Little Ice Age, there was widespread malaria in northern Europe, Russia and the US, and the reason it is now gone is not down to climate fluctuation, but because, today, these countries can afford to prevent it. On average, malaria has tended to disappear when a country's GDP capita has exceeded $3,100.[330]

◆ Polar bears are not dying out because of global warming. First, it is a variant of the brown bear, with which it therefore can breed. Second, the polar bear population was, in 2013, at around 20,000-25,000; the population was significantly less around 1970, and Canada has been selling about 700 annual hunting licenses annually for polar bears. Finally, polar bears survived the last interglacial period when temperatures were much higher than today.[331]

◆ When the world's media writes that temperatures are the highest "on record", it does not, as many readers probably assume, mean that they are the highest ever or since the last Ice Age. The term refers to temperatures measured by satellite or thermometer where previous warm periods per definition are not "on record".

Not everything we have heard about environmental problems is true, whether it concerned DDT, extinctions, global cooling, acid rain, sea-, air- and river pollution, global warming or many other subjects, and some of the alleged threats we hear have virtually no basis at all. But in spite of this, it is still fair to question whether Western civilization, with its growth and technological innovation, is dangerous. What is the truth?

The truth is that intense creativity, advanced technology and increased prosperity are the most effective elements in the creation of a better environment. Conversely, romanticising the past, rejecting new technologies, embracing zero growth, falling for undocumented fads and refusing to weigh costs and benefits of different scenarios against one another will make the challenges unsolvable.

To see who is best at protecting their environment, one can check the so-called Environmental Performance Index (EPI), which is based on 25 different environmental indicators measured in each of a number of countries. This was first developed in 1999 by two of the world's leading universities, Yale and Cornell, both in the US, along with the World Economic Forum and the European Commission. The results show a clear, positive correlation between income levels and a healthy environment. As stated in an EPI report from 2008: "Not surprisingly, per capita GDP is correlated with higher performance on the EPI. In particular, overall EPI scores are higher in countries that have a per capita GDP of $10,000 or higher."[332]

So, the richest countries are the cleanest, and these are predominantly Western. The highest scoring countries for cleanliness in 2014 were Switzerland, Luxembourg, Australia and Singapore, in that order, while the most polluted were impoverished Somalia, Mali, Haiti and Lesotho. Poor North Korea has developed into an ecological disaster and has lost much of its forest cover, while wealthy South Korea's forests are stable.[333] The island of Hispaniola consists of the poverty-stricken Haiti on the one hand and the (close to 10 times) richer Dominican Republic on the other. Haiti has destroyed nearly all its forests, while the Dominicans have maintained theirs effectively.[334] If we also bear in mind all our previous examination of environmental history, including UK's, the picture gets pretty clear: economic growth begins with a deterioration in the environment, but is subsequently better than if the country had remained poor. Seen over a longer perspective, the sequence is roughly this:

◆ Phase one: Mass extinction. The earliest tribesmen are hunters and perpetrate mass extinction, primarily of big animals and island birds, combined with regular torching of forests which creates prairie, savannas and heathers.
◆ Phase two: Further deforestation. Early farmers undertake permanent clearing of forests for conversion to farmland.
◆ Phase three: Big smoke; big stink. During early industrialization, air and water initially suffers massive pollution.
◆ Phase four: Clean-up. As societies grow rich, they introduce modern environmental technology combined with growth in natural parks and so on. The environment improves incrementally.

The key observation is that the West has, for a long time, been at stage four above. Yes, the environment grew worse in the past, but the trend turned a long, long time ago. Economists sometimes describe this phenomenon as "the environmental Kuznets curve". The turning point is typically reached when GDP per capita rises to somewhere between $2,000 and $8,000 dollars a year; some studies indicate that the average is $4,000 dollars, and specifically for loss of forest, the average turning point has been in the region of $4,600. When a country later exceeds GDP per capita of approximately $10,000, there will typically be a significant improvement in the environment. In Denmark, for example, forest cover in the early 1800s was only 2-3%, but it has since increased to approximately 11%, even as the country has become a massive exporter of farming products.[335] Development in forest cover is actually rather symptomatic of what is happening to our environment. An inventory of the global forest cover for the period 2000-2010 revealed that 13 million hectares had either been reclassified or had disappeared entirely, compared with16 million hectares having been reclassified or lost over the previous decade (reclassification typically means that the forest remains, but it has been converted to intensive forestry or other human activity). However, at the same time, 95 million hectares were converted to national parks.[336]

The main issue with forest cover concerns jungle (because of its immense biodiversity), and according to an analysis by the United Nations in 2007, around 154,000 km2 jungle was destroyed every year. However, at the same time, no less than 8.5 million km2 of jungle was growing back after having previously been farmland.[337] Now, of course, "destroyed" and "growing back" are not directly comparable units at all, but it is somehow interesting that the latter figure was 55 times larger than the former and that the area where jungle was coming back was equal to the size of US. The reason that this was happening was urbanization and greater use of technology-intensive farming, which required much less land.[338]

Here, we will also get help from an unexpected side, namely the so-called aerial fertilization effect, i.e. fertilization by increasing atmospheric CO_2 content.[339] The dry matter in plants consist mainly of carbon, which they extract from the CO_2. As natural CO_2 concentrations are low, greenhouse owners often double or quadruple the CO_2 artificially, since plants typically grow 25-65% faster at a CO_2 concentration of approximately 1,500 ppm (parts per million), which is optimal for many plants. Conversely, plants often die, if the concentration falls below 150-200 ppm. Similarly, an increase in atmospheric CO_2 to 500 – 1,000 ppm, which we may see at some point in this century, will enable many plants to grow much faster.

On average, forest coverage has been increasing in most wealthy nations for a long time. In fact, the growth of forest land in rich countries continued to be so swift that it has almost compensated for forest loss in poorer nations. According to statistics from the Food and Agricultural Organization of the United Nations (FAO), which is the only organization that has closely-measured global forests over the long term, global forest cover today is much the same as it was when it began to calculate it in 1949.

All this does not mean that there hasn't been forest loss over the long term, because there has. It is estimated that approximately 37% of the globe was covered with forests before humans existed, and this figure has been reduced to 30% today. But most of the destruction was carried out in, or before, the Middle Ages, and over recent years, forest cover has actually increased in Asia, Europe and the US.[340]

UN official forecast of 2013 for world population predicts the global population will increase from approximately 7 billion people today to more than 9 billion by 2050 and up to 10 billion in 2100 (it also has scenarios in which world population drops after 2050). The high estimate, however, is based partly on the expectation that rich countries have increasing, rather than decreasing, populations, and partly on a number of African countries not reaching their demographic turning points.

These assumptions look increasingly unrealistic. When a country's GDP reaches about $5,000 per capita, birth rates (fertility) typically begin to decline, and at around $10,000, the typical pattern is that fertility drops below equilibrium level - often even far below.

This decline will often happen very quickly. Birth rates can even fall by up to 40% within 15 years, if incomes grow fast enough.[341] Among the more extreme examples is Iran, which from the end of World War II to 1990 had birth rates of 6-7 children per woman. However, within a single generation, it dropped to 1.88 – far below replacement level.[342]

In 2011, Sanjeev Sanyal from Deutsche Bank published an analysis which included calculations based on the same statistics, the UN used, but with very different conclusions.[343] His argument was based on the total birth rate. For various reasons, this has to be a little over two children per woman to ensure a stable population, but in the 1950s, for example, it was 6.1 in China and 5.9 in India. This figure, however, had, in 2012, decreased to 1.8 in China and 2.6 in India. Furthermore, there were around 119 boys born for every 100 girls in China, and in India the ratio was 110:100. If you adjust for this, Sanyal pointed out, effective birth rates were just 1.5 in China and 2.4 in India. This meant China faced a rapid population decline and India had already come very close to a level that would provide stabilization.

Around the middle of this century, China stands to lose 20-30% of its population per generation, and other countries will lose up to 50% per generation. The effect of all this will be a world that is very different to what many envisage. In 2009, ecologist Stewart Brand made this assessment, based on the corrected data:

"The UN's median estimate in 2008 was that the world population would reach little over 9 billion, but that figure is based on the assumption that birth rates in emerging markets will start rising again for some reason. Because that seems unlikely, I think a more probable peak is 8 billion followed by a descent so rapid that many will consider it a crisis." [344]

There's more: global GDP per capita has just reached the critical $10,000, which usually heralds demographic peak, and there is currently not a single country in the world which has a higher birth rate than it had in 1960. In fact, as already mentioned, the global population growth rate peaked in 1963, and it has since declined steadily.

From 1970 to 2010, the global birth rate dropped by 33% for the world as a whole, by 34% in developing countries and 41% in Islamic nations. It is overwhelmingly likely that birth rates will continue to decline significantly from year-to-year, and then population growth will halt completely. If you adjust for imbalances between girls and boys born in Asia, the indication is that, between 2020 and 2025, the human race will reach the magic tipping point where the global sex-adjusted birth rate falls below the equilibrium level. Approximately one generation after that, the globe will begin to depopulate, perhaps even rapidly. It should here be noted that Japan, China, Russia, Brazil, the US, South Korea and most of Europe are now below replacement birth rates.

However, here is an obvious question: what if China drops its one-child policy, which has already been liberalized slightly? A clue to the answer can be seen from the Chinese populations in Hong Kong and Taiwan, which are much richer, but have no one-child policies. In both territories, the estimated birth rate in 2013 was only 1.11, so significantly lower than China's. In even richer - and 74% Chinese – Singapore, the birth rate is as low as 0.79%. Given Hong Kong's birth rate, the eighth generation, totalling one million people, will only have 11,527 children, and with Singapore's birth rate it would only be 1,066 children.

Why is the average birth rate so extremely low in Hong Kong, Taiwan and Singapore? Because when people grow richer, life offers them better opportunities for pleasure, which reduces their willingness to be limited by children. In addition, far more women get tertiary (high) educations and seek career, which again comes into conflict with having children - especially having many children. This is an important aspect, because over the past few decades we have seen a dramatic transformation, so that now, globally, more women than men participate in higher education.

There is another important factor driving down birth rates almost everywhere: urbanization. As farming becomes more technology-driven and compact, farmland is turned into national parks and former farmers move to the cities. Actually, one of the main reasons the birth rate is so low in Hong Kong and Singapore is simply that they are city-states, and city-dwellers have fewer children than people in the countryside. In developing countries, this difference is indeed extreme - in poor countries, an abundance of children equates to cheap labour for a farmer, but in cities children are an economic burden to their parents. This urbanization factor is important, because the world is undergoing a huge urbanization transformation. The global rural population has already peaked and is predicted (also by the UN) to start declining in a few decades. Especially in China, the government plans to move hundreds of millions of people to cities over the coming decades. So a huge demographic transition is underway.

Here is the conclusion: In order to reverse population growth, we have to focus on creative technology, urbanization and rising prosperity - not on zero growth, back-to-nature romanticism and forced abortion.

We must remember that the world's population doubled during the 40 years from 1970 to 2010, but even according to the pessimistic UN estimates, numbers will only increase by approximately a third over the next 40 years, and according to Sanyals and Brand's forecasts, they will even grow by much less than that – perhaps only by 15%. In either scenario, the most intense period of population growth is well behind us.

This can actually been summed up in a very simple way: there has always been a race between population growth and innovation, and since 1450, innovation has evolved fastest.

But how can we keep this up? Obviously, we cannot now know which environmental technologies will be invented over the coming decades, but we can gain a hint by studying examples of new environmental technologies that either seem imminent or have been introduced recently.

We have already looked at possibilities such as thorium reactors, travelling wave technology, nuclear fusion and transmutation of nuclear waste. In Belgium, scientists work with a technology called Myrrha (Multi-purpose Hybrid Research Reactor for High- tech Applications), which converts nuclear waste into substances that degrade themselves within about 200 years.[345] In 2006, France amended its laws on the storage of nuclear waste so that, henceforth, it should remain available for 100 years; this meant that opportunities to transmute it or to extract the rest of its energy potential (which is approximately 98-99%), through new technologies, would not be missed.

Another interesting field is the treatment of conventional waste in land-fills. This can be done with a new waste-to-energy technology called plasma arc waste disposal, whereby mixed waste is heated to between 3,700 and 14,000 degrees centigrade without access to atmospheric oxygen. This rips apart molecules and the result is a stream of gas and slag, the latter akin to the lava spewing out of volcanoes. This process reduces the contents of landfills by about 99%, and the gas it generates is so plentiful that, in addition to operating the incinerator, it provides an energy surplus. As for the slag, this comes out in liquid form, which makes it imminently suitable for casting stones like building materials, just as one can extract recyclable metals from it. And if there is excess slag after metals have been extracted, well, when it cools down, it is simply stones. The US and Japan have started to remove and partially recycle the waste in old landfills with these technologies.

Similarly, new technologies to eliminate toxins from past pollution in nature have been developed. For example, scientists have created a genetically-modified poplar tree, which collects mercury from the soil. Once the poplar is felled, the mercury can be extracted and sold commercially. Another example is the aforementioned genetically modified bacteria that can break down oil spills in the oceans.

More problematic, however, is halting the extinction of species. But we are getting far better at tackling this. The vast majority of the losses of species occur on small islands (60%, 81% and 91% of extinct mammals, birds and reptiles, respectively lived only on islands.[346]), and, to a lesser extent, in tropical rainforests.

To prevent future extinction in affected areas, there is now a strong focus on restoring original streams and planting trees that capture nitrogen to improve soil fertility. There is also implementation of fishing quotas combined with fish farms and modified agricultural practices such as protecting small areas containing wild species in between patches of farmland. Perhaps most important is a huge effort to enhance natural parks, and the world's natural parks actually increased ten-fold between 1970 and 2010.[347]

In addition, there are now more than 1,000 gene banks (or seed banks), where the seeds of an increasing number of plant species are kept safe and regularly planted for renewal. An international collaboration between aquariums and botanical and zoological gardens has also helped bring back many species from the brink of extinction.

While we are on this subject, it is worth noting that people say "extinction is forever", but is it really? Not if you believe what you saw in the 1993 film *Jurassic Park*, which was about the recreation of dinosaurs. The method (in the movie) was to drill into ancient amber pieces that contained mosquitos and extract dinosaur blood from the stomachs of these insects. Scientists could then take this dinosaur DNA and insert it into birds' eggs, possibly by first-sequencing a lot of samples and recreating full DNA strings. The idea was that the eggs cells would hatch and dinosaurs emerge.

That was a cool plan, but there were several problems with it, including the fact that the dinosaurs ate the scientists. This was admittedly what made the story excellent movie material, but as well as that, scientists watching it generally found it too far-fetched. "I laughed when Steven Spielberg said that cloning extinct animals was inevitable," said Hendrik Poinar of McMaster University in an interview with *National Geographic* in 2009. Poinar was an expert in ancient DNA and scientific advisor for the film. However, he has since changed his mind: "I'm not laughing anymore, at least about mammoths. This is going to happen. It's just a matter of working out the details."[348]

When the film was made, no one had ever deciphered DNA. Now, this is routine, and the same goes for synthesizing new DNA. Furthermore, scientists have found relatively well-preserved DNA strands of hair from frozen mammoths in Siberia. By decoding and comparing many of these, they have reconstructed the entire code, and they now believe they can produce artificial mammoth DNA and implant it into eggs, which would then be inserted into elephants.

Such a process is now called "de-extinction", and there is already a technical precedent. In 2003, a company called Advanced Cell Technology cloned a banteng, which is an endangered ox from Java. The clone was made from frozen tissue taken from an animal that had died 23 years earlier. The scientists achieved this by putting the dead animal's genome into several cow's egg cells, and one of the cows gave birth to a healthy banteng. If you can do it with an animal that died-out 23 years previously, you can, in principle, do it with one that became extinct 10,000 years previously - if you can sequence its DNA, and if there is a reasonably close-living relative that can breed it. You don't even need to extract an intact DNA string, as long as you can identify its sequence by comparing numerous damaged DNA samples. Once you know the code, you can synthesise a new DNA string using standard machinery.

Here it should be noted that some of the species scientists hope to recreate lived in cold climates. These include megafauna such as the Tasmanian tiger, mammoths, sabre-toothed cats and woolly rhinos, which lived in the recent ice age. So if we end up developing a real-life Jurassic Park, it might have to be in Greenland, Siberia, Canada, Chile o Argentina, all of which today have areas with suitable climates (and it will not be Jurassic, but Mesolithic).

All this brings us back to the story of the environmental disaster on Easter Island. After Jared Diamond had published his bestseller *Collapse*, where he described how the people on this island felled all their big trees and subsequently ate each other in desperation, several later books were published that painted a very different picture; two such examples were *Questioning Collapse* and *The Statues that Walked.*[349]

These argued, convincingly, that it was actually the rats that arrived with the Polynesian immigrants, which had caused the island's deforestation, since that kind of thing is normal on islands and because approximately 99% of old nuts found on the island had traces of rat bites. To illustrate how swiftly such things can happen, laboratory experiments have shown that a single rat couple can multiply to 17 million individuals in just over three years. Terry Hunt and Carl Lipio concluded in *Questioning Collapse*:

"The ecological catastrophe of Rapa Nui had a complex history that cannot be reduced to psychological motivations of people who cut down the last tree. Indeed, the "last tree" may simply have died, and rats may have simply eaten the last seeds. What were the rats thinking?"

A more fundamental comment on the same matter comes from aforementioned nuclear physicist David Deutsch:

"It would be astonishing if the details of a static society's collapse had any relevance to hidden dangers that may face our open, dynamic and scientifically-based society, let alone what we should do about them." [350]

The problem on Easter Island was precisely that the locals had a static society without an innovative culture, so when they encountered problems, they didn't come up with solutions. They did not know how to develop traps or make rats into chicken feed. Nor did they manage to make nets and other fishing gear that could have made them effective fishermen. When, in 1786, J F G de la Perouse brought them sheep, goats, pigs and crops for breeding-purposes, they just ate them. They were not creative.

But others were, and we should not forget that while Homo sapiens has destroyed a lot of things, it is also the only species on the planet that deliberately tries to preserve and protect other species; so, if a 100 or 500 years from now, a giant comet rushes towards Earth with the potential to eradicate half of all living species, there will be, perhaps for the first time in its multi-billion-year history, one species, among the millions of species, that is capable of preventing disaster for all the others: we humans, because we are creative.

Let's bring this chapter to a close by summarizing the environmental challenge in as simple a way as Paul Ehrlich would have done. As mentioned earlier, he launched the IPAT equation, which read as follows:

Environmental Impact = Population × Affluence × Technology

So, in his opinion, the richer we become and the more new technology we introduce, the worse things become. This is wrong, because as we have seen, the more advanced the technology a society has, the less damage it does to the environment.

But Ehrlich's equation is even worse than that, because he describes wealth as being part of the problem even though the richest nations, statistically, are the cleanest and have stable or declining populations on top, which means that affluence should also appear as a divisor. So here is a better version:

Environmental Impact = Population / (Affluence × Technology)

The solution to our challenges is not to stand still or to reverse, as they did on Eastern Island, but to move forward. The key to our future environmental solutions is not to curb technology and economic growth, but to incourage creativity, prosperity, technology and growth.

PART 5

THE SILTING OF SOCIETY

The West originally created a unique civilization via tremendous creativity and dynamism. However, today, many Western nations suffer from stagnation, debt burdens, unemployment and pessimism. Many of these problems seem eerily similar to those of the Western Roman Empire shortly before its fall.

In this section we shall look at both their symptoms and causes.

CHAPTER 16:
The legal tangle

CHAPTER 17:
The public productivity problem

CHAPTER 18:
Over-taxation and public borrowing

CHAPTER 19:
The donation delusions

16.
THE
LEGAL
TANGLE

One day in November 2011, 87-year-old Danish farmer Niels Kristensen was standing inside the steel shovel of his front loader, 115cm above the ground, cleaning his gutters. Unfortunately for him, a representative from the Working Environment Authority passed by and reported him to the police for violation of health and safety regulations. This resulted in a fine of 20,000 kroner, which, on appeal, was commuted to a fine of 10,000 kroner or 10 days in jail. "I accept the alternative penalty of 10 days in jail rather than paying the fine," he later said in an interview. "I admit that I was standing in the front loader. But I have not posed any danger, and it is completely impossible to fall out. I simply cannot imagine a safer place to clean the gutter than from the front loader."[351]

Less than three months later, on 2 February 2012, the successful Danish juice chain, Joe & The Juice, received a message from the Food and Drug Administration: its juice bars could no longer call their fruit-and-vegetable juices "Hangover Heaven", "Stressless", "Go Away Doc", "Stress Down", "Strong Bones" or "Immunity" and they would have to pay substantial fines if they kept doing it. The reason, the authorities explained, was that such product names violated labelling regulation 76 which set out how you could describe a product. Why? Because if you bought a "Go Away Doc", for instance, you could not be sure you wouldn't need a doctor afterwards - so the name was misleading. The same could be said of the other ones. That was a big problem for the chain because the brands had been expensive to develop and were very popular.

Less than a month later, a new law was passed requiring vendors of seafood to quote all fish names in Latin. *Berlingske*, a Danish newspaper, subsequently interviewed fish wholesaler Axel Jessen, who explained what this new law meant to him:

"I had to hire a secretary to come in the morning and fill out all this stuff on my bills because I do not have time to do it. In the morning, when the fish come in, I have to sell my fish to customers, which by the way show blind indifference to what a hake is called in Latin. What matters to them is whether the fish is fresh." [352]

The following month, the Danish parliament began debating whether trac-tors were considered "single offices" as trucks were considered to be, because if they were, then they should be covered by the smoking ban.

Many such laws in Europe originate from the European Union (EU) - includ-ing the aforementioned marketing law and the law demanding Latin naming of fish. By 2015, the EU had issued more than 35,000 binding regulations, 5,000 non- binding directives and 50,000 standards, plus 12,000 judgements by the European Court of Justice, all of which had led more than 80,000 pages of legislative text.

The original thinking behind the EU was that it would ensure free move-ment of capital, services, goods and labour. To meet those objectives it was necessary to develop certain shared standards, so that member states would, for example, recognize each other's education programmes, product stan-dards and services. The idea was that the EU would remove bureaucratic barriers and make life easier for companies and citizens, and that is exactly what it did in the beginning.

The original plan for the EU was also to respect what is known as the sub-sidiarity principle, which means that central leadership may only act (make laws) where the action of individual communities (here EU member-nations) is insufficient. In fact, this very principle was established in the EU via the European Charter of Local Self-Government in 1985, and was reaffirmed in the 1992 Treaty of Maastricht.

However, in the EU the reality has been an ongoing creep towards central-ization, where lawmakers write evermore detailed manuals about how life should be lived, governments run and companies managed.

Don't get this wrong. Centralization and indeed international laws can serve good purposes such as providing rules for diplomacy, aviation, postal systems, international navigation, free trade and more. However, the trend within EU has increasingly been to make international laws about labour rights, expulsion rights, minority protection, marketing norms, and many other issues, without respecting parliamentary majorities in the nations concerned. In fact, when local politicians have failed to get their proposals through their domestic legal systems, they have often subsequently succeeded via the EU.

A specific problem is that decisions made via the EU are typically made by haggling, where each group or nation manages to extract concessions and exemptions. Thus, in March 2005, former EU Competition Commissioner Mario Monti described, in a speech in Monaco, how EU decision-making was a "total chaos", in which every decision required negotiation between the EU 's (then) 25 member states, which, individually, could demand compensatory measures before agreeing to anything; this, in turn, tended to trigger an endless cascade of special rules, grants, footnotes and exceptions.

In the EU you are no longer allowed to serve olive oil in a bowl in a restaurant or sell food per dozen (price should be per unit weight). Nor may you point out that water prevents dehydration (which it does) or that plums prevents constipation (they do). It is forbidden to eat your own horse, if it is a pet (why?). If pollen represents more than 0.9% of honey, you should indicate whether any of the bees have visited GM plants (how can the farmer know that?), and vacuum cleaners may only use 900 watts (doesn't work).

Since 2013 it has been illegal for EU citizens to plant any seeds that are not approved by the EU Plant Variety Agency. Children under the age of 13 can no longer deliver newspapers, and children under eight years old should not blow up balloons, unless supervised by an adult.

The US is no better. In 2010, the "Land of the Free" introduced the so-called FATCA system, under which foreign banks had to collect taxes from Americans living abroad on behalf of the US state or be sued for billions. By mid- 2014, more than 77,000 non-American institutions had agreed to do this, which probably involved an additional administrative workforce of 300,000-400,000 people.[353] For the seven million Americans abroad, it meant thousands of dollars spent filing tax forms to another country (the US) than the one in which they actually reside.

While many financial institutions chose to comply, a large number reacted to the regulation by terminating their relationship with US clients which obviously made life very difficult for these seven million people and the US companies, for which they worked. It is hardly surprising that the number of Americans renouncing their citizenship rose. Of course, it was only a question of time before an US citizen sued a Dutch bank for kicking him out. He won, and this implied that the US could force other nations to collect its taxes. The US Congress estimated the system would generate approximately $800 million in extra revenue for Americans, but the cost to non-American financial institutions, plus the affected expatriates, was a very large multiple of that.

On 6 May 2011, the EU called on all its members to ban the use of WiFi in classrooms. The motive was to protect children from a potential radiation hazard; this is despite the fact that the ban prevents modern education, and even though WiFi is used virtually everywhere else and constitutes no proven hazard.

And so it goes, but without the least element of consistency. You are not allowed to clean your own gutters in the safest way possible, but sky-diving, performing on a circus trapeze or taking part in heavy-weight boxing is perfectly fine. You cannot call a drink "Go Away Doc", but calling it "Sex on the Beach", "Sex With an Alligator", "Death in the Afternoon" is ok, even if

the promised sex or death doesn't always come with it. And "Gorillas Milk "
is acceptable, even though it doesn't come from an ape, as indicated. It takes
$1.3 billion to register a scientifically-based medication, but next to nothing,
if it isn't. If a bank sends out an analysis of a company or currency, it comes
with pages of legal disclaimers and any major bank is entangled in thousands of lawsuits, but if an environmental organization inaccurately states
environmental data by a factor of approximately 5,000 times while collecting
money, that's fine.

The bureaucratic law machine becomes an undemocratic political machine
that prevents experimental activity and choice. For example, *The Maastricht
Treaty* provides for a "Social Charter" which, in direct contradiction to its own
aforementioned subsidiarity principle, says that member states should harmonize their social policies, apparently to a level that would turn the entire
EU into a new Argentina.

In November 2011, *The Economist* reported on three young Spaniards who
(heroically) decided to open a combined bookstore and cafe in Madrid. It took
them three years to gain the required licences to sell books, coffee and wine.
Furthermore, in Spain, as in many other European countries, it has - for many
years - been extremely expensive to sack employees. The consequence had
been that many small businesses simply closed in bad times, where the alternative in a freer market could have been to reduce staff numbers or working
hours temporarily. This contributed to an unemployment rate which exceeded 25% in 2013.

Laws have become so complicated that people often have no idea
whether they are doing something illegal, which means they often seek
permits to do something that is already legal, while violating laws they have
never heard about.

One of the problems people experience is that public offices tell them what
they cannot do but not what they can do. And there is rarely a public office
with the guts and authority to say "enough is enough" and issue a general permit to start your business, build your bridge or whatever it is you want to do.
This means you never know for sure whether there is yet another permit you
didn't know about and for which you have failed to apply that could stop you
in your tracks after you have invested all your money.

In 2009, President Obama initiated a programme to weather-proof 607,000
homes, but this virtually ground to a halt because a law from 1931 said that
weather proofers should be paid the local prevailing rates. Instead of weather-
proofers now going to work, an army of bureaucrats began a massive work to
find out what the going rates were for weather-proofers in each of thousands
of local counties involved. In California, the number of houses that should
have been weather-proofed by 2009 was approximately 30,000, but the actual

total was 12. When the port authority of New York and New Jersey needed to raise the road on an existing bridge to accommodate the new global standard size for container ships, it required 47 permits from 19 government bodies and included a mandatory survey of 2,500 historical buildings in the community that were not in any way affected by the project. One law said that an environmental study should include participation from native tribes, and Indians from all over the nation, including Nebraska and Oklahoma, were thus invited to oversee it. A number of years after the start of the process, the authorities were bogged down in paperwork and lawsuits with no end in sight, even though the modest change proposed had huge environmental and economic advantages.[354]

American workers, whether in the public or private sector, are often so restricted by what they can and cannot do that nothing is done. When a manager fires or reassigns an employee, he or she is so afraid of being sued for the cause given that none is given. It's a case of: "You are fired and we will not tell you why". If anyone brings home-cooked food to school parties or charities, they are shut down or sacked for violating food regulations. If children sell lemonade to raise money for charities, they can be stopped by the police and prosecuted.

One of the problems with legal jungles is the lack of focus on eliminating outdated or ineffective laws. We continuously add new laws to existing ones, and the total volume of legal tangle grows unceasingly. In March 2012, US lawyer and writer Philip K Howard pointed this out:

"At this point, democracy is basically run by dead people. We elect new representatives, but society is run by policy ideas and political deals from decades ago. Congress has a tragic misconception of its responsibility -- it sees itself as a body that makes new law, not one that makes sense of old laws." [355]

This created many problems, he pointed out. The first was the sheer accumulated amount of laws and prohibitions, which often made it increasingly difficult for people and businesses to manoeuvre. In addition, the laws typically created unintended consequences that required adjustment via new laws, and they often reflected outdated priorities. For instance, US farmers were given subsidies in the 1930s, because they had major financial problems then. These problems ended in 1941, but the subsidies continued. When Brazil sued the US for subsidizing cotton farmers, it was awarded the right essentially to confiscate $800 million worth of intellectual property rights from US companies at its choosing. Instead of cancelling its subsidies, the US responded by negotiating a deal whereby it would also subsidize Brazilian cotton farmers, so that these also could compete unfairly.

In the US, total federal tax regulations constituted 400 pages in 1913. In 1969, they had grown to 16,500 pages and in 2013, they filled 72,513 pages full of cross-references.[7] This, and many other legal areas, are now so complex that no one can know for sure where they stand, and when politicians want to streamline or cut, they routinely run into so much complexity that they give up and leave the existing structures as they are. They are no longer in charge; the bureaucrats are. As Howard writes:

"Nothing today is legally feasible. Nothing. Government is on autopilot, its legal flaps locked in an unsustainable position' headed towards a stall and then a frightening plummet towards insolvency and political chaos." [356]

Everything a politician wants to touch is tied up in a web of cross-referencing laws, rules and regulations that make change almost impossible. And if you try to effect change, you will be hit by an avalanche of lawsuits that can go through cascading appeals lasting decades. US regulations concerning the production and sale of hamburgers involve in the region of 200 laws as well as 41,000 rules and precedents derived from 110,000 related lawsuits.[357] In addition, there is a tradition that lawyers offer to sue people and companies based on profit-sharing with the lawyer's client. Such lawsuits often end with the defendant paying to have the case dropped even if he is completely innocent – a concept that is not materially different from paying protection money to the Mafia. Examples from outlandish lawsuits include a man who attempted to commit suicide by jumping under a train in Manhattan. He was injured, but survived, and afterwards, sued New York City Transit Authority, because they had not been better at stopping the train.[358] Due to this extreme lawsuit culture, US products are often labelled with absurd warnings and instructions, such as ones that advise people to seek medical advice before using a kayak.

The US has more than twice as many lawyers per 1,000 inhabitants as Germany and more than five times as many as France; the number of US court cases has tripled within just 30 years.[359]

Overall, the legal maze the Western world is constructing is as absurd as the way the Eastern Islanders built statues as their societies atrophied, and just as stifling, and it is a symptom of a drift towards centralization of government. One of the reasons is simply this: To start with, a society may have a high degree of freedom and local self-rule. Then someone makes a mistake somewhere. The press picks up on this and puts pressure on government politicians to intervene. These then issue standard rules for all local communities so that this mistake can't happen again. In this way, step by step, over time, everything becomes standardized, centralized and ruled from afar. This stifles creativity and de-motivates people, and it creates another problem: overdependence on statistics. When you rule from afar, you only see quantities, not quality. Ruling from afar is ruling by numbers; not by insight, intuition or compassion.

It's hard to measure exactly to what extent exaggerated legal mazes and litigation culture damage the implicated economies, but in the US, studies have shown that the 7,800 lawsuits that, in 2010, were started daily, cost society the equivalent of 8% sales tax on all products or 13% income tax on all wages.[360]

Often, public lawsuits (where tax payers bear the costs) are conducted without any consideration for the costs. The trial of former Yugoslavian president Slobodan Milošević, which had to be terminated without judgement (he had died) had already accumulated bills of more than €160 million (or $200 million), even though it wasn't even finished.

International comparisons show that the smaller the proportion of a country's academics that are engineers, and the greater the proporption of lawyers, the slower its economy will grow.[361] The reason is, arguably, that engineers primarily engage in win-win activities, while lawyers often work with win-lose or lose-lose transactions.

One of the reasons for this ever-growing Mandarin-style legalism is that the bureaucrats and politicians who make all these laws and appeal bodies have rarely experienced how frustrating it is for normal people to live with them. US Democratic presidential candidate George McGovern left the Senate in 1981 and then had to support himself, after which he invested in the hotel Stratfort Inn. In 2008, he explained what it was like suddenly to be on the other side of the table - to be among those who must follow the laws instead of make them:

"In retrospect, I wish I had known more about the hazards and difficulties of such a business, especially during a recession of the kind that hit New England just as I was acquiring the inn's 43-year leasehold. I also wish that during the years I was in public office, I had had this first-hand experience about the difficulties business people face every day. That knowledge would have made me a better U.S. senator and a more understanding presidential contender." [362]

There are three basic ways to pursuit the delivery of good products and services:

◆ **Legalism (command and control)**. Central bureaucrats write rules, manuals and forms, have police and inspectors check that people act accordingly and punish them if they don't.
◆ **Principles (guide and consult)**. Bureaucrats describe broad goals and

use "guided discretion" rather than detailed commands, but empower the people actually doing the jobs to figure out how to meet such guidelines. If they are not met, it is resolved through dialogue with stakeholders.

◆ **Markets (vote with your feet)**. Suppliers are free to work out ways of attracting and pleasing customers; and if they are not good at this, they go under.

Western societies have, for decades, moved further away from markets and principles and towards greater legalism. The over-reliance of rules can easily turn people irresponsible and disengaged. If everything you have to do is written down in laws and manuals, you will no longer feel free and you will not be engaged and creative. To do a job well often requires performing tasks that cannot be described in writing, but which require intuitive decision-making on the spot.

Increasingly, there is also a risk that people who are subject to an excess of rules will inadvertently feel compelled, or be forced, to act immorally. In 2012, the Floridian life guard Thomas Lopez was sacked for saving the life of a drowning person outside his own area of the beach. In 2013, an elderly resident of a care home collapsed and somebody called 911 for an ambulance and handed the phone to a nurse, who spoke with the call-handler. When the call-handler asked the nurse to perform CPR (Cardiopulmonary Resuscitation), she declined on the basis that she was not authorized to do so. "Is there anybody that's willing to help this lady and not let her die?" the dispatcher later asked. Refusal again. And then it went:

Dispatcher: This lady is going to die.

Nurse: Yeah.

Dispatcher: Well, if you get anybody, any stranger that happens to walk by, who is willing to help ... I understand if your boss is telling you can't do it. But if there's any ... it's a human being. I don't, you know ... is there anybody that's willing to help this lady and not let her die?

Nurse: Not at this time.

The patient died.[363] US teachers are now scared to put their arms around crying children for risk of being sued. People walk pass the injured or dying without acting for fear of being held liable. In 2011, firefighters stood on a beach in Alabama watching a suicidal man battling the waters for an hour before drowning. They didn't intervene because they were not authorized to do so and had been told by their superior about the legal liabilities for performing uncertified rescues.

Legalism has made it ever more risky to do the right thing and evermore difficult to be an innovator. Many countries have whole sectors of people collecting "speed money" for helping gain permissions to do business faster (you don't want to know how). The intentions may be good, but the consequences are negative, and what we are recreating is the stifling mentality of Chinese mandarins of the past.

17.
THE PUBLIC
PRODUCTIVITY
PROBLEM

The legal jungle and lawsuit culture is all about the over-institutionalization and centralization, which can kill creativity, but there are many other examples of this. In February 1991, William W Lewis - who was a partner in the renowned consulting firm McKinsey and co-founder of their research arm McKinsey Global Institute - organized a meeting to discuss the fundamental health of the US economy. Participants included Nobel laureate Robert Solow, Professor Francis Bator from Harvard University and editors from The Wall Street Journal and The Economist.[364]

After much discussion, the group concluded that the main difference between the performances of various economies mainly came down to their long-term productivity growth, by sector. Thereafter, the McKinsey Global Institute, along with local McKinsey offices worldwide, began to analyze what promotes and prevents productivity for each country and industry, and these studies have resulted in thousands of pages of research.

In 2005, after this work had been carried out for 16 years, Lewis published in the book *The Power of Productivity*, where he summarized the main conclusions. One was that high productivity occurs if the government abstains from prioritizing some business areas over others, and if companies are subjected to maximum pressure of competition in their quest to give consumers what they want.

Consumers are key, he concluded. If you give consumers maximum choice, that will bring about maximum competitive pressure, and this will force productivity to increase via innovation and cost-control. Private companies are under constant competitive pressure and often measure current productivity and efficiency almost in real time in order to keep up. Public organizations, however, generally operate without competition. This weakens incentives for creativity and thus provides less innovation and lower productivity growth.

So how slow is productivity growth in the public sectors? McKinsey finds the hair-raising fact: that the long-term productivity growth in the public sector is, typically, around zero. Of course, there have been exceptions to this where the growth rate was slightly positive, but also some where it was found to be negative.

The results of such studies about the (lack of) productivity growth in the public sector is also supported by the fact that countries in which everything is public -

socialist economies – have typically, after a first transitional stage, stagnated and then almost always collapsed or evolved into static zombies.

From time-to-time,the UK government publishes productivity studies for the country's public sector, and these have shown aslight decline in productivity over time.[365] While productivity in the UK private sector, for example, grew by 28% within the period 1997-2007, it *declined* by more than 3% in the state over the same period. This has enormous effects, because if the UK public sector had had the same productivity growth the private sector, it would only have needed to charge half as much in taxes.[366]

An aspect of the problem can be a focus on the wrong incentives. A classic example of the effect of incentives happened when, in the 19th century, England shipped high numbers of prisoners to Australia. They paid their captains a fixed fee for each prisoner that boarded a boat, but only 40% survived the trip. In 1862, the politician Edwin Chadwik proposed to change the payment method, so that captains instead were paid for each prisoner who arrived alive in Australia. That took the survival rate from 50% to 98.5%. Incentives always matter and McKinsey Global Institute found that, in Japan, hospitals were paid per bed-night, and that meant that patients were hospitalized for an average of 24 days compared to six days in the US, where hospitals were paid for the relevant illness/transaction. However, when it came to diagnosis, Japanese doctors were paid per consultation unit, while the US was paid for consultation time. And guess what? On average, Japanese consultations lasted just five minutes, whereas they lasted 24 minutes in the US.

Wrongly-targeted incentives can lead to bottleneck problems. In many countries with public healthcare, people complain about long waiting lists for, say, hip replacements, and often poor service. Paradoxically, these are the same countries that may offer excellent service and minimal waiting times, if you need surgery for a cat or dog at a vet, or if you want cosmetic surgery. The reason for this enigma is that these tasks are considered less important, which is why the state leaves them to the private sector.

One of the clearest differences between public and private sector services is their different tendency to exhibit creativity and innovation. A curious example is seen in the very different Christian churches in Europe and the US. In Europe, a visit to a church is a trip back in history – virtually nothing has changed over the past 600 years. By contrast, the US Christian churches are highly creative and constantly evolving. Their services feature numerous Christian radio and television channels, amazing gospel music and religious rock groups like best-selling band *Jesus Culture*. Additionally, there are trendy Christian youth and lifestyle magazines, summer camps, rock operas, passion conferences, online communities and mega churches like Lakewood Church, Second Baptist Church of Houston and North Point Community Church, which every week bring together tens of thousands of worth shippers in giant events, which are broadcast live and can be replayed on the internet. Why are the US churches so creative while the European ones aren't? It is because the former are not funded by the state like those in Europe.

Another classic example of private versus public creativity is that of universities, where a majority of the top-ranked in the world are private sector organisations, although these represent only a very small proportion of all universities. For example, globally top-ranked universities such as Harvard, Yale, Princeton, Columbia, Chicago, MIT, Duke, Columbia, Brown, Richmond, Stanford, Carnegie Mellon, Pennsylvania and University College are all private.

In the same way, products will be far better when delivered by private companies under competition. When Germany was divided into the market-based West and socialist East after World War II, the East Germans manufactured Trabants and the West Germans produced BMWs, Porches, Mercedes, Audis and VWs.

When the governments' spending grows as proportion of GDP, a nations' apparent GDP growth can become very misleading. This happens partly because private services are included in the national accounts in terms of what people have been willing to pay for them, whereas public services are counted on the basis of what they cost, which is often far greater than what people would willingly have paid, or what it would have cost in a competitive market. Also, when we institutionalize services that were previously provided in the homes, they suddenly become part of GDP. For instance, when you take care of your child personally, it doesn't boost official GDP, but if you let an institution do exactly the same work, it does. This is especially alarming if there is a disproportionate growth in government-driven win-lose or lose-lose transactions, such as administration and controls which the private sector has to match by defensive activities such as tax advice, legal assistance, and so on. Control systems and tax lawsuits add to a nation's GDP, but not to people's well-being.

Apparent GDP growth can also be disguised through public lending. Many Western states essentially became static several decades ago and have since only been able to grow through public lending (and by paying evermore people for non-work, from the public purse). Borrowed money may be used for public prestige projects - typically in the capitals and other major cities – that are highly visible. In Roman times, the capital's inhabitants could watch with awe as the emperors built marble palaces and performed grandiose spectacle shows in Roman arenas, but they did not see that more and more farmland in the province was simultaneously fallowed. Similarly, no one who visited the cafes in Paris or London in 2010, for example, would have sensed that these two countries had lost 25-30% of their industries within the preceding ten years while accumulating massive government debt.

Another reason why deceptive GDP growth together with over-institutionalization comes creeping is this: in the private sector, wages increase in line with productivity, but in the public sector their increase just follows the private sector wage increases, even though there is no productivity increase. The consequence is that the tax burden or government borrowing continues to climb, even if public services are completely unchanged. Or to put it another way: the public sector will constitute a constantly-increasing share of GDP, even if the benefits it provides do not increase at all.

Just think about how important this problem really is: even if we change nothing, it will just get worse and worse until society collapses. The phenomenon is called the "Baumol effect" after the economist William Baumol, and it explains why growth in public debt and constant tax increases just keep going.[367]

The overall problem is this: when the public sector's share of the economy grows, the majority, or all, of the growth in GDP can be misleading. The growing GDP number captures the fact that more money is spent, but it does not pick up on whether the money actually creates greater value or was earned before being spent or was, in fact, simply borrowed.

From all these observations, one can conclude that it is important to rein in and, at some point, halt growth in the public sector. However, this turns out to be very difficult to implement in practice.

Why is that? One reason was given as long ago as in 1955, when the magazine The Economist carried an article by English professor and marine historian Cyril Northcote Parkinson, which introduced what is now known Parkinson's Law. This states that: "Work expands so as to fill the time available for its completion".[368] In addition to this observation, Parkinson noted a tendency for administration, and especially the number of managerial functions within administration, to grow relentlessly, even if the task they had to solve didn't grow or was in fact declining.[369] After studying a lot of statistics, Parkinson concluded that public bureaucracy spontaneously grew by 5-6% a year, regardless of whether their primary mission grew at all. For example, he made a study of what had happened with the English Navy between 1414 and 1928:

Number of large battleships in use:	- 67%
Number of officers and enlisted men in the Navy:	- 32%
Number of shipyard workers:	+ 10%
Number of office workers:	+ 40%
Number of officers:	+ 78%

Parkinson's analysis was entertaining and a bit of an eye-opener, but it was not based on a particularly scientific study. However, since then, lots of deeper analyses of these problems have been carried out. One of the findings is described in the "budget-maximizing model". This was launched in 1971 by university professor William Niskanen, who, among other things, worked as chief economist at Ford, as well as being a consultant for the US government.

Niskanen noted that public sector managers often try to increase their own organizations' budgets so that they can gain more subordinates and greater power. To justify rising budgets, they will gradually increase the number of tasks their organizations are undertake.

This phenomenon is an example of what is known as "mission-creep", whereby an organization spontaneously begins to pursue a different mission than originally intended. One example is the EU's aforementioned transition from being a free-trade organization towards a more paternalistic power-centre.

Niskanen's main proposal for solving the problem was simply to introduce competition, which simultaneously reduced costs and improved innovation and quality, and also allowed people to get a sense of the reasonable cost/price for any given service.

Another reason for constant public sector growth is that societies normally, at some time, reach a point where you get a so-called "welfare coalition", where the majority of people now live from the state, why they keep voting for increased public spending. And a final reason can be found in the so-called "Mouritzens 1-3 rule". As Poul Erik Mouritzen, who is a political scientist from University of Southern Denmark, explains:

"If the government implements an improvement of a certain size, is may perhaps gain an electoral win of 1000 votes. If later, for example for financial reasons, it feels compelled to remove the improvements, the electoral loss according to the 1-3 rule will be 3,000 votes." [370]

So according to this rule, in a democracy, voters will predominantly elect those who give more benefits, for which reason the government will tend to grow as part of GDP, at least until an acute economic crises stops and reverses it for a while.

The problems do not only arise because of what happens among bureaucrats and voters, but also from the behaviour of benefit receivers. They experience a scenario akin to sharing a table in a restaurant with 20 people you don't know. So each person orders a far more expensive meal than would have been the case, if the person should have paid for it alone, or if it knew the others personally and thus felt an obligation for constraint. So everybody will shamelessly overindulge while each hope, that the others are more responsible. When the bill finally arrives, everyone is chocked. This is an example of what economists call "the called the tragedy of the commons".

Five additional issues should be mentioned here. The first is political leaders' occasional infatuation with the power that you can gain by having a large state. Many politicians are, in fact, preoccupied with the idea of becoming a global power (or at least be "heard in the world") through centralization. However, their citizens are seldom particularly interested in global political power - they'd rather have jobs, pensions, a good environment and low crime rates.

Another reason why the states just keep growing is that welfare transfers create changes to moral norms and social behaviours, which means that people in an "entitlement society" become less and less shy about dipping into the public purse (more about that later). The consequence of this is that social transfers increase beyond what was predicted, which is then compensated for with higher taxes, lending or by cutting down on basic services.

Lack of monetary incentives is also a factor. First, if public sector employees receive big bonuses, it may easily cause a public outcry. Second, the public sector has, on average, a higher union density and more centralized wage-bargaining than private sector industries, which prevents strong individual performance-based pay schemes.

Further to that we have the so-called "insider takeover" problem, whereby the employees of an institution begin to primarily serve themselves instead of focusing on clients (this is also a variation of the mission-creep phenomenon). Insider takeover is extremely common in both the private and public sector, but within private companies it is contained by competitive pressures. Within the public sector, on the other hand, it is far more frequently allowed to continue, and the effect is typically seen after privatization of state functions, after which it is not uncommon for a very large proportion of the workforce to be let go while customer service is improved significantly. Good examples were the European telecom monopolies before privatization, which were massively over-staffed, while it could take months or even years to get a phone line.

When an organization is subject to insider takeover, it is more likely to become "extractive", as economists Acemoglu and Robinson have called it (we looked at that in chapter six).[371] The classic example is the public institution which identifies an opportunity for savings but evades this for fear that its budget will then be reduced in the following year. This pattern is quite well known among those who sell capital equipment such as car fleets or computers to private and public institutions, who note that public sector managers often seek to accumulate expenses during the last months of the current fiscal year, whereas private managers are more likely to push them into the beginning of the following year. The obvious reason is that public sector managers are seeking to maximize their costs and thus justify the same budget the following year, whereas private sector managers want to maximize their profits in the current year to win bonuses.

Both actions are selfish, but the consequences for society are different. In private companies, people try to maximize their profits through creativity and cost-savings. In the public sector, on the other hand, they optimize by increasing their budgets and organization as much as possible. In fact, it is not unusual that the state responds to a lack of results in a project by expanding its budget instead of closing or revising the activity.

Another issue that goes some way to explain the lack of productive growth in the provision of public services is the so-called "flypaper effect", which allows bodies that distribute public funds to keep much of them for their own organizations.[372]

The third problem is the so-called "Kronos effect", named by American professor Tim Wu.[373] Kronos was a god in Greek mythology, who ate his own sons to prevent them from taking the throne from him. What Tim Wu pointed out was that a service provider's instinct is to attempt to stifle innovation from outside their organization that could harm their own position of power. He saw examples of this in IT organizations which gained initial success through innovation, but which forever after would fight any attempt from outsiders to develop innovations that would make their own redundant. These attempts would almost always fail, after which they would lose out. The Kronos effect is also widespread in public organizations, which try to prevent private competitors entering their field. The typical arguments used here are that "all citizens should have the same service", "private services will only be for the rich", or "it is dangerous if the relevant services are provided by someone with a profit motive." If the same principles were applied to other sectors such as the car industry, we would all be driving Trabants.

WIKIPEDIA COMMONS.

TRABANT 601 S DELUXE. THIS IS WHAT A CAR MADE BY GERMANS WITHOUT A PROFIT MOTIVE LOOKED LIKE IN 1988. IT NEEDED 36 SECONDS TO REACH 100 KM/H (60 MPH), WAS HIGHLY POLLUTING AND TENDED TO RUST VERY QUICKLY.

All those phenomena are elements of a broader theory complex called public choice theory, which describes how bureaucrats often will act collectively against the interest of society, while acting perfectly rationally from their own perspective.

The sum of it all is lack of innovation and productivity growth. The reason is wrong incentives. It can be summarized as follows:

13 CAUSES OF THE PUBLIC PRODUCTIVITY PROBLEM

1. There is no competition to force innovation.
2. Employees have no financial incentive for innovation and rationalization.
3. There is no process to repeal laws and regulations, so their numbers keep growing without end.
4. There is "insider takeover" compelling public employees to increasingly prioritize themselves over the customers/users. They use mission creep to expand their original task definitions, and the organizations thus become "extractive".
5. Bureaucrats create work for each other, and work expands to fill the time allocated.
6. Managers seek more power by taking on more staff and seeking bigger budgets.
7. A majority of voters become dependent on the state and create an informal welfare coalition voting for ever more benefits.
8. Voters give three times as many votes to politicians who increase benefits as to those who remove them (the 1-3 rule).
9. The "flypaper effect" allows offices disbursing funds to take more and more of these for themselves.
10. According to Baumol's cost disease, the state pays the same wage as private sector companies, but without the commensurate increase in productivity. Therefore, the state automatically increases its share of GDP even if its services remain unchanged.
11. Via the "Kronos effect", the government tries to stifle innovation that might threaten its power monopoly.
12. Each citizen takes far more from the public purse than he would if he should pay these services by himself. This is the "tragedy of the commons".
13. As tax pressure rises, an increasing proportion of GDP is allocated to tax collection and control.

18.
OVER-TAXATION
AND PUBLIC
BORROWING

On 10 March 1976, the Swedish newspaper *Expressen* carried a satirical story entitled *"Sagan on Pomperipossa with the Långa näsan"*. This was written by author Astrid Lindgren about a writer of childrens' fiction who, despite her hard work, had almost nothing to live on, since she paid 102% in marginal tax.[374] It was rumoured that the story was about Lindgren herself.

This story immediately became a "hot political potato" in parliament, where the leader of the Moderate Party, Gösta Bohman, read it aloud. Afterwards, the leader of the Social Democrats, Gunnar Sträng, took the podium, explaining that the article was an interesting combination of stimulating literary ability and deep ignorance about how tax policy works. He added mockingly: "Yes , she can tell stories, but she cannot count."

The very next day, Lindgren was interviewed on the radio where she said: "If there is anyone who has calculated incorrectly, it is the IRS (Inland Revenue Service), because I have the numbers from them." She added a remark that the media loved: "Sträng can tell tall tales, but he obviously cannot calculate. We should probably swap jobs, he and I."

It was actually Lindgren who was right, and when this became clear to the public, the foundation was laid for the Social Democrats' loss of votes at the next election. Since then, the Swedes have lowered their marginal tax considerably.

It evidently doesn't work to maintain a marginal tax of 102%. However, many believe that top tax rates that are only slightly lower do not hinder communities' dynamism and creativity. "People have to spend their money, whether they are taxed heavily or not, so what difference does it make?", they might argue. Some would even add that "high taxes force people to work harder, so it increase GDP." None of this sounds particularly counter-intuitive, so do very high taxation levels undermine a society's creativity?

Before we look for the answer, we should perhaps note that very high taxation is a relatively new phenomenon, generally speaking (although there have been fairly rare historical episodes, such as in the latest stages of the Roman empire,). From the Middle Ages until 1900, people in the UK typically paid 8.5% or less of their income in taxes, and in the US, the figure from initial colonization until 1900 was never more than 6.5%. From the year 1900 to 1929, it increased to 12%, but was never higher.

One taxation issue to consider is what taxation level maximizes tax revenues (if that is something one should to aim maximize and not minimize). The answer to that lies somewhere in what is known as the "Laffer curve". The gist of this is simple: If the tax rate is zero, there will be zero tax revenue. If it is 100%, there will be perhaps a bit in the beginning, but in the long run, it will again be zero, as everyone will emigrate or stop working. Revenues must therefore follow a curved path between these two points.

There have been many attempts to calculate the taxable optimal point and thus the drawing of the Laffer curve diagram, but these tend to lead to very different conclusions (for example, the contradictory suggestions that maximum tax revenues are reached at marginal tax rates of above 60 % or below 20%). Instead, we can look around in the world and learn from practical experience. In 1921, the marginal tax rate in the US was 73% for people earning in excess of $100,000. In that year, the state collected approximately $700 million in income tax, of which 30% came from these high earners. In 1929, after the marginal tax rate was lowered dramatically to 24%, the tax revenue increased to more than $1 billion, while the share paid by the richest had risen to 65%.[375] So, contrary to what one might expect intuitively, the lower marginal tax rate brought in much greater revenue. After the stock market crash of 1929, the government introduced tariff barriers and raised the marginal tax rate dramatically, which probably contributed greatly to the creation of the 1930s depression.

Similar effects have been seen in Capital Gains Tax, where, in the US, there was a clear inverse correlation between tax rates and actual revenues collected during the 50 years between 1954 and 2005:[376]

The same phenomena have been seen in recent times. Russia had, until 1998, an expensive and complicated tax system that people contrived all sorts of schemes to dodge - the actual tax yield in 1998 was only 8.6% of GDP. Then the system was simplified and marginal taxes were lowered with introduction of a flat income tax of 13%. The result was dramatic; tax revenues rose to 16.1% of GDP in 2001 - almost a doubling within three years (the proceeds exceeded the tax rate due to certain commodity taxes and so on.)[377]

In the US and the UK, various recent experiments with lowering and raising the top tax bracket have shown similar effects. Between 1980 and 1988, tax revenues from the richest Americans more than tripled after the US lowered marginal tax rates from 70% to 28%. So this was an effect very similar to that seen in the 1920s. In 2007, when the US state of Maryland decided to raise the top tax bracket from 2008 so as to increase revenue collected from

CAPITAL GAINS REALIZATIONS AND TAX RATES

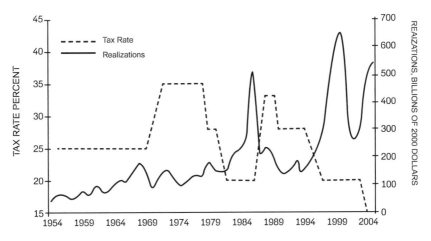

MOORE, S & T. GRIMM, THE BUSH CAPITAL GAINS TAX CUT AFTER FOUR YEARS: MORE GROWTH, MORE INVESTMENT, MORE REVENUES, NCPA POLICY REPORT NO. 307., JANUARY 2008

CAPITAL GAINS TAX RATES AND REALIZATIONS IN THE US BETWEEN 1954-2005. THE DOTTED LINE SHOW THE TAX RATES AND THE UNBROKEN LINE SHOWS THE AMOUNTS ACTUAL COLLECTED BY GOVERNMENT FROM CAPITAL GAINS TAX.

the richest by a projected $106 million, revenues instead fell by 22%, leading to a loss of $257 million. Nearly a third of the millionaires, it turned out, had suddenly "disappeared".[378]

You see the same thing over and over again. In 2010, the then Labour British prime minister Gordon Brown increased the top tax level in the UK from 40% to 50%. The following year, the number of registered taxpayers with income of more than £1 million fell from in excess of 16,000 to just 6,000 - an even greater fall than in Maryland. When the subsequent Conservative-led coalition government lowered the top tax bracket to 45%, the number of top tax payers immediately rose to 10,000. In reality, the previous increase in the top tax bracket was, here as elsewhere, a loss-making decision for society, and had the coalition government lowered it to its original level or even lower, it would probably have resulted in an even better deal in the long term.

Similar conclusions are found in Swedish studies that have shown that there is a strong negative correlation between the tax burden and economic growth in rich countries.[379] Indeed, they found, by studying many countries, that 10% less tax in affluent countries was associated with 0.5-1% higher annual economic growth. Specifically, Sweden had, in the period 1994-2010, had an average economic growth per capita of 2.2% per year, which surpassed the US (1.5%) and the EU15 (1.4%) over the same period. This coincided with a period in which Sweden, after the mid-1990s, had reduced spending and tax by approximately 10 percentage points.

However, if you want to study natural tax experimentation, there is no better place to look at than Switzerland, where the vast majority of taxes are collected and spent locally by the 26 individual cantons (federal states, with an average population of 300,000) and local communities (average population: 2,800). Switzerland has the subsidiarity principle (mandating decentralization) inscribed in its constitution and is the most decentralized nation in Europe and possibly the world, which means that each canton and local community is free to decide a whole lot of things themselves.

Immediately after World War II, the canton of Zug was amongst the poorest of Switzerland's cantons. However, Zug citizens voted to reduce marginal tax rates significantly. This helped business flourish and, soon after, a series of neighbouring cantons followed suit. The entire region of Central Switzerland has since become one of the richest areas in Europe and indeed of the world, with extremely low unemployment and crime plus high social stability and therefore putting very little pressure on the public purse. At the same time, Switzerland was one of the only nations in the world that managed to reduce its already moderate public debt during the financial crisis 2008-13.

Switzerland has one of the lowest levels of public expenditure and taxes in OECD, but it scores extremely highly on virtually all indicators of welfare, safety and cleanliness. For instance, it scores very highly on PISA scores (school performance), university rankings, human development, average lifespan, environmental performance, creativity and competitiveness index, patents filed, Nobel prizes per million inhabitants and so on. In fact, in many of such rankings, it takes the top spot. And it scores very low on crime levels, unemployment, illness-related absence from workplaces, tax dodging, alcoholism and other social ills. So how does that work?

It works because of competition and creativity. The Swiss cantons compete intensely, and keep experimenting. Each canton has its own schools, its own police, its own flag and its own tax system right down to individual taxation for car ownership. Furthermore, the healthcare system is private, with fierce competition between healthcare providers.

Unterwalden, also located in Central Switzerland, is a single canton, but the administration is split into two half-cantons, with individual autonomy, (named Obwalden and Nidwalden) since they couldn't agree on policy. Over a number of years, Obwalden chose to stick with relatively high tax rates in order to maintain a high level of public service. Nidwalden, on the other hand, did rather as Zug had done, reducing tax bracket.[380] By 2005, Nidwalden's GDP per capita was 44% higher than Obwalden's GDP and it was again demonstrated that lower tax rates often yield higher long-term revenues. Obwalden now faced the consequences of its policy and voted to adopt an extreme tax system with declining marginal tax. However, this was over-ruled as "unconstitutional" by the state, after which, in 2007, the Obwalders (with a voting majority of more than 90%) decided to introduce a flat tax on income of 10,000 Francs and a corporate tax of 6%.[381]

The hyper-competitive cantons of Central Switzerland have taken and kept the lead in Switzerland, but all of Switzerland has low tax rates and maintains a VAT rate of 8%, which is far lower than in most other European nations. The result of all this is local districts that compete with one another, and this "race to the bottom", as critics might call it, has really become a race to the top. In 2013, Switzerland took first place on both the Global Innovation Index and Global Competitiveness Report. So Switzerland solves social challenges less via collecting money from the public and more by creating private jobs.

Singapore follows a similar strategy. As in Switzerland, there is no Capital Gains Tax. In addition, both corporate and income tax are below 20% (2013). Through this strategy, Singapore had, until 2012, accumulated surplus funds totalling around $500 billion; equivalent to approximately $100,000 per citizen. From being fairly poor and far behind Western Europe and North America two to three generations ago, Singapore has become the world's second richest country, not including small oil nations. According to the IMF, Singapore's GDP per capita in 2010-2011 was approximately $60,000 against, for example, an average of $31,000 in the EU. So again we see that low taxes lead to higher creativity, growth and prosperity and hence high revenue.

The pattern repeats itself over and over again, where countries with low taxes such as Chile, Hong Kong, Singapore, Switzerland and the United Arab Emirates (UAE) are doing better than neighbouring countries with higher tax rates. Many do not understand this, but former US president John F Kennedy clearly did, as he once said: "It is a paradoxical truth that tax rates are too high today and tax revenues are too low, and the soundest way to raise the revenues in the long run is to cut the tax rates."

So why don't all countries cut marginal tax rates to, for example, 20%?

The typical argument against lowering marginal tax rates is that they assume a trickle-down economy that actually doesn't work. However, it is extremely difficult to find a supporter of lower marginal tax rates who mentions this trickle-down model as their motive for reducing the tax burden. It is certainly not an official, standard theory mentioned in textbooks on economics or the history of economic thought. In reality, the closest thing to this argument one is likely to hear is that ideas will trickle down from entrepreneurs to those around them.

When people argue in favour of lowering tax brackets, it's not trickle-down economics they use to support their argument, but other factors such as the simple statistical observation that it simply works.

But why? We can start with the observation that lower tax leads to less tax evasion. Data from the IMF and Eurostat from 2012 show that countries with small public sectors and thus low taxes, on average, experience less tax-dodging. For instance, in 2012 this constituted only 7% of the economies of moderately-taxed Switzerland and the US, whereas it was respectively 13, 14 and 14% of the higher-taxed Danish, Swedish and Norwegian economies. Similar figures were found in a study from the German IFO institute same year.[382]

The increased amount of undeclared work, which heavy taxation induces, has a negative effect which many may not consider. Undeclared work is easiest done by people who are either officially registered as unemployed or on disability benefit. So incentives to avoid tax also work as incentives to seek public benefits. This means that high-tax countries will have many welfare beneficiates who are actually better off than people with an official job. This provides a demoralizing effect and destroys public finances from two sides. Of course, the same applies to career criminals, who do not pay tax. The higher the tax rates, the bigger the relative advantage of seeking a criminal career.

Another negative effect of high taxes is that the derived black economy creates a massive hidden competitive advantage to very inefficient companies, since they are the ones who can most easily get away with undeclared work. The result is a kind of hidden wealth transfer from effective to ineffective businesses.

High taxes also mean that people have lower private savings, and it compels them to hide their wealth in passive investments such as art, expensive watches, jewellery or precious metals rather than investing in business. So high taxes move money from active to passive investments.

In addition to these aspects, it should be mentioned that high taxes remove incentives to work hard. Former US President Ronald Reagan began his political career as a Democrat, but one of the experiences that led him to switch to the Republican side was a marginal tax rate of 90%, which meant that, each year he only worked until he reached the top tax bracket, after which time he went on holiday at his ranch.

There's more. High taxes lead to brain drain, whereas low taxes promote brain gain, as Switzerland and Singapore would testify. And high taxes lead to higher collection costs for the government and more money wasted by citizens trying to protect their money from the state. This cost to society has been estimated to be equal to up to 15% of total tax revenues in the US.[383] One more important argument against high taxes is seldom raised, but is very important: until recently, in many societies you would expect that, if you received a good education and worked hard, you would end up owning your own primary dwelling plus possibly a holiday home and a decent pension, even if your spouse didn't work. That was the middle class lifestyle. Today, many may feel they need two incomes to create such financial security, or that they simply cannot obtain it. The reason is that in many countries you now pay approx. half your income or more in direct and indirect taxes, whereas your parents or grandparents might have paid only around 20% or so. So the missing wealth has gone to taxes.

These arguments against high taxes are all relatively well-known, but there is a different, and probably much more important, problem: high taxes prevent division of labour. A high tax burden is a direct barrier to the voluntary win-win transactions that are the very essence of creativity and which Adam Smith used as his main explanation for why market economies are efficient.

US citizens are known to work a lot and take much less leave than, for example, the Swedes, but here is a peculiar observation: two Swedish scientists found, in 2010, that while headline statistics indicated that Americans worked more than Swedes, there was virtually no difference in how much work people in these two nations did, when you took into account private work such as cooking, repairs of home and so on. The difference was that people in the US were more likely to eat out and call a tradesman to fix things for them, whereas Swedes did more themselves.[384]

In societies where income tax and VAT rates are low, people are far more likely to eat out every day – for breakfast, lunch or dinner, and they find it more effective to call a plumber when their taps drip than to (try to) fix it themselves. This division of labour solves a lot of social and practical issues and makes everything far more efficient.

Conversely, if you live in a high-tax society it doesn't make sense to undertake many of these voluntary win-win transactions. Let's imagine that the artisan Smith offers to paint a wall for the homeowner Johnson. Smith will bill $1,250, of which $250 goes to VAT and $500 to his marginal tax. Johnson also pays the 50% marginal tax rate and must therefore earn $2,500 to pay Smith's bill, of which Smith himself only can keep $500. This only makes sense for Johnson if Smith is at least five times as efficient at painting as himself. Five times!

And that is the biggest problem: high taxes drive a wedge between people, so they refrain from division of labour. It prevents the win-win transactions that drive creativity and growth. It also discourages acts of friendship and compassion, as if you help a friend, you risk being punished for not billing the job and thus paying taxes.

If Western civilization enters a state of permanent crises, and if someone 100 years from now writes books about why it happened, this problem, alongside the Baumol Effect, will probably be among the core explanations.

A major argument for high taxation is that the revenue it generates helps the poorest with better education, healthcare and so on. This is obviously often the case.

10 MAIN DISADVANTAGES OF HIGH TAXATION

1. Encourages tax dodging
2. Incentivizes people to seek welfare recipient status as a cover for undeclared work
3. Increases the relative economic incentives of criminal careers
4. Provides relative favouritism of inefficient companies that have an easier time evading tax
5. Moves savings from growth-stimulating investments in business to tax-dodging hideouts like jewellery, art and precious metals
6. Reduces willingness to work hard
7. Causes high administration costs and legal costs for both state and tax payers
8. Promotes brain drain and difficulties in attracting talent from outside
9. Makes it impossible for the middle-classes to save enough to feel secure
10. Reduces division of labour, marginalizes people and discourages acts of friendship and compassion.

However, as we have seen above, there are also many negative social effects of high taxes: they make people more dishonest, criminal and lazy; they induce individuals to seek welfare instead of work, they hamper business development, entrepreneurship and thus job creation, and they drive a wedge between people, which marginalizes many and criminalizes acts of friendship and compassion.

Now, let's consider the Laffer curve again, which was a kind of illustration of the over-fishing principle: if you fish too aggressively, you catch fewer fish in the long term, and thus, according to Laffer, if you tax too aggressively, you also gain less tax revenue in the long term. However, the objective is to maximize net social gains, not maximize taxes collected, and it is to do this over the long term; not the short term. Because net social gains are the result of the social benefits from government spending minus the social disadvantages of taxation, the social taxation optimum must be at a lower tax level than the Laffer optimum point.

It is impossible to determine with any certainty where the social taxation optimum lies. First, it must be somewhat different from nation-to-nation depending on cultural inclination for crime, tax dodging, brain drain, and so on. Second, some of the social disadvantages of high taxation evolve slowly over many generations as they gradually undermine honesty, entrepreneurial drive, compassion and economic growth. This means that the long-term Laffer tax optimum and social tax optimum are at lower tax rates than the short-term optimums. People adapt to high tax rates, but some of that adaptation takes shape as a slow shift in culture and values that lasts generations.

What we can say with great certainty, though, is that a country like Switzerland, where typical top income tax brackets in 2014 were approximately 30% (and, in Central Switzerland, typically 20%) and where VAT was 8%, had placed itself far closer to the optimum taxation rate than France, where top tax was 75% and VAT was 19.6% or Denmark where top tax was approximately 52% and VAT was 25%. Switzerland beat these two countries on virtually any indicator of social wellbeing such as health, wealth, unemployment, security, education, crime, environment, etc. as well as on indicators of financial sustainability such as fiscal debt, central bank reserves and balance of payment.

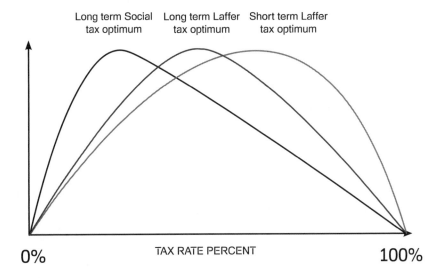

Speaking of France: in 1981, France had a public debt equal to 22% of GDP and a relatively small deficit, even though the country was in recession. Its socialist president François Mitterrand then decided to stimulate the economy by hiring 250,000 more people in the public sector and increasing civil service salaries. At the same time, he shortened the working week from 40 to 39 hours to distribute the work on more hands. He also increased transfer payments, increased the money supply and raised the minimum wage. Furthermore, he nationalized 38 banks and seven major companies. All this led to a tripling of the budget deficit, brain drain, an inflation rate of 14%, 10% unemployment and complete economic stagnation, while other Western economies, by contrast, expanded rapidly out of their recession.

Fortunately, he learned on the job, so in 1983 he made a U-turn where he indexed public sector wage increases to a level that was below inflation, put limits on money supply and deregulated the labour market. This brought inflation down to 4% and reduced the budget deficit significantly.[385]

However, the French electorate seems to have forgotten the lessons of that experience. In 2000, the French government forbade people to work more than 35 hours a week. French newspapers reported afterwards that taxmen drove around in the evenings looking after offices with lights turned on, so that they could fine people working. In 2012, the country announced that it would raise the marginal tax rate for the highest earners to 75%, which meant the actual marginal income for successful business leaders and entrepreneurs, when they took into account other taxes such as VAT and excise duties, came close to 90% marginal tax. They also introduced an exit tax to prevent entrepreneurs from leaving, which they did in droves anyway.

In 2014, French government debt had exceeded 90% of GDP, after the country had not had a single fiscal surplus since 1974 (that's 40 years of deficits). In 1974, the French GDP per capita was 1.13 times that of the UK and 0.81 times that of the US. By 2012, it had fallen to 0.83 times the UK GDP/capita and 0.61 times that of the US. Meanwhile, the French public sector, as a share of its GDP, had become one of the world's five highest. The reality was that France had evolved into an essentially static society which would only grow by borrowing money.

When a civilization embarks on sustained over-taxation and systemic government borrowing, it is probably on a countdown to collapse. Over-taxation turns an entrepreneurial culture into a culture of cheaters and welfare beneficiaries, and systemic government borrowing shows lack of respect for the property of future generations, who will foot the bill.

In 2000 and 2001, three scientists from Harvard, MIT and the University of California published a study of the economic performance in former European colonies. Their conclusion was remarkable: Statistically, three-quarters of the differences between the economic performance in these nations could be explained by a single variable. This was the extent to which private property was respected. If the state or others confiscated people's valuables, this was more damaging to economic growth than any other economic variable.[386]

Systemic over-taxation and government borrowing are both symptoms of a static world-view which underestimates the power of incentives, and the main difference is that the former (over-taxation) hits current taxpayers, while the latter (borrowing) hits future generations. There can be moral arguments for and against high taxation, but the main argument against it is pragmatic. It simply does not pay for a society to have high taxes. It kills the creative dynamism, and its negative social effects will, over the long-term, massively outweigh the positive ones. Overtaxed societies get stuck in a rut like the Roman empire, and societies financing growth with borrowing end like Greece, Venezuela or Argentina.

19.
THE
DONATION
DELUSIONS

In the Medieval Age, the central political struggle in the West was between the privileged classes and the rest. Being "bourgeois" (in French), or "burgerlich" (in German) meant being part of the rest, and these people defended the view that all citizens should have equal opportunities, in the same way as we now expect that all are equal before the law, or the players on a football field must all follow the same rules.

The opposition to these bourgeois were people who enjoyed innate privileges such as royals and nobles. These people were born with much better opportunities than the rest.

This power struggle was gradually won by the bourgeois, who managed to create societies largely based on merit, where people were rewarded in accordance with their skills and effort. This "meritocracy" incentivised creativity and industriousness and was central to the creative explosion that followed.

The next big idea was socialism, which pointed out that people are not equally fortunate from birth, which is why meritocracy isn't fair. Fair is when everyone receives roughly the same.

However, as many (former) socialists later realized that pure socialism didn't work, they would often, instead, aim for combinations of highly-regulated market economies and strong welfare states. Some of this was not entirely new. At least since the early medieval ages there had been local informal welfare communities organized primarily around either gilts or churches. These would organize funerals, pension aid for widows, etc, but always with a focus on getting people to work, if they could. However, as people increasingly migrated to cities to work in big factories after the industrial revolution, these decentralized and often rather informal welfare structures were broken up. Within the cities people would oftentimes experience brutal mass layoffs, and this inspired the creation of both unions and welfare states, where the latter was pioneered by Otto von Bismarck of Germany. The early versions of welfare systems tied welfare to companies, but this led to excessive demands for protection against redundancy and thus lack of flexibility in the job markets. Some countries then transferred welfare systems to the state and created thus so-called "flexicurity", and this is how the big centralized welfare states happened.

Later some countries went further and used the tax systems to create more general income equalization. This was the beginning of the Western entitlement societies.

Reward system		
Privileges	Merits	Entitlements
Lucky people are rewarded, regardless of effort	All are rewarded in accordance with skill and effort	All are rewarded regardless of skill and effort

It should soon become clear that something in the entitlement societies didn't pan out as expected. Even when welfare programs began to grow in the 1970s, early signs of adverse side-effects turned up. First, contrary to predictions, the trend in inequality, which had been falling steadily before the build-up of the welfare states, stopped or reversed in some countries, as argued by aforementioned scientist Thomas Piketty.

One reason could be that the welfare institutions compelled more people to stop working. For example, in 1960 the US was home to 687,000 registered disabled people, and one would expect that this figure would fall rather quickly, as medical treatments improved rapidly on many fronts. After all, previously debilitating diseases such as malaria, polio and smallpox had disappeared, and one could now remedy or cure many other diseases that had previously been debilitating. However, since disability support was raised, the opposite happened: In 1965, the number of disability pension claiments rose to 1.739 million – in fact, it almost tripled in just five years, and in 1975 it even reached 4.352 million.[387] This was an increase of 533% in just 15 years. Then it remained largely stable as a proportion of the population for several years, after which it increased further by approximately 50% between 1994 and 2010.[388] As a proportion of the workforce, disability rose almost seven-fold from approx. 0.8% to about 4.6%. A similar effect has been observed in other countries, where in the UK, for example, the number of registered disabled people grew from approximately 400,000 in 1970 to 2.6 million in 2011 - more than six times as many within 40 years.[389]

In spite of longer life expectancy and better healthcare, similar patterns have been seen in other countries with welfare states, and the more generous the disability insurance systems are, the more sick people there appear to be. In Norway, which has one of the world's healthiest populations and therefore highest average life span, 9 % of the workforce was registered as disabled in 2012, and another 5-6% of workers were, on average, absent from work due to illness.

What about helping the poor? In 1960 22.2% of Americans lived in poverty, but this had fallen to 12.6% in 1970, while the country had very limited social spending. After 1966, it began significant increases in marginal tax rates and social spending programmes, and by 1970 social spending had more than doubled. Then something amazing happened: the previous decline in the number of poor ceased, and in 1980 it had, for the first time since World War II, begun to increase.[390]

But the situation was actually even worse when you included what is known as the "latent poor". This describes people who would have been poor if they had not received benefits. The number of latent poor in the US had fallen evenly and steadily until 1967. However, with the introduction of greater entitlements and increased social spending, the number of latent poor soared. And after a delay, the number of actual poor people also started to rise.[391]

Clearly, the welfare states had unintended consequences, and we now know a great deal about why it goes wrong.[392] The first problem is that entitlements and welfare offerings can change people's moral compasses. In earlier times, people often took great pride in fending for themselves. You had a pleasure in getting a meal on your table, but also in knowing that you had earned it. Here, it was important for parents to teach their children to work hard and take the initiative, perhaps also because parents could expect that they would have to help their children, if they didn't help themselves. If people knew that they had to work in order to live decently, they made a virtue of necessity: it became a question of pride and self-esteem to support yourself. However, as the concept of welfare and entitlements spread, the mindsets of many changed. An international study from 2013 showed a clear and significant negative correlation between the degree of redistribution via taxes and welfare systems and the average work ethics in different societies.[393] In the previously mentioned World Values Surveys, respondents are asked whether they think it is important that parents teach their children the value of hard work. Among Chinese, 86% agreed with that. Similarly, many Poles (86%), Singaporeans (64%), Turks (74%) and Vietnamese (75%) agreed that hard work was important. In the Western world without large welfare states, a smaller but significant proportion of the populations also agreed.

However, when it came to countries with large welfare states, the picture was quite different. In the Netherlands, only 14% felt that parents should teach their children the value of hard work. In Sweden the figure was 4%, and in Denmark only 2% - the lowest in the world. So 98 % of the Danes did not think that it was a good thing to teach children to test themselves through hard work. This is vital, because a society will be far more innovative if a fair proportion of the population is willing to work very hard. That's how you start companies.[394]

This question related to hard work. But what about work in general? A study of Danes showed that, among those born before World War II, 45% believed that it was a "duty" to work. However, among those who were born between 1955 and 1963, the figure was just 12%, although this figure has since risen to approximately 15-20%.[395] But even with these higher numbers, what it means is that 80-85% of Danes no longer believe that working is a duty – living off others people's money is fine.[396]

Studies of attitude changes as well as behavioural changes indicate strongly that the option of avoiding work offered by welfare states has led to a change in culture. Working tends to mean you rise early in the morning, dress smartly and go to a job where you have to work co-operatively with colleagues and clients. This means that you stay sober, go to bed at a reasonable time, and generally take care of yourself. All of these memes form a part of a culture, which can erode if many people don't work, and if children of such people have never seen a normal, responsible lifestyle practised by their own parents.

It's all about incentives, and the problem inherent in entitlements is that they very often give incentives that displace merits. However, the welfare state in its current form is not the only example of state dependency systems that create unintended side-effects: Corporate subsidies (sometimes called "corporate welfare" by critics) and foreign aid have parallel problems. This does not mean that these activities are always wrong or damaging, but upon closer scrutiny, it turns out that they surprisingly often are.

Let's start with business subsidies. The philosophy behind these may be that a country benefits from having business activities in special locations that are short of jobs or are becoming depopulated. Or it may mean stimulating particularly promising sectors.

However, in practice, the vast majority of Western business subsidies have been given to farmers. This has led to widespread fraud, costly and bureaucratic administration and unfair competition for producers in developing countries. Partly to compensate developing countries for this loss, Western nations have provided foreign aid, which, unfortunately, also has led to significant administration overheads, fraud and other problems – we shall return to that shortly.

One of the countries in the world that is most dependent on food exports is New Zealand, which up until 1984, provided subsidies amounting to approximately 30 % of the farm turnover. However, then the country experienced major economic problems, including inflation rates of around 15%. Its Labour government consequently decided to abolish subsidies for agriculture while lowering corporate and income taxes and deregulating across the economy. Over the following ten years, New Zealand increased its GDP per capita by more than 50%, while inflation fell to 3-5%. Still today, New Zealand's agriculture operates without support and is highly competitive.

Perhaps the previous farm subsidies in New Zealand had their benefits, but they were clearly outweighed by their overall costs, and this brings us to the need to do cost-benefit analysis. For instance, a university study of the Spanish government's very ambitious attempt to create "green jobs" showed what happens if you don't calculate costs against benefits, as it included the following conclusions:

"The study calculates that since 2000 Spain spent €571,138 to create each 'green job', including subsidies of more than €1 million per wind industry job. The study calculates that the programs creating those jobs also resulted in the destruction of nearly 110,500 jobs elsewhere in the economy, or 2.2 jobs destroyed for every "green job" created. Each 'green' megawatt installed destroys 5.28 jobs on average elsewhere in the economy: 8.99 by photovoltaics, 4.27 by wind energy, 5.05 by mini-hydro. These costs do not appear to be unique to Spain's approach but instead are largely inherent in schemes to promote renewable energy sources.[397]

In this case, the government proudly promoted the benefits, but it didn't understand (or communicate) the much bigger costs. It was even worse in the US, where a government programme to create green jobs cost, on average $11 million per job.[398]

The general fallacy behind this is the issue of concentrated benefit versus scattered expense. Those who benefit from public spending are easy to identify, and they have strong motives to fight for it, while those who pay will each pay so little that they do not find it worth their while to take up the fight against it. This scenario of concentrated benefits versus dispersed damage is precisely the opposite of what happens in business. In the private sector, the pain of cost-cutting is typically focused, but the collective gain dispersed. This makes the pain more visible, but this process tends to be far more effective for society. What business undertakes was coined "creative destruction" by Joseph Schumpeter, whereas what the public sector achieves, when it does the opposite, seems to amount to "destructive creation".

Another complication with business subsidies is that politicians and bureaucrats are rarely good at foretelling the future. On 24 March 2000, for example, the EU issued the *Lisbon Strategy Declaration*, where you could read that "the Union is experiencing its best macro-economic outlook for a generation" and it was said that this was "a result of stability-orientated monetary policy supported by sound fiscal policies". The declaration also informed readers that "the Euro has been successfully introduced and is delivering the expected benefits for the European economy." Furthermore, Europe's goals for 2010 included increased employment and "to become the most dynamic and competitive knowledge-based economy in the world, capable of sustainable economic growth with more and better jobs".[399]

It took just three days from the publication of this upbeat report before one of the biggest stock market crashes in history began, followed by recessions and countless bankruptcies. This did not deter the EU from issuing a directive on working time in June the same year, under which it was to be forbidden for all EU citizens to work more than 48 hours a week, even if entrepreneurial projects and small independent companies often require people to work 60-80 hours a week to have even the slightest chance of survival.

With regard to the EU prognosis that the EU would be the world's most competitive economy by 2010, the actual situation in 2010 was a massive crises, 10% unemployment in the Euro area and a huge build-up of national debt burdens.

The private sector is much better positioned to identify growth opportunities than is the state because it has more relevant and better distributed information. It has private angel investors (private investors in entrepreneurial ventures), banks, investment funds, hedge funds and private equity funds to identify investment opportunities. In particular, many equity-and-venture funds are led by former successful entrepreneurs from high-tech companies who are well positioned to choose what to invest in and who would know, for instance, that you need to work more than 48 hours a week in order to succeed with a start-up project. Conversely, civil servants and politicians rarely have any direct management experience from the private sector and can have quite naive attitudes to these things, no matter how intelligent, well educated, well-meaning and hard-working they might otherwise be.

The impact of state aid will often become completely absurd, such as when the US government offered tax credits of $6,000 for each electric car, which meant that golf carts became free. The American television host John Stossel then picked up a free golf cart, which he gave to a park, but one of his friends picked up seven for nothing.[400]

What about foreign aid? Presumably only evil people can have any objections to that? Well, no. It turns out that many people who have vast experience with foreign aid conclude that it often creates similar problems as the welfare state and business subsidies.

Foreign aid, it should be said, comes in three different forms: disaster relief, private charity projects and state aid. The first two can work extremely well, especially when they focus on helping people to help themselves (which, it should be said, is rarely relevant for acute disaster relief).

The problem comes, predominantly, when rich states transfer money to governments of poor countries, which they have done on a massive scale and over a very long period. In fact, during the years after World War II, rich nations have pumped in the order of $2.3 trillion in foreign aid into poor countries, of which approximately one trillion went to Africa.[401] This corresponded to approximately 15% of the continent's GDP, and compared to the GDP over the period, it has corresponded to approximately four times the level of the Marshall Plan for Europe after World War II.

One of the world's leading experts on the effects of foreign aid is William Easterly, who after working for 16 years with foreign aid projects in the World Bank became a professor specializing in foreign aid at the University of New York in the US. Easterly has made a number of statistical studies of the effects of foreign aid, and many of his findings are surprising, to put it mildly.

Here is an example: he examined statistics from 138 developing nations to clarify whether - as is generally believed – there was a statistical correlation between increased investment and higher economic growth. He could only find that in four of them (Tunisia, Israel, Liberia and Reunion), of which, only Tunisia had received foreign aid to increase investments.[402] So if you give state aid to increase investments with the aim of creating growth, you seem to be wasting your money.[403]

Another popular aid model has been to support birth control via provision of free condoms. However, this has also disappointed for the simple reason that about 90% of births in countries with high birth rates actually are wanted, which is why condom-dissemination is mostly ineffective.[404]

But giving people aid in the form of education most surely be good? No, generally not. A well known World Bank study called *Where Has All the Education Gone?* concluded, that on average, there had been no positive effects of giving people in emerging markets education - in fact, more sophisticated statistical methods indicated, that if anything, the effect was statistically significant and ... negative.[405]

Actually, there is a similar problem in rich nations. In 2012, Ulf Berg, a former director of the Swiss industrial giant Sulzer, assembled European statistics on the correlation between gaining a high school diploma and youth unemployment in a number of European countries. The correlation he found was astonishing: the greater the number of students, the higher the level of youth unemployment. He then examined the same for German federal states (länder) and Swiss cantons, and the pattern was, in both cases, replicated: high numbers of high school graduates equated to increased youth unemployment.[406]

The previously mentioned social scientist Charles Murray found similar results in the US and concluded that America produced too many high school graduates and academics (plus drop-outs). He pointed out that one of the problems with academic study is that it mostly works for students who have unusually high analytical talents and typically with a special emphasis on literacy and numeracy skills. If you are instead - as goes for the vast majority - more gifted in intuitive, practical, social, physical or artistic areas, an academic education is often useless or worse. A US study from 2010 showed that 45 % of 2,300 students showed no significant improvement in Collegiate Learning Assessment (CLA) scores after two years in college, and 36 showed no improvement at all. That is 81% who showed little or no improvement of two years of studies.[407] Another study concluded that: "a reasonable conclusion is that over-education remains the persistent and even growing situation of the US labor force with respect to skills."[408]

The result of excessive education is too many sadly wasted years, student loans that cannot be paid back, dispelled illusions, unemployment and bitterness, whereas vocational educations often could have led to a much better lives and the launch of new companies. The state is trying to create winners through education, but the opposite is all too often the consequence.

Going back to foreign aid, the money the West has spent on this has largely been wasted or caused damage. A large meta-analysis from 2008 concluded as follows:

"Our central conclusion is there is no robust positive relationship between foreign aid and growth." [409]

Another study showed equally that foreign aid did not provide growth, and scientists here could not find a single example anywhere in the world where foreign aid had led to higher economic growth. Not one. In fact, they concluded that foreign aid on average did economic damage to recipient countries:

"We find that aid inflows do have systematic adverse effects on growth, wages, and employment in labor intensive and export sectors." [410]

So it has been a general disaster, and in her book *Dead Aid*, African economist Dambisa Moyo suggest why. The problem, she says, is that aid programmes support bureaucrats and rent-seekers in both donor countries and (worse) in the recipient nations. Donor countries have approximately half a million aid workers, and, in recipient countries, the funds are often used by governments to finance networks of cronies, rewarded for their loyalty via contracts, government jobs and cash under the table. They do this because the societies are tribal, and in tribal societies, you favour your own and make extractive institutions. So the money, says Moyo, create a dependency culture, corruption and crony capitalism, and it attracts talent to the public bureaucracy rather than to private entrepreneurship. It simply provides nourishment for extractive organizations.

So how do you create growth in poor countries? Moyo recommends stopping giving foreign aid to governments and instead just giving it directly to end-users in return for reciprocal concessions, such as sending their children to school every day. Moreover, one can focus on micro-credit, where groups of local business people can borrow small amounts for personal business investments of mutual or individual liability. Such micro-finance projects have been implemented in a number of countries with enormous success.

Another take on the matter comes from William Lewis from McKinsey Global Institute, whom we met earlier. In the long term, he says, it is predominantly productivity growth that will move the load, and the key ingredient to this is to create a clear commercial incentive to do business. This will stimulate entrepreneurship and attract business and talent from abroad. In either circumstance, these businesses will ensure that their staff receives the relevant training.

Of course, institutions such as fair courts, efficient police and land registries, are critical, but in many cases, very simple barriers at the micro-level prevent growth. One example, among many possible ones, is practical obstacles to the establishment of supermarkets. Supermarkets are often an extremely important driver of growth, because supermarkets place huge demands on suppliers' efficiency and affordability. If you only have small "mum-and-dad" retail outlets, you will lack such pressure for efficiency and that will be reflected along the entire supply line.

So in the long term, it is primarily - if not entirely - attractive framework conditions for the private sector, which have a positive effect - not public aid. These framework conditions can include low taxation, few bureaucratic obstacles, an efficient and reliable rule of law, effective protection of private property, and the possibility of attractive lifestyle for creative and executive officers.

There is a common denominator in the histories of the welfare state, foreign aid, business subsidies and educational over-kill and it is this: donating substantial quantities of tax money to solve social problems is rarely as efficient as facilitating voluntary win-win transactions within the respective fields.

In their book *Why Nations Fail*, Daron Acemoglu of MIT and James Robinson of Harvard concluded something similar after 450 pages of analysis:

"Nations fail because their extractive economic institutions do not create the incentives needed for people to save, invest, and innovate."

So it's actually pretty simple: If individuals or businesses enjoy strong incentives and few hindrances to innovate and grow, it will usually happen. If this requires training and learning, training and learning will follow. And people typically have amazing untapped creative potential that can be released, if the incentives are right.

In this context, it is interesting that Harvard professor Jacob Schmookler made an extensive literature study of the causes of 934 groundbreaking innovations in agriculture, petroleum, paper manufacturing and railway industry in the 157 years 1800-1957 and concluded:

"...in a significant majority of cases, the stimulus is identified, and for almost all of these that stimulus is a technical problem or opportunity conceived by the inventor largely in economic terms. When the inventions themselves are examined in their historical context, in most cases either the inventions contain no identifiable scientific component, or the science that they embody is at least 20 years old." [411]

Note how radical this really is. Out of 934 inventions, almost none were directly triggered by scientific discoveries. Instead, the driver was the desire to make money by solving a practical problem. Of course, as Schmookler also noted, in many cases the innovations could not have been made without previous scientific discoveries. But that is not the point. The point is that these discoveries are only turned into products and services because someone wants to make money by solving a practical problem. This again shows how great ideas and clear incentives to undertake voluntary win-win transactions are far more powerful drivers of progress than welfare and aid systems.

Here there is just something we have to note: typically all the net employment growth in developed nations comes from the creation of new businesses. Studies in the US show, for example, that virtually all net job growth between 1980 and 2010 came from firms that were less than five years old, and that approximately one third of all existing jobs in the country in 2010 were within firms that had been founded after 1980. In contrast to young companies, the well established ones will typically seek profit growth, predominantly via rationalization. [412]

Another important finding is the aforementioned alchemists' fallacy, which means that entrepreneurs, on average, only retain approximately 4% of the value they create; the rest goes to society as a whole. An obvious conclusion is that the creative community should stimulate entrepreneurs and inventors significantly by giving them very strong incentives (such as keeping most of their 4 %) and by removing barriers to their activities (such as legal tangle).

So that works, but if people, conversely, have incentives to receive benefits without working for them, they will also adapt to this and they will do this individually as well as collectively by developing extractive institutions for that purpose. The classic example is countries that have natural resources and therefore focus on creating institutions that can create unearned gains from that. Having resources can be like having a constant flow of foreign aid (and vice versa), and that's why such resource-rich nations often end up being poorer than those who had no resources and no aid. As an example, Acemoglu and Robinson point out that the countries in South America that had the most natural resources, developed the most extractive institutions, neglected human potential and experienced widespread corruption, inflation and often civil war. Conversely, North America had fewer resources and focused instead on efficient human transactions.

The rich, Western countries were once destitute, and they did not become rich because of foreign aid, business support, welfare states or free university education for all, since they had none of this in their strong growth phases. But they had clear incentives to save, invest and innovate. No one asked them to read thousands of pages of legal text or demanded taxes that were so high that artisan Smith would have to be five times as efficient as Johnson before it made sense for the two to co-operate.

The core reason why systems primarily built on voluntary win-win transactions in a state of competition become most successful is because co-operation generates creativity. Donations are also voluntary, but they are only win-win, if it makes the donor happy. And they become lose-lose, if they are forced on the donor and have negative, behaviourally- pacifying effects on the receiver.

The donation delusion is about always sending money to fix problems. The much better alternative is often to organize society so that people are strongly incentivized to show creativity, take initiative and thereby help themselves.

PART 6

THE ENEMIES
OF REASON

The rise of the West was largely based on the Age of Enlightenment, which replaced superstition, irrationality and baseless dogma with science, systematic doubt and rationality. It also replaced group-think with individual reasoning and insularity with openness. And it made people optimistic instead of fatalistic. "We can fix things", was the new mentality. "We can figure them out." "We can make something beautiful."

However, enlightenment has always had its enemies, from Medieval clerics to the Sturm und Drang movement, which rejected rationality and aesthetics.

It still has enemies today, and in this section, we shall study these. Who are they? Why do they think the way they do? And what damage can they do?

CHAPTER 20:
Neo-Luddites and panic-mongers

CHAPTER 21:
Eco-fascists and pseudo-scientists

CHAPTER 22:
Babblers, cynics, charlatans

CHAPTER 23:
Utopians and social engineers

20.
NEO-LUDDITES
AND PANIC
MONGERS

One of the West's current problems - especially in Europe - is growing Luddism and panic mongering. Luddism, it should be said, is named after an anti-technology movement that existed in England from 1811 to 1817, where the so-called Luddites regularly stormed into factories and smashed their machines. Modern Luddites are increasingly inhibiting the West's creative machinery, which, as we have seen, is vital for providing the solutions to many challenges.

In 1841, the Scottish writer and journalist Charles Mackay published a magnificent book, which now seems as relevant as ever. Its title is *Extraordinary Popular Delusions and the Madness of Crowds*, and it's about how people move from one irrational mass movement, euphoria or panic, to the next.

One of its chapters is about a period in which Westerners frequently poisoned one another. The trick, which prevailed for hundreds of years and culminated in the 1700s, was to poison the enemy so slowly that people thought they were just dying of natural causes. The murderers would often wear finger rings with hidden poison chambers from which they could easily and unobtrusively pour a little arsenic or other poison into their enemy's food or wine. It may not be very surprising to hear that many people seriously feared being poisoned during that time.

But now? Western civilization is largely built on the use of science-based technology, however recently people have started rejecting new scientific discoveries and technology, because they consider it unnatural and its fruits possibly toxic. Today, when life is safer than ever, Westerners are driven from one irrational panic to the next.

The fluoride panic is a good example. In the 1930s, scientists noticed that children living in the town of Minonk, Illinois had significantly better teeth than people who came to the town later in life. The explanation, it soon turned out, was that their drinking water had unusually high levels of fluoride. It was consequently decided to add fluoride to drinking water elsewhere, which on average halved people's dental problems. Dental problems, it must be pointed out, do not concern only the teeth; they also often cause atherosclerosis and other health problems as a result of chronic inflammation.

However, this fluoride dispersion soon created a panic because the atom fluoride appears within certain poisons. Of course, so do common atoms such as oxygen, hydrogen and carbon, but no matter. Furthermore, the concerned people pointed out that large doses of fluoride could be dangerous, according to some studies. However, in order to receive such a dose though drinking water, one would have to drink approximately 500 bath tubs filled with fluoridated water within a short time. That would indeed kill anyone (even before they exploded), but this is because the water from a tenth of the first bath would cause death, since all substances are toxic in local overdose. In this case, therefore, the water dose was 5,000 times as toxic as the fluorine dose within it.

The Fluor panic was an example of the widespread Luddism in Western civilization, but vaccine panic has caused more damage, and we can take the story of polio vaccine as an example. Polio often leads to few or no symptoms, so people can carry this infection without knowing. However, in approximately 5% of cases, people have clear symptoms and the disease is sometimes called "infantile paralysis", because, in bad cases, it will destroy the patient's nervous system within a few hours, so they become partly or wholly paralysed for life or die. This gruesome outcome occurs in an estimated 0.5-1%.

In 1916, however, an epidemic with a variant of the strain broke out in New York City, which killed between 20 and 25% of those infected and led to countless cases of paralysis. This soon grew so awful that police sealed off the entire area so no one could leave. As this local epidemic finally subsided, it left many paralyzed, 9,023 dead, the vast majority of whom were young children.[413]

Many years later, in 1953, scientist Jonas Salk announced that he believed he had developed an effective vaccine for polio. People were now invited to take test shots, and only six months later, 1.8 million children were vaccinated. A Gallup poll that year showed that there were more Americans who knew about this vaccination programme than the incumbent president's first name. Authorities then selected virologist Thomas Francis to examine whether all these tests vaccinations had been effective.

A few months later, Francis held a press conference about his findings in a packed lecture hall covered by a number of live TV and radio networks. His speech lasted 90 minutes and he revealed that the vaccine was indeed effective. Air sirens now went off, church bells started ringing across the country, and traffic lights were set to flash red. In the schools, students were invited to a minute's silence in gratitude for the discovery, and in many places you could find parents crying in relief. The day after the press conference, the story covered more than half of the front space in many newspapers around the world, and the *New York Times* devoted almost its entire front page and another five full pages inside to describing this story in all its aspects. To many people, this was simply the biggest event since the end of World War II.[414]

Polio was far from the only infectious disease that sowed fear in the hearts of past Western populations. Another was the more dangerous smallpox, which according to ancient records probably killed 300-500 million people worldwide during the 20th century, including approximately 10 % of the children in Europe. Before the introduction of mass vaccination, it was therefore quite common to have family members or acquaintances who had died of smallpox. About 80% of those infected were children, of whom 20-60% died. The survivors could often be recognized by their heavily-scarred faces and sometimes blindness and deformed limbs.

Other common diseases include diphtheria, which is a serious throat infection that probably killed around 30% of those infected. There was also measles which today kills more than 30 % of those infected in developing countries, but only about 0.3% in developed countries. In addition, there was mumps that could cause sterility in men, whooping cough, which could kill young children, and rubella, which caused damage to foetuses of pregnant women and led to abortions or severe birth defects.

All these can be easily prevented today, and children in the West are thus routinely vaccinated against diphtheria, tetanus, polio, Haemophilus influenzae type b (a bacterium that can cause a number of dangerous diseases such as meningitis), pertussis and pneumococcus, and against even more, if they have to travel to exotic areas. The one disease against which we do not vaccinate anymore is smallpox because this is the first disease ever to be eradicated via a determined global vaccination programme.

Vaccination programmes do not only protect the vaccinated individual, but also, via so-called herd immunity, those who have not been vaccinated. This is because an epidemic becomes unlikely, if a sufficiently large section of the population is vaccinated. Herd immunity mainly protects babies not old enough to be vaccinated and the very weak, who cannot take vaccines.[415]

Here comes the problem: despite all these obvious benefits of vaccination, there is a growing group of Luddites in society who decline vaccination because it is unnatural or because, for instance, they think it can cause autism. The latter (linked to the measles, mumps and rubella (MMR) vaccination) has been thoroughly investigated and clearly rejected. Because of this, many diseases that were close to being eradicated, have started to spread again, where they not only affect the deliberately unvaccinated children and adults, but also the weak and the newly-born.

Luddism also affects our relationship with medicine. Most countries have very liberal laws for natural medicine, even though it rarely works. The world's first university professor of alternative medicine, Edzard Ernst, made during his long career 160 meta-analyses of the effects of alternative medicine and alternative therapies. He concluded that approximately 95% were no more effective than placebos. In other words, if they had an effect, it was typically due to a psychological impact on the patient – in themselves, they were ineffectual.[416]

And so what? People can take any medicine they want, can't they? Well, yes, but there are two paradoxes here. The first is that science-based medicine, unlike alternative medicine, needs to live up to such enormous licensing requirements that it typically cost 1.3 billion dollars to get a single licence - approximately 100 times as much as 60 years ago.[417] The second paradox is the mere fact that many people are distrustful of medicine that is based on scientific research, and instead consciously prefer something that is not. This is luddism.

An instinctive fear of technology is most common in Europe; probably because it is a direct cultural extension of the German Romantic movement from the 1800s, where people longed for a simpler and less technological past.

Western Luddism has also affected the energy sector. In the 1960s, many workers in the nuclear power industry viewed themselves as environmentalists, as their technology cleaned up the pea-soup air produced by coal-firing. In fact, their vision included, for instance, that the US, around the year 1990, could be completely free of fossil fuel-use. However, to their surprise, violent demonstrations broke out against this new technology, which was therefore largely stopped it in its tracks. And the Western world maintained a large dependency on coal.

Coal is, arguably, the most dangerous and polluting energy form known, and although it sounds anti-intuitive, it actually creates hundreds of times as much radioactivity waste as the same amount of energy produced by nuclear power. Yes, it's true, because while there is very little radioactive material in each tonne of coal, this is more than offset by the amount of coal necessary to gain the same quantity of energy. And radioactive materials from coal are not stored in containers for later transmutation, reprocessing or burial. No, they are pumped into the atmosphere.

If an average person's lifetime supply of energy comes from coal, it creates approximately 68 tonnes of solid waste and 77 tonnes of CO_2.[418] Alternatively, uranium-based nuclear power for one person creates no more waste than could fit into a can of Coca-Cola, and its radioactivity decreases to just 0.00001 times its original radioactivity over 175 years.[419]

Average coal mining fatalities were approximately 100,000 in the 1970s - a figure that has only gradually decreased to about 15,000 today. Similarly, fatal haze pollution from coal still stands at approximately 350,000 annually in China alone.[420] All of this means that several million people have been killed by coal that could have lived if nuclear energy had been used instead. Meanwhile, the burning of coal in poor countries let to significant local pollution and was obviously a main source of CO_2 emissions.[421]

Of course, nuclear power has killed too. Between 1970 and 2014 there have been two fatal civilian nuclear accidents: Chernobyl in 1986 and Fukushima Daiichi in 2011. Both plants were designed in the 1960s and were thus based on highly out-dated technologies when their accidents occurred. The first of these led to 28 immediate deaths. Furthermore, a survey in 2005 attributed to it a further 15 deaths from thyroid cancer. Altogether, it led to some 4,000 cases of thyroid cancer, which, however, has a cure rate of 96%.[422] So by 2014 – this is 28 years after the accident - the death count was 43 people. More may come to light, but scientists have not registered an increase in any other types of cancer since the accident, although some theoretical models indicate that this should have happened. By comparison, it went almost unnoticed when a coal mine explosion in Soma, Turkey, killed more than 240 miners and injured countless others in May, 2014.[423]

As for the Japanese nuclear accident, two people were killed in the explosion, but it did not immediately lead to radiation-related deaths - and one should bear in mind that it was a consequence of a huge natural disaster that killed in the region of 25,000 by drowning, building collapses and so on. A subsequent analysis by the World Health Organization (WHO) concluded:

"A comprehensive assessment by international experts on the health risks associated with the Fukushima Daiichi nuclear power plant (NPP) disaster in Japan has concluded that, for the general population inside and outside of Japan, the predicted risks are low and no observable increases in cancer rates above baseline rates are anticipated." [424]

In other words: they did not expect more than those two deaths from radioactivity, despite the fact that the plant actually exploded. It should be said that some elderly and sick peole may have died as an indirect result of being moved to temporary housing due to either flooding or radioactivity and that the fear of cancer (even if unfounded) can cause stress. However, everything is relative, and the point about the death numbers from nuclear is that for each person killed by nuclear energy, several thousand have been killed by coal.

The fact is that nuclear – even old-fashioned uranium-based nuclear and not the newer and improved designs or even thorium technologies - is very safe. The US Department of Labor has, for instance, concluded that it is safer to work in a nuclear power plant than in the real estate or financial industries.[425] Moreover, a study of 54,000 employees at nuclear power plants found, in 2004, that they, on average, had lived longer than the rest of the population and (get this) had experienced significantly less cancer. In fact, they concluded as follows: "The cohort displays a very substantial healthy worker effect, i.e. considerably lower cancer and non-cancer mortality than the general population.[426]

Overall, nuclear power is - by a fairly wide margin – simply the safest-known form of energy, and yet, it is the one about which people are most scared. The table, compiled by the WHO, compares different energy technologies.[427]

Energy form	Number of deaths per TWh (terawatt-hours)	Mortality compared to nuclear power
Coal	100	2.500 times
Oil	36	900 times
Biofuel	12	300 times
Peat	12	300 times
Natural gas	4	100 times
Hydro	1,4	35 times
Solar panels	0,44	11 times
windmills	0,15	3.75 times
Nuclear power	0,04	-

Who would have thought that solar panels are 11 times as dangerous as uranium-based nuclear power? But the main point is that it really is coal that nuclear energy would have replaced.

Here is a question, though. Why can't we just go with clean solar, biofuels and wind energy, because even though they are more dangerous, they don't produce any waste...?

Well, they do leave waste if you count the energy and materials that go into making them and recycling them after they are worn down (how do you recycle a giant windmill with fibreglass blades or a square kilometre or mirrors or solar panels?) But let's leave that issue, because the main problem is another one. The serial entrepreneur Saul Griffith – who has won a number of awards for innovation and entrepreneurship – made, in 2009, some calculations that provide a useful perspective. The world used, at the time, some 16 terawatts of energy, and Griffith calculated the effort that would be needed, if six of those 16 terawatts were to come from solar power, wind and biofuels.

Here we go: if two terawatts were to come from solar panels and if we assumed 30% efficiency - which is a reasonable estimate - we would be required, by Griffiths' estimate, to install 50 m2 panels per second (yes, per second) for 25 years. This corresponds to an astronomical 4.3 million m2 a day - every day for 25 years.[428]

That was two of the 16 terawatts. Should we wish to achieve another two via biofuel, we would additionally have to install four Olympic pools with genetically modified algae per second. And we could then add two terawatts of wind power by constructing a hundred metre high wind turbine every five seconds. Taken together, this would give us six terawatt out of the 16 and thus make us somewhat renewable.

Even if all this could be done, we would have to take into account the planet's growing energy demand due to growth in emerging markets. Suppose it increases to 24 megawatts in 25 years and all of this were required to come, in equal parts, from solar power, biofuels and wind. We would then have to install four times as much of each, equivalent to installing 17 million m2 of solar panels, half a million Olympic swimming pools with biofuel as well as more than 1,100 new giant wind turbines - every single day, for the next 25 years, which essentially amounts to industrializing a significant part of our landscape.

So what some of the modern Luddites seem to propose is that we shut down our safest energy form (uranium-based nuclear fission), abstain from implementing far safer alternatives (thorium-based fission and nuclear fusion) and instead do roughly what we have just described above. Good luck with that.

If there is one group of technologies that can instil even more fear and rejection among Luddites it is perhaps genetic engineering.

However, as we have already seen, genetic engineering has been a central part of human history for millennia, and not only have we modified ourselves genetically, but also through selective breeding, the creation of hybrids, and so on, we have genetically modified almost everything we eat. These are the modified species that people, including environmentalists, today grow as "organic". So what is new about genetic engineering is actually only that it is done with deeper insight and greater precision by deliberately moving individual atoms in DNA chains instead of letting it happen more randomly.

There is an overwhelming consensus among scientists that genetic engineering, when carried out under standard safety norms, is safe for humans and the environment. In October 2014, German scientists published a meta-study covering all 147 studies of the effects of the use of genetically modified (GM) crops published in English since 1995, where GM production took off.[429] Since all major research is indeed published in English, these 147 studies represented all available scientific knowledge gathered over these 19 years. The analysis, which was financed by the German government and the EU, concluded: "On average, GM technology adoption has reduced chemical pesticide use by 37%, increased crop yields by 22%, and increased farmer profits by 68%."

By the same time, more than 3,400 scientists, including 25 Nobel Prize winners, had signed the *Declaration of Support for Agricultural Biotechnology*, which expresses support for modern genetic engineering.[430] In China, which supports such technology strongly, the Chinese Academy of Science estimated that, through the use of genetic engineering, it could reduce the use of pesticides by about 80%. In the US, the American Medical Association has issued a strong statement of support for modern genetic engineering, and the EU Environment Commissioner Margot Wallström has described restrictions against modern genetic engineering as "illegal and not justified."[431] Many ecologists also support it strongly, and the Rockefeller Foundation, Bill and Melinda Gates foundation as well as the US Agency for International Developments view it as a vital tool for improving our environment and people's lives.

However, modern Luddites consider it would be a disaster, if we were to make modified versions of just a fraction of a thousandth of the world's species through such technology, even if it is clear that this can solve significant environmental and resource challenges and/or save millions of people from disease and death. Besides the fact that virtually everything they eat is actually engineered already, these people somehow ignore the fact that the global biosystem constantly creates an astronomical number of natural mutations - presumably many trillion per second. An example: in 2009, the first results from the so-called Cancer Genome Project were published and they showed that, on average, there were 23,000 mutations in each lung cancer cell tested and 33,000 mutations in each skin cancer cell.17 Mutations are simply happening everywhere and constantly where they create not only cell damage, but also new ideas.

In 2004, Craig Venter, who is arguably the world's most famous expert in genetics and the main pioneer behind the first sequencing of human DNA, explained in a speech how extensive the biological experimentation really is. Venter and his team had sailed around the Earth to collect samples of seawater which they filtered so that they could extract and analyze its DNA material. Here, they discovered that a single barrel of water from the Sargasso Sea contained 50,000 unknown species with 1.2 million unknown genes. And every time he sailed 200 nautical miles, he and his team took another sample and saw that, on average, 85% of the genes differed from what he had found in the previous sample.[432] Here is how he explained real time evolution:

"In the air in this room—we've been doing the air genome project—all of you just during the course of this hour will be breathing in at least 10,000 different bacteria,

and maybe 100,000 viruses. I would look closely at the person sitting next to you to see what they're exhaling. This is the world of biology that we live in, that we don't see, where evolution takes place on a minute-to-minute basis." [433]

And this is the point; evolution happens all around us and within us, in a massive scale and on a minute-to-minute basis. Genes come naturally from one's parents, but can also be imported via viruses, and much of our genetic material looks suspiciously similar to some in viral genes. Genes may be introduced from one's surroundings as naked DNA fragments or even as whole DNA strands. As mentioned earlier, mitochondria are probably bacteria whose DNA was copied into other cells, and the same goes for chloroplasts in plants.

So here is what anyone who is scared of genetic mutation should know: nature changes all the time, and 99 % of all species had perished before the first human evolved. You are a mutation yourself, and almost everything you eat and may consider to be "natural" has been mutated by your ancestors. If you are white, then it is because your black ancestors mutated and changed colour. If you can tolerate milk, that is a mutation too because of the invention of farming. Each of your own body cells has mutated massively since you were born, but 90% of the cells in your body are, in fact, not even human cells, but bacteria that also mutate all the time. You are also absolutely full of viruses, many of which are messing with the genes in your cells at any time. So if you are afraid of even the slightest change in any genes, then you are either not very well informed or not very rational. You are a Luddite.

There is something that we need to understand: we cannot go back to nature, living like the Amish or !Kung- people – there are too many of us for that now.

If we were to live without modern technology, there would only be room for the ten or so million people who probably constituted the entire global population shortly after the last Ice Age. But there are seven billion people now.

And even if we just wanted to go a little bit back in time along the line of the German Romanticism and convert to organic farming, we would also have a problem. Here is why: a European meta-study based on 109 scientific studies of organic farming concluded as follows:

"The results show that organic farming practices generally have positive impacts on the environment per unit of area, but not necessarily per product unit. Organic farms tend to have higher soil organic matter content and lower nutrient losses (nitrogen leaching, nitrous oxide emissions and ammonia emissions) per unit of field area. However, ammonia emissions, nitrogen leaching and nitrous oxide emissions per product unit were higher from organic systems." [434]

The reason why organic farming has a net positive effect per soil unit but not per food unit is that it takes up more land. This specific aspect has been thoroughly investigated in another meta-study, which found that organic farming, on average, requires 25% more land per produced food unit.[435] If the entire world's food were organic, we would need to increase our agricultural land by an area corresponding to approximately. seven times the area of France. If, conversely, it were produced as intensively as in the Netherlands, we would be able either to feed 60 billion people or to convert nearly 90% of our current farmland to national parks.[436]

But is organic food at least more healthy than non-organic food? In 2012, a research team at Stanford University conducted the, hitherto, largest meta-study into that question. The scientists examined the results of 17 previous scientific analyses of health conditions in people who ate organic and non-organic food, respectively. In addition, they studied 223 studies of nutrients and various forms of pollution in many common foods that were either organic or non-organic. They did not find any clear difference between the two cultivars.

Does oganic food taste better, then? Here we also have a meta-study, and its conclusion was that if and when organic tasted better, it was only because it was dryer, so the taste components were more concentrated.[438]

To protect nature, it is vital that we drop romanticism and make our farming as compact as we can. The scientist Indur M Goklany has calculated that if the world had not used technology to boost agricultural productivity between 1950 and 2002 (which it fortunately did) we would have needed almost twice as much agricultural land in 2002 as is actually used. This difference is similar to that of India, Brazil and South Africa's total land area. If we take an even longer perspective of 100 years – from 1900 to 2000 - the positive effect of technology on farming is even more pronounced, because over that period, we managed to multiply productivity per land unit by a factor of five. Had we not done that, we would have used the entire suitable landmass and still starved. If we focus on high-tech farming going forward, we could decrease the farmland needed even as consumption grows considerably.[439]

The reality is that Luddism and irrational romanticizing of the past actually harms the environment as well as the economy and the poor (and few things harm the environment more than harming poor people). In his book *Whole Earth Discipline* the ecologist Stewart Brand commented aptly:

"I dare say the environmental movement has done more harm with its opposition to genetic engineering than any other thing we've been wrong about. We've starved people, hindered science, hurt the natural environment, and denied our own practitioners a crucial tool. In defence of a bizarre idea of what is 'natural', we reject the very thing Rachel Carson encouraged us to pursue—the new science of biotic controls.

We make ourselves look as conspicuously irrational as those who espouse 'intelligent design' or ban stem-cell research, and we teach that irrationality to the public and to decision makers." [440]

Luddism, irrationality and panic-mongering are probably symptoms of very natural human instincts, but the lack of major, real threats has led us to become evermore frantic about ever less.

An example is how we reacted to "mad cow disease". In 1996, the UK health minister announced that there was a possible link between bovine spongiform encephalopathy (BSE) and a similar disease that had been observed in humans. He was right, and this disease was a real problem which could cause a horrible illness. That evening on a news programme on television channel BBC2 newsnight, the UK government's chairman of the Spongiform Encephalopathy Advisory Committee, John Pattison, appeared on screen, where he, with little encouragement from television presenter Jeremy Paxman, conceded, that the disease could kill half a million people. The following weekend Sunday newspaper *The Observer* referred, in a major article, to a forecast by Professor Richard Lacey, who said that the disease would kill half a million people...a year...in England alone by 2016

The actual global number of human deaths from mad cow disease has since been estimated to be at in the region of 280 - equivalent to about 0.056 % of the government's estimate. Lacey's estimate that the disease would kill half a million UK citizens annually was also wrong; the actual death toll was, over the following ten years, a total of 176 people (0.0035 % of the professor's prediction). [441]

This was a typical example of how we massively overstate dramatic risks, but just two years later, came another instance. This was centred on potential major computer problems at the turn of the millennium because many computer systems only registered the last two digits of the year and were thus not prepared to deal with the transition to a new millennium, when they would register the year as "00". The panic became known as "Y2K", which is short for "year two thousand" and "the millennium bug". At a Senate hearing on the subject in 1998, senator Chris Dodd said: "I think we're no longer at the point of asking whether or not there will be any power disruptions, but we are now forced to ask how severe the disruptions are going to be." In July of the same year, *BYTE magazine* quoted technology writer Edmund DeJesus calling Y2K "a crisis without precedent in human history", which would bring it right up there with the world wars and the medieval plague.

So a disaster of epic proportions seemed inevitable, which is why the most pessimistic people stocked up on canned food and medicine as they prepared for the downfall of Western civilization. As a precautionary measure, the

Federal Reserve began, well before the turn of the millennium, to increase liquidity in the market, so as to be able to whither the coming storm better.

However, when the clock struck midnight on New Year's Eve 1999/2000, life continued as before. Subsequent analysis indicated that the only serious Y2K-related technical error worldwide occurred in England, where 154 women were sent wrong amniocentesis test results.

Just three years later came the next panic; this time it was a bird flu pandemic which, according to the UN, could kill 150 million people worldwide – more than Hitler, Stalin, Pol Pot and Mao combined. However, the actual death toll was about 200 people, or 0.00013% of what was predicted.

These panic outbreaks follow a typically pattern. Since 1980, such a panic has, on average, broken out every three years, and the scenarios have included descriptions of millions of deaths, global depression or mass annihilation of plants and species. Many panics are reinforced by reports from UN institutions and other public authorities as well as in books and newspaper articles by intellectuals, which all describe the incredible horrors that await people.

So we have a panic culture, and this is also playing out at the individual level. The Red Cross was founded by Swiss businessman Jean-Henri Dunant after he arrived, by coincidence, in the Italian town of Solferino on June 24, 1859 and found 40,000 soldiers, who had been injured or killed in battle between a French and a Sardinian army with virtually no-one to assist them. Who could have guessed that this same organization would, in April 2013, launch an emergency phone line to provide psychological treatment to Norwegian teenagers who had failed to obtain tickets for a Justin Bieber concert in Oslo?[442]

The increasingly widespread use of crisis therapy is not just odd, it is also problematic, because it means people lose the ability to face resistance and to overcome problems by themselves. In fact, quite apart from the erosion of norms and culture that such activities create, in many individual cases excessive crisis therapy can do more harm than good due to "counter-transference", whereby the victim feels worse because their therapist "feels" with them and reinforces their perception that their experience is a clinical problem.[443]

The phenomenon of increasingly exaggerated fear of anything new or unexpected is very similar to what happens to the human body if it does not experience enough natural infections. Many studies have shown that the body can not only endure many infections in small doses, but it actually needs them, as they stimulate the immune system. A healthy immune system is not only useful for the control of bacterial infections, but it also kills the thousands of more or less cancerous cells that the body naturally creates. In addition, in the absence of real problems to work with, the body may compensate for this via autoimmune reactions (attacking its own healthy cells and organs) and allergies.

A similar phenomenon is known with toxins, which if given regularly in small doses, stimulate the production of degrading enzymes, which then keep the body fit and prepared for any greater shock. When testing the responses to toxic substances, scientists often seek the lowest concentration that gives a quantifiable health problem in test animal such as rats. They will then define a maximum exposure level for humans, which may, for instance, be one promille of that dose. However, such experiments often show that the test animals do better if they are given small concentrations of poison than if they receive none at all. Thus, a large meta-study from 2000 showed that 245 out of 668 toxins (37%), were, in fact, healthy in low doses when tested on animals, plants or cells.[444]

Yes, healthy poison, and this phenomenon is called hormesis and signifies that for many dangerous toxins, whereas large intake is unhealthy or deadly, a low intake has positive effects. This stands in contrast to the so-called LNT model (Linear, No Threshold), which says that any load of a given poison is harmful.

The important observation is that while hormesis doesn't apply for all poisons or infections (such as AIDS), it actually applies to a large quantity of them. Even radioactive exposure seems quite healthy in moderate doses, because it stimulates the body cells' genetic repair and protection mechanisms. DNA is frequently damaged, and we therefore have chemicals that do proofreading and fill in missing atoms. These don't know what the code should be, but they can see if one of the two atoms in a base-pair is missing, which they then fill in. Of course, the fact that radioactivity, which messes with genes in the first place, also triggers a correction process that exceeds the damage, does sound odd when you first hear it, but it has been demonstrated in thousands of studies. Hormesis expert Thomas D Luckey thus estimated that the healthiest radioactive exposure for humans is about 6,000 millirem. After having gone through almost 3,000 different scientific analyses of the health effects of radiation, he concluded:

"We live with a subclinical deficiency of ionizing radiation. By ignoring the scientific data in almost 3,000 reports, advisory committees and government practices have caused, and are now causing, premature cancer deaths for millions of people. We need more, not less, exposure to ionizing radiation. There is proven benefit and no known risk from low-dose irradiation. Health and increased average life-span, not risk and death, should be the guide for new recommendations and laws. With the exception of suicides and abortions motivated by fear, people do not die from low-dose irradiation."[445]

So, on average, people would live longer and have fewer cases of cancer if they received more radiation than they actually do. To put Luckey's recommendation of 6,000 millirem in perspective, the natural background radiation in most places is about 300 millirem, so only 5% of the optimum he described. For another comparison, the maximum allowable radiation from nuclear power plants in the US is just 15 millirem. The real danger of radiation, Luckey explained, typically doesn't come from the exposure itself, but rather from the anxiety created by the mass hysteria that often surrounds nuclear technology. In another meta-analysis, Professor Joel Kauffmann from Philadelphia University concluded:

"The prevailing view of regulatory agencies and advisory groups is that all radiation is bad for health, and exposure to any form of it should be minimized. While high-dose radiation, regardless of source or intention, is harmful to health, evidence is presented that chronic doses up to 100 times those of normal ambient (including medical) exposures are beneficial, mainly due to lower cancer rates. Further evidence is presented that single, acute doses of up to 50 rad are beneficial, including in treatment of cancer and gangrene. Data are cited to show that below-ambient radiation levels are unhealthful, and that some radiation may be essential for many life-forms." [446]

Hormesis is akin to what happens when you grow stronger by training muscles hard or gain more energy in general by periodically draining your energy through jogging. If you carry out a blood test on an athlete in the middle of his tough training, you will typically see a lack of oxygen and overdose of free radicals, which, in itself, seems unhealthy. And yet, sport is healthy in moderation and even quite large doses. The same applies to moderate mental stress and much more, as shown in the table below.

Potentially beneficial effects of moderate physical and psychological stress	
Impact	Possible beneficial effect
Tough sport	Stimulates blood circulation, muscle building, bone strength and immune systems
Infections	Strengthens the immune system; prevent autoimmunity and allergy
Mental stress	Promotes happiness, ability to concentrate and ability to cope with future stress
Poison	Promotes the production of toxic degrading enzymes
Radioactivity	Triggers DNA repair mechanism

All these panic stories show that Western civilization, as a whole, has developed severe autoimmune and allergic reactions to the fruits of its own creativity, and this undermines the spirit that made Western societies great in the first place.

This value shift is reflected in gradual changes to how societies make decisions about risk. The traditional principle is simply to weigh expected benefits and risks against each other, and this is called a "cost-benefit analysis" (or common sense).

The aforementioned "linear no-threshold" or LNT model (the one assuming that the negative effect is directly proportional to exposure) can provide input to cost-benefit analysis, which is correct unless there is a hormesis phenomenon in play. However, the increasing trend is first, to ignore any hormesis and thus always use the LNT model; and second to use its results as input to "precautionary principle" models instead of cost-benefit models. The precautionary principle states that nothing new can be done unless it can be proven, without doubt, that it can cause no harm whatsoever. This is called "proving a negative", which is in most cases theoretically impossible.

There are even people who go further and use the so-called "slippery slope" argument, which says that even if a technology or behaviour is acceptable according to both cost-benefit analysis and the precautionary principle, it should not be used because that would be a slippery slope leading to a more malicious use of the same technology later. For instance, one should not do video surveillance of dark streets, because this is a slippery slope towards watching people everywhere. And one should not clone extinct mammals, because that can be a precursor to cloning a T-Rex, which eat people.

If we really were to model our lives on the LNT model, the precautionary principle and/or the slippery slope argument, no one would drive a car or start a business. Nor would we eat cherries, apples, tomatoes, raw almonds, apple cores or potatoes, as all of these contain toxins. Nor would anyone eat shellfish, peanuts, sweet dairy products, kiwi, sesame, corn, egg, soy or wheat, as these can trigger dangerous allergies and digestive problems. Beer, wine, coffee, mushrooms, red peppers and much more probably couldn't be approved either, if someone invented or discovered them today.

What about table salt? No, this poison is extremely dangerous in large quantities. Extremely! And you would not be able to play football, go cycling or have sex - not to mention get pregnant.

In 2003, a group of scientists organized a conference In London called "Panic Attack: interrogating our obsession with risk". This included presentations of many other examples of technologies that would not have been possible according to the modern precautionary principle. These included innovations such as antibiotics, birth control pills, blood transfusion, organ transplant, hybrid crops, microwave ovens, radar, refrigerators, telephones, televisions, water treatment, and X-rays.

When you really think about it, Vikings and Columbus would never have discovered America had they followed the precautionary principle, as their ships were not safe. And the Wright brothers would never have shown us how to fly.

The problem, if you refuse to make cost-benefit analysis, is that you end up rejecting better solutions because they are not perfect, which leaves you stuck with the old ones which are worse. For example, many of environmentalists oppose fossil fuels, nuclear power and hydroelectric dams, which together make up about 90% of world energy supply and almost 100% of that of many Western nations. Or they are against modern agricultural technology and deforestation, although rejection of the former will inevitably lead to the latter. They will often oppose sea fishing, but also fish farms. They oppose wealth growth, even though this has been shown to be the best way to stop population growth. They just want to stop the world, because it is dangerous, so they end up opposing each step that could make it less dangerous.

In his story *The Fable of the Steak Knives*, previously mentioned Wikipedia founder Jimmy Wales describes how absurd the mentality of the Neo-Luddites really is. If one were to launch the world's first steak restaurant today and suggest that people should be provided (armed) with knives at the table, the precautionary principle would probably require diners to be shielded in cages to avoid bloodshed.

Wales could also have used the slippery slope argument here. What is the next step, if we really let people use arms in restaurants? Samurai swords? Guns? No, it's a slippery slope!

We started this chapter with a discussion of toxins, so let's end it with a little more about them - this time with a focus on how they may stimulate cancer. One of the world's leading researchers into the relationship between toxins and cancer is Bruce Ames of the University of California, who invented the famous Ames Test to get a swift indication of whether a substance is carcinogenic (cancer stimulating). Based on several decades of research in the field, he and his staff concluded:

◆ Approximately 99.9% of the foods modern humans eat is natural; the remaining 0.1% is artificial.
◆ Similarly, 99.9% of all the pesticides that humans eat are natural toxins produced by plants to defend themselves against fungi, insects and other animal predators such as ourselves. So only 0.1% of the pesticides we eat are artificial.[447]

This means that natural and artificial food contains approximately equal proportions of toxins, but because 99.9% of what we eat is natural, 99.9% of the toxins we eat are also natural. And even though we spray plants with artificial toxins (and organic farmers do it with insect-killing bacteria, copper, etc.) artificial toxins (but not cobber) sprayed on the plants typically degrade before or after harvest (but before we eat the plants). The plants, on the other hand, produce their own pesticides constantly until the time when they are harvested.

So what do these numbers mean for us? Ames illustrated this with an example: a single cup of coffee contains as many natural pesticides as an average American consumes in artificial pesticides during an entire year. Put in another way, just 80 cups of coffee gives us as much poison as all the artificial toxins we will consume throughout our entire life. And yet, despite this, most studies show that moderate daily intake of coffee is quite healthy for most people. So if we get cancer, it is extremely unlikely that it came from anything produced with modern technology.

How unlikely? Studies by Richard Doll and Richard Peto concluded in the 1980s, that just 2% of all cancers could be attributed to artificial compounds in food and elsewhere; the rest came from smoking, unbalanced diets, infections and hormonal imbalances. In fact, tobacco and unbalanced diets alone accounted for two-thirds of all cancers.[448]

Moderation is the key word here. The body likes a balanced diet and lifestyle, but it can actually also benefit from hard work, mental stress, infections and even many toxins and increased nuclear radiation, as long as everything is moderate. Not too much, but (and this is the important part) not too little either. And yes, even steak, coffee and red wine seem to be healthy when consumed in moderation

Luddism, irrationality, panic and refusal to weigh costs against benefits are all elements of the same story. It's about excessive self-taming that inhibits innovation, and the slippery slope argument plus the precautionary principle can, in themselves, pretty much destroy it. As Robert Bailey of *Reason Magazine* wrote aptly in 2003, you can describe thee precautionary principle as this: "Never do anything for the first time."

China became static when its inhabitants were prevented from sailing out to sea, and the Ottomans lost their dynamism when they forbade the search for new knowledge in printed books. Many in the West have now become intellectually autoimmune, allergic to innovation, enemies of science, and instinctive opponents to doing something for the first time. This irrational longing for a static society costs society billions and leads to unnecessary loss of animal and human life. The problem is, as Franklin D. Roosevelt put it in his inaugural address in 1933:

"The only thing we have to fear is fear itself." [449]

21.
ECO-FASCISTS
AND
PSEUDO-SCIENTISTS

On November 29 2012 Rebecca Rubin gave herself up to FBI agents in Blaine, Washington, having been wanted for eco-terrorism for seven years. Her organization had previously arranged at least 20 arson attacks or attempted arson, including firebombing of administrative offices, a ski resort, a barn and a timber company.[450]

Eco-terrorists commit a lot of violence, but they usually confine it to vandalism, for example by throwing paint on fur-clad people or destroying scientific research laboratories. A survey of 1,000 biomedical researchers showed that approximately a quarter had been affected by violence from activists, and before the 9/11 terror attack in the US, the FBI listed the environmental movement Earth Liberation Front as the country's leading terror group after it had conducted some 600 attacks between 1996 and 2004.[451]

However, it is clear that many of these people fantasize about greater destruction. For instance, editor John Davis of the World Wildlife Fund has, for one stated that: "Human beings, as a species, have no more value than slugs", and that he "suspects that eradicating small pox was wrong. It played an important part in balancing ecosystems."

"I think if we don't overthrow capitalism, we don't have a chance of saving the world ecologically", stated Judy Barr from the Earth First! movement correspondingly, and elaborated: "I think it is possible to have an ecologically sound society under socialism. I don't think it is possible under capitalism." However, it was really much more than capitalism, some of these people were after. It was humanity. In its early days, Earth First! used the slogan "Back to the Pleistocene" (which ended about 2.6 million years ago, when there were not even ape-men). In their newsletter of December 1989, they wrote that "if radical environmentalists were to invent a disease to bring human populations back to sanity, it would probably be something like AIDS." David Foreman, who was their spokesman, said to *Backpacker Magazine* in September 1988 that "man is no more important than any other species. It may well take our extinction to set things straight." On another occasion he said that "phasing out the human race will solve every problem on Earth, social and environmental."

Charles Wurster was co-founder and senior scientist for The Environmental Defence Fund, and he evidently didn't like DDT, as he was the man we met earlier who put alcohol into sea water to suggest that DDT could stop photosynthesis. He was once asked whether a ban on DDT would lead to people switching to other toxins that were more dangerous to humans, to which he replied "probably". When the reporter asked if this would not kill people, he replied: "So what? People are the cause of all the problems. We have too many of them. We need to get rid of some of them, and (malaria) is as good a way as any."[452]

Michael Oppenheimer of the same organization elaborated: "If China, where there's one car for every 500 people, gets the same kind of cars and the same ratio of cars to people that the United States does, where there's one car for every two people, the world is essentially going to go through the roof environmentally. We can't let that happen."[453]

So keep them poor. It should be said here that Oppenheimer later left the organization because he believed it was infiltrated by Marxists and anarchists, which sounds about right.

Getting rid of the poor hasn't been the only objective of radical environmentalists; democracy could also seem a hindrance, as James Lovelock, author of The Gaia Hypothesis, stated in an interview:

"Even the best democracies agree that when a major war approaches, democracy must be put on hold for the time being. I have a feeling that climate change may be an issue as severe as a war. It may be necessary to put democracy on hold for a while." [454]

Actually, neither the US nor UK resorted to dictatorship, even as when they fought the dictators in World War II, but no matter. The Finnish Literature Prize winner and winner of The Environmental Prize by Finnish Association for Nature Conservation and founder of The Finnish Natural Heritage Foundation, Pentti Linkola, has for years argued that democracy is a "death religion" and that:

"Any dictatorship would be better than modern democracy. There cannot be so incompetent a dictator, that he would show more stupidity than a majority of the people. The best dictatorship would be one where lots of heads would roll and government would prevent any economical growth." [455]

According to him, a "transnational organization like the UN" should attack the cities with nuclear bombs or biological or chemical weapons. Linkola has also argued that the Stalinist and Nazi extermination campaigns were "massive thinning operations," which have "not overturned our ethical norms."[456]

Speaking of thin, he also didn't like people weighing too much: "That there are billions of people over 60 kg weight on this planet is recklessness," he said. In 1994, he gave an interview to the Wall Street Journal, in which he stated:

"If there were a button I could press, I would sacrifice myself without hesitating, if it meant millions of people would die." [457]

Kill, kill, kill!

Of course, most environmentalists are not fascists, and the environmental movement includes some of worlds' greatest friends, which we should never forget. But it also includes some of its worst enemies, which we should never ignore.

In 2009, the American writer and author Alex Steffen introduced a way to distinguish between environmentalists. His first, and by far the largest, group is "light green", which are those who try to exercise personal environmental awareness - for example by driving fuel-efficient cars, better insulating their houses or support tree planting. That can't be wrong.

The second type of environmentalist, according to Alex Steffen, is "bright green". These believe that environmental problems must be solved with modern technology, such as genetic manipulation and new forms of nuclear power. Among the most prominent individuals who hold such believes are Stuart Brand, founder of the publication series Whole Earth Catalogue and think tank organisation The Long Now Foundation. This group also includes ecologist Patrick Moore, physicist and mathematician Freeman Dyson, Microsoft founder Bill Gates, Amazon founder Jeff Bezos, Nobel laureate James Watson (who helped discover the structure of DNA), democratic politicians George McGovern and Jimmy Carter plus financier Warren Buffet and many more. Many of those people have launched or supported creative environmental solutions that have brought the world forward.

However, there is also a third environmental movement: "dark green", represented by the likes of Paul Ehrlich, Charles Wurster and Pentti Linkola, who portray technological progress and economic growth as core problems and therefore want them stopped.

Many dark green ecologists favour very authoritarian and perhaps global government. They are typically against globalization and international trade, and their arguments often contain attacks on multinational firms, market economies and the profit motive. The main organizations with dark environmentalism leanings are probably Die Grühne, Friends of the Earth, Earth Liberation Front, Greenpeace, Environmental Defence Fund, Earth First!, the Sierra Club, the Union of Concerned Scientist and the World Wildlife Fund.

Ideology can have complex roots, but at some point, it needs some simplicity. Arguably, the roots of dark environmentalism go back to the aforementioned German counter-enlightenment movement Sturm und Drang from the late 18th century, which was opposed to enlightenment, rationality, science, aesthetics and universalism. This reappeared as the German Luddite and anti-enlightenment Romantic Movement. This romanticism spread from Germany across Europe, where Frenchman Rousseau became one of its better-known advocates, but it always had the strongest grip among Germans. Its main theses were that technology and, in part, civilization were artificial phenomena and thus dubious and that the past was better than the present. They also believed there was an important bond between a given people, its traditional culture and the area from which they originated, which is why the Romantics were typically strong nationalists and against international trade or mixing of races.

Simplicity entered the picture when, in 1866, the German biologist and philosopher Ernst Haeckel, who was enthusiastic member of the Romantic Movement, introduced the concept of "ecology". To view all of nature as a whole was rather new, and Haeckel argued that this view should replace religion.[458]

On the heels of this came the German Blut und Boden (blood and soil) movement. This emphasized the spiritual and genetic purity (blood) and a dream of returning to nature (soil). The movement supported organic farming, conservation of nature, natural medicine, self-sufficiency and traditional German heritage. In 1913, the philosopher Ludwig Klages published the book *Mensch und Erde* (Man and Land), where he elaborated on the philosophy and deemed new technology and advanced farming technology to be destructive to the land. After this book, the Blut und Boden movement would increasingly condemn capitalism, industrialization, urbanization, new technologies, as well as Jews and Christianity. Cities were seen as unnatural phenomena, while peasants doing organic farming with traditional means were elevated to the noblest of all people.

The movement had other facets, and its basic ideas can be described roughly as follows:

1. There may not be a God, but nature and genes are sacred.
2. Human beings are part of nature, and we must protect ourselves by keeping our genes clean and our food and medicines free of modern technology, and by limiting our numbers.
3. Man is spiritually and culturally related to the land from which he came. Urban life and modern technology is inversely unnatural and create a wedge between us and the Earth.

4. Rootless cosmopolitans such as immigrants and urbanites miss the bond with the land and are therefore often corrupt and decadent.[459]

The movement was an example of an austere and static mentality, which focused on protecting and cleaning what existed, while rejecting the new and alien. At the edge of this philosophy came homeopathy and other alternatives to science-based medicine.

Some of those ideas meshed well with communism, and in the 1940s Stalin launched a campaign against "rootless cosmopolitans" (безродный космополит), which he apparently thought were mainly Jews.[460] However, the ideas resonated even better with the Nazis, or NSDAP, which it was officially called, an abbreviation which translates to National Socialist German Workers' Party. One of the Nazis, biologist Ernst Lehmann, explained the essence of their philosophy with these words: "We understand that the separation of man from nature, from the whole of life, leads to man's own downfall and death of nations." He elaborated as follows:

"This quest for connectedness with life's totality, with nature itself, a nature that we are born into, this is the deepest meaning and the true essence of National Socialist thought." [461]

Lehmann described Nazism as "politically performed biology", and in his opinion, the return to nature is not only a part of the Nazi spirit, but it was its very core. Hitler expressed similar ideas in his book *Mein Kampf*, where he wrote: "When people try to go against nature's iron law of logic, they come into conflict with the very principles that have given them their existence as a people. Their interventions against nature must lead to their downfall."

He meant it. After his inauguration, Nazis implemented Europe's most advanced nature protection laws, including the Tierschutzgesetz, Reichsjagdgesetz, Dauerwald and in 1935 Reichsnaturschutzgesetz. The Nazi Party also created Europe's first nature reserves, and Hitler banned medical experiments on animals (but not on Jews).

How high a priority the Nazis gave to nature and farming was also reflected in the fact that the German Ministry of Agriculture, even until the middle of the war, retained the fourth-largest budget of all ministries. Agriculture minister Richard Walther Darré often made stirring speeches under the Blut und Boden banner, in which he argued for organic farming and, with agro-technical terminology, described Jews as Earth's "weeds". One source indicates that, in the end, it was he who was convinced Hitler and Himmler that Jews and Slavs were to be "weeded out" with poison gas.[462]

The Nazi Reichsminister of Food and Agriculture , Richard Walther Darré, holds a speech under the Blud und Boden banner in Goslar on December 13th, 1937

The Nazis were, in other words, obsessed with clean food, clean minds, healthy genes and clean bodies. Hitler himself was a dedicated ecologist and a supporter of homeopathy and also, at least from 1941, a vegetarian, as was Rudolf Hess, who was second to Hitler in terms of rank.

Nazis saw the Jews as enemies of nature and as alien to German soil. In the book, *Giftpilz* (poisonous fungus) the contrast between Jewish financiers and the Germanic rural population was highlighted. Jews lent money to farmers, it was explained, and then they forced them from their farms, when they could not pay these debts. In this way, these evil financiers separated Germans from their land and severed the vital blood ties.

The Blut und Boden movement formed a key element of the German zeitgeist and was reflected in many romantic books and plays, which idolized self-sufficiency and the romantic life of the country. There were also many Blut und Boden-inspired art exhibitions showing paintings of the romantic Germanic rural life. These would almost always show people performing manual labour without the presence of machines or other forms of new technology.

The movement had a broad support among German youth, including via Wandervogel, a youth group that aimed to get back to nature and freedom, and celebrated the "great outdoors". It also fared well among conservationists, and an inventory from 1939 showed that 60% of the members of natural conservation associations also were registered members of the Nazi party, compared with only 10% of the general population.[463]

Perhaps one would think that all of this ended after the Nazis were crushed in World War II. However, it really didn't, because the Blut und Boden movement soon reappeared in a new guise, and the essence remained largely the same: self-sufficiency, romanticizing traditional peasant life and the past, rejecting new technology and, to some extent, science, and supporting a general thinning of the human population. It has to be said, though, that few would now publically oppose racial mixing, although cultural mixing was often rejected. And as a clear example of the civilizing process in practice, no one advocated killing Jews anymore.

People considered inferior were another matter, though, and World Wildlife Fund co-founder Sir Julian Huxley had, in 1941, given his support to the forced sterilization of the unemployed and weak, and he had also suggested making it difficult for the weak to access healthcare, so they became less likely to survive and breed. He remained chairman of the British Eugenics Society from 1939 to 1962. Within the auspices of The World Wildlife Fund, he also worked also with Herbert Gruhl, who envisaged a strongly-armed ecological dictatorship that would provide "an optimum of military preparedness with a minimum of consumer satisfaction and therefore a much smaller utilization of natural resources." Gruhl authored the bestselling book *A Planet is Looted*, where he suggested introducing a "dictatorship stricter than Stalin to ration the world's resources." He also co-founded the green Ökologisch-Demokratischen Partei (Ecologic Democratic Party). His main concern, apart from immigration and the mixture of cultures, was lack of resources, because as he explained:

"There is no doubt that the wars of the future will be fought over shares in the basic foundations of life -- that is, over the basis of nutrition and the increasingly precious fruits of the soil. Under these circumstances, future wars will far surpass in frightfulness all previous wars." [464]

One of the renewed movement's strongest forces, however, became the German party Die Grühne, founded in 1979 by Gert Bastian, his wife Petra Kelly and August Haussleiter, who became its first leader. However, in 1980 Haussleiter was forced to resign due to public criticism of his political background. He had, it turned out, in 1933, been editor of the Nazi and strongly anti-Semitic weekly magazine *Fränkischer Kurier*. Then he had volunteered as an SS officer and had served as such during World War II. In 1952, he described the Nuremberg war tribunal as the "most stupid and vile of all criminal courts."

POPULAR NAZI EMBLEMS. TO THE LEFT, AN EMBLEM FOR WAFFEN SS, IN THE MIDDLE FOR THE PARTY, AND TO THE RIGHT FOR ITS BLUD UND BODEN MOVEMENT.

So Haussleiter still appeared somewhat Nazi-like in many people's view, and it didn't help that, after the war, he had co-founded an extremist party called Deutsche Gemeinschaft, which supported the incorporation of parts of Eastern Europe under a greater "socialist Germany." This party was later banned under the country's anti-Nazi legislation. Haussleiter's interest in founding a German green party was mainly evoked by seeing how big, popular forces could be mobilized against nuclear power.

Gert Bastian, the second of the three founders of Die Grühne, was a former Nazi major general, who after the war, had been a founding member of the organization Krefelder Appell, which was supported by the East German Communist Party. His partner, Petra Kelly was the third founder. However, in October 1992, Gert shot Petra and then himself. The reason is unknown, but just before it happened, he had been informed that the Stasi archives were about to be opened, so it could have been out of fear of what one would find there – however, his file turned out to be empty.

Today, the Blut und Boden concept continues to offer broad appeal, and it constitutes the core of the dark green environmental mindset. Among those who, in recent years, have studied its roots and worldview more closely is Professor Peter Staudenmaier from Marquette University in Wisconsin. In his book *Ecofascism: Lessons from the German Experience,* he concludes about the dark green:

"The "green wing" of the NSDAP was not a group of innocents, confused and manipulated idealists, or reformers from within; they were conscious promoters and executors of a vile program explicitly dedicated to inhuman racist violence, massive political repression and worldwide military domination. Their 'ecological' involvements, far from offsetting these fundamental commitments, deepened and radicalized them. In the end, their configuration of environmental politics was directly and substantially responsible for organized mass murder."

Greenpeace is now recruiting members under the promise that they can be "eco-warriors" and, in April 2010, the following comment from Greenpeace's Indian communications director Gene Hashmi appeared on its website:

"We must break the law to make the laws we need: laws that are supposed to protect society, and protect our future. The proper channels have failed. It's time for mass civil disobedience to cut off the financial oxygen from denial and scepticism."

So, just like James Lovelock, Herbert Gruhl, Arnold Reize, Pentti Linkola and others, Hashmi apparently seemed to think that it could be ok to abolish democracy for the sake of the environment. He continued the statement by making personal threats against people with divergent opinions:

"If you're one of those who have spent their lives undermining progressive climate legislation, bankrolling junk science, fuelling spurious debates around false solutions, and cattle-prodding democratically-elected governments into submission, then hear this: We know who you are. We know where you live. We know where you work. And we be many, but you are few."

That was as plain-speaking as it gets, and the message disappeared from their site a short time later. Meanwhile, Greenpeace co-founder Paul Watson has moved on to found the Sea Shepherd Conservation Society which, for whatever reason, shows a human cranium on a black background.

A widely used strategy among dark greens has been to harass or terrorize scientific research, scientists and engineers until the latter's work became so expensive that it had to be abandoned. Among their important tools are LNT, the precautionary principle and slippery slope arguments.

The dark green organizations are not democratically elected, and their activists are fortunately few, but their power is immense, and not many people dare speak openly against them. We have already looked at some of the typical consequences of their harassment in the form of extensive wasting of resources, often millions of unnecessary deaths, and paradoxically, also deterioration of our environment. We saw, for instance how their campaigns against nuclear energy led to resurgence of coal use with millions of additional deaths as a consequence, and how their campaign against DDT arguably killed additional tens of millions, via malaria. But here it is important to keep in mind that many dark green activists, in line with Malthus, actually welcome such side effects as ways of keeping down the population. As Pentti Linkola said: "When the lifeboat is full, those who hate life will try to load it with more people and sink the lot. Those who love and respect life will take the ship's axe and sever the extra hands that cling to the sides."[465] And this: "Who misses all those who died in the Second World War? Who misses the twenty million executed by Stalin? Who misses Hitler's six million Jews? Israel creaks with over crowdedness; in Asia minor, overpopulation creates struggles for mere square meters of dirt."[466]

Yeah, cut them off! But surely, not all dark environmentalists can be evil; most are probably uninformed idealists, but as Nobel Prize winner TS Eliot once wrote, the indifference to the actual reality lead to much suffering:

"Half the harm that is done in this world is due to people who want to feel important. They don't mean to do harm; but the harm does not interest them. Or they do not see it, or they justify it because they are absorbed in the endless struggle to think well of themselves." [467]

Along with sister movement Friends of the Earth, Greenpeace has been a key player in preventing the use of golden rice, which, as previously described, is modified so that it contains a lot of beta-carotene, which alleviates vitamin A deficiency. A study in 2005 showed that 190 million children and 19 million pregnant women worldwide suffered from vitamin A deficiency which led to 1-2 million deaths annually, typically among children. This makes it almost as big a killer as malaria. In addition, every year, it leads to around 500,000 (some estimate 2-3 million) new cases of blindness and millions of cases of impaired vision and dry eyes and so on.[468] This is a truly terrible problem, and in February 2012, the director of the Consultative Group on International Agricultural Research, Ismail Serageldin, posed this question:

"I ask opponents of biotechnology, do you want 2 to 3 million children a year to go blind and 1 million to die of vitamin A deficiency, just because you object to the way golden rice was created?" [469]

In September that year, bright green-ecologist Patrick Moore wrote an article which concluded:

"It is clear from the facts that Greenpeace is guilty of crimes against humanity as defined by the International Criminal Court. They claim that "Golden Rice is a failure" while they are the ones responsible for preventing the cure that is so desperately needed by millions of civilians. The fact that Greenpeace perpetuate lies about Golden Rice while at the same time doing nothing to solve the problem themselves constitutes gross negligence on top of the crime against humanity. Will someone please bring them to justice?" [470]

It should be noted that Patrick Moore actually was a co-founder of Greenpeace, but later left the organisation when he felt that it had been hijacked by people with destructive, anti-humanist and anti-scientific attitudes.

Technology and science is, as previously mentioned, central to Western civilization's progress and future, and we have already looked at science's most important principles such as impartiality, objectivity, logic, reasoned assumption, systematic doubt, source check, falsification, replicability, verification, peer reviews, and openness to criticism. The vast majority of scientists work roughly according to these principles, and scientists are therefore generally held in high esteem. However, not all live up to the fine reputation of this profession.

Aforementioned environment professor Stephen Schneider, who in 1970 published warnings of coming Ice Age and later changed his mind, became senior writer for the IPCC on global warming, and explained his mindset in 1989:

"On the one hand, as scientists we are ethically bound to the scientific method, in effect promising to tell the truth, the whole truth, and nothing but — which means that we must include all the doubts, the caveats, the ifs, ands, and buts. On the other hand, we are not just scientists but human beings as well. And like most people we'd like to see the world a better place, which in this context translates into our working to reduce the risk of potentially disastrous climatic change. To do that we need to get some broad based support, to capture the public's imagination. That, of course, entails getting loads of media coverage. So we have to offer up scary scenarios, make simplified, dramatic statements, and make little mention of any doubts we might have." [471]

So he thought it was acceptable for scientists to distort the truth, if it served a good purpose, and he concluded further as follows: "Each of us has to decide what the right balance is between being effective and being honest. I hope that means being both."

Don't we all, but it doesn't always work out that way. Climate scientist Michael Mann is among those who have been criticized for giving particular priority to being efficient. The first time his name appeared in a wider circle, was in 1998, when he and two other researchers had an article published in the highly- regarded scientific journal *Nature*. It contained a reconstruction of the climate of the northern hemisphere from 1400 to 2000. "MBH98", as this reconstruction was technically called, was soon renamed "the hockey stick", as its graphic depiction looked a bit like a hockey stick – first straight for a long time, then suddenly rising sharply. The following year, it was updated to stretch from the year 1000.

The message of this graph was shocking: Between the year 1000 and the early 20th century, temperatures had been very stable with fluctuations rarely exceeding 0.5 degrees, but when CO_2 emissions had increased sharply after World War II and especially after the 1970s, they had suddenly exploded upward. The conclusion seemed obvious: anthropogenic (man-made) emissions of CO_2 were creating an unprecedented warming. This graph created a huge stir and appeared on thousands of websites and was notably distributed to all households by the Canadian government. Soon, it was by far the world's most used illustration of the problem of global warming.

However, there were aspects of it that caused some raised eyebrows here and there. For example, what on earth had happened to the Little Ice Age, which was so well described in historical records? And what about the well-documented warm periods?

Shortly after the hockey stick graph had appeared, the magazine *Climate*

Research published an analysis by two astrophysicists from Harvard, which contradicted Mann's graph and concluded that recent climate variations were well within the normal range.[472]

What happened next is extraordinary. We have an unusual behind-the-scenes insight into the case, as an anonymous person leaked thousands of emails and other documents spanning a period of 13 years from the Climatic Research Unit (CRU) at the University of East Anglia in England. Many of the climate scientists around Michael Mann immediately began to discuss how they could prevent researchers with different results than their own from getting these published. Thus wrote the director of the CRU, Phil Jones, on March 11th 2003 to some colleagues: "I will be emailing the journal to tell them I'm having nothing more to do with it until they rid themselves of this troublesome editor."[473]

Yes, that editor was really annoying, and Phil Jones had already complained to the magazine because they had published articles that contradicted his own on global warming. The editor that Jones wanted fired had acted quite correctly: He had sent the Harvard physicists' article to an external scientist and asked him to send it on to five other experts of his choosing for peer review and thus also for an assessment of whether it was scientifically solid. The five had concluded that it was, and that was why it was published.

No matter, Michael Mann suggested his colleagues boycott the magazine by refraining from sending it articles for publication and never quoting research that had been printed in it. On April 22, Phil Jones wrote to his colleagues that he had told the magazine's editor-in-chief that he would boycott the magazine.

Over the following months and years this pattern of trying to block the scientific debate was repeated in a number of other cases where leading climate scientists discussed how they could use boycotts, layoffs or withholding of data to prevent researchers with differing views from doing research and publishing results.[474] When one scientist pointed out that a number of Chinese temperature data used in a report by Phil Jones were very sketchy, Kevin Trenberth of the National Center for Atmospheric Research suggested the following in an email to Mann on April 21 2007: "So my feeble suggestion is to indeed cast aspersions on their motives and throw in some counter rhetoric. Labelling them as lazy with nothing better to do seems like a good thing to do."

However, it was difficult for them to shut off all criticism. The same year that Mann's hockey stick graph appeared, a Canadian mathematician named Stephen McIntyre asked Michael Mann if he could give him access to the hockey stick model used and the data behind it for checking, as McIntyre also wondered where previous temperature fluctuations had gone. McIntyre had, as a student, won a national mathematics competition and studied as a mathematician at Oxford University. Later, he had founded and managed a mining company and had subsequently worked as a consultant specializing in finding errors in statistical models. However, as he realized that the task at hand was significant, he asked Ross McKitrick, a Canadian economist specializing in environmental economics and policy analysis, to help him analyse the hockey stick.

It soon turned out that Michael Mann was not particularly welcoming to McIntyre and McKitrick. As shown in the correspondence - which went on for more than ten years and was later published on the internet and in various books - Mann first sent some wrong data and then announced that some of the information was missing. At one point they were told that they could not get the rest of Mann's underlying climate data, as contracts with other countries' climate research institutions prohibited the release to a third party. As McIntyre and McKitrick discovered that they had actually delivered the same data to other climate scientists, the explanation was changed to that the data could only be released to professional climate scientists and not to the Canadians. McIntyre and McKitrick arranged, therefore, that other climate scientists asked for the same data, but now the explanation was again changed; the data had been lost, they were told.

The general attitude to discussion and openness was quite clearly expressed as the Australian climate scientist Warwick Hughes after a month-long period of e-mail correspondence with Phil Jones about gaining access to raw climate data and formulas behind the Institute's analyzes February 21, 2005 received the following final rejection:

"Even if WMO agrees, I will still not pass on the data. We have 25 or so years invested in the work. Why should I make the data available to you, when your aim is to try and find something wrong with it?" [475]

As Phil Jones was summoned to a hearing by the UK government in March 2010, he explained away the extreme data secrecy among the climate scientists by saying that it was not standard practice among climate scientists to release data. [476]

As for McIntyre and McKitrick's request for the software code (the statistical model), Mann refused to give it out on the grounds that it was verbally-described in his article and that it was, in any case, his private property, even though he was working for a public and taxpayer-funded university.

When no one could gain access to the code, it was evidently difficult to check Mann's graph, and in 2005, the US government also asked for the code, to which Mann responded:

"My computer program is a piece of private, intellectual property, as the National

Science Foundation and its lawyers recognize. It is a bedrock principle of American law that the government may not take private property "without [a] public use," and "without just compensation." [477]

So still no code after seven years of trying, and against this background, it seemed impossible to test how Mann had arrived at his graph.

The two Canadians tried to replicate Mann's procedure based on his oral description of the code, but they could not, which process they described in an article published in 2003.[478] However, a breakthrough came when they found some important lines of code between data series that Mann had sent them. These algorithms selected any data series that had been particularly volatile towards the end of the period and amplified them compared to other data series.

By inserting these in their replication model, McIntyre and McKitrick could finally get it to make hockey sticks. In fact, so much so, that when they combined combinations of random data (so-called red noise) more than 10,000 times, the model generated hockey sticks in over 99% of cases. And again: this was out of combinations of completely random data. When using the model on Mann's actual data, they found that its hockey stick shape was generated by amplification of a single one of the many time series used: tree rings from California trees. This statistical time series went back to year 1404. Between the years 1421 and 1447 it was based on two trees, between 1404 and 1421 on a single tree, and before that, Mann had just added some fictitious numbers. The numbers came from an analysis by other scientists, who had concluded that the reason why three rings had been larger in recent years was not warming, but aerial fertilization (the aforementioned tendency for plants to grow faster, if the air contains more CO_2).[479]

The biggest problem in all this is actually not that a small group of academics sacrifice basic scientific principles and choose to act as stealth political activists. The problem is that they get away with it and are even widely praised for it.

In the third assessment report from the leading science body, the Intergovernmental Panel on Climate Change (IPCC), in 2001, Mann's hockey stick graph was reproduced no fewer than five times, including a very prominent colour illustrated version on page 29. This, despite the fact that Mann, who was then a relatively unknown scientist, still refused to hand over the data and code, which was why the graph had never been verified independently. It was also despite the fact that the graph totally contradicted a number of other climate reports and archaeological information as well as what had been stated in previous IPCC reports. It is therefore difficult to conclude anything else than that the graph was strongly promoted because the IPCC team liked its political power: it was effective.

The problem doesn't end here, though, because Michael Mann has since been awarded a number of honours for his scientific work. And so has our serial catastrophist Paul Ehrlich; in fact, so much so, that a simple list of his honours and awards would fill approximately two A4 pages. Among the many organizations that have praised his research in such ways (and often with prizes totalling millions of dollars) are The Sierra Club, World Wildlife Fund, the Royal Swedish Academy of Sciences, Volvo, the UN, the Albert Einstein Club, Ecological Society of America, the American Institute of Biological Sciences and the Royal Society of London. If these organizations have a problem with a scientist being completely divorced from reality, they certainly don't show it.

Oh, and we shouldn't forget that Erlich also received the MacArthur Foundation "genius" award, along with a substantial pot of money. This was in 1990, where it was clear that his forecasts had been spectacularly wrong.

You couldn't make this up, but there is another side to the matter that is equally grotesque. For while this circus is continuing, there are tens of thousands of serious scientists who are indeed interested in the impartial and objective search for the truth, but who spend their careers in relative anonymity and economic modesty. Day after day, these scientists actually stick to the dry figures and the scientific methods, which mean they are less likely to receive big awards, let alone genius prizes.

And they find it hard to go against the politically-tainted mass movements. On 12 April 2006, Richard Lindzen, who was a professor of atmospheric physics at MIT, wrote an article in the *Wall Street Journal* in which he stated: "Scientists who dissent from alarmism have seen their grant funds disappear, their work derided, and themselves libelled as industry stooges, scientific hacks or worse."

Julian Simon experienced the same phenomenon in 1980 when, in the journal *Science*, he showed that the scientific statistics in no way indicated that population growth had created a lack of resources; rather the contrary. Ehrlich responded that to explain to someone like Julian Simon that commodities would become scarce when the population grew "would be like attempting to explain odd-day-even-day gas distribution to a cranberry." Of the peer reviewers who had approved Simon's article, Ehrlich wrote: "Could the editors have found someone to review Simon's manuscript who had to take off his shoes to count to 20?" Similarly Bjørn Lomborg received an explicit political firing from the Danish government after he published the book *The Skeptical Environmentalist*, where he referred to the 2,930 sources step-by-step to explain how certain environmental scientists and activists often had misrepresented data massively.

The Economist, in October 2013, published a story about increasing problems with scientific errors, which pointed out that private companies often found it very difficult to replicate the results of public research.[480] For instance, the biopharmaceutical company Amgen had tried to replicate 53 leading international studies about cancer and was unable to replicate 47, even though they often worked closely with the public researchers who had made the initial experiments.[481] Similarly, Bayer HealthCare could only replicate approximately one-quarter of 67 published health studies.[482]

One of the problems here is that it is far easier to get analysis published, if it shows something new, surprising or dramatic, like Mann's hockey stick graph did. However, the reason such results meet those criteria are often that they are actually wrong - there have been deliberate or unintentional errors in the research process.

One might assume that such errors are likely to be discovered quickly by other researchers? Not necessarily. Since new and dramatic research provides much more publicity (and thus more research grants and awards), fewer and fewer scientists deal with the so-called "negatives" - studies that attempt to verify others' research while looking for erroneous data and conclusions, as McIntyre and McKitrick did with Mann's work. This is confirmed by a study of 4,000 research reports from between 1990 and 2007, which showed that the proportion of published negatives decreased from 30% to 14% during the period.[483] In addition, it is quite normal for scientists to publish insufficient information to enable others to test their results properly. In a study of 238 biomedical reports published in scientific magazines, 84 concluded that more than half omitted information necessary for replicating their experiments.[484]

Let's conclude this chapter by simply noting, that while pursuit of science and technology has been absolutely central to our progress for centuries, it has always had its enemies and abusers; from clerics and others imposing scientific censorship to political agitators bending scientific principles and Luddites opposing new technologies to romantics turning blind eyes to whatever contradict their illusions. Similar problems are clearly still with us today.

22.
BABBLERS, CYNICS, CHARLATANS

Artist Salvador Dali once said that he had never ordered lobster in a restaurant and then been served a fried phone as a result. In other words, parts of life are fairly predictable – if you order lobster, that's probably what you will get, just as next Wednesday will typically play out in a similar way to last Wednesday. However, there exists a minority of people who live in a world in which repetition is totally unacceptable - namely artists. In this profession, you are either innovative or you are nothing.

In 1990, a book with the intriguing title *The Clockwork Muse: the predictability of Artistic Change* was published. The author was psychology professor Colin Martindale, who for 20 years, had studied the history of art market. Based on advanced statistical methods he had shown that this followed a surprisingly predictable pattern, which he called The Law of Novelty.[485] It goes like this: first, someone develops a new form of artistic expression. If this is successful, others develop variations of it. However, in order to attract attention, each new artist must find a somewhat more radical expression than the previous. Therefore, the new art form grows evermore strident, exaggerated or loud, and eventually it becomes so grotesque and decadent that the audience drops it and moves on to something entirely different, which will go through the same process.

Martindale mapped this phenomenon in the art world, and it also applies to other forms of creativity that do not serve a direct, measurable purpose such as philosophy, as we shall now see.

Social Text is a magazine published by Duke University Press which deals with social, cultural and philosophical topics. In 1996, its editorial committee received an article proposal submitted from physics professor Alan Sokal. This provided a long (35 pages when printed) philosophical investigation into the relationship between quantum physics and so-called postmodern philosophy.[486] It contained many great flights of rhetoric, such as "the postmodern sciences deconstruct and transcend the Cartesian metaphysical distinctions between humankind and Nature, observer and observed, Subject and Object."

The magazine's editors really liked this article, so they decided to put it in a special issue of the magazine dedicated to the defence of postmodern philosophy and especially of "social constructivism", which Sokal's article exemplified so well.

They would later regret that, because as soon as the issue (and Sokal's article) had been printed, Sokal announced, far and wide, that his article was actually designed to be a mere parody of postmodern philosophy - he had deliberately written the whole thing so it was totally meaningless babble. This was evidently rather funny, but it brought with it a lesson, which the critic Katha Pollit described rather well:

"The comedy of the Sokal incident is that it suggests that even the post-modernists don't really understand one another's writing and make their way through the text by moving from one familiar name or notion to the next like a frog jumping across a murky pond by way of lily pads." [487]

Sokal was not the only one entering the murky pond. The philosophical superstar Ludwig Wittgenstein enchanted his fans with profundities such as" My propositions are elucidatory in this way: he who understands me finally recognizes them as senseless, when he has climbed out through them, on them, over them. (He must, so to speak, throw away the ladder, after he has climbed up it." [488]

That was in 1922, and since then the fog has only thickened. Some modern philosophers have thus introduced a kind of non-realism, according to which experimental tests only tell us about the outcome of the relevant trial, but nothing about reality. For instance, the leading thinker of the social constructionist school Bruno Latour has told us that nature is a result of our own thoughts, which is why it would be meaningless to use its behaviour as a source of knowledge. In fact, one of his *Seven Rules of Method* sounds like this:

"Since the settlement of a controversy is the cause of Nature's representation, not the consequence, we can never use the outcome -- Nature -- to explain how and why a controversy has been settled."

Perhaps we need to chew on that for a while, but once we are finished, we probably gather from it that experimental science doesn't work. Enlightenment and science were illusions.

Many of the new philosophers have also rejected rationalism. For example, in his books *Against Method* and *Farewell to Reason* Paul Feuerabend argued against use of logic and science. Add to this "deconstruction ", which is popular among post-modern philosophers, and we realize we actually cannot know an objective reality. Everything is subjective, we learn here, and a statement is merely the results of language which, in turn, is a subjective social construct.

Therefore, one cannot say, with certainty, that something is true.

Nor can one know whether something is good. To say, for instance, that freedom or love are positive values for all people, is called "totalizing" by deconstructionists and rejected in the strongest terms. So if you add all that up, it really isn't easy to know anything much.

But we aren't done yet. The so-called "relativists" tell us that any objective truth is culturally determined, which is why all cultures, in principle, may be equally worthy. Therefore, any given individual cannot really know anything about what is good or bad other than his own personal preferences.

All these anti-rational, anti-scientific theories are part of post-modern philosophy, which originated in France after World War II and has later spread throughout the West where it gained a significant foot-hold in many academic circles and beyond.

The philosophers' strategy seem to be to serve meaningless twaddle as phrases and vocabulary so complex that even the keenest reader will hopefully give up and conclude that the writers are simply too clever to be understood. To make sure of this, the philosphers will often decorate their writing with seemingly learned references and analogies to, for example, Einstein, Gödel and Niels Bohr.

For Sokal, the record-holder for academic nonsense - at least within the single-sentence category - may be celebrated cultural theorist Paul Virillio. In his book *L'Espace Critique*, he delivered a sentence comprising193 French words, which when (with some difficulty) translated to English, starts like this:

"When depth of time replaces depths of sensible space; when the commutation of interface supplants the delimitation of surfaces; when transparency re-establishes appearances; then we begin to wonder whether that which we insist on calling space isn't actually light, a subliminary, para-optical light of which sunlight is only one phase or reflection..."

Much, much later it ends with these words of wisdom:

"... transferred into the eternal present of a relativity whose topological and teleological thickness and depth belong to this final measuring instrument, this speed of light possesses one direction, which is both its size and dimension and which propagates itself at the same speed in all radial directions that measure the universe."

"Universe", it must be said, is pompous enough to be a quite popular word among post-modernist thinkers, together with incomprehensible stuff such as "fallogocentric, "multimodalities", ""post-colonial others", "intertextual" "hyper-contemporaneity" "spatialities", "teletopic" , "derrideanism", "commutation" and so on.

They don't make things easy, and the general clouding and inherent contradictions of the postmodernist arguments are such that it gets really hard to define what it is, if you believe in it. Indeed, when Jacques Derrida, who is credited with developing "deconstructionism", was once asked how he defined it, he answered:"I have no simple and formalisable response to this question. All my essays are attempts to have it out with this formidable question".[489]

Perhaps his problem was that the language you would need to use in order to explain it would be deconstructed by it, which is akin to the impossible concept of eating oneself. Among the most radical post-modern postulations are claims that we cannot be sure that there is a reality at all. Of course, if that claim is true, then we do not really exist, so perhaps we shouldn't worry.

If "philosophers who can help us solve the world's problem"'s can be considered to be "the lobster the world's citizens have ordered", then one might argue that they were served "a fried phone" when the post-modernist philosophers turned up instead.

This doesn't mean that all philosophers have been negative. In fact, the world has had many great philosophers such as the aforementioned Montesquieu, John Locke, Thomas Hobbes, Thomas Aquinas, Alexis de Tocqueville, Max Weber, Richard Dawkins, Robert Wright and many others, all of whom had something important to say, tried to speak clearly and managed to change people's minds for the better. As an excellent example of the latter (speaking clearly) we should include writer Hans Christian Andersen, who even managed to get his messages across in the form of entertaining fairy tales, such as the ever relevant story about *The Emperor's New Clothes.*

Speaking of which: in September 2007, the English restaurant reviewer AA Gill of *The Sunday Times* visited an office of auction house Christie's to ask if they would sell a portrait of Stalin for him, which he had previously bought for £200. They would not do this. However, Gill then asked if they would have sold the Stalin painting had it been by the post-modern artists Andy Warhol or Damien Hirst. They said they would have done. He then called Hirst, whom he knew, and asked if he would paint a red nose on the Stalin painting, to which Hirst agreed. The painting was subsequently sold for £140,000.

Evidently, Damien Hirst is a big name in the art business, which he had partly earned by creating installation art such as a series of 12 medicine cabinets and dead animals preserved in formaldehyde. The latter started when he bought a tiger shark for some £8,000 (approximately $12,000), after which he prepared it with formaldehyde, put it on display in a tank and called this *"The Physical Impossibility of Death in the Mind of Someone Living".* He then sold it to collector Charles Saatchi for £50,000, who later re-sold it to a hedge-fund manager for an amount rumoured to be $12 million.

Soon after, the shark began to rot. Hirst agreed to replace it, which, however, raised the question of whether this would still constitue the original work of art worth 12 million dollars worth, or would merely be a copy, which would make it worth closer to 12 thousand dollars worth - a dilemma that wasn't reduced by Hirst also producing replica of the first work.

Such dilemmas were, in fact, common, because Hirst had an art factory, where, for instance, paint was poured onto a twisting spinning wheel over a canvas, which he would then sign. This raised a problem: had he been in the room when the wheel was spinning, or not? If not; could one still call the art work "Hirst"? Because if you couldn't; what was it worth? Millions or thousands?

The value of such things are all in the eyes of the beholder, as a post-modern philosopher might have said, and this was illustrated by a simple experiment conducted in 1964 by Åke "Dacke" Axelsson, a journalist from Sweden's Göteborgs-Tidningen. Axelsson exhibited some abstract paintings in an art gallery, claiming that they were by avant-garde artist Pierre Brassau. These soon generated great acclaim, and a critic wrote:

"Brassau paints with powerful strokes, but also with clear determination. His brush strokes twist with furious fastidiousness. Pierre is an artist who performs with the delicacy of a ballet dancer." [490]

Little did this critic know that the paintings were actually made by a four-year chimpanzee from Borås Zoo called Peter.

A similar incident occurred when the director of the National Arts Foundation Museum in Moritzburg was shown an abstract painting and thought was by the famous and award-winning painter Ernst Wilhelm Nay. In this case, the painter was the chimpanzee Gambhi.

THE POSTMODERN ARTIST PETER;
ALSO CALLED PIERRE BRASSAU,
AT WORK. [491]

In 2011, scientists at Boston University asked 72 students of art or psychology to evaluate 30 pairs of abstract paintings in order to choose 1) which they preferred and 2) which they thought was technically better. In each comparison, one painting was by a very famous abstract painter such as Rothko or de Kooning and the other by a toddler, monkey, elephant, chimp or gorilla. Among art students, 37% of stated preferences were for the paintings by toddlers and animals, and among psychology students, works by animals and toddlers were preferred in 44 % of the cases. Works of toddlers and animals were given highest technical ratings in approx. 1/3rd of the pairings.[492]

People pay hundreds of thousands of dollars for works by On Kawara, which are simply paintings of dates on a canvas, which the artist says never take more than two hours to paint. Or they pay $456,000 for a pile of blue and white candy by Felix Gonzalez-Torres.

The art world's "new emperors" can apparently sell anything – and often for a fortune, such as $690,000 for a work by Jim Hofges, constituting a leather jacket thrown into a corner. The emperor's new clothes really do spring to mind here, quite literally.

"They will buy what you fucking give them", Hirst once explained, but it helps an artist's reputation to be provocative. In 1997, the Royal Academy of Arts in London held an exhibition called "Sensation", in which one of the main attractions was a giant portrait of a woman named Myra Hindley, an infamous murderess, sentenced to life imprisonment for helping her boyfriend, Ian Brady, kidnap and torture children in northwest England in the 1960s. Outside the exhibition, the desperate parents of the murdered children took part in demonstrations in an attempt to have the painting removed, which presumably just added to the artistic sensation. Inside the rooms, you could see various sliced-up animals exhibited in a formaldehyde solutions, portraits of people with rectums as mouths, a close-up of a bullet hole in a head and paintings with titles such as *"Beautiful, kiss my fucking ass"* or *"Space Shit"*, where the latter was decorated with faeces from an elephant. The award-winning artist behind the this (Chris Ofili) often sold these stool-images in so-called *"Shit Sales"*, and among his greatest hits was a depiction of The Madonna mixed with pornographic pictures and elephant faeces.

According to Martindale's aforementioned Law of Novelty, this should continue until it cannot become any more ludicrous, although Italian artist Piero Manzoni, who sold his own faeces in cans to private collectors and public museums for staggering prices, already seem to have achieved this.

This is a world in which the brand matters infinitely more than the content, and where a vacuum cleaner or a urinal on a pedestal is considered as expressive as a Picasso or Rembrandt. Talking of urinals, there was actually an artist by the name of Duchamp, who exhibited just such a thing entitled "Fountain", for which he won many awards and honours. However, this made the world's most famous art historian Sir Ernst Gombrich to comment in an interview that:

"This century has been more influenced by scientific progress than artistic. In art, there is no parallel to the discovery of chromosomes. If you think of the deciphering of the genes and compares that to the enthusiasm for Duchamp, when he exhibited a urinal, the contrast becomes all too clear." [493]

Many of the philosophers tell us that we cannot test anything, cannot know anything, should reject rationality and science, should never judge or compare anything, and for good measure also add that it is doubtful whether anything (including themselves) exist. Many of the post-modern artists and their followers tell us that what really counts is obscurity and a brand.

The commonality of both forms of post-modernism is rejection of the West for the fun of it - it is deliberate contempt of the Renaissance, enlightenment, science, rationality, logics, aesthetics and ethics. If people do not buy art for the actual emotional experience it brings, but instead for being seen as avant-garde, then we open the floodgate to charlatans and, yes, the emperor's new clothes. And if we join the new philosophers in thinking that nothing can be known, nothing exists, and expression does not matter, everything is equally good, and our civilization is of no particular value.

With such attitudes, progress becomes impossible or undesirable. Scientists who have worked tirelessly around the clock to seek truth are no better than mystics and visionaries. Michelangelo, Newton and Niels Bohr were nothing. People, who gave their lives so that we may live in peace and freedom, were no better than others. Everything disappears in the anti-realist and anti-rational murky waters flanked by urinals on pedestals and faeces in cans. Eternally blinded by the newest fad, we try to dig our own graves. But it is all extremely modern, and that's what counts.

The ancient Greeks had their cynics who rejected much of what was the greatest culture the world had ever seen. The medieval age saw an initial decline in the quality of its art that has been mirrored elsewhere through history, and the medieval church insisted for long that the Bible should deliberately be written in Latin only so that common people could not read it. It is safe to say that neither culture nor enlightenment always advances, and we should thus be prepared to question if what we hear or see really advances anything or not.

23.
UTOPIANS
AND SOCIAL
ENGINEERS

In 1516, Sir Thomas More, who was Lord Chancellor to English King Henry VIII, published a book describing an imaginary dream society, in which there was no private property, so that everyone lived in similar houses and shared everything equally. Meals would be shared in community dining halls, and each community had the perfect number of inhabitants (6,000). In order to secure these perfect arrangements against violation, the state would issue internal passports and control where everyone lived.

The name of the book was *Utopia*, and ever since it was published, the dream of a society with state-enforced equality has captivated millions; after Karl Marx's *Communist Manifesto* in the 19th century, the idea gained even further ground. So much so, in fact, that by 1965, approximately 32% of the world's population lived in pure socialist economies, for example, the Warsaw Pact countries, Mao's China, Kim's North Korea, Pol Pot's Cambodia and Fidel Castro's Cuba. Another 23%, including Egypt, India and Indonesia, had socialist-inspired leadership with a focus on self-sufficiency and strong re-distribution policies (except, perhaps, when it came to the political leaders themselves). In other words: just over half of the world's population then lived in nations pursuing More's and Marx's utopians dreams.

Socialism and communism are examples of what is sometimes called "social engineering". This is the large-scale pursuit of centrally-controlled social programmes, within which citizens are commandeered in the pursuit of Utopian goals.

Of course, such social engineering does have its costs, because you cannot tightly control people and at the same time have them do what they please, so the Greek ideas of liberty and democracy don't really work in these projects, and neither does Montesquieu's separation of powers, nor John Locke's protection of private property nor Adam Smith's free trade. You also need to control where people live and forbid them from undertaking private enterprises. In reality, though, that's not enough. You also have to control the information they receive and prevent the best and the brightest from escaping your regime.

This is why the Communist regime in the Warsaw Pact countries spied on inhabitants, conducted systematic brainwashing, mass deportations, political murders, incarceration of political prisoners, and restricted internal movement, prohibiting most attempts to escape (via the Berlin Wall, for example).

Overall, the leading French expert on the history of Communism, Stéphane Courtois, has estimated that, through executions, famine, deportations, physical confinement and forced labour it has killed 94 million people as follows:[494]

- 65 million in China
- 20 million in the Soviet Union
- 2 million in Cambodia
- 2 million in North Korea
- 1.7 million in Africa
- 1.5 million in Afghanistan
- 1 million in the Communist states of Eastern Europe
- 1 million in Vietnam

These people all died for a dream, but it probably wasn't their dream.

Fascism is another example of social engineering. While it does allow some market forces, the common denominator between fascism and socialism or communism is a strong preference for state control over the individual. Indeed, the German Nazis, as well as the Italian fascists, always called themselves socialists. Mussolini was, in his early years, editor of the communist weekly publication *Avanti!*, and he described his aim as: "Everything in the State, nothing outside the State, nothing against the state." Hitler was, as a young man, sent by the German military to spy on the Deutsche Arbeiterpartei, but he came to sympathize with them and joined as their 55th member. He later renamed it Nationalsozialistische Deutsche Arbeiterpartei, which was since known as the "Nazis".

Various shades of socialism and fascism have always had a following in Central, Southern and Eastern Europe. For instance, fascists came to power in Italy in 1925 and in Poland the following year. After the start of the Depression, fascism spread quickly to Croatia (1930); Portugal (1932); Austria (1934); Germany (1934), Spain (1936) and Greece (1936). These regimes implemented various degrees of persecution, mass killings or genocide. The Nazis alone murdered some six million Jews, almost two million Poles, between 220,000 and 1.5 million Romanians, 200-250,000 disabled people, 20-25,000 Slovenians, 5-15,000 homosexuals and 2,500 to 5,000 Jehovah's Witnesses. All together, European fascists and Nazis deliberately murdered more than 10 million civilians during the 20th century. On top of that came victims of

World War II, which led to 50-60 million additional deaths. In 1942, Europe had only four liberal democracies left; England, Ireland, Switzerland and Sweden; elsewhere, it was lights out, and if Hitler or Stalin had won the war, they would surely have put a definitive end to what the Athenians had started approx. 2,300 years before.

Grand-scale social engineering doesn't work, and there are two main reasons for this;

◆ Technical impossibility of central planning
◆ The public productivity problem

Central planning of a country may sound easy to somebody who has never tried to run a business. This would explain, as the British historian Paul Johnson has noted, that European dictators pursuing social engineering have this in common: they showed very little interest in how wealth was created and had never personally been engaged in wealth creation.[495] For instance, Lenin wrote that the operation of enterprises involved "extraordinarily simple operations" which "any literary person can do".[496]

However, all centrally-planned economies have ended up with huge logistical problems that often descended into pure farce. One of the major mistakes of central planning is to trust in the value of experts. Even if the typical knowledge among governing elites is, for example, ten times that of the average citizen, these elites will still, in combination, hardly possess more than a tiny minimum of society's entire knowledge. They are unlikely to have any real concept of the daily tasks of farmers, fishermen, school teachers, software engineers or factory managers. So let's be extremely generous and assume that the country is ruled by elites which, together, hold 1% of its total knowledge. The remaining 99% is held by the rest of the population. That means that people who have 1% of the relevant knowledge tell people who have the remaining 99%, what they must do, which evidently doesn't work well.

In order to understand why you cannot run a complex society from the top, you need to consider the alternative: what happens when it is operated largely by a free market. In this scenario everyone use price mechanism and profit motives as real-time information tools and motivators. Prices settle at levels that attract customers, and profits settle at levels that signal where markets are relatively undersupplied. Both phenomena are fluid and adapt in real-time - the system is organic and an excellent example of large-scale crowdsourcing.

Perhaps such a system sounds extraordinarily simple if you are Lenin, but it only works because millions of people spontaneously and simultaneously adjust constantly to the behaviour of one another. In the Soviet Union, it was discovered how utterly impossible it was for the central government to set prices for the 24 million different products which the country apparently had, in spite of its relative simplicity.

The lack of market-based pricing and profits meant that there was frequently an over-supply of certain products and (more often) a shortage of others. Therefore, the large factories in the Soviet Union often resorted to self-sufficiency. For example, a car factory would produce its own window glass, screws, rubber bands and tyres, because that was the only way to be certain that these would be available. So, without specialization, competition and incentives, everything regressed to an appalling quality.

Meanwhile, a lack of market-based pricing made it utterly impossible to calculate which investments made most sense, which meant that many things for which there was a natural demand were simply missing. Stories about life in the communist Soviet Union told of hour-long queues to buy the most basic groceries.

The lack of pricing signals also applied to wages, which were rigid and largely unrelated to effort, skills, ingenuity and demand, so that nothing showed whether a given person would be more valuable in another position than where he was, or whether that person ought to work harder (to get richer) or less (to prioritize family life, health or hobbies). This lack of price signalling meant that people who worked more than others were, in fact, often abused by colleagues for being "eager beavers" raising expectations for everyone else.

As early as 1921, Austrian economist Ludwig von Mises predicted in a book that the Soviet Union would collapse, merely because of such planning problems.[497] The philosopher and economist Friedrich Hayek elaborated in 1944 that, as an economy developed, it would become evermore complex, and this would make it ever less suitable for socialism. He stated here, more specifically, that the collapse of the Soviet Union would occur before the end of the 20th century.

He was right, and a modern society has far more than the Soviet Union's 24 million different products. After all, a Boeing 737 aeroplane consists of 367,000 parts, provided by countless suppliers around the world. To create each of these parts requires further commodities, materials and machines, each of which requires thousands of other parts. This means that, when you add it all up, it must require co-operation between countless millions of specialized people to produce a single aircraft or even a single modern car. The same goes for virtually any product beyond stone axes and the like.

The only way this can work for all products is via the equivalent of what IT people call massive, parallel, real-time computing; overall, this could be called "the silent knowledge of market economy" – the unplanned ability to enable co-operation between millions of people. Socialism, on the other hand, is based on the equivalent of sequential, central computing. Comparing socialism with a market economy is a bit like comparing an old mainframe computer with an internet-based crowd-sourcing and social network.

The other big problem with centralized control and social engineering is the public productivity that we have already examined. It causes the problems described by Parkinson's Law, Mancur Olson's accumulation of special interests and privileges, Niskanens public growth sickness, Tim Wu's Kronos effect, Acemoglus' and Robinsons' extractive organizations. If everything is run by the state, it becomes very difficult to check these issues, which is why productivity soon slows down further and further.

Especially within socialism, things happen through rules, coercion, manuals and punishment and there is rarely anyone who smiles, says "thank you" and thinks about how to do it better next time. Coercion and commands creates resentment and motivation problems, and socialism creates a negative, unco-operative and ineffective culture.

Motivation is key. When agriculture is changed from collective to private ownership, history shows that there is typically a marked increase in productivity, in the manner of the quick doubling of productivity that was seen in China when it privatized agriculture from 1978-84. Conversely, when a shift is made from private farming to forced collectivisation, the consequence has often been starvation.

While socialism lacks the positive incentives to work hard and think creatively, it also lacks the negative pressure of competition. This, combined with centralization, explains why virtually no technological innovation has been observed in socialist/communist economies except for in the arms industry and space exploration sectors, where people were offered incentives similar to that in market economies. Nor was there any significant innovation in art, fashion, design and lifestyle, and the typical attitudes in the service sectors were lousy.

Socialism and fascism are based on using force to make individuals comply with imposed plans, and this never works as intended. The systems end up undermining honesty and creativity. Despite numerous attempts over the years, there is not a single example in history of socialism serving a country's citizens well. In fact, all countries that have tried it have been forced to prevent their citizens from escaping and have introduced censorship to prevent uproar. In the Soviet Union, access to photocopying machines and even printing paper was tightly controlled and foreign radio and TV signals blocked with noise transmitters.

Virtually all socialist states have imprisoned political opponents, and many have resorted to state-sponsored mass murder. They have experienced shortages of all sorts of basic goods including toilet paper. Finally, the lack of technological and cultural innovation has led to depressing, grey communities with poor environments, corruption, poor resource utilization, increasing dishonesty, widespread crime and comprehensive substance misuse.

Actually, after a time, both Hitler as Mussolini changed most socialistic aspects of their models to corporatism instead. This is a concept, under which private businesses are allowed, but where all companies are expected to work for society as a whole, rather than for their owners and clients, under observance of the law. Corporatism can involve control of salaries, prices and profits, and it works better that pure socialism, but not necessarily much better, as Argentina and Venezuela have discovered. Milder forms are simply "corporate social responsibility" with buzzwords such as "people, planet and profit" and "triple bottom line", where public bureaucrats, union leaders or environmentalists may be de-facto co-managing companies which they would never have been capable of creating personally.

The world will always have people dreaming of utopian social engineering, and the reason is that they imagine a better world and wants to ensure that it gets implemented. The problem is always the same: if their systems predominantly involve force rather than encouragement, they are on the wrong side of history, because, as Robert Wright correctly pointed out: its cooperation; not coercion, that drives success. Success comes to those who bet on voluntary win-win transactions, which large scale social engineers definitely don't.

PART 7

SAVING CREATIVITY

Are we moving toward the end of history, where all societies will be "liberal democracies", as Francis Fukuyama suggested? Perhaps, but the road to that destination hasn't been easy thus far, and it probably won't be in the future either.

Why? - because once people take future wealth and security for granted, they often become dangerously complacent and oddly irrational, and they also tend to over-institutionalize their societies. These three phenomena can destroy healthy nations. Successful liberal democracy is therefore not a steady state, and once you have reached it, you must constantly defend it against armies of paper-shufflers, rent-seekers, Spartans, cynics, scaremongers, eco-fascists, babblers, charlatans, naysayers and social Utopians.

However, there are ways to protect creativity and keep societies agile and dynamic that we could pursue. If we do that, the future could actually be rather bright.

CHAPTER 24:
The 12 threats to creativity

CHAPTER 25:
The creative state

CHAPTER 26:
The possible world

24.
THE
12 THREATS
TO CREATIVITY

We have covered a good deal of ground in this story; so let's here high-light the main conclusions from it all.

The first is that creativity generally thrives in systems that combine:

◆ Small units
◆ Change agents
◆ Effective networks
◆ Shared memory systems
◆ Competition

Such systems create spontaneous experimentation and progress through "survival of the fittest", but perhaps surprisingly, these "fittest" tend to be whoever, through innovation, has become better at co-operating (such as humans). There are now far more humans than chimpanzees on the planet because we became better at co-operating than they did, and this started a relentless genes-culture co-evolution for us, but not for them.

The introduction of pair-bonding among pre-humans was an excellent early example of improved co-operation, but our greatest hit in that respect is surely the later invention of trade. This concept of cooperation is so radical, that not a single other species has made it. Nor did the Neanderthals, which is probably why our ancestors overcame them.

Voluntary co-operation under competition creates innovation, and this gives us a self-perpetuating creative design space, which again stimulates better use of our social space. The result is constant positive feedback loops between innovation, social networking and genes. This process is exponential; since most new innovations are re-combinations of old ones, the greater the number of ideas we have already had or implemented, the more new ones are within our reach. And innovation is not a pot we are emptying, but an infinitive process, only limited by the laws of physics, which tend to be very generous. For instance, if we learned to smash together deuterium and tritium in an orderly fashion, we would have safe and clean energy for billions of years; if all farming was as effective as in Holland, we could feed 60 billion people and if we could accelerate a rocket to 20% of the speed of light, it would circumvent the Earth in less than a second.

However, innovation only happens if we maintain a system conducive to it, and here we should note how important the prevalence of small units is. All else equal, whenever a system grows more decentralized and thus populated by larger numbers of smaller units, its creative processes will accelerate. Conversely, centralization slows down or kills creativity. When a private company makes a new innovation, it will typically be a question of a few weeks or months before most of its competitors have responded with the same or more. In government, it is not so at all. Government may fall decades after what happens in private business.

Throughout this book we have seen many examples of this. For starters, we saw that ecological speciation is biggest on islands, as Darwin discovered. Another example: the runaway development of the human species from CHLCA (chimpanzee–human last common ancestor) and, in particular, the fast development of the human brain was possible because the population was frequently separated into smaller tribes which mutated and then reconnected with others for co-operation and competition. The third obvious example is ancient Greece, which was highly creative when it consisted of approximately 700-1,000 city states, but became virtually static after becoming part of empires. Creativity also exploded in Western Europe during the Middle Ages exactly in the areas that, like ancient Greece, were divided into countless mini-states, whereas it slowed down in the more centralized areas. In this particular case, it happened because parts of Western Europe, during this era, had the following essential criteria for innovation:

- **Small units**, since Western Europe consisted of up to several thousand independent and competing mini-states.
- **Change agents** in the form of constant migration, trade and blending of peoples such as Celts, Anglo-Saxons, Latinos and Jews within the countless mini-states.
- **Networks** in the form of the Roman ports and road network combined with a sailing culture that was facilitated by accessible Western rivers and natural ports.
- **Shared memory systems** in the form of common Latin written language, standard measurement units, shared calendar, common legal concepts and so on.
- **Competition** between the many states which again typically had internal power balance between Masonic lodges, councils, church, nobility, private companies, army and royalty.

This led to an extraordinary chain reaction, which can be summarized by these development phases and new core ideas:

Development phases	New core ideas
1 The Renaissance	1 Logic and rationalism
2 The Enlightenment	2 Depersonalization
3 The Age of Discovery	3 Freedom
4 The reformation	4 Tolerance and individualism
5 The Scientific Revolution	5 Meritocracy
6 The Industrial Revolution	6 Democracy
7 The Female Liberation	7 Separation of powers
8 The Information Revolution	8 The rule of law
9 The Crowdsourcing revolution	9 Private property/freedom of contract
10 The Biotech Revolution	10 Free competition

Alongside these developments came a certain optimism and can-do mentality, and, as one thing led to the next, the creative design space grew gradually for a few hundred years. Then, around 1450, it virtually exploded, and it has kept growing frantically ever since. This has created such extensive innovation that the West has arguably produced more than 95% of all global creative output ever - even though its population has never constituted more than a small minority of the world's total population.

A creative process such as Western creativity has begun in other civilizations as well. However, the historical tendency is that a period of creativity and optimism is extinguished - from within. Once this happens and societies become static again, win-win transactions are replaced with win-lose activity; freedom with coercion and growth with stagnation. Once they become static, people increasingly assume that one man's gain must be another man's loss. Of course, they will make the same assumption if they believe that it ought to be static even as it still grows. People in static societies are typically more hostile, envious and aggressive than in expanding ones, and when a society is in decline, you typically get tyranny and/or civil war.

However, even though there were countless attempts to halt the creativity in Medieval Western Europe (censorship, monopolization of trade, anti-enlightenment, Luddism, mad monks), it could never be achieved, as freedom had too many escape routes – when tyranny grew in one place, the creative people and the money just moved on to another, which would then gain power and wealth. Creativity was thus constantly rescued by decentralization.

The most convincing onslaught on Western civilization happened in the 1930s and 40s, where communists, Nazis and fascists almost killed it off entirely in Europe, but because liberal democracy had previously spread to the US and other areas, these new liberal nations became liberators and saved the day.

Western civilization is largely built on ideas that evolved in Greece more than 2,000 years ago, and as we have seen, getting from there to here was a Herculean task. Indeed, each and every victory along the way involved enormous work and much human suffering. Millions were killed in battles to make the present possible, and high numbers of people perished in prisons or were executed for defending values such as freedom, democracy, science, religious tolerance, the rule of law or rationality. Equally, the mere development of the enormous infrastructure and the technology we control today involved vast efforts, with countless people essentially working themselves to death to give us what we take forgranted today

But we made it, and since the spring of innovation can apparently run forever unless we cut it off, should we now safely assume all is fine and dandy? It may certainly feel that way if you are sipping a cafe latte in Vienna, Vancouver or Wellington, and as previously mentioned, in 1992 Francis Fukuyama published his book *The End of History and the Last Man*, with its central claims that: 1) Western-style liberal democracy (market economy and democracy) is the best model and 2) everybody will eventually figure that out, so that 3) the end-point for history is a world full of such liberal democracies.

At the time of his book (1992), he saw Denmark as the best example of such a well-functioning liberal democracy, and therefore used the term "getting to Denmark" for how you arrived at a democracy of this kind. Perhaps Switzerland is the new Denmark with Australia as the runner-up, but in any case: the West still rocks. Take, for instance a look at the table below, which shows how Western-style liberal democracies receive most of the global top scores for humanistic, economic, environmental and financial excellence:

Global Rank	Human Development Index, 2014[498]	Environmental Performance Index, 2014[499]	Where to be Born Index, 2013[500]	World Happiness Report, 2013[501]	Country Strength Index 2014[502]
1	Norway	Switzerland	Switzerland	Denmark	Switzerland
2	Australia	Luxembourg	Australia	Norway	Hong Kong
3	Switzerland	Australia	Norway	Switzerland	Singapore
4	Netherlands	Singapore	Sweden	Netherlands	Denmark
5	United States	Czech Republic	Denmark	Sweden	Netherlands
6	Germany	Germany	Singapore	Canada	Australia

7	New Zealand	Spain	New Zealand	Finland	United Kingdom
8	Canada	Austria	Netherlands	Austria	Belgium
9	Singapore	Sweden	Canada	Iceland	Ireland
10	Denmark	Norway	Hong Kong	Australia	Norway

As we have seen, people living in Western-style societies anywhere have undergone a very strong civilizing process that has made them much more co-operative, peaceful, rational, confident, tolerant, freedom-seeking, individualistic, democratic, creative and even intelligent than in the past. Also, Westerners consistently rank as the happiest people on the planet, whether you measure that as pure happiness or through broader indicators such as satisfaction with life. So it's no wonder there is a constant flow of people from the outside trying to get in, while the flow of insiders trying to get out (they are free to leave) is tiny.

And these happy Westerners have largely benefitted the world, even as they evidently also did it harm. In essence, Westerners have historically been good at spreading their ideas, capital and technologies to other nations who benefitted tremendously from them. Indeed, quite a few of these have now adapted many or most Western ideas to great effect; for instance, South Korea, Chile, Japan, Hong Kong and Taiwan, spring to mind.

They are still beneficial. In the "Good Country Index", which compiles a large number of indicators for how much good a nation does for the entire world, the top 20 "good" countries in the 2014 ranking were all Western (led by Ireland, Finland, Switzerland, The Netherlands and New Zealand).[503]

So obviously Fukuyama was right to claim that liberal democracies work very well (especially, as the tables above shows, in small nations). However, he didn't really dwell on the complication that once civilizations have reached apparent perfection (having "got to" Denmark), they have an inherent tendency to swing around again and head towards Argentina. Empires always collapse, nations often fail and civilizations sometimes decay, and there are, as we have seen three systematic reasons for that:

◆ Naysayers, who don't believe in the project
◆ Over-institutionalization, which leads to unintended stagnation
◆ Enemies of reason, who reject enlightenment, culture and
   voluntary co-operation

Let's summarize them, starting with the naysayers. These people are the equivalents of the cynics in ancient Greece and Rome; the people who simply did not believe in the project. The modern cynics have some or all of the following wrong conceptions:

◆ End-of-ideas misconception: ideas are resources that we are tapping, and we must be very close to the limit of anything that is possible. So we must prepare for a more static society.

◆ Exclusivity misconception: market economies concentrate information, power and money in ever fewer hands, which could destroy them. To avoid that destruction, the state must redistribute and control everything.

◆ Resource depletion misconception: economic growth in creative societies will lead to depletion of our resources, so it must be stopped.

◆ Environmental destruction misconception: the increasing wealth and technology created by economic growth will destroy the planet, so it should be stopped

As for the end-of-ideas misconceptions, we have seen that there is nothing in the dynamics of creative design spaces that suggest we are close to a natural boundary in terms of innovation or that such a boundary even exists. New technologies keep coming through recombination of older ones, and those that do reach maturity become subject to ever-changing fashion trends. Furthermore, each new core technology stimulates its own mini creative design space with evermore applications for it. So, if anything, the more ideas we have already had, the more we can have in the future, and this is an exponential process. The reality is this: there is no end to innovation in sight, because it has no end.

Our second group of naysayers argue (as they have done for almost 200 years) that liberal democracy brings increasing concentration of knowledge, money and power in ever fewer hands, which will lead to its collapse. This is the stuff of countless novels and movies such as *Hunger Games* or *In Time*, but on a more serious note, it has also been the expectation of Karl Marx (*Das Kapital*), Baran and Sweezy (*Monopoly Capitalism*) or Thomas Piketty (*Capital in the Twenty-First Century*). However, capitalism hasn't collapsed because of capital concentration as predicted by Karl Marx. Nor are we all run by a military-industrial complex as Baran and Sweezy expected.

Instead, free markets have created evermore diversity, pluralism and mobility. For instance, instead of mass-produced standard products, we have moved towards "segment of one", "mass-to-class", "Do-it-yourself" (DIY) communities and "maker movement" manufacturing, which has brought the total number of products available to well over 100 million. Furthermore, we have introduced more products that are entirely customizable, just as well as we have moved many from central locations into the homes (the "I-movement"). For instance, the central mainframe is replaced by the home computer or smartphone, the central printer by home printing, the central cinema with home cinemas, central movie production with home movies and so on.

Company average sizes have also declined as their mentality changed from corporate to crowd and from pyramid to cloud. And their shareholder bases have broadened, partly due to public listings, crowdfunding and new use of stock options. Education has opened up with Massive Open Online Courses, and more women than men go on to higher education. Creative crowd-sourcing is exploding and providing us with collaborative filtering, mass ratings, prediction markets, mass-edited wikis, open innovation contests, and much more. And finally, social mobility has not declined, but has instead increased to the point where being among the very rich now tends to be a very temporary affair. Furthermore, as Piketty's own numbers actually showed, wealth concentration is not a long-term rising trend.

The third popular delusion among naysayers is based on the seemingly eternal idea that we are on the verge of running out of resources, as was predicted by Thomas Malthus more than 200 years ago or in countless recent best-selling doomsday books such as *Our Plundered Planet* or *Limits to Growth*. And since wealth equals resource depletion, the naysayers argue, there should be no room for unnecessary and wasteful luxury lifestyles.

One can understand how Malthus got it wrong, because people had limited knowledge in 1798, but it is harder to see why anyone keeps assuming it now. Since Malthus' time, the world's population has grown seven-fold, yet we eat far more per capita.

Most limits-to-growth catastrophists vastly underestimate the creativity of scientists, engineers and businessmen. And even if any of them do understand that power, they might think that this just accelerates our dash to the bottom of the jar. But as we have seen, what actually happens is quite the opposite; we are innovating towards infinity. Resources therefore become increasingly abundant as we grow richer, and this happens precisely because we are getting richer, due to the combinations of efficiency, recycling, compression, substitution, digitization, virtualization, biological cultivation, synthesizing and sharing that money can buy. Meanwhile, the same wealth increase leads to a declining population, which makes the resource problem even smaller.

The idea that we should stop enjoying ourselves because we are running out of things brings to mind the Venetian monk Girolamo Savonarola, who in 1497 arranged public burnings of luxury objects – the so-called "bonfire of the vanities".

The fourth popular delusion among naysayers sounds roughly like this: "Modern technology and economic growth destroys the world's environment, so we should have less technology and less wealth." In the minds of these naysayers, who are often called dark environmentalist, much of science is very dangerous, and should therefore be halted by ethics committees, using the slippery slope argument, the LNT model and the precautionary principle.

However on many fronts, the reality is that the West's worst environmental problems have long since passed, and there exist very elegant technological solutions to those that remain – and many more are on their way. Strong statistical evidence shows that the cultures and nations that actually create greatest environmental devastation are poor and static, not rich and dynamic. In fact, the worst offenders of all seem to have been some of the Neolithic (pre-civilization) people, and the worst offenders in modern times have been poor or socialist nations.

Dark environmentalism is typically propagated in various forms by such organizations as Die Grühne, Friends of the Earth, Earth Liberation Front, Greenpeace, Environmental Defence Fund, Earth First!, The Sierra Club, the Union of Concerned Scientist, World Wildlife Fund and by bizarre scientists such as Paul Erlich. Their typical aim is to save the planet with an iron fist. The philosophical roots of dark environmentalism are the Germanic Sturm und Drang, Romanticism and Blud und Boden movements (which are much alike and appeal to the same mindsets), and they tend to tie in with opposition to free or global trade and support of centralization. There are clear parallels between such dark environmentalists and the likes of Sultan Selim, who in 1515 forbade the printing press, or with Chinese Emperor Hongzhi, who in 1500 banned maritime navigation. If the dark environmentalists' power truly matched their ambitions, the creative Western civilization would perish and mayhem follow. However, even the limited influence which they do wield has caused significant unnecessary pollution and millions of deaths and disabilities – possibly more than those caused by Nazism and communism combined.

Even if we don't agree with the naysayers that the Western project will or should be ended, we may end up destroying it anyway, accidentally, via Carol Quigley's over-institutionalization, which is the unintended road "from Denmark toward Argentina."

◆ The public productivity problem. Due to Parkinson's Law, Mancur Olson's accumulation of special interests and privileges, the development of welfare coalitions, Mouritzens 1-3 rule, the Tragedy of the Commons, Niskanens public growth sickness, Tim Wu's Kronos effect, Acemoglus' and Robinsons' extractive organizations and so on, the public sector keeps expanding while becoming far less efficient and creative than the private. This leads to Baumols' cost disease, whereby they automatically absorb an ever bigger part of any economy.

◆ The legal tangle. We move towards evermore mandarin-style legalism, which compromises intuition, freedom, personal moral and creativity.

◆ Over-taxation and public borrowing. The constantly-growing public sector requires ever-increasing taxation. This works like over-fishing in the oceans: we move far beyond the long-term and social optimum on the Laffer curve. The derived funding gaps are then met with unsustainable public borrowing, whereby money that could have been invested in companies and ventures is instead used for public over-spending.

◆ The donation delusions. We instinctively believe that any social problem or struggling business sector must be healed by donating money. The money is then collected from well-functioning people and businesses, and we all feel good. But, surprisingly, the donations often worsen the problems we seek to heal over the longer term. And it contributes to the aforementioned widespread over-taxation and public borrowing, which has its own social costs.

As if all this wasn't enough, we have even more challenges to creativity and growth, because many modern Westerners take peace, freedom, culture, science, enlightenment, aesthetics and prosperity so much for granted, they treat it with cavalier indifference or even think it trendy to mock it. This is the bizarre netherworld of people – often state-funded academics - who make it their mission or (publicly-funded) job to fight against science, freedom, technology, trade, culture or entrepreneurship:

◆ Neo-Luddites and panic-mongers. Rooted in the German Romantic Movement and the British Luddite Movement, there is constant panic-mongering and increased rejection of new technologies such as vaccines, genetically-modified food and nuclear energy. This follows a refusal to weigh costs and benefits of new technologies against one another in a rational manner, so that we instead embrace an increasing culture of "can't".

◆ Eco fascists and pseudo scientists. Largely divorced from reality, a small, but vocal group of environmentalists and environmental scientists use scientific fraud or pseudo-scientific media schemes to stop economic growth and technological development. Some go even further and call for global government, suspension of democracy or even use of violence to get what they want. This is echoes of the Blud und Boden movement, if not worse.

◆ Babblers, cynics, charlatans. Post-modernists oppose enlightenment, science and artistic achievement by claiming we cannot test or know anything, should never judge or compare anything, should not assume that the West is better in any way and should reject rationality, science, discovery, beauty and aesthetics. This reflects Colin Martindale's Law of Novelty, but it has historical parallels in the Islamic Al Ghazali and the Ash'ari schools, which also argued against discovery, rationality, arts and science.

◆ Utopians and social engineers. These are people who believe centralized systems such as fascism and socialism or modified versions of these (corporatism) through wide-scale social engineering can provide fairer and more efficient societies than those based on freedom.

We have now listed the 12 internal challenges to creative, free societies, and these may feel like *The 12 Labours of Hercules*, although that they do not seem to end as swiftly as his did. One of their consequences is simply widespread pessimism, which can become self-fulfilling. Just listen to these words:

"Will this be the world that your grandchildren will thank you for? A world where industrial production has sunk to zero. Where population has suffered a catastrophic decline. Where the air, sea and land are polluted beyond redemption. Where civilization is a distant memory. This is the world that the computer forecasts."

This was on the back cover of the aforementioned global best-seller *Limits to Growth* from 1972. Of course, since this was written, the global economy has grown approximately five-fold, civilization remains and, if anything, is somewhat overdone by now, and air and water quality have improved in most places. So the grandchildren to whom the quote refers to, and who should be alive and well, might be wondering what was wrong with the computer that made the forecast, but they might equally be relieved that people behind the book didn't succeed in convincing the world that it should limit growth. Here is another quote reflecting pessimism:

"Humanity stands at a defining moment in history. We are confronted with a perpetuation of disparities between and within nations, a worsening of poverty, hunger, ill-health and illiteracy, and the continuing deterioration of the ecosystems on which we depend for our well-being."

These words are from the opening statement of the Agenda 21 Declaration from 1992, which was, believe it or not, signed by government leaders from 178 countries. What makes this so incredible is that it was written (and signed) in a year in which the global average life expectancy had never been higher; where most of the poor countries had a high and accelerating income growth; where the proportion and numbers of malnourished and starving people in the world had been declining for decades; where illiteracy was rapidly diminishing; and where the air and water were cleaner in most countries than they had been for 100 years. Three years later, in 1995, Jared Diamond wrote:

"By the time my infant sons reach retirement age, half of the world's species will be extinct, the air radioactive, and the seas polluted with oil." [504]

Negativism, scaremongering and promotion of zero-growth philosophy are not new phenomena, as one can read in the book *The Idea of Decline in Western History* by Arthur Herman. Indeed, such ideas are central to many religions; perhaps because they reflect basic instincts of the human mindset, or perhaps because scaring people is an effective way of concentrating power. But while the expectation of decline is not new, it has become unusually widespread in recent decades, possibly since external threats are now viewed as remote and also because, if you can convince people that growth must halt, the next logical step is to implement socialism as the dynamic effects of market economies are no longer needed or desired. That, at least, would explain why so many socialists don't believe in growth, and vice versa.

Just as well, as the rejection of growth is destructive, so is a Spartan rejection of fashion, art or luxury products, which is, in effect, a rejection of our cultural experimentation and enjoyment of life. As American journalist and satirist H. L. Mencken once wrote about Puritans, they have "the haunting fear that someone, somewhere, can be happy". Luxury, art and fashion items can be expensive, but it isn't a big part of our economies. For instance, luxury products which exemplify the pinnacle of craftsmanship, design and technology, constitute approximately 0.8% of the overall world economy.[505] However, they serve a great purpose by inspiring better products, and by giving society more colour, charm and ambition in just the way that elite sports people inspire amateur sportsmen.

Pursuers of zero growth may not realize that our societies have made many explicit and implicit promises that can only me met if we keep growing. If we turn to zero growth, hospitals will no longer be able to afford the newest technologies, governments will not be able to pay back their debts, and as most government bonds sit in pension portfolios, people will not be able to retire as planned either.

Finally, there is this: if you believe that growth is impossible, undesirable or immoral, it must follow that one person's gain is at the cost of others, so that those who work hardest and take biggest risks should be met with envy and contempt rather than be viewed as sources of inspiration and admiration.

The Western pessimists typically argue that people are essentially sinners who should live Spartan lives under the firm guidance of the authoritarian and centralized leadership of a large state. Science and technology are viewed with scepticism, and fear or panic leads to the precaution principle plus the slippery slope argument and the demand for zero growth.

It would be a tragedy if Western ideas would finally succumb. But they certainly don't have to, because, as Quigley pointed out, civilizations can oscillate repeatedly between "Denmark" and inner conflict (France?) without necessarily getting as far as North Korea.

To save Western ideas, the task is to overcome the cult of decline, the legal tangle, the Luddite lunacy, the monopoly mentality, the max tax madness and the culture of "can't". We must confront the Neo-Luddites, rent-seekers, neo-Spartans, panic mongers, eco-fascists, pseudo-scientists, babblers, charlatans and social Utopians and keep calling their bluff as Friedrich von Hayek, Alan Sokal, Julian Simon, Bjørn Lomborg and many others have done in times past.

We must also defend growth and experimentation and explain to everyone willing to listen, that when dynamic nations encounter challenges, they find solutions, and as they become richer, their solutions become evermore amazing.

In the following chapter we shall try to outline some thoughts about how we can make it happen.

THE 12 HERCULEAN TASKS OF MODERN TIMES

Convincing the naysayers
1. Overcome the expectation that we will soon run out of ideas
2. Overcome the belief that free markets concentrate wealth and power and will therefore collapse
3. Overcome the delusion that we are now draining the world's last resources
4. Overcome the misconception that technology and wealth destroys the environment

Avoiding over-institutionalization
5. Counteract the public productivity problem
6. Reduce the legal tangle
7. Stop and reverse over-taxation and public lending
8. Reduce over-reliance on welfare and transfers

Defending Enlightenment, culture and reason
9. Challenge the neo-Luddites and panic mongers
10. Call the bluff of eco fascists and pseudo scientists
11. Unmask the babblers, cynics and charlatans
12. Reject the utopian social engineers

25.
THE
CREATIVE
STATE

How do we make a state more creative?

One suggestion that may sound too simple, but which could have an enormous effect, is to eliminate the right to take out unsecured government loans. In the 1700s, the brilliant Irish politician and philosopher Edmund Burke described society as "a partnership not only between those who are living, but between those who are living, those who are dead, and those who are to be born." That sounds right, and the current generation should respect the partnership by not borrowing money, squandering and then leaving the bill for the next generations to pick up. Especially, if they in the process of overbuilding the state destroys society's growth potential so that these children may have less wealth than their parents and grandparents who borrowed from them. And yet, this is exactly what has been happening, and on a massive scale. To solve this, it should be illegal, by constitution, for governments to borrow, unless it goes to fund defensive war or to finance investments in specific assets, where these, and only these, assets may be pledged as collateral. In other words, if the state borrows money to build a bridge, the lenders would only have this bridge as collateral, and coming generations would not be liable in any way.

As these pay-as-you-go states would always need buffers for stabilization during recessions but couldn't resort to borrowing, they should have sovereign wealth funds, into which they could tap during recessions. There could be strict, rules for when a government could spend some of this wealth for stabilization purposes and when it must replenish the fund, and if any government failed to meet these rules, that should trigger an automatic election, in which none of the previous ministers are allowed to run for office.

A sovereign wealth fund of around 30% of GDP should be enough for even the worst crises, but some countries such as Singapore have much more (nearly 70% in 2013). Such a model for the management of state finances would prevent public financial crises, such as we saw in 2008-13, and this would instil much more trust in private entrepreneurs and investors. Furthermore, as there would be far less (and ultimately no) government bonds, more money would be invested in private companies instead. This combination of cash and confidence would give a major boost to creativity.

States should also replace the precautionary principle with the cost-benefit principle for approval of scientific research and new technologies. The fact that a new technology may cause problems should not prevent its introduction, if it can be shown to remove even bigger problems.

The centralized state can also stimulate innovation through conscious use of standards, mandates and strategic purchases. Let's start with standards. States have an obvious position to impose certain requirements and open standards, and the web standards were actually launched by the US Department of Defence, while the GPS system came from the US Air Force.

Mandates are akin to common standards but define a performance requirement rather than an implementation methods. Such mandates are often environmental, but a future example might be that any new car with an internal combustion engine should be able to switch between gasoline and methanol. Methanol has, for years, been trading at far less than half a dollar per litre on the world market and it can be produced from biomass or via chemical catalysis driven by power from the nuclear, wind or solar panels.

States may also stimulate innovation with strategic purchases optimized to stimulate private innovation. For instance, large orders from the US government were instrumental in helping companies like Intel and HP, when they were small.

What about the legal tangle? How can the state make life simpler and reduce the bureaucracy that comes with too many laws and prohibitions? A place to start is working time regulations. There are significant differences between how much and how long different people can and do work. Some would like to work full- time and others part-time while their children are growing up. Some save up to start their own businesses and would prefer, therefore, to work 16-hours a day; seven days a week, and others have already started their businesses and have to work 16-hour days. Some prefer to work to their dying day, while others would rather wind down gradually over many years or stop abruptly when they reach a certain retirement age. So why restrict people with rigid laws that have no relationship to individual preference?

A second proposal is this: judges should be able to toss out any civil suit in just the same way as they must approve a search warrant. A large proportion of lawsuits are frivolous, and many are completely baseless and filed by people suffering from paranoid personality disorders.[506]

Any government could also establish a deregulation office in government, with a sole purpose of continuously simplifying or abolishing laws and prohibitions. The motto should be: "If we didn't have this law today, would we then introduce it now?" Such an office should publish independently-audited figures to show how many laws have been implemented and removed in the past year; they should represent this, long-term, in the form of a graph .

The concept of systematically reducing legal mazes has been tried from time-to-time by different governments, and has been popular. The Roman emperor Justinian commissioned a major clean-up of the legal jungles in the sixth century and Napoleon Bonaparte did the same. The Danish government did it in a big campaign in 1982-88, and in January 2011, the American state of Kansas introduced "The Office of the Repealer", whose only task was to find redundant laws that could be repealed. Similarly, in 2013, the UK government embarked on a determined campaign to reduce the number of laws with the stated objective of becoming the first UK government (at least in modern times) to leave behind fewer laws than it inherited.

However, much can be achieved by having a more conscious process of cost-benefit analysis of new laws, which might be done like this:

◆ Before a Bill is sent for parliamentary vote, it is sent for public consultation via a standard crowdsourcing platform. Here, one might even experiment with letting people try to write the draft law-text together like a wiki. There should also be a forum through which people can present relevant criticism and suggestions.
◆ The Bill is then be submitted to an office for a cost-benefit analysis, including costing of wasted time and money among everyone affected.
◆ If it is implemented, it should be with a so-called "sunset clause" (unless it is a criminal Bill), meaning that it will automatically expire after a set number of years.
◆ Before the automatic expiry date, a new cost-benefit analysis is made, so that the results are known when parliament votes either to renew it or accept the expiry.

Such a process is similar to the routine cost-benefit analysis and marketing control carried out by well-run private companies, and it will draw bureaucrats' and politicians' attention to the enormity of the law burden as well as its true costs to the state, its citizens and to companies.

Here are some other possible initiatives to reduce the legal burden:

◆ Use legal "harm done" clauses stating that people can only be punished for offenses if they caused actual damage to a third party
◆ Use "opt out" clauses whereby companies can opt out of some regulation as long as they clearly state that they have done so.
◆ Always follow the subsidiary principle stating that matters should be handled by the smallest, lowest, or least-centralised authority capable of addressing that matter effectively (such as is actually inscribed into the Swiss constitution)

◆ Develop a concept for law-writing that makes it easy for analytical software to interpret them immediately (make laws computer readable)

◆ Replace, when possible, the command-and-control approach with "advise and consult" (by stating basic principles and objectives rather than specific implementation rules in the laws).

◆ Set a time limit for public approval processes.

◆ Develop one-stop approval procedures, so that you only have to file a single application for an activity and will either receive a "yes" or a "no" within a specified maximum timescale.

◆ Develop prediction markets, in which people can place bets on the impact of different laws and the progression of social metrics.

Furthermore, it should be made possible to submit complex application,s including building applications, for online pre-approval by computers. All this to halt or reverse the legal inflation.

Why do states have anti-trust regulation? It's evidently because monopolies normally deliver services that are expensive and poor. This is correct, but why, then, have the states delivered most of their own services as monopolies while growing ever larger?

The alternative to monopolies can be so-called "open architecture", a term that was introduced among IT companies in the 1980s. This started primarily with the operating system UNIX, which, unlike, for example, the systems used on IBM mainframes, as a system for which anyone could write applications and change.

Many people at IBM were not impressed with that, because, as demonstrated by the aforementioned Kronos effect, they preferred things they had invented themselves and fought things they hadn't created. "Not invented here" could be the company's unofficial motto, or "we-will-make-it-all-ourselves"

But IBM was actually heading towards a crisis, which is why it's new CEO, Louis Gerstner, decided to turn the thinking on its head and replace its "we-will-do-it-all-ourselves" approach with a culture of "the-customer-is-king". In line with this strategy, IBM would figure out what its customers needed and then assemble solutions for them, whether these were made by IBM or not. So the company became solution provider rather than mere product-pusher.

This was a big success, and the concept soon spread. However, Apple took it to new heights when it launched its iPhone in 2007. Rather than just developing all the phone's software applications itself, the company invited others to write "apps" they could sell via an "App Store". This triggered an explosion of creativity - about 800,000 different apps were written for the App Store within the first five years of its launch, and these were downloaded a approximately 40 billion times by users. It was wildly popular in other words, and the competition in the App Store was so fierce that average prices of software packages quickly dropped at just $1.5.

This became one of the most amazing creative explosions and price drops ever seen in any sector. It was so overwhelming that competitors such as Nokia, which had stayed closer to the "we-do-everything-ourselves" philosophy, were almost wiped off the map.

Western states today (in fact, all states) function predominantly as IBM did before Louis Gerstner, or as Nokia did before Apple attacked it. They operate largely as closed, monopolistic dinosaurs characterized by "we-will-do-it-all-ourselves" mentalities. Of course, governments generally don't build their own hardware (such as cars or office buildings), but they do tend to deliver their own services as monopolies, which, as we have seen, leads to weak innovation and generally zero or negative productivity growth.

The alternative way is to create what we can call "open architecture states", where citizens are treated more as commercial customers and given commercial choices, and where decisions are moved away from expert committees to the masses. Such states will be built on a combination of :

1. Monopolized public services: the obvious ones are the legal system, the legislative function, the central bank, the intelligence services, diplomacy and the core of the armed forces and the police.
2. Outsourced services: where a given service task is licensed to a single company for a given duration of time. This is suitable for natural monopolies where democratic control is less important. The typical areas are operation of utilities, environmental protection, security services, control functions, the penal system and some social services.
3. Open Service Shop: this is similar to Apple's App Store, but offering services rather than software. Citizens have access to these services via free coupons but can buy add-on services with their own money. The most obvious areas are education and healthcare.
4. Crowdsourcing: through which anyone can get involved in public problem-solving. This is most relevant for scientific, technical, social and administrative tasks and may take the form of crowdfunding, social impact bonds, crowd voting, prediction markets and inducement contests such as innovation awards.

Crowdsourcing can take an incredible number of shapes. Imagine every citizen in a community can take a photo of any problem such as graffiti or a lamp that doesn't work and send it to authorities tagged with the GPS coordinates. Authorities can then post it online and offer a small amount to the first one who offers to fix it – a concept a bit like the Uber service. Or make a competition for the best idea for ideas to fix this type of problems more permanently. In order to create a really creative public sector, it is important that as few activities as possible are delivered by monopolies. As an example, in a dynamic economy, 30% of its economy may be public, out of which 5% is monopolized, 5% outsourced, 15% in service shops and 5% crowdsourced.

Now, let's look at outsourcing. As mentioned, this is suited to functions that are best run as local monopolies (such as air traffic control), but which do not need to be provided by the government's own staff.

It can be achieved for many functions, and there is nothing particularly controversial, for example, in outsourcing a control function. The private sector already has countless companies that are specialized in all sorts of control functions on a consultancy basis. Examples are private inspection firms Veritas Group, SGS and Intertek, which in 2014 had approximately 75,000, 50,000 and 35,000 employees, respectively. Each of these had in the region of 1,000 offices worldwide, and they were in intense competition with one another and countless other local companies.

Similarly, it is not controversial to outsource military services to private companies (which are known as private military companies (PMCs)). PMCs' share of US military personnel has increased from approximately 2.5% of the total staff in the 1990s to 10 % in 2013, because they are often more efficient and cheaper than government-hired personnel. These help with security planning, training, logistics, translation, monitoring, bodyguard services, protection of critical installations, computer security and cryptography. Some advantages of using such companies are that they can move their staff from country-to-country and from job-to-job, so there is less or no periodic idleness or associated cost.

You can use private police forces as well. This is particularly common in the US, where private police outnumber public police by a ratio of approximately 3:1.[507] Private police in the US are often given public authority to make arrests and carry weapons.

This can reduce the state's costs significantly. One example is the US city Reminderville, which asked its own police staff, as well as some private companies to bid on provision of surveillance and alarm services. Their own police staff calculated they to do it for $180,000 a year with a guaranteed response time of 45 minutes. The city, however, chose instead to give the job to the company Corporate Security, which for half the price, offered a response time six minutes and twice the number of patrol cars.

There are four important variations to the outsourcing concept:

◆ Outsourcing via tender
◆ No cure, no pay consulting
◆ Sponsored outsourcing
◆ Social impact bonds

Outsourcing via tender is the classic one. An example: a government needs to run a security service, so it outlines the task and writes a tender. A number of companies make bids and the government chooses the best for a period of, say, five or 10 years, after which a new tender is developed.

No cure, no pay consulting is a bit different. Let's say that the state is running a service, but suspects it could be done more efficiently by someone else. So it makes a contract with a private management company, which takes over the management with the promise of receiving, for example, half of any savings made. Many private companies do this, with Accenture being among the leaders. In 2014, this company had approximately 280,000 employees worldwide and has had great success in taking over operations of IT departments, applications development and maintenance teams, help desk services plus human resources. It will often do this largely with the same employees who previously performed the task, "re-badged" as Accenture employees for the duration of the contract.

Sponsored outsourcing is where a sponsor offers to manage a public task because it can use it as a promotional tool. In addition to bearing the costs, the sponsor may even pay for the right to operate the service – this can be achieved through an auction process. The classic examples are private sponsors for sports and music events.

An intriguing case to consider is protection of endangered species, where a company can be paid to protect plants or animals against performance-based remuneration and the branding rights. General Electric or Google might, for instance, own a nature reserve with rhinos and continuously report on their website, what has happened to the stock (of rhinos, that is). If their reputation is at stake, they will probably publish some good news about rhinos.

The fourth form of outsourcing is the use of social impact bonds (contracts where private providers are paid performance fees for solving social tasks). For instance, in 2014, a Boston-based non-profit organization called Roca offered to help reduce crime in Massachusetts by working with young men released from jail to prevent them from committing more crimes. The work was financed by bonds, which had Goldman Sachs as prime investor. Goldman would get its full investment back, if the men targeted by Rocas programme spent 22% less time in jail than their peers. If they performed even better, Goldman would make a profit.[508]

That was outsourcing, so let's now move on to the public service shop (the parallel to an App Store), where obvious sectors include healthcare, care of the elderly, prisons and education.

Healthcare is always a big cost item and a big source of frustration for policymakers as well as for patients. The most efficient solution could be a modified combination of the Swiss and the Singaporean systems. That would work out something like this:

◆ Every resident needs to sign up for a private healthcare system.
◆ The providers of these insurance policies are not allowed to reject anyone or discriminate in price unless for lifestyle-related factors such as smoking.
◆ They are not allowed to earn profit (on average) for selling basic insurance, but they are allowed to sell for-profit add-on insurances and make money on that.
◆ There is partial coverage for personal fitness training.
◆ If the basic insurance cost exceeds x% of the insured person's' income, the state pays the rest.
◆ The insured people have unlimited coverage for dangerous and serious diseases, but only an annual maximum allowance for "trivial" illnesses (such as common cold). If they do not use this whole allowance within a given year, they are credited half the savings.
◆ Treatment of the trivial illnesses is not performed by doctors, but by medical students and nurses in walk-in centres/clinics at shopping malls, large work places and train stations.
◆ No matter which clinic a patient visits and or for what, patients always need to make a symbolic payment.
◆ Serviced homes for the elderly are included in the healthcare schemes.

This would give people a very direct, personal economic interest in staying healthy and in avoiding abuses of the health insurance system, and it would put every healthcare provider under competitive pressure, which would force them to innovate constantly. Indeed, most would think twice about seeking medical care for none-issues or out of boredom. It would also motivate them to seek low prices when they need help, which again would stimulate a market for low price treatments.

The consequence would be less time-wasting in doctors' surgeries and less waste of highly-trained physicians' time on banalities, so they could focus on more on complex diseases. It would cost much less and be more innovative. Nursing homes and protected/services homes for the elderly could also be private and offered under competition on an service store platform; one could imagine international nursing home chains which tried to attract clients by, for instance, combining locations where they elderly live and holiday locations, so that the elderly spent some of their time "under the sun".

An even bigger and more complex task for the open state and its service store is education, which in its basic structure, has changed surprisingly little over the past century. A complete rethink would be to offer all education via single courses from a public service shop, to which each citizen would receive vouchers for, say, 15 years or free life-long education. Some of the steps taken could be this:

◆ Primary and secondary school plus vocational education would be financed with vouchers granted to all citizens at birth.
◆ Tertiary education (university/college) would be financed in part by tax payments from their own graduates (and drop-outs); covering perhaps 10 years from the date they began studying there. Universities would also be entitled to sell their innovations (it should be said that many already are today, although few are good at it).

The latter would mean that if an institution provided education that didn't lead to many good job opportunities, its funding would automatically dry up, so it would either have to improve its education, educate fewer people or close down.

Please note how all this would change the behaviour of educational institutions. If the administrators of these knew their income would depend on the tax payments from their students, they would do everything possible to make these very successful and hopefully nourish a few superstars who would start the next Facebook or Microsoft. So they would behave much more like venture capital funds and venture incubators and less as certificate pushers.

How could they do that? By establishing so-called technology transfer offices, which sell licensing rights for the technologies. This works best by using standard licensing contracts or even "express license agreements". Universities could also promote their innovations by making joint innovation databases such as iBridge, through which people could gain an overview of the technologies a number of universities owned and offered for licensing.

This brings us to another great area to explore: innovation contests. We have already looked at modern examples such as X Prize and DARPA and historical competitions organized by the British government, Napoleon and others. An obvious way to combine education and public work is to develop structures so that far more tasks are solved through competitions. The state may, for instance, run fact-finding contests, cost-saving contests and, of course, technical and scientific contests. Students in primary, secondary and technical schools and universities may then spend a substantial parts of their study time competing for these awards. Here is why such competitions can be positive: it is well-known that most people who buy an electronic device normally start fiddling with it before they even open the manual. It is simply in our genes to solve tasks on our own rather than to receive instructions. MIT conducted an experiment in which researchers studied 230 million clicks on their online course material and 100,000 comments on class discussion boards, and were surprised to learn that more than half the students started solving a given task before they had studied the relevant training video.[509] So giving young people instructions for many hours every day during 13-17 years must be less efficient than constantly giving them tasks – real tasks – which motivate them to seek the required information.

Such approaches would simultaneously solve several problems. First, people would love to get involved, for the fun or sport of it, out of mere academic interest or as a commercial marketing/branding tool. Second, it would make education far more interesting. Third, it would foster lots of new ideas. And finally, much of what full-time employed bureaucrats and scientists do could probably be done better and more cheaply that way. This would mean that public sponsored science – the projects that employ full-time public sector employees – would be more focused on the most capital intensive mega-research projects.

When discussing education we should be aware of a phenomenon that the economist Joseph Schumpeter once discovered, to his horror, which was that most people who demonstrate great creativity do so before the age of 30 (Schumpeter was almost 30 when he discovered it, thus his horror). The same discovery was made by the philosopher Thomas Kuhn, as he delved into the scientific processes and paradigm shifts through history and noted: "Those who have achieved fundamental inventions of a new paradigm have generally been either very young or very new to the field whose paradigm they changed."[510]

It would be much more effective if more people took a short training course, combined with real-life project work, and then got a job or started a company at fairly young age, after which they could follow up with single, targeted courses from time-to-time during the rest of their lives. You are much more motivated to learn, when it is directly relevant to your current work and distributed in smaller modules spread over a lifetime, and when you gradually discover where your talents and opportunities lie. As it is today, the vast majority of learning in an academic education is irrelevant to what the graduates end up doing, which is a massive waste of time and creative potential.

Another area that could stimulate entrepreneurship would be use of entrepreneur colleges, wherein students at an economic institution that have founded companies live together, so they network more easily.

Entrepreneurship can also be promoted via business plan competitions such as those promoted on iStart. Some universities also created upstart mentoring programmess for students who have started their own businesses. Among the highly-successful examples are MIT Mentoring Service and the University of Miami Launch Pad. Within its first two years alone, the Launch Pad programme was used by approximately 1,000 students, who formed 50 new companies under its supervision. An analysis from 2009 concluded that graduates of MIT together had founded 25,800 companies that had a total of 3.3 million employees and generated sales of $2 trillion.[511]

There is an illusion that we need to address here. You do not gain a creative community simply by giving a lot of people higher education. A creative community should have a good balance between large and small, old and new, high-tech and industrial and service-oriented and crafts-based businesses.

One reason for this is that services often find a large customer base in industrial companies. Also, creative start-ups often have great synergy with larger technology firms, which end up taking on distribution and production of the young company's inventions.

Furthermore, the importance of handicrafts and other practical vocations such as being musician or professional athlete should not be underestimated. These people exhibit what is sometimes called "silent knowledge" (even if noisy when applied by musicians) – stuff you cannot just define in words, but which has to be learned through practice, with guidance. The Japanese understand this; they have employed 4,700 craftsmen who they call "Living National Treasures of Japan" to ensure that the finest craft skills are passed down the generations. Also, Germany, Switzerland, Holland, Austria and Scandinavia have traditionally been good at training craftsmen to levels at which they can work autonomously, and thus creatively.

Well-trained craftsmen are vital for premium and especially luxury markets, and there are lots of these involved in producing for brands like Lancôme, Gulfstream, Royal Huisman, Feadship, Ferrari, Chanel, Hermès, Cartier, Patek Philippe, Wilson Audio or Prada. Although luxury turnover only amounts to some 0.8% of the world economy, eight of the world's 100 most-profitable brands in 2014 were actually pure luxury producers (Louis Vuitton, Gucci, Coach, Hermés, Rolex, Prada, Chanel and Burburry) and another four (German car manufacturers) made a good part of their profits from luxury.[512]

The trend in the West, in recent decades, has been for fewer and fewer young people to undertake vocational education and more and more to take academic courses. This is probably because they can postpone the time when they commit to a given career path and partly because "academic" is widely seen as the "A-team". But this creates imbalanced jobs markets, economic waste, unemployment, student loan crises and social problems. A solution could be to merge vocational schools with universities so that students can combine modules of a more practical and a more theoretical nature as they see fit.

Fortunately, due to the spectacular growth in free, online courses from universities (the aforementioned massive open online courses, or MOOCs) it is getting far easier for anyone to attend individual training courses throughout life, and the whole concept of studying at university for five or more years and then applying for a job should be replaced with something far more flexible.

Private schools will often develop individualized and innovative approaches. In New York, for example, an average 62% of pupils pass their exams in third, fourth and fifth grade but in the privately-owned Harlem Success Academy, the figure is 99%. This is despite the fact that this school is located precisely in the socially deprived area of Harlem and that it selects its students via a lottery. Other private schools in Harlem, such as KIPP and Democracy Prep also manage to produce better results for Black students than those seen among White students in the more affluent suburbs.[513] These are and should not only be new ways of passing standard tests. Why not give higher freedom to specialize schools more, so that there are sports schools, fame schools, technical schools, nerd schools, etc. Children are extremely different, and this should be used as an opportunity; not seen a problem.

Private schools make good use of "carrots and stick". If schools do well, they grow, if they disappoint, they close down. Countries that have high proportion of private schools consequently have quite high average scores on the global PISA scale of students' academic abilities, and in the OECD as whole, students in private schools also score significantly higher in all areas than those in state schools.[514]

Unfortunately, it is complicated to measure the impact of private schools precisely, but a study from 2010 concluded that an increase in the proportion of private schools by 10% led to a decrease of 5% in average tuition cost at all schools, while also leading to better exam results.[515]

Of course, an alternative to private schools is state-funded, none-selective schools which either run with great autonomy or have private ownership. This has, for instance, been tried in England, where the majority of public schools in many areas were converted to autonomous so-called "academies", which could control their own budgets, staffing and curriculums. The results of this have been very impressive.[516] Similarly, the US has privately run charter schools, which have done well. Overall, a focus on private schools can save money, stimulate useful innovation, and improve education.

Let's now look at crowdsourcing. It would be highly-efficient if all sorts of government bureaus routinely did what American military research institute DARPA did and launched public competitions to find solutions to its challenges. These could be innovation awards, but also public competitions to identify cost- savings, reduce red tape, optimize the tax system, develop a better traffic plan, or anything at all, really. This could be tied in with reality-style TV shows where problems were initially presented and where finalists (those with the best solutions) would present to an audience and judges.

Another approach to crowdsourcing would be simply to pursue openness. Instead of letting state employees alone crunch numbers and issue reports, it could be efficient simply to release the raw data and possible calculation models to the public in standardized formats, after which anyone (including students) could analyse it in their own way.

Experience shows that this would trigger a lot of activity with people trawling through it and analysing it in many different, and sometimes highly-creative and surprising, ways and discussing it on social media. Quite apart from the creativity this would unleash, any errors made by the experts would then soon be discovered.

This would be a step away from authoritarian rule by experts with credentials and towards more popular creativity and decentralized knowledge. And it would avoid situations like the aforementioned controversy with the hockey stick graph, where the public had access to the analysis conclusions, but was unable to see the underlying data and formulas that had let to it, despite having paid for it. In fact, many states have already taken steps in that direction; for example, when President Obama launched the "Open Government Initiative", in which data of public relevance (not state secrets) are published in XBRL format - a standard that makes it possible for individuals to analyse large amounts of data in a standard Excel spreadsheet.

Another useful area of crowd-sourcing is that of whistleblower laws, whereby any citizen can gain immunity from prosecution and a percentage of any fines paid by perpetrators, by disclosing lawbreakers such as tax cheaters, corrupt officials or corporate swindlers.

Governments should also facilitate crowdfunding of start-ups and young companies. A major barrier for start-ups, is raising funds in the three-to-ten years, it often takes to reach break even. These may be funded by so-called angel investors or venture capital funds, but many such investors, and in particular venture capital funds, tend to prefer stepping in at later stages. Hence, the need for another public funding source in the form of crowdfunding, where people raise money through websites such as Kickstarter. Governments can help here by exempting crowdfunding up to, say, $10 million from many of the financial fundraising requirements that otherwise apply. They should, in other words, have some opt-out clauses from some financial regulation. Sovereign wealth funds could also allocate a specific part of their investments to such venture funding.

There are two more possible uses of crowdsourcing in government: It should be possible for people in a community or country to call a referendum via the collection of signatures. And there should be a system so that people can vote for a monthly subject, via text message or email that has to be debated in a televised session in parliament. Both initiatives would mean that people were more engaged in the political debate and that they felt that they had a direct say in policy. Furthermore, it would give politicians a better feel for what was on people's minds.

A final note: how do you pay for it all?

Of course, one way is to reduce the bill directly by cutting corporate subsidies, government-to-government foreign aid transfers and those welfare offerings that pacify recipients or by letting people make symbolic payments for healthcare and contribute to the bill, if they take a higher education. Another way is to privatize government assets, which often bring both short term revenue and long term benefits. For instance, Europe has privatized a bigger proportion of its main airports than the US, which can be seen by the much higher standards these airports now have. Apart from such initiatives, the dynamic effects of a more creative society where money is invested in new businesses rather than government bonds will be higher tax revenues, which also enable lower tax rates.

But there will still be a bill, and the perfect sort of tax is placed on activities that have so-called negative externalities, i.e. negative impact on others, such as pollution. The second best is tax on individual usage of common goods, such as on driving on highways. Conversely, the worst sort of tax is on something you want to simulate, such as work, savings and business investment.

In practice, however, the former two kinds of taxes can hardly pay for everything, so more is needed, even if it may hamper work, savings and business investment. One possible tax structure that can be effective without hampering creativity (much) is this:

◆ Negative income tax for earned income ("earned" means by working) up to a defined poverty line. There might, for instance, be a 10% subsidy on this income
◆ For income above that, a flat tax of, say, 20%, with income deductions for up to two children, but for absolutely nothing else
◆ VAT of approximately 10%
◆ Corporate tax of approximately 10%

◆ Alternative annual wealth tax of 0.5% for wealth exceeding, for instance, $5 million, which is offset against income tax, so that if a person pays enough income tax, there is no wealth tax
◆ European-style tax on fossil fuels
◆ No capital gains tax on company or common-equity investments, but 10% capital gains tax on property gains, as these are not equally productive for society
◆ Annual drivers' tax per registered driver. This should be designed to be enough to finance the road system; but no car tax (apart from the VAT)
◆ Mandatory private health insurance, where the state pays any part exceeding, say, 5-10% of personal income

A tax system roughly like what is described above (except for the watermark issue) is very similar with what has been practised in Singapore, Switzerland and other successful, hyper-creative and economically sustainable economies, and it also reminds of what Denmark looked like in the 1960s, when it had very high economic growth, whereby it had "got to Denmark", as Francis Fukuyama described, For instance, total taxation in Denmark was less than 30% of GDP in 1965, and the country had extremely high average growth rates and virtually no unemployment and minimal crime in the 1960s. Of course, a variation in a highly-decentralized state might be that the government collects VAT and fossil fuel taxes and leaves everything else to the local communities. Switzerland is not so far from that.

Finally, when we consider what a creative state is like, it is useful to hold a few core concepts in mind that separate how we think and act if we assume or want a static and dynamic society, respectively.

HOW WE THINK		
	Static world-view	Creative world-view
Our destiny	"Everything is controlled from the outside, and we are subject to fate."	"Our lives are in our own hands and we can change the world."
Resources	"We shall soon run out of resources."	"The ultimate resource is our creativity."
Inequality	"If someone is rich, he probably took this wealth from others."	"If someone is rich, he probably created something new."
History	"The past was better."	"The best is yet to come."

Being good	"A good person must submit."	"A good person accomplishes something."
Problems	"If something goes wrong, we are probably victims."	"If something goes wrong, we must do better next time."
Change	"We must cleanse ourselves of the new and protect ourselves against the unknown."	"The new, the unknown and the future offer many opportunities."

HOW WE ACT		
	Static society	Creative society
Safety standards	Precaution principle LNT assumption Slippery slope argument	Cost-benefit principle
Public services	State monopolies, standard services fro all	Outsourcing, service shop, crowd-sourcing, segment of one marketing
Legal concepts	Firm laws, manuals, command-and-control	Broad principles, guide-and-consult, opt-out and harm-done and sunset clauses, subsidiarity principle
Investments	Government bonds to finance government overspending	Equities and venture capital to finance growth and private job creation
Education	13-17 years in the classroom and then apply for a job; sharp distinction between academic and vocational education	Start work much earlier; follow up with single courses. Modular education; use educational institutions as venture incubators and reward them financially for their student's commercial results
Taxes	High tax on work and savings	Low tax on work and savings

26.
THE
POSSIBLE
WORLD

Francis Fukuyama may well have been right when he assumed that, in spite of all the turmoil and setbacks, we are on a march towards an end of history in which liberal democracies completely dominate. Equally, Robert Wright's assumption that the destiny of mankind is win-win for evermore may also be correct.

However, creative societies have never had it easy, and they are now battling the aforementioned 12 internal threats. Similar battles have always been fought, and as we have seen, in most of history, creativity actually lost more often than it won. Indeed, if the West were just one big nation, its creativity would almost certainly also have been extinguished by now. It was saved by its decentralization.

The essential lesson, above anything else, is probably that "small is cool". Ancient Greece and medieval Western Europe became so creative because of their many city states. Today, small nations typically score higher on humanistic, economic and environmental criteria than the big ones, and international opinion polls typically show that local mayors are far more popular than national leaders, who are again more popular than international leaders.[517]

Could it perhaps be that the best model, ultimately, is a return to city states - small units loosely aligned in bigger, open networks? Why should we not have combinations of hippy states, economic Singapore-style power centres, international metropolises, and even perhaps a small Stone Age country for those who may prefer that? People are, indeed, very different, and we should embrace that rather than try to "harmonize" them. If we really decentralize our communities, but also keep them open to trade, we will, in many ways, have copied the robust structure of natural ecosystems, Ancient Greece, free markets or the internet as a way to defending creativity.

In this connection, there is an observation about democracy that we should not ignore. We think of democracy is "rule by the people" as opposed to "rule by dictator". However think about this: when we go shopping in a market economy, we compare offers from countless companies that may each be ruled in dictatorial ways by their CEO and/or owner. And yet, in spite of all these dictators, we are free. We are free, because we can vote with our feet; if we don't like any of the offerings in a bakers shop, we don't call for a hand-vote to have them changed, but we can instead to another shop, and this is how our transaction remains based on voluntary win-win. The bigger and more centralized a democracy becomes, the less freedom we have. It is increasingly rule by a majority with whom we may disagree.

One thing is for certain: we can never establish a single utopia in which everyone is happy, because we are far too diverse for that. But we can make a network of open and dynamic communities akin to the Greek or medieval mini-states, each of which is unique, constantly experimenting and always fiercely competing, so that *together* they find the better solutions.

If we really choose this way, here are some examples of what the future might well offer us:

◆ As wealth keeps growing, the world's population peaks before or around 2050 at 8-9 billion, after which it plummets, so that 100 years later it is only 3-4 billion.

◆ The average productivity in the most professional farms quadruples through genetic engineering combined with computer-controlled drip irrigation, robotic precision planting and precision weeding and so on.

◆ This, combined with a declining population, means that approximately half the globe is nature reserves by year 2100. These are predominantly owned or operated by private benefactors and companies, which combine protection with gentle tourism.

◆ We use travelling-wave reactors and transmutation to utilize and degrade our existing nuclear waste. However, in parallel we have introduced first thorium based fission, which has been followed by compact nuclear fusion.

◆ Landfills with mixed waste have virtually all been reprocessed with plasma arc technology, and the metals in them have been recycled.

◆ Most cars are electric, but you still see sports cars with internal combustion engines (beautiful noise!). These use biofuels made with gene-modified algae.

◆ Centralistic societies have largely gone the way of the central mainframe computer; we have instead entered the age of decentralized rule, small city-states and loose federations.

◆ In the same vein, antitrust regulation is widely applied to public services, so that these are offered by tens of thousands of private companies via outsourcing or public service shops. This has fostered great creativity plus extreme drops in the prices of most "public" services.

- We have truly entered the age of crowdsourcing, and states initiate tens of thousands of new innovation prizes, idea competitions and so on every year. Much of the education activities in schools and universities are centred on participation in these.

- Most learning has become based around online lectures and instructive multiplayer games, which people call "geek games". The number of students studying simultaneously at each top university therefore exceeds millions, and the best professors gain global rock star reputations (and salaries). The art of giving an absolutely captivating lecture reaches new highs all the time, and universities make much of their money from advertising related to their online courses.

- Almost no states take out unsecured loans anymore, and most large pension funds now refuse to invest in unsecured government bonds for ethical reasons. Instead, most states have sovereign wealth funds for stabilization purposes, and since this shift took place, there have been no major economic crises in any of the relevant states.

- Realizing that taxes kill creativity and marginalize people, most communities have settled for top tax rates of approximately 20% and VAT and corporate tax rates at or below 10%. However, tax structure and taxation levels are largely left to local communities, who are not obliged to mirror others.

- For the first time in several centuries, there is now a steady decline in the number of laws and regulations. Furthermore, many of those that remain can now be read and understood by computers which can tell anyone within seconds whether, for instance, a proposed house would be legal to build or a proposed financial transaction violates any rules.

- Lightweight aircraft powered by nuclear thermal rockets can leave the atmosphere and fly from Europe to Australia within three hours. Space- travelling rockets using the same technology can reach 20% of the speed of light and are commuting regularly between the solar system's planets. Mars is only 20 minutes away at that speed, but when you factor in acceleration and deceleration, it takes eight hours for an unmanned rocket to get there. Numerous robotic camps have been set up within the planetary system, and there are tourist hotels on Mars and the Moon.

- The survival of virtually all known species has been secured by genetic and/or biological backups; the latter via a collaboration between zoos, botanical gardens and aquariums across the globe. Furthermore, using genetic reconstruction ,we have also begun restoring selected extinct animal and plant species. The first "Mesolithic Park" with mammoths, sabre-toothed tigers and woolly rhinoceros has been established in

Chile, where it has become one of the world's major tourist attractions. Russia, Greenland and Canada plan to take up the competition.

◆ Earth has established an effective missile-based defence against comets that might otherwise trigger mass extinction of millions of species and threaten ourselves, and we have mapped most of these potential threats for several decades out.

◆ The dreaded labour-shortage due to global ageing has been totally avoided via the use of hundreds of millions of super-smart robots.

◆ Self-driven cars have become so safe that they are allowed to drive 200 km/h on many highways except in Germany, where the limit is set at 300 km/h and in Texas, where it is 300 mph. The number of traffic accidents has decreased markedly.

◆ People can be vaccinated against most cancers to which they are genetically predisposed, and also against alcoholism, drug addiction and an ever-increasing variety of common diseases.

◆ Via vaccination programmes and knock-out genes, we have eradicated yellow fever, malaria, dengue fever, guinea worm, smallpox and polio.

◆ Golden rice and other genetically modified crops, combined with modern agricultural technologies, have eliminated malnutrition around the world and Africans have, by 2100, become as rich as the Germans were in 2000. The African population has consequently begun falling rapidly.

◆ Global life expectancy has risen to 120 years, where people with healthy lifestyles can expect to be in really good shape until they reach around 100 years of age.

◆ You can have a meaningful discussion with computers over the internet. This AI technology is used for fact-finding and many other purposes, but it is particularly popular for providing mentoring services related to education and for developing scientific hypothesis and technical opportunities.

This book started by quoting Alan Shepard talking about his moonwalk in 1971. Like the other astronauts, this man obviously had many skills, but most important was perhaps his incredible optimism. Ten years before he came to walk on the Moon, he was destined to be the US's first astronaut, and on May 5, 1961, he sat strapped in his seat at the top by a ten-story, 33-ton rocket loaded with highly explosive fuel; waiting to be shot into space.

And he waited.

And he waited, because the control centre said there was a "technical problem". That sounds rather nerve-wracking, but when he after four hours of waiting contacted the control centre, it was not to ask for crisis therapy or legal assistance. No, he just asked them this: "Why don't you fix your little problem and light this candle?" They did, and he blasted off with his golf gear and all.

We should also get going, because while we do have problems, there are actually excellent solutions available, and the results could be heavenly.

REFERENCES

1. IMF, List of countries by GDP (PPP) per capita, http://en.wikipedia.org/wiki/List_of_countries_by_GDP_(PPP)_per_capita
2. Fukuyama, F.: *Political Order and Political Decay: From the Industrial Revolution to the Globalization of Democracy* Farrar, Straus and Giroux, 2014
3. Tattersall, I.: If I had a hammer, *Scientific American*, Sept 2014
4. Wade, N.: *A Troublesome Inheritance*, Penguin Press, 2014
5. http://stoneageskills.com/articles/pdf/Human_technology_timeline.pdf, http://en.wikipedia.org/wiki/Timeline_of_human_prehistory
6. Wolf, G.: Steve Jobs: The Next Insanely Great Thing, *Wired*, Apr. 1996
7. Wade, N.: *Before the Dawn, Recovering the Lost History of our Ancestors*, Penguin Books, 2006
8. Wikipedia Commons
9. How Neanderthals met a grisly fate: devoured by humans, *The Observer*, 17 May 2009
10. Dawkins, R.: *The Selfish Gene*, 30th Universary Edition, Oxford University Press, 2006
11. Wright, R.: *Nonzero: History, Evolution & Human Cooperation: The Logic of Human Destiny*, Abacus, 2001
12. A precursor for Wright's thoughts was the book *Mutual Aid: A Factor in Evolution*, which was published by Peter Kropotkin in 1902
13. Horan, R.D., E. Bulte & J.F. Shogren: How trade saved humanity from biological exclusion: An economic theory of Neanderthal extinction, *Journal of Economic Behavior and Organization*, 2005
14. Gunligge, B.: Europe between the Oceans, Yale University Press, 2008
15. Vernon Henderson, J., A. Storeygard & D. Weil: Measuring Economic Growth from Outer Space, *American Economic Review*, 2012
16. Bristow, M.: Ex-leaders head for North Korea, *BBC News Asia-Pacific*, 25. april 2011
17. Shreeve, James: *The Genome War: How Craig Venter Tried to Capture the Code of Life and Save the World*, Ballantine Books, 2000
18. Wade, N: Nice Rats, Nasty Rats: Maybe It's All in the Genes, *New York Times*, 25 July, 2006
19. Benton, M. J., 2001, Biodiversity on land and in the sea, *Geological Journal* 36, p. 211-230
20. John Doebley - http://teosinte.wisc.edu/images.html
21. Dixon, G.R.: *Vegetable brassicas and related crucifers*, Wallingford, 2007
22. Gibbons, A.: European Skin Turned Pale Only Recently, Gene Suggests, *Science*, 20 April, 2007
23. Henrich, J. et al.: 'Economic Man' in Cross-cultural Perspective: Behavioral Experiments in 15 Small-scale Societies, *American Economic Review*, 2001
24. Henrich, J. et al.: In Search of Homo Economicus: Behavioral Experiments in 15 Small-Scale Societies. *American Economic Review*, 91, 2001
25. Knack, S. & P.J. Zak: Building trust: Public policy, interpersonal trust and economic development, *World Bank*, 2001
26. Wade, N.: *Before the Dawn, Recovering the Lost History of our Ancestors*, Penguin Books, 2006
27. Chagnon, N.: Life Histories, Blood Revenge, and Warfare in a Tribal Population, *Science* p.239, 2988
28. Chagnon, N.A.: Yanonmamo, *Thomason learning*, 1992
29. Your Brain Is Smaller Than a Caveman's. Here's Why, *Bloomberg Business Week*, 22 May, 2014
30. Chagnon, N.A.: Yanonmamo, Thomason learning, 1992
31. Gordon, P.: Numerical Cognition Without Words: Evidence from Amazonia, *Science*, Vol. 306, 2004
32. Nordhaus, W.D.: Schumpeterian Profits and the Alchemist Fallacy, Revised, *Yale Working Papers on Economic Applications and Policy*, Discussion Paper No. 6, 2005, Yale University Department of Economics
33. Ibid
34. Huntington, S.P.: The Clash of Civilizations?, *Foreign Affairs*, summer 1993.
35. Fromkin, D.: *The Way of the World: From the Dawn of Civilizations to the Eve of the Twenty-first Century*, Vintage, 2000
36. Keay, J.: *China A History*. Harper Press, 2009
37. Wikipedia, "List of Largest Empires"
38. Murray, C.: *Human Accomplishment*, Harper Collins Publishers, 2003

39. Ferguson, N.: *Civilization, The West and the Rest*, Penguin Books, 2011
40. Kennedy, P.: *The Rise and Fall of Great Powers*, Random House, 1987
41. Ferguson, N.: *Civilization, The West and the Rest, Penguin Books*, 2011
42. Starr, C.G.: *A History of the Ancient World*, Oxford University Press USA, 1991
43. Wikipedia Commons
44. Cowel, E.R.: *Everyday Life in Ancient Rome*, B.T. Bratsford, 1961
45. Fromkin, D.: *The Way of the World: From the Dawn of Civilizations to the Eve of the Twenty-first Century*, Vintage, 2000
46. Ibid.
47. Johnson, P.: *Enemies of Society*, Weindenferld & Nicholson, 1977
48. Tainter, J.A.: *The Collapse of Complex Societies*, Cambridge University Press, 1988
49. Fromkin, D.: *The Way of the World: From the Dawn of Civilizations to the Eve of the Twenty-first Century*, Vintage, 2000
50. Gibbon, E.: The History of the Decline and Fall of the Roman Empire, *Penguin Classics*, 1996
51. Dudley, D.R.: *A History of Cynicism from Diogenes to the 6th Century AD*, Cambridge University Press, 1937
52. Wikipedia Commons
53. Nimura, C.: *Rock art and coastal change in Bronze Age, Scandinavia* Department of Archaeology and Classical Studies, Stockholm University, 2012
54. Gunliffe, B.: *Europe between the Oceans*, Yale University Press, 2008
55. Dudo af Saint-Quentin: *Libri III de moribus et actis primorum Normanniae ducum*, 1015
56. How Vikings navigated the world, *Science Nordic*, 9 October, 2012
57. Westwood, J & S.: *Kingshill, The Lore of Scotland: A guide to Scottish legends*, Random House Books, 2009
58. Goody, J: *The Development of the Family and Marriage in Europe*, Cambridge University Press, 1983. See also: Domesday Book, http://www.nationalarchives.gov.uk/domesday/
59. http://www.domesdaybook.co.uk/
60. Maddison, A.: *Growth and Interaction in the World Economy: The Roots of Modernity*, Aei Press, 2005
61. Burringh, E. & J. L van Zanden: Charting the "Rise of the West": Manuscripts and Printed Books in Europe, A Long-Term Perspective from the Sixth through Eighteenth Centuries, *The Journal of Economic History*, Vol. 69, 2009.
62. Gay, P.: *The Enlightenment: The Science of Freedom*, W.W. Norton & Company, 1996
63. Condorcet, M.J.: *Sketch for a Historical Picture of the Progress of the Human Mind*, Hyperion, 1980
64. Bergreen, L.: *Columbus: The Four Voyages, 1492-1504*, Penguin Books, 2012
65. http://commons.wikimedia.org/wiki/File:Travels_of_Marco_Polo.svg
66. Bergreen, L.: *Columbus: The Four Voyages, 1492-1504*, Penguin Books, 2012
67. http://en.wikipedia.org/wiki/File:Viajes_de_colon_en.svg
68. Martin, L.: Fetal Alcohol Syndrome in Europe, 1300-1700: A Review of Data on Alcohol Consumption and A Hypothesis, *Food and Foodways*, XI, 2003
69. Russell, J.C.: *Late Ancient and Medieval Population Control*, American Philosophical Society, 1985
70. http://commons.wikimedia.org/wiki/File:European_empires.png
71. Maddison, A.: *Growth and Interaction in the World Economy*, The AEI Press, 2004
72. Davis, R.C.: *Christian Slaves, Muslim Masters: White Slavery in the Mediterranean, the Barbary Coast, and Italy, 1500-1800*, Palgrave Macmillan, 2003
73. Headrick, D.R.: *The Tools of Empire: Technology and European Imperialism in the Nineteenth Century*, Oxford University Press, 1981
74. Wikipedia: Demographics of Portugal
75. Boxer, C.R.: *The Portuguese Seaborne Empire, 1415-1825*, Alfred A. Knopf, 1969
76. Wikipedia lists, see following footnote.
77. Luxury brands are listed in Tvede, L.: *Supertrends*, Wiley & Sons, 2011. Restaurant-ratings are from Restaurant Magazine 2014 rating. University rankings are average of 2014 ratings by QS World University Rankings, Times Higher Education World University Rankings and Academic Ranking of World Universities. Biotech company rankings are based on Wikipedia search on "List of biotechnology companies", which unfortunately was based on 2006 numbers. The remaining numbers are from 2014 Wikipedia searches "list of best-selling books", "list of most expensive sculptures", "list of most expensive paintings", "list of highest-grossing movies" and "list of best-selling music artists".

78. http://www.nobelprize.org/nobel_prizes/lists/all/. See also http://stats.areppim.com/stats/stats_nobelhierarchy.htm
79. Martin Prosperity Institute, http://martinprosperity.org/
80. http://en.wikipedia.org/wiki/International_Innovation_Index#cite_note-1
81. http://www.globalinnovationindex.org/gii/index.html
82. Murray, C.: *Human Accomplishment*, HarperCollins Publishers, 2003
83. Ibid
84. http://en.wikipedia.org/wiki/Book_printing#mediaviewer/File:Printing_towns_incunabula.svg
85. Murray, C.: *Human Accomplishment*, HarperCollins Publishers, 2003
86. Ferguson, N.: *Civilization, The West and the Rest*, Penguin Books, 2011
87. http://www.eupedia.com/europe/Haplogroup_R1b_Y-DNA.shtml
88. Bartlett, R.: *The Making of Europe: Conquest, Colonization and Cultural Change*, Princeton Universtity Press, 1993
89. http://www.eupedia.com/forum/threads/26956-Map-of-Individualism-(vs-Collectivism)
90. Henrich, J: Demography and cultural evolution: How adaptive cultural processes can produce maladaptive losses: the Tasmanian case, *American Antiquity*, 69, 2004
91. McGhee, R.: Disease and the Development of Inuit Culture, *Current Anthropology*, vol. 35, 1994
92. Quigley, C.: *The Evolution Of Civilizations*, Liberty Fund Inc., 1979
93. Olson, M.: *The Rise and Decline of Nations*, Yale University Press, 1982
94. Ridley, M.: *The Rational Optimist*, Harper Perennial, 2011
95. Soto, H.d.: *The Mystery of Capital: Why Capitalism Triumphs in the West and Fails Everywhere Else*, Basic Books, 2003
96. Al-Ghazali, A.H.: *The Incoherence of the Philosophers*, Brigham Young University, 2002
97. Al-Andalusi, I.H.: *In Pursuit of Virtue*, Basic Teachings, 1990
98. Reilly, R.R.: *The Closing of the Muslim Mind*, ISI Books, 2010
99. Ibid.
100. Reilly, R.R.: *The Closing of the Muslim Mind*, ISI Books, 2010. Also Pococke, E: Bar Hebraeus: Historia Compendiosa Dynastiarum, Oxford, 1663
101. Reilly, R.R.: *The Closing of the Muslim Mind*, ISI Books, 2010
102. Ferguson, N.: *Civilization, The West and the Rest*, Penguin Books, 2011
103. Acemoglu, D. & Robinson J.A.: *Why Nations Fail*, Crown Business, 2012
104. Gruber, C.: *The Islamic Manuscript Tradition: Ten Centuries of Book Arts in Indiana University Collections*, Indiana University Press, 2009
105. *Arab Human Development Report 2002: Creating Opportunities for Future Generations*, United Nations, 2002
106. http://gulfnews.com/news/gulf/uae/education/reading-risks-being-a-generation-s-loss-1.724410
107. Pervez Amirali Hoodbhoy Science and the Islamic World – The Quest for Rapprochement, *Physics Today*, august 2007
108. Allawi, A.A.: *The Crises of Islamic Civilization*, Yale University Press, 2009
109. 2014 Edelman Trust Barometer, http://www.edelman.com/p/6-a-m/2014-edelman-trust-barometer/
110. Acemoglu, D. & Robinson J.A.: *Why Nations Fail*, Crown Business, 2012
111. Ibid.
112. Huff, T.E.: *The Rise of Early Modern Science: Islam, China, and the West*, Cambridge University Press, 1993
113. Waley-cohen, J: *The Sextants of Beijing: Global Currents in Chinese History*, W. W. Norton & Company, 2000
114. Mokyr, J.: *The Lever of Riches: Technological Creativity and Economic Progress*, Oxford University Press, 1992
115. Brewer, J.: *The Pleasures of the Imagination: English Culture in the Eigtheenth Century*, HarperCollins, 1997
116. Acemogly, D. & Robinson J.A: *Why Nations Fail*, Crown Business, 2012
117. Ibid
118. Capell, C. et al: A Y Chromosome Census of the British Isles; *Current Biology*, Volume 13, 2005.
119. Weber; M, P.R. Baehr & G.C. Wells: *The Protestant Ethic and the "Spirit" of Capitalism and other Writings*, Penguin, 2002
120. Acemogly, D. & Robinson J.A.: *Why Nations Fail*, Crown Publishing, 2012

121. Long, J.B.D. & Shleifer A.: Princes and Merchants: European City Growth before the Industrial Revolution, *NBER Working Paper No. 4274*, 1993

122. Fowler, B.: *Iceman, Uncovering the Life and Times of a Prehistoric Man Found in an Alpine Glachier*, Macmillan, 2000

123. 123 Thomas, E.M.: *The Harmless People*, Vintage, 1989

124. 124 Lee, R.B.: *The !Kung San: Men, Women and Work in a Foraging Society*, Cambridge University Press, 1979

125. 125 Heider, K.: *Grand Valley Dani: Peaceful Warriors*, Wadsworth Publishing, 1996

126. 126 LeBlanc,S.A.: *Constant Battles*, St. Martin's Press, 2003

127. 127 Gat, A.: *War in Human Civilization*, Oxford University Press, Oxford, 2007

128. 128 Ibid

129. 129 Curtis, E.S.: *The North American Indian, Volume 9*, Classic Books, 1913

130. 130 Schwager, R: *Must There Be Scapegoats?: Violence and Redemption in the Bible*, Gracewing, 2000

131. White, M: *The Great Big Book of Horrible Things: The Definitive Chronicle of History's 100 Worst Atrocities*, W. W. Norton & Company, 2012

132. Fromkin, D.: *The Way of the World: From the Dawn of Civilizations to the Eve of the Twenty-first Century*, Vintage, 2000

133. Pinker, S.: *The Better Angels of Our Nature: Why Violence Has Declined*, Penguin Books, 2012

134. Ibid

135. http://www.allempires.com/article/index.php?q=fate_of_roman_emperors

136. Ibid.

137. Kincaid, D.: *British Social Life in India, 1608-1937*, Routledge & Kegan Paul Books, 1973

138. Olson, M: *Power and Prosperity: Outgrowing Communist and Capitalist Dictatorships*, Oxford University Press, 2000

139. Pinker, S.: *The Better Angels of Our Nature: Why Violence Has Declined*, Penguin Books, 2012

140. Morris, I.: *War, what is it good for?*, Profile Books, 2014

141. Elias, N.: *The Civilizing Process: Sociogenetic and Psychogenetic Investigations*, Blackwell Publishing, 2000

142. Taheri, A.: *The Spirit of Allah*, Hutchinson , 1987. The words were spoken in a radio broadcast from Qom on 20 August 1979.

143. Fromkin, D.: *The Way of the World: From the Dawn of Civilizations to the Eve of the Twenty-first Century*, Vintage, 2000

144. Hegre, H., Oneal J.R & Russett B.M.: Trade Does Promote Peace: New Simultaneous Estimates of the Reciprocal Effects of Trade and Conflict, *Journal of Peace Research*, 47, 2010

145. Friedmann, B.M.: *The Moral Consequences of Economic Growth*, Vintage, 2006

146. Regarding corruption, see Transparency International, http://cpi.transparency.org/cpi2012/results/

147. Wikipedia Commons

148. Friedmann, B.: *The Moral Consequences of Growth*, Vintage, 2006

149. Przeworski, A. et al.: *What Makes Democracies Endure?, Journal of Democracy*, January 1996

150. The pursuit of happiness, *The Economist online*, 24 May, 2011

151. Hashim, M.S.B.: *Problems and Issues of Higher Education Development in Malaysia*, Regional Institute of Higher Education and Development, 1973

152. Knox, R.: *The Races of Men: A Philosophical Enquiry into the Influence of Race over the Destinies of Nations*, H. Renshaw; Enlarged 2nd edition, 1862

153. Tocqueville, AD.: *Democracy in America*, Penguin Classics, 2003

154. Sowell, T.: *Black Rednecks and White Liberals*, Encounter Books, 2005

155. Ibid.

156. Sowell, T.: *Intellectuals and Society*, Basic Books, 2011

157. Flynn, J.R.: *Are We Getting Smarter?: Rising IQ in the Twenty-First Century*, Cambridge University Press, 2012

158. Lynn, R. & Vanhanen T.: *IQ and the Wealth of Nations*, Praeger Publishers, 2002

159. Wechsler, D.: *The Measurement of Adult Intelligence*, Williams & Wilkins, Baltimore, 1944

160. Mingroni, M.A.: The secular rise in IQ: Giving heterosis a closer look, *Intelligence*, Volume 32, Issue 1, 2004

161. Jensen, A.R.: *Straight Talk about Mental Tests*, The Free Press, 1981

162. Boivin M.J.: Effects of early cerebral malaria on cognitive ability in Senegalese children, *Journal of Developmental & Behavioral Pediatrics*, October 2002

163. Thomas, R.M.: *Human Development Theories: Windows on Culture*, SAGE Publications, 1999

164. Vernon, P.E.: *Intelligence and Social Environment*, Methuen & Co., 1969
165. G. Cochran, J. Hardy, Harpending H.: Natural History of Ashkenazi Intelligence, *Journal of Biosocial Science* 38 (5), p.659–693 (2006),University of Utah
166. G. Cochran, J. Hardy, H. Harpending. Natural History of Ashkenazi Intelligence", University of Utah, *Journal of Biosocial Science* 38 (5), p 659–693, 2006
167. Lynn, R. & Longley, D. On the high intelligence and cognitive achievements of Jews in Britain." *Intelligence*, 34, 541–547, 2006
168. Engels, F.: *Origin of the Family, Private Property, and the State*, Pathfinder Press, 1972
169. Feynman, R.P.: *There's Plenty of Room at the Bottom*, speech December 29th 1959 at the annual meeting of the American Physical Society at the California Institute of Technology (Caltech), http://www. zyvex.com/nanotech/feynman.html
170. Cressler, J.D.: *Silicon Earth: Introduction to the Microelectronics and Nanotechnology Revolution*, Cambridge University Press, 2009
171. Brock, D.: *Understanding Moore's Law: Four Decades of Innovation*, Chemical Heritage Foundation, 2006
172. *Report to the President and Congress, Designing a Digital Future: Federally Funded Research and Development in Networking and Information Technology on the Fourth, Executive Office of the President President's Council of Advisors on Science and Technology*, 2010
173. Kelly, K.: Was Moore's Law Inevitable?, *The Technium*, 17 July 2009, http://www.kk.org/thetechnium/archives/2009/07/was_moores_law.php
174. Tvede, L.: *Supertrends*, Wiley & Sons, 2011
175. West, Geoffrey.: Growth, Innovation, Scaling and the Pace of Life, *Proceedings of the National Academy of Sciences*, 2007
176. Bornstein, M.C & H.G. Bornstein: The Pace of Life, *Nature* 256, February, 1976
177. Carlino, G. A., Chatterjee S. & Hunt, R.M.: Urban Density and the Rate of Invention, FRB of Philadelphia Working Paper No. 06-41, 2006
178. Turing Test breakthrough as super-computer becomes first to convince us it's human, *The Independent*, June 08, 2014
179. Craig Venter Wants to Solve the World's Energy Crisis, *Wired*, 18 May, 2012.
180. *Pet kitten cloned for Christmas*, BBC News, 23 December, 2004, http://news.bbc.co.uk/2/hi/americas/4120179.stm
181. *Cloning Man's Best Friend: How Far Would You Go to Keep Fido?* - ABC News, abcnews.go.com. 21 May, 2008
182. First Gene Therapy Successful Against Aging-Associated Decline: Mouse Lifespan Extended Up to 24% With a Single Treatment, *Science News*, 14 May, 2012
183. Peng C., Zuo Y., Kwan K.M. et al.: Blueberry extract prolongs life span of Drosophila melanogaster, *Exp Gerontol.*, 472, Feb, 2012
184. Ingenious, *The Economist*, February 8th, 2014.
185. Macer, J., J. Azariah & Srinives P.: International Attitudes to biotechnology in Asia, *International Journal of Biotechnology*, Vol. 2, No. 4, 2000
186. Cao, X. Et al: Maintenance of superior learning and memory function in NR2B transgenic mice during ageing, *Bioscience*, 25 March,2007
187. Dubal, D. E. et al: Life Extension Factor Klotho Enhances Cognition, *Cell reports*, 8 May, 2014.
188. Scientists in Germany Draft Neanderthal Genome, *New York Times*, 12 Feb, 2009
189. Judson , O.: A Bug's Death, *New York Times*,25 Sept , 2003
190. Galizi, R. Et al: A synthetic sex ratio distortion system for the control of the human malaria mosquito, *Nature Communications* 5, 2014
191. A new challenge, *The Economist*, October 11, 2014
192. Crosby, F.: *The Complete Guide to Fighters & Bombers of the World*, Hermes House, 2006
193. Anderson, C.: How I Accidentally Kickstarted the Domestic Drone Boom, *Wired*, 22 June, 2012
194. Lakhani, K. R. et al: *The Value of Openness in Scientific Problem Solving, Working paper*, Harvard Business School, CBS, Innocentive, 2007
195. Sobel, D.: *Longitude: The True Story of a Lone Genius Who Solved the Greatest Scientific Problem of His Time*, Walker & Company, 2007
196. And the Winner is..., *McKinsey & Company*, 2009
197. Berg, J.E., Forsythe R., F. Nelson & Rietz, T.A.: *Results from a dozen years of election futures market research, Technical report*, University of Iowa, 2000. Se også Berg, J.E., F. Nelson & T.A. Rietz: Accuracy and Forecast Standard Error of Prediction Markets, Working draft, Henry B. Tippie College of Business and Administration; University of Iowa, 2003

198. Tvede, L.: *Business Cycles*, Wiley, 2006
199. Sunstein, C.R.: *Infotopia*, Oxford University Press, 2008
200. Bajarin, T.: Why the Maker Movement Is Important to America's Future, *Time.com*, May 19, 2014
201. The Success of Small Countries, *Credit Suisse Research Institute*, 2014
202. www.edx.org
203. www.coursera.org/
204. www.udacity.com, www.udemy.com
205. The digital degree, *The Economist*, 28 June, 2014
206. www.khanacademy.org
207. Ridley, M.: *The Rational Optimist*, Harper Perennial, 2011
208. Ricardo, D: *On the Principles of Political Economy and Taxation*, John Murray,1817
209. Sherman, H. J.: Monopoly Capital-An Essay on the American Economic and Social Order.*American Economic Review*, 56, 1966
210. Becker G.S. et al: The Quantity and Quality of Life and the Evolution of World Inequality, *National Bureau of Economic Research*, Working Paper 9765, 2003
211. Murray, C: *Coming Apart: The State of White America, 1960-2010*, Crown Publishing Group, 2013
212. Irwin, M.: Did Thomas Piketty Get His Math Wrong?, *International New York Times*, 24 May, 2014
213. Moving one Up, *Wall Street Journal*, 13 Nov, 2007
214. The 400 Individual Income Tax Returns Reporting the Highest Adjusted Gross Incomes Each Year, 1992-2008, *IRS*, http://www.irs.gov/pub/irs-soi/08intop400.pdf. The relevant numbers appear in table 4.
215. Warner, B. The 25 Richest People Who Ever Lived – Inflation Adjusted, April 14, 2014, *Celebrity Network*, http://www.celebritynetworth.com/articles/entertainment-articles/25-richest-people-lived-inflation-adjusted/
216. The figures covering 1960-2010 are from Connors, J.: *The Scope of Government and the Wealth of Nations Revisited, Joseph Department of Political Science*, Duke University, 2012. The earlier numbers are from Taming Leviathan, *The Economist* March 17th, 2011.
217. Roosevelt, T.: *Conservation as a National Duty*, Speech Text, Voices of Democracy, http://voicesofdemocracy.umd.edu/theodore-roosevelt-conservation-as-a-national-duty-speech-text/
218. Ibid
219. Governers Cheer Roosevelt's Talk, *New York Times*, 14 May, 1908
220. Cyprianus, T.C.: *Address to Demetrianus*, Amazon Digital Services, Inc., 2011
221. Fagan, B.M.: *The Little Ice Age: How Climate Made History, 1300-1850*, Basic Books, 2001 Malthus, T.: *An Essay on the Principle of Population*, CreateSpace Independent Publishing Platform, 2010
222. Jevons, W.S.: *The Coal Question: An Inquiry Concerning the Progress of the Nation, and the Probable Exhaustion of Our Coal Mines*, A.M. Kelley, 1865
223. Fairfield, O.: *The Plundered Planet*, Faber and Faber Limited, 1948
224. Vogt, W.: *Our Road to Survival*, William Sloane Associates, 1948
225. Ehrlich, P.: *The Population Bomb*, Buccaneer Books, 1995
226. Erlich, P. R.: Looking Backward from 2000 A.D. *The Progressive*, April 1970.
227. Paddock, W. & Paddock, P.: *Famine – 1975!*, Little, Brown, 1967
228. World Health Organization: *Diet, nutrition and the prevention of chronic diseases*, WHO Technical Report Series 916, 2003
229. Devereux, S.: *Famine in the Twentieth Century*, IDS Working Paper 105, 2000
230. Ehrlich, P.: *The Population Bomb*, Buccaneer Books, 1995
231. A Generation in Search of a Future, edited by George Wald from his speech given on March 4, 1969, at the Massachusetts Institute of Technology, http://www.elijahwald.com/generation.html
232. Lomborg, B.: *The Skeptical Environmentalist: Measuring the Real State of the World*, Cambridge University Press, 2001
233. Simon, J.: *Population Matters.* Transaction Publications, 1990
234. Barnett, H.J. & Morse C.: *Scarcity and Growth: The Economics of Natural Resource Availability*, RFF Press, 1965
235. Simon, J.: Paul Ehrlich Saying It Is So Doesn't Make It So, *Social Science Quarterly*, Vol. 63, No. 2, June 1982
236. Simon, J.: *The Ultimate Resource*, Princeton University Press, 1981. Tierney, J.: Betting on the Planet, *New York Times*, December 2002, 1990, http://www.nytimes.com/1990/12/02/magazine/betting-on-the-planet.html?src=pm

237. McClintick, D. & Emmett R.B.: *Betting on the Wealth of nature*, The Simon/-Ehrlich Wager, PERC Report, Volume 23, No. 3, Fall 2005. Middleton, D.: The Simon-Ehrlich Wager at Seven Billion People, Whatsupwiththat, 25 January, 2012, http://wattsupwiththat.com/2012/01/25/the-simon-ehrlich-wager-at-seven-billion-people/

238. Walter, E.: *The Immorality of Limiting Growth*, State University of New York Press, 1981

239. http://www.iea.org/aboutus/faqs/gas/

240. Wellinger, A.: Algal Biomass – Does it save the world?, *IEA Biooenergy*, April 2009

241. Institute for Energy research, http://instituteforenergyresearch.org/analysis/growth-sake-humans-just-sake-growth

242. Sivak, M.: *Effects of Vehicle Fuel Economy, Distance Travelled, and Vehicle Load on the Amount of Fuel Used for Personal Transportation: 1970-2010*, The University of Michigan Transportation Research Institute, 2013

243. *Fuel Comparison*, European Nuclear Society, 2013, http://www.euronuclear.org/info/encyclopedia/f/fuelcomparison.htm

244. Kadak, A.C.: A future for nuclear energy: pebble bed reactors, *Int. Journal of Critical Infrastructures*, Vol. 1, No. 4, 2005

245. Evans-Pritchard, A.: Obama could kill fossil fuels overnight with a nuclear dash for thorium, *The Telegraph*, 23 April, 2013

246. Ongena, J. et al.: Energy for Future Centuries – *Will Fusion be an Inexhaustible, Safe and Clean Energy Source?*, European Fusion Development Agreement, 2001

247. Clark, G.: *A Farewell to Alms*, Princeton University Press, 2008

248. Nanosats are go!, *the Economist*, June 7th, 2014

249. George, H.: *Progress and Prosperity*, Amazon Digital Services, http://rapgenius.com/Henry-george-progress-and-poverty-book-ii-chap-3-lyrics

250. Lomborg, B.: The truth about the environment, *The Economist*, 2 Aug, 2001 See also: Lomborg, B.: The environmental Litany and data,

251. http://www.fringer.org/wp-content/writings/litany.pdf

252. Hesser, L.: *The Man Who Fed the World: Nobel Peace Prize Laureate Norman Borlaug and His Battle to End World Hunger*, Durban House, 2006

253. Charles, D: *Lords Of The Harvest: Biotech, Big Money, And The Future Of Food*, Basic Books, 2002

254. Ibid.

255. A positive step towards a more sustainable approach to animal feed, Agricultural Biotechnology Council, 12/04/2013, http://www.abcinformation.org/index.php/media-centre/press-releases

256. Monsanto Will Undertake Three-Point Commitment to Double Yield in Three Major Crops, Make More Efficient Use of Natural Resources and Improve Farmer Lives, Monsanto http://monsanto.mediaroom.com/index.php?s=27632&item=76958

257. *The Millennium Development Goals Report*, UN, 2008

258. Santen, R.v., D. Khoe & B. Vermeer: *2030: Technology That Will Change the World*, Oxford University Press, 2000

259. Lumber Statistics, US Geological Survey, http://minerals.usgs.gov/ds/2005/140/wood.pdf

260. Iron and Steel Statistics, U.S. Geological Survey, http://minerals.usgs.gov/ds/2005/140/ironsteel.pdf

261. Middleton, D.: The Simon-Ehrlich Wager at Seven Billion People, Whatsupwiththat, 25 January 25, 2012 http://wattsupwiththat.com/2012/01/25/the-simon-ehrlich-wager-at-seven-billion-people/

262. Glanvill, C.B. (ed.): The voyage of Captain Don Felipe González in the ship of the line San Lorenzo, with the frigate Santa Rosalia in company, to Easter Island in 1770-1. Preceded by an extract from Mynheer Jacob Roggeveen's official log of his discovery of and visit to Easter Island in 1722, Hakluyt Society, 1908

263. Ship Logs and Journals of Don Felipe Gonzalez, 1770, http://www.easterislandtraveling.com/easter-island/history/ship-logs-and-journals/don-felipe-gonzalez-1770/

264. Horwitz, T.: *Blue Latitudes: Boldly Going Where Captain Cook Has Gone Before*, Picador, 2003

265. Peiser, B. From Genocide to Ecocide: The Rape of Rapa Nui, *Energy and Environment*, Volume 16 No. 3 & 4, 2005

266. Carson, R.: *Silent Spring*, Houghton Mifflin Company

267. Myers, N.: *The Sinking Ark: A New Look at the Problem of Disappearing Species*, Pergamon, 1979

268. Lovejoy, T.E.: *A Projection of Species extinctions, in Council on Environmental Quality (CEQ)*, The Global 2000 Report to the President, Vol. 2. CEQ, Washington, DC, p.328-31

269. Myers, N.: *The Sinking Ark: A New Look at the Problem of Disappearing Species*, Pergamon, 1979.

The meeting he refers to in this quote is described in Scientists Talk of the Need for Conservation and an Ethic of Biotic Diversity to Slow Species Extinction, *Science Magazine*, May 10, 1974

270. Raven, P.: Biological resources and global stability, I S. Kawano, J.H. Connell & T. Hidaka (eds.): Evolution and Coadaptation in Biotic Communities, 1988

271. Waters. J. Running scared, http://www.mywvhome.com/forties/scared.html

272. Foster, M.: Running behind the DDT truck, http://www.cospringsrealestatenews.com/running-behind-the-ddt-truck/

273. Wayland J. H. Et al: The Effect of Known Repeated Oral Doses of Chlorophnothane (DDT) In Man, *Journal of American Medical Association*, October 27, 1956

274. Laws, E. R. Jr., et al.: Toxicology of Abate in Volunteers, *Archives of Environmental Health*, Vol. 15, 1971.

275. Silinskas, C. & A. E. Okey, Inhibition of Leukaemia by DDT, *Journal of the National Cancer Institute*, Vol. 55, 1975

276. Bulletin of the Virginia Department of Agriculture, May, 1967

277. McLean, A.E.M. & McLean E.K: Diet and Toxicity, *British Medical Bulletin*, Vol. 25, 1969

278. Charles F. Wurster, Jr.: DDT Reduces Photosynthesis by Marine Phytoplankton, *Science* 159, no. 3822, 1968

279. Jukes, T.H.: Silent Spring and the Betrayal of Environmentalism, *21st Century Science and Technology*, 7, no. 3 1994

280. Edwards, G.J. : DDT: A Case Study in Scientific Fraud, *Journal of American Physicians and Surgeons*, Volume 9 Number 3 Fall 2004

281. Sweeney, E.M.: Consolidated DDT Hearing: Hearing Examiner's Recommended Findings, Conclusions, and Orders, Environmental Protection Agency, 25 April, 1972

282. http://www.greenpeace.org/india/en/news/new-findings-reaffirm-presence/

283. Reversing its policy, UN agency promotes DDT to combat the scourge of malaria, UN News Centre, September 15th, 2006

284. Mora, C. et al.: How Many Species Are There on Earth and in the Ocean?, *PLoS Biology*, 2011

285. Bailie, J. & B. Broombridge (eds.): 1996-1997 IUNC Red List of Threatened Animals, 1997; K.S. Walter & H.J. Gillet (eds.): 1997-1998 Red List of Threatened Plants, 1998; Reid, W.V.: How Many Species Will There Be?, Whitmore, T.C. & J.A. Sayer: *Tropical Deforestation and Species Extinction*; Frankham, R., J.D. Ballou & Briscoe D.A: *A Primer Of Conservation Genetics*, Cambridge University Press, 2007

286. Fisher, D.O. & S.P. Blomberg: Correlates of rediscovery and the detectability of extinction in mammals. *Proceedings of the Royal Society of London B* 278, 2011

287. Meyer, A.: Phylogenetic relationships and evolutionary processes in East African cichlids, *Trends Ecol. Evol.*8, 1993

288. Dead as a Moa, *The Economist,* 14 Sept, 2013

289. Ridley, M.: *The Rational Optimist*, Harper Perennial, 2011

290. Martin, Paul S., & Richard G. Klein (eds.): *Quaternary Extinctions: a Prehistoric Revolution*, University of Arizona Press, 1984

291. Olson, S.L.: Extinction on islands: Man as a Catastrophe, In: Pearl, M. & Western D. (eds.): *Conservation Biology for the Next Century*, Oxford University Press, Oxford, 1989

292. Hames, R.: Game conservation or efficient hunting? In McKay, B.I. & I.M. Acheson (eds): *The Question of the Commons: The Culture and Ecology of Communal Resources*, University of Arizona Press, 1987. See also Alvard, M.S.: Conservation by Native Peoples – Prey Choice in a depleted habitat, *Human Nature*, Volume 5, 1994; Vickers, W.T.: From opportunism to nascent conservation: the case of the Siona-Secoya, *Human Nature* 5, 1992 and Stearman, A.M.: Only Slaves Climb Trees: Revisiting the myth of the ecologically Noble Savage in Amazonia, *Human Nature* 5, 1994

293. Sedjo, R.A.: *Forests – Conflicting Signals*, In: Baily, R.: Ecoscam, St. Martins Press, 1993

294. Budiansky, S.: *Nature's Keepers: The New Science of Nature Management, The Free Press*, 1995

295. Jones, M. & R. Sawhill: Just Too Good to Be True: Another reason to beware of false eco-prophets, *Newsweek*, 4 May, 1992

296. Smith, H.A.: Scraps from a Diary: Chief Seattle – A Gentleman by Instinct His Native Eloquence, etc., etc., *Seattle Sunday Star*, 29 October, 1887

297. Abruzzi, W.A.: The Myth of Chief Seattle, Department of Sociology and Anthropology, Muhlenberg College, Allentown, 2000

298. Kaiser, R.: Chief Seattle's Speech(es): American Origins and European Reception, In*: Recovering the Word: Essays on Native American Literature*, University of California Press, 1987. See also Buerge, D.:

299. Seattle's King Arthur: How Chief Seattle continues to inspire his many admirers to put words in his mouth, Seattle Weekly, 17 July, 1991
300. Stone, L.: *The Family Sex and Marriage in England*, 1500-1800, Penguin Books Ltd, 1990
301. 300 Brimblecombe, P., London air pollution, 1500-1900, *Atmospheric Environment* 11, 1977
302. Frost, M.: The Great Stink, www.martinfrost.ws/htmlfiles/great_stink.html
303. Observations on the Filth of the Thames, contained in a letter addressed to the Editor of *The Times Newspaper*, by Professor Faraday, http://www.chemteam.info/Chem-History/Faraday-Letter.html. See also
304. Green Wheels, *The Economist*, 20. april 2013
305. *Teeming with fish, Thames is cleanest for two centuries, London Evening Standard*, 14 July 2009
306. Goklany, I.M.: *The Improving State of the World*, Cato Institute, 2007
307. Don't Be Very Worried, *Wall Street Journal*, 23. maj 2006
308. Pollution prospect a Chilling One, *The Owosso Argus-Press*, 26 January, 1970
309. Rasool, S.I., & Schneider S.H.: Atmospheric carbon dioxide and aerosols: Effects of large increases on global climate, *Science*, 173, 1973
310. Maximus, F.: An important letter sent to the President about the danger of climate change, 21 October, 2009, www.fabiusmaximus.com
311. Ponte, L.: *The Cooling: Has the Next Ice Age Already Begun?*, Prentice-Hall, 1976
312. The exact quote is "Die ersten großen Wälder werden schon in den nächsten fünf Jahren sterben. Sie sind nicht mehr zu retten". This was given in an interview with *Hamburger Abendblatt*.
313. "Saurer Regen über Deutschland. Der Wald stirbt.", *Der Spiegel* 47/1981
314. Integrated Assessment, The National Acid Precipitation Assessment Program, 1990
315. Integrated Assessment, The National Acid Precipitation Assessment Program, 2011
316. Kauppi, P.E., Mielikäinen, K & K. Kuusela: Biomass and carbon budget of European forests, 1971 to 1990, *Science*, 1992.
317. Erisman, J.W. & G.J. Hei (eds.): Acid Rain Research: Do We Have Enough Answers?, *Elsevier Science*, 1995 (see the chapter "Evaluation, integration")
318. Donavan, J. Climate Change, Acid Rain Could Be Good for Forests, *Michigan Tech News*, July, 2009
319. Petit, J.R., et al.: Vostok Ice Core Data for 420,000 Years, Center for Paleoclimatology Data Contribution Series #2001-076., 2001
320. CharvaÁtova, I.: Can origin of the 2400-year cycle of solar activity be caused by solar inertial motion?, *Ann. Geophysicae* 18, 399±405, 2000.
321. Alley, R.B: The Younger Dryas cold interval as viewed from central Greenland. *Quaternary Science Reviews* 19, 2000
322. Solanki, S.K. et al.: Unusual activity of the Sun during recent decades compared to the previous 11,000 years, *Nature*, 431, 2004
323. Lamb, H.H.: *Climate, History and the Modern World*, London, Routledge, 1995
324. Zick, M.: Die Spur des Schweizer Ötzi, *Der Tagespiel*, may 16, 2005. See also Growe, J.M: Glacial geological Evidence for the Medieval Warm Period, Climatic Change 26, 1994
325. Data collected by Permanent Service for Mean Sea Level, http://www.psmsl.org/data/obtaining/
326. Spencer, R.: Maybe That IPCC 95% Certainty Was Correct After All, www.drroyspencer.com, 14 October, 2013
327. Bjørk, C.A. et al.: An aerial view of 80 years of climate-related glacier fluctuations in southeast Greenland, *Nature Geoscience*, 5, 2012
328. Coral reefs rarely get over 30-45 meters tall. However, some have grown much higher, and the highest know are in the Bokak Atoll, where they can reach 1.400 meters. http://en.wikipedia.org/wiki/Bokak_Atoll
329. Mahlman, J.D.: Uncertainties in Projections of Human-Caused Climate Warming, *Science*, Vol. 278, 1997
330. Tola, R.S.J. & Dowlatabadic H.: Vector-borne diseases, development & climate change, Centre for Marine and Climate Studies, *Integrated Assessment*, Vol. 2, Number 4, 2001
331. Unger, Z.: Are Polar Bears Really Disappearing?, *Wall Street Journal*, 9 February, 2013
332. Environmental Performance Index 2008, Yale University, Columbia University, World Economic Forum and the EU, 2008.
333. Engler R. et al.: An Assessment of Forest Cover Trends in South and North Korea, From 1980 to 2010, *Environ Management* 53, January, 2014
334. Robin, E. et al,: Haiti and the Dominican Republic: One island, two worlds, *Environmental Management*, Vol 53, 2014

335. Skovene og Skovbruget i Danmark, Skovinfo, 1997
336. 336 FAO Global Forest Resources Assessment, FAO 2010
337. 337 State of the World's Forests Report, UN, 2005
338. 338 Rosenthal, E.: New Jungles Prompt a Debate on Rain Forests, *New York Times*, 29 Jan, 2009
339. 339 Idso, K.E. & Idso S.B: Plant responses to atmospheric CO2 enrichment in the face of environmental constraints: A review of the past 10 years' research. *Agricultural and Forest Meteorology*, 69, 1994
340. Gore, Al: *Our Choice: A Plan to Solve the Climate Crisis*, Rodale Books, 2009. See also Lomborg, B.: *The Sceptical Environmentalist: Measuring the Real State of the World*, Cambridge University Press, 2001, og Cunningham, W.P. & A.M. Cunningham: Environmental Science: A Global Concern, McGraw Hill, 2009
341. Goldman, D.P.: *How Civilizations Die (and Why Islam is Dying Too)*, Regnery Publishing, 2011
342. Abbasi-Shavazi, M.J.: United Nation's Population Division, Completing the fertility transition, United Nations; Recent changes and the future of fertility in Iran, 2002. See also CIA World Fact Book 2013
343. Sanyal, S.: The End of Population Growth, The Wide Angle, Deutsche Bank, 13 May, 2011. http://globalpublicsquare.blogs.cnn.com/2011/10/31/the-end-of-population-growth/
344. Brand, S.: *Whole Earth Discipline*, Penguin Books, 2009
345. Vandeplassche, D. & Medeiros L,: Accellerator Driven Systems, Proceedings of IPAC2012, 2012
346. Frankham, R., Ballou J.D & Briscoe D.A.: *A Primer Of Conservation Genetics*, Cambridge University Press, 2007
347. Growth in global number of protected areas (1911-2011), http://www.wdpa.org/Statistics.aspx. See also Harrabin, R.: Marine Protected Areas increase 10-fold in a decade, *BBC*, 13. October, 2012
348. Mueller, T.: Cloned Species, *National Geographic*, May, 2009, http://ngm.nationalgeographic.com/2009/05/cloned-species/mueller-text. See also Brand, S.: The dawn of de-extinction: Are you ready?, YouTube
349. McAnany, P.A. & N. Yoffee (eds.): *Questioning Collapse, Human Resilience, Ecological Vulnerability and the Aftermath of Empire, Cambridge University Press*, 2010. See also Hunt, T. & Lipo C.: *The Statues that Walked: Unraveling the Mystery of Easter Island,* Counterpoint, 2012
350. Deutch, D.: *The Beginning of Infinity: Explanations that Transform The World*, Penguin, 2012
351. 89-årig renser tagrende – ryk direkte i fængsel, *Børsen*, Feb. 8th, 2013
352. Johansen, M.Ø.: Fiskehandlere skal lære latin, *Berlingske Business*, 18. februar 2012
353. Dropping the Bomb, *The Economist*, June 28th, 2014
354. Howard, P. K.: *The Rule of Nobody*, W. W. Norton & Company, 2014
355. Howard, P.: It's Time to Clean House, *The Atlantic*, 6. marts 2012
356. Tax reform in America, Simpler, fairer, possible, *The Economist*, 13. july 2013
357. Howard, P. K.: *The Rule of Nobody*, W. W. Norton & Company, 2014
358. Dixon, P.: *Futurewise – Six faces of Global Change*, Profile Books, 2007
359. *The 13 Dumbest Lawsuits in Recent History* http://www.ranker.com/list/the-13-dumbest-lawsuits-in-recent-history/williammtx?page=3#TFZLbIQpliskYkkY.99
360. http://wiki.answers.com/Q/What_country_in_the_world_has_most_lawyers_per_capita
361. Overview over the number appears in *US Tort Liability Index 2010 Report* (Pacific Research Institute, 2010). Overview of associated costs are in: Baker, J., H.M. Kritzer & N. Vidmar: *Jackpot Justice and the American Tort System: Thinking Beyond Junk Science*, School of Law, Duke University, 1. July 2008
362. Shleifer, A., R.W. Vishny & K.M. Murphy: *The Allocation of Talent: Implications for Growth*, NBER Working Paper No. 3530, December 1990, NBER
363. McGovern, G.: A Politician's Dream Is a Businessman's Nightmare, *Nation's Restaurant News*, Wall Street Journal, September 1992 http://online.wsj.com/article/SB10001424052970203406404578070 5 43545022704.html
364. Dramatic 911 tape reveals dispatcher's fight to save patient; nurse refuses to help; kerngoldenempire. com
365. Lewis, W.W.: *The Power of Productivity*, University of Chicago Press, 2004
366. Public Service Productivity, UK Statistics Authority, Office for National Statistics, Publication Hub, Gateway to UK National Statistics, Public Service Productivity, UK Statistics Authority, Office for National Statistics, Publication Hub, Gateway to UK National Statistics, http://www.statistics.gov.uk/hub/government/central-and-local-government/public-service-productivity
367. Hopkins, K.: Public sector inefficiency claimed to cost £58.4bn, *The Observer*, 23. august 2009

368. Baumol J.W. et al.: *The Cost Disease: Why Computers Get Cheaper and Health Care Doesn't*, Yale University Press, 2012
369. Parkinsons Law, *The Economist*, November 19th, 1955
370. Parkinson, C.N.: *Parkinson's Law*, Buccaneer Books, 1957
371. Mouritzen, P.E.: *Spændinger i Velfærdsstaten, Kommunestyrets fremtid*, Norstrand, R & N. Groes (ed.), AKF-Forlaget, 2001. p. 379-404.
372. Acemogly, D. & J. A. Robinson: *Why Nations Fail: The Origins of Power, Prosperity, and Poverty*, Crown Business, 2012
373. Amy Ellen Schwartz: Flypaper effect, *Encyclopedia of taxation and tax policy*, s. 152, Courant, 2005. See also Hines, J.R. & R.H. Thaler: Anomalies: The Flypaper Effect, *The Journal of Economic Perspectives*, vol. 9, nr. 4, 1995
374. Wu, T.: *The Master Switch: The Rise and Fall of Information Empires*, Atlantic Books 2012.
375. *Astrid Lindgren och Pomperipossa*, http://sverigesradio.se/sida/artikel.aspx?programid=1602&artikel=776215. Se også http://www.expressen.se/noje/pomperipossa-i-monismanien/
376. Sowell, T.: *Intellectuals and Society*, Basic Books, 2011
377. The Effect of Capital Gains Tax Rises on Revenues, Adam Smith Institute, May 21st, 2010
378. Bartlett, B.: Cutting taxes in Russia, Townhall.com, 12. april 2002
379. Maryland's Mobile Millionaires Income Tax Rates Go Up, Rich Taxpayers Vanish, *Wall Street Journal*, 12. marts 2010
380. Henrekson, M & A. Bergh: *Government Size and Implications for Economic Growth*, AEI Press, 2012
381. Bessard, P.: Tax Competition: The Swiss Case, Liberal Institute, 2008
382. Obwalden votes for flat rate tax, *Swissinfo.ch*, Dec. 16th, 2007
383. Tax Evasion in Europa, *CES IFO*, sommer 2012
384. Who will tame the taxman?, *The Economist*, 25. maj 2013
385. Bergh, A. & M. Henrekson: *Government Size and Implications for Economic Growth*, The AEI Press, 2010
386. So much to do, so little time, *The Economist*, 17. november 2012
387. Acemoglu, D., S. Johnson & J.A. Robinson: Colonial Origins of Comparative Development: An Empirical Investigation, *American Economic Review*, 2000. See also: Acemoglu, D., S. Johnson & J.A. Robinson: *Reversal of Fortune: Geography and Institutions in the Making of the Modern World Income Distribution*, NBER Working Paper No. 8460, 2001
388. Murray, C.: *Loosing Ground*, Basic Books, 1994
389. Eberstadt, N.: *A Nation of Takers: America's Entitlement Epidemic*, Templeton Press, 2012
390. Beatty, C. & S. Fothergill: Incapacity benefits in the UK: an issue of health or jobs?, Centre for Regional Economic and Social Research, 2012, Sheffield Hallam University, UK
391. Murray, C.: *Losing Ground*, Basic Books, 1994
392. Ibid
393. Melzer. A. H. & S. F. Richard: A Rational Theory of the Growth of Government and the Distribution of Income, The Wharton School Research Paper No. 67, 2014,
394. Dahl, C.H.: Velfærdsstat og arbejdsmoral, CEPOS arbejdspapir Nr. 22, CEPOS, 2013
395. Ericsson, A.K. et al.: The Making of an Expert, *Harvard Business Review*, juli-august 2007
396. Inglehart, R. et al.: *Human Beliefs and Values: A cross-cultural sourcebook based on the 1999–2002 values surveys*, 2004
397. Olesen, O.B.: *Taberfabrikken*, People's Press, 2007
398. Álvarez, G.C., R.M. Jara, J.R.R. Julián & J.I.G. Bielsa: Study of the Effects on Employment of Public Aid to Renewable Energy Sources, Universidad Rey Juan Carlos, 2009
399. The Department of Energy Committed $11 Million Per Job, Institute for Energy Research, May 2013
400. Lisbon European Council 23 and 24 March 2000, Presidency Conclusions, 2000
401. Stossel, J.: *No they Can't: Why Government Fails – but Individuals Succeed*, Treshold Editions, 2012
402. Easterly, W.: *The White Man's Burden; Why the West's Efforts to Aid the Rest have Done So Much Ill and so Little Good.* Penguin Books, 2007
403. Easterly, W.: *The Elusive Quest for Growth, Economists' Adventures and Misadventures in the Tropics*, First MIT Press, 2002
404. Ibid
405. Pritchett, L.H. : Desired Fertility and the Impact of Population Policies, *Population and Development Review*, Vol. 20, No. 1, marts 1994

406. Pritchett, L.: Where has All the Education Gone?, World Bank Policy Research Working Paper Series number 1581, 1996

407. Berg, U & Y Vontobel: Am Hang, *Schweizer Monat*, September 2012

408. Arum R. & J. Roksa: *Academically Adrift*, University Of Chicago Press, 2010

409. Cappelli, P: Skill Gaps, Skill Shortages and Skill Mismatches: Evidence for the US, NBER Working Paper No. 20382, 2014

410. Rajan, R.G. & A. Subramanian: Aid and Growth: What Does the Cross-Country Evidence Really Show?, *The Review of Economics and Statistics*, vol. 90, nr. 5, 2008

411. Raghuram, R. & A. Subramanian: What Undermines Aid's Impact on Growth?, International Monetary Fund, 2006

412. *Schmookler, J.: Invention and Economic Growth,* Harvard University Press, 1967

413. Litan, R.E. & C.J. Schramm: *Better Capitalism: Renewing the Entrepreneurial Strength of the American Economy,* Yale University Press, 2012

414. Mnookin, Seth: *The Panic Virus, A True Story of Medicine, Virus and Fear,* Simon & Shuster, 2011

415. Ibid.

416. History and Epidemiology of Global Smallpox Eradication, in *Smallpox: Disease, Prevention, and Intervention,* CDC & The World Health Organization

417. Think Yourself Better, *The Economist*, 19. maj 2011; Sing, S. & E. Ernst: *Trick or Treatment?: Alternative Medicine on Trial,* Corgi, 2009

418. Enriquez, J.: Medicine's Missing Measure, *The Atlantic*, 31. maj 2012

419. Brand, S.: Nuclear Power is Safe, Sound …and Green, *Earth Island Journal,* Winter 2011, http://www. earthisland.org/journal/index.php/eij/article/brand/

420. Chen Y. et al.: Evidence on the impact of sustained exposure to air pollution on life expectancy from China's Huai River policy, *Proceedings of the National Academy of Sciences*, vol. 110, nr. 32, 2013

421. Tu, J.: Safety Challenges in China's Coal Mining Industry, AFAR, 15. marts 2006, http://www.asianresearch.org/articles/2997.html

422. Chernobyl's Legacy: Health, Environmental and Socio-Economic Impacts, Chernobyl Forum assessment report, Chernobyl Forum, 2005

423. As it happened: Turkey mine disaster, BBC News Europe, May 13, 2014

424. Global report on Fukushima nuclear *accident details health risks*, World Health Organization, 2013

425. *Safety Indicators Show U.S. Nuclear Industry Sustained Near-Record Levels of Excellence in '07*, Nuclear Energy Institute, April 14, 2008

426. Howe, G.R. et al.: Analysis of the mortality experience amongst U.S. nuclear power industry workers after chronic low-dose exposure to ionizing radiation, *Radiation Research* 162, 2004

427. *Wang, B.:* Deaths per TWh for all energy sources: Rooftop solar power is actually more dangerous than Chernobyl, *Next Big Future, 14. marts 2008*

428. Griffits, S.: *Climate Change Recalculated*, Long Now Foundation, jan.16, 2009, http://longnow.org/seminars/02009/jan/16/climate-change-recalculated/

429. Qaim, M. & W. Klümper: A Meta-Analysis of the Impacts of Genetically Modified Crops, PLoS ONE, Nov. 03, 2014

430. Scientists In Support Of Agricultural Biotechnology, http://www.agbioworld.org/declaration/petition/petition.php

431. United States Trade Representative: *U.S. and Cooperating Countries File WTO Case Against EU Moratorium on Biotech Foods and Crops*, April 2003

432. Craig Venter on DNA and the Sea, TED Talks, Feb. 2005, http://www.ted.com/talks/craig_venter_on_dna_and_the_sea.html

433. Life: A gene-centric view, Craig Venter & Richard Dawkins: A Conversation in Munich (Moderator: John Brockman), Edge 235 – 6. 6th, 2008, http://www.edge.org/documents/archive/edge235.html

434. Tuomisto, H.L., I.D. Hodge, P. Riordan & D.W. Macdonald: *Does organic farming reduce environmental impacts? – A meta analysis of European research*, Wildlife Conservation Research Unit, Department of Zoology, University of Oxford

435. Seufert, V., N. Ramankutty & J.A. Foley: Comparing the yields of organic and conventional agriculture, *Nature*, vol. 485, 10. maj 2012

436. Chang, K.: Stanford Scientists Cast Doubt on Advantages of Organic Meat and Produce, *New York Times*, sep. 3rd, 2012. See also Johnson, P.: Enemies of Society, Weindenferld & Nicholson, 1977

437. Smith-Spangler, C. et al.: Are Organic Foods Safer or Healthier Than Conventional Alternatives?: A Systematic Review, *Annals of Internal Medicine*, vol. 157, september 2012

438. Williams, C.M.: Nutritional Quality of Organic Food: Shades of Grey or Shades of Green?, *Proceedings of the Nutrition Society*, vol. 61, 2002

439. Goklany, I.M.: *The Improving State of the World*, Cato Institute, 2007

440. Brand, S.: *Whole Earth Discipline*, Penguin Books, 2009

441. Booker, C. & R. North: *Scared to Death, From BSE to Global Warming: Why Scares are Costing Us the Earth*, Continuum, 2007

442. Carlsen, D.G. & T. Steen: Flere unge Bieber-fans ringer Røde Kors, *Dagbladet* (NO), april 7th, 2013

443. Regehr, C.: Crisis Debriefing Groups for Emergency Responders: Reviewing the Evidence, *Brief Treatment and crises Intervention*, Sep. 1st. 2001, http://www.buentrato.cl/pdf/est_inv/interv/ic_regehr.pdf

444. Calabrese, E.J. & L.A. Baldwin: The Frequency of U-Shaped Dose Responses in the Toxicological Literature, Toxicological Sciences 62, 2001. See also Dish the dirt and keep healthy, *New Statesman*, 03 July 2000, http://www.jameslefanu.com/articles/science-dish-the-dirt-and-keep-healthy

445. Luckey, T.D.: Radiation Hormesis Overview, *RSO Magazine*, 1998

446. Kaufmann, J. M.: Radiation Hormesis: Demonstrated, Deconstructed, Denied, Dismissed, and Some Implications for Public Policy, *Journal of Scientific Exploration*, Vol. 17, 2003

447. Swirsky, L.G., T.H. Slone & B. Ames: *Pesticide Residues in Food and Cancer Risk: A Critical Analysis*, University of California, Berkeley, i Krieger, R. (ed.): *Handbook of Pesticide Toxicology, Second Edition*, Academic Press, 2001

448. Doll, R. & R. Peto: The Causes of Cancer: Quantitative Estimates of Avoidable Risks of Cancer in the United States Today, *Journal of the National Cancer Institute* 66, no. 6, 1981

449. http://www.whitehouse.gov/about/presidents/franklinroosevelt

450. North Vancouver woman pleads guilty in eco-terrorism case, *CBC News*, Oct. 10th, 2013

451. Animal Research: Battle Scars, *Nature*, vol. 470, Feb. 2011, http://www.nature.com/news/2011/110223/full/470452a.htmlhttp://www.nature.com/news/2011/110223/full/470452a. html

452. Reagan, T: *Earthbound: New Introductory Essays in Environmental Ethics*, Waveland, 1990

453. M. Oppenheimer on This Week with David Brinkley, 31 May 1992

454. Hickman, L.: James Lovelock: Humans are too stupid to prevent climate change, *The Guardian*, 29. marts, 2010

455. http://www.anus.com/zine/philosophy/resources/pentti_linkola.pdf

456. Linkola, P.: *Can Life Prevail?*, Integral Tradition Publishing, 2009

457. Milbank, D.: A Strange Finnish Thinker Posits War, Famine as Ultimate Goods, *The Wall Street Journal Asia*, 24. maj 1994

458. Haeckel, E.: *The Riddle of the Universe*, Harper and Brothers, 1900

459. Bramwell, A.: *Blood and Soil: Walther Darre and Hitler's Green Party*, Kensal Press, 1985

460. Figes, O.: *The Whisperers: Private Life in Stalin's Russia*, Metropolitan Books, 2007

461. Lehman, E.: *Biologischer Wille: Wege und Ziele biologischer Arbeit im neuen Reich*, 1936

462. Manvell, R. & H. Fraenkel: *Hess: A Biography*, London, 1971

463. Biehl, J. & P. Staudenmaier: *Ecofascism: Lessons from the German Experience*, AK Press, 1995

464. Gruhl, H.: *Ein Planet Wird geplundered*, S. Fischer Verlag, 1975

465. Linkola, P.: *Can Life Prevail? A Radical Approach to the Environmental Crisis*, Integral Tradition Publishing, 2009

466. Linkola, P.: *Johdatus 1990-luvun ajatteluun*, WSOY, 1989

467. Eliot, T.S.: *The Cocktail Party*, Faber and Faber, 1974

468. Dole, K., C. Gilbert, M. Deshpande & R. Khandekar: Prevalence and determinants of xerophthalmia in preschool children in urban slums, Pune, India – a preliminary assessment. *Ophthalmic Epidemiology*, 2009

469. Bailey, R.: Dr. Strangelunch, *Reason*, January 2001

470. Former Greenpeace co-founder Dr. Patrick Moore rips 'Greenpeace's Crime Against Humanity' for opposing Golden Rice which can eliminate vitamin A deficiency, *Climate Depot*, sep. 2010

471. *Discover* Magazine, Oct 1989, pg. 47.

472. Soon, W. & S. Baliunas: Proxy climatic and environmental changes of the past 1000 years, nature, *Climate Research*, 2003

473. There is substantial coverage of these episodes in the literature. Among the most comprehensive descriptions are Montford, A.W.: *The Hockey Stick Illusion*, Stacey International, March 2001, Montford, A.W.: *Hiding the Decline*, Biddles, 2012 and Mosher, S & T.W. Fuller: *Climategate, The Crutape letters*, Createspace, 2010

474. Montford, A.W.: *Hiding the Decline*, Biddles, 2012
475. Memorandum submitted by Warwick Hughes (CRU 35), Parliamentary Business, February 2010
476. Phil Jones in the British Parliament, March 1st, 2010, YouTube, http://www.youtube.com/watch?v=AK0oGnqtVXo
477. Turne, S. P.: *The Politics of Expertise*, Routledge Studies in Social and Political Thought, 2013
478. McIntyre, S. & R. McKitrick: Corrections to the Mann et al. (1998) Proxy Data Base and Northern Hemispheric Average Temperature Series, *Energy & Environment*, vol. 14, 2003
479. Graybill, D.A.& S.B. Idso: Detecting the Aerial Fertilization Effect of Atmospheric CO2 Enrichment in Tree-ring Chronologies., *Global Biogeochemical Cycles* 7, 1993
480. Trouble at the Lab, *The Economist*, Oct. 10th, 2013
481. Begley. C.G. & L.M. Ellis: Drug development: Raise standards for preclinical cancer research, *Nature*, vol. 483, 2012
482. Prinz, F., T. Schlange & K. Asadullah: Believe it or not: How much can we rely on published data on potential drug targets?, *Nature Reviews Drug Discovery*, vol. 10, 712, 2011
483. Fanelli, D.: Negative results are disappearing from most disciplines and countries, *Scientometrics*, vol. 90, 2012
484. Handel, M. et al.: On the reproducibility of science: Unique identification of research resources in the biomedical literature, *PeerJ*, oct. 9th, 2013
485. Martindale, C.: *The Clockwork Muse, The predictability of Artistic Change*, Basic Books, 1990
486. Sokal, AD.: Transgressing the Boundaries: Towards a Transformative Hermeneutics of Quantum Gravity, *Social Text*, Spring/Summer 1996
487. Pollit, K: Polomotov Cocktail and Selected Responses, *The Nation*, June 10, 1996
488. Wittgenstein, L.: *Tractatus Logico-Philosophicus*, CreateSpace Independent Publishing Platform, 2011
489. Derrida, J.: Letter to a Japanese Friend, (Prof. Izutsu)." In: *Derrida and Differance*, ed. Wood & Bernasconi, Warwick: Parousia Press. 1985
490. http://en.wikipedia.org/wiki/Pierre_Brassau
491. Hawley-Dolan, A & E. Winner: Seeing the Mind Behind the Art: People Can Distinguish Abstract Expressionist Paintings From Highly Similar Paintings by Children, Chimps, Monkeys, and Elephants, Psychological Science, March 2011
492. Wikipedia Commons
493. *Weekendavisen*, December 1999
494. Courtois, S.: *The Black Book of Communism: Crimes, Terror, Repression*, Harvard University Press, 1989
495. Johnson, P: *Modern Times Revised Edition: World from the Twenties to the Nineties*, Harper Perennial, 2001
496. Lenin, V.I.: *State and Revolution*, International Publishing, 1932
497. *Mises, L: Socialism: An Economic and Sociological Analysis*, Liberty Classics, 1986
498. http://hdr.undp.org/en/data
499. http://epi.yale.edu/epi/country-rankings
500. http://en.wikipedia.org/wiki/Where-to-be-born_Index
501. http://unsdsn.org/wp-content/uploads/2014/02/WorldHappinessReport2013_online.pdf
502. The Success of Small Nations, Credit Suisse Research Institute, 2014
503. The Good Country Index, http://www.goodcountry.org/overall
504. Diamond, J.: *The Third Chimpanzee*, Harper Perennial, 2007
505. Tvede, L.: *Supertrends*, Wiley & Sons, 2011
506. Eddy, W.A.: "It's All Your Fault!" - Working With High Conflict Personalities, http://www.continuingedcourses.net/active/courses/course075.php
507. Dixon, P.: *Futurewise – Six faces of Global Change*, Profile Books, 2007
508. How Goldman Sachs Can Get Paid to Keep People Out of Jail, *Bloomberg*, May 8th, 2014
509. Professors take lessons from online teaching, Boston Globe, Jun 9, 2013
510. Kuhn, T.S.: *The Structure of Scientific Revolutions*, University of Chicago Press, 1996
511. Roberts, B.E. & C. Eesley: Entrepreneurial Impact: The Role of MIT, MIT Sloan School of Management, 2009
512. http://www.forbes.com/powerful-brands/list/
513. Riley, J.L.: Charter Schools Flourish in Harlem, *Wall Street Journal*, 8. marts, 2010
514. Programme for International Student Assessment, Wikipedia, http://en.wikipedia.org/wiki/Programme_for_International_Student_Assessment
515. West, M.R. & L. Woessmann: *Every Catholic Child in a Catholic School: Historical Resistance to State Schooling, Contemporary Private Competition and Student Achievement across Countries*, The Economic Journal, August 2010

516. The new school rules, *The Economist*, October 11th, 2014
517. Barber, B. R.: *If Mayors Ruled the World: Dysfunctional Nations, Rising Cities*, Yale University Press, 2013

ABOUT THE AUTHOR

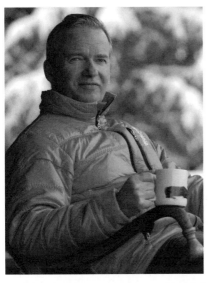

Lars Tvede (www.larstvede.com)
A serial entrepreneur who holds a
Master's degree in Engineering and
a Bachelor's degree in International
Commerce, Lars is also a certified
derivatives trader from National
Futures Association in Chicago.
Lars spent 11 years in portfolio
management and investment
banking before moving to the
high-tech and telecommunications
industries in the mid 1990s, where
he has co-founded and seed-funded a
number of award-winning
high-tech companies in the satellite
communication, Internet and mobile space. He is also founder of Beluga,
a successful financial trading company.

He has authored a number of books on marketing strategy, technology,
financial markets, general economics and the future, which between them
have been published in 11 languages and more than 50 editions. He has been
a frequent participant in international media, including TEDTalks. Lars
was listed in *The Guru Guide to Marketing* as one of the world's 62 leading
thinkers of marketing strategy.

A Danish national, Lars lives in Switzerland with his family. His main
hobbies include sailing, skiing and collecting Italian sports cars.

Dialogue

THE ONLY CONVERSATION THAT MATTERS

Dialogue is an original, practical and world-class journal, which focuses on key issues and challenges encountered by business leaders and managers around the world.

The journal provides a vital source of fresh ideas for top executives creating, leading and developing businesses in today's world.

Dialogue provides and explains the best of leadership thinking together with original insight and analyses from a range of experts, thinkers and practitioners.

Make sure you receive every copy in print, on your computer, on your phone or on your tablet. **Subscribe today...**

BEYOND
THE WRITTEN WORD

Authors who speak to you face to face.

Discover LID Speakers, a service
that enables businesses to have
direct and interactive contact with
the best ideas brought to their
own sector by the most
outstanding creators
of business thinking.

- A network specialising in business
  speakers, making it easy to find the
  most suitable candidates.

- A website with full details and videos,
  so you know exactly who you're hiring.

- A forum packed with ideas and
  suggestions about the most interesting
  and cutting-edge issues.

- A place where you can make direct contact
  with the best in international speakers.

- The only speakers' bureau backed up
  by the expertise of an established
  business book publisher.

LIDspeakers.com

Sure value.